THE HISTORY OF PARLIAMENT

Honour, Interest and Power:
an Illustrated History of the House of Lords,
1660–1715

Edited by
Ruth Paley and Paul Seaward

with Beverly Adams, Robin Eagles
and Charles Littleton

*View of Old Palace Yard around
1700, by an unknown artist,
looking north towards the east end
of the Henry VII chapel, and the
south gable of Westminster Hall.
The entrance to the House of Lords
is on the right, with a coach
standing in front of it.*

HONOUR, INTEREST & POWER

AN ILLUSTRATED HISTORY OF THE HOUSE OF LORDS, 1660–1715

The Boydell Press, for the History of Parliament Trust, 2010

First published 2010

Published by The Boydell Press
an imprint of Boydell & Brewer Ltd
PO Box 9, Woodbridge, Suffolk IP12 3DF, UK
and of Boydell & Brewer Inc.
668 Mt Hope Avenue, Rochester, NY 14620, USA
website: www.boydellandbrewer.com

ISBN 978-184383-576-9

A catalogue record for this book is available from the British Library

The publisher has no responsibility for the continued existence or accuracy of URLs for
external or third-party internet websites referred to in this book, and does not guarantee
that any content on such websites is, or will remain, accurate or appropriate

Mixed Sources
Product group from well-managed
forests and other controlled sources
www.fsc.org Cert no. SGS-COC-005091
© 1996 Forest Stewardship Council

Papers used by Boydell & Brewer are natural, recyclable products
made from wood grown in sustainable forests.

Book designed by Simon Loxley.
Printed in Great Britain by Butler Tanner & Dennis Ltd, Frome and London

Foreword

By the Chairman of the History of Parliament Trust

For more than fifty years The History of Parliament has been publishing a series of increasingly magisterial volumes on the House of Commons. However, Parliament consists of two Houses and no history of Parliament can ever claim to be complete or comprehensive unless it encompasses the history of the House of Lords. The Trustees of the History of Parliament decided a decade ago to embark upon that history, and this volume introduces a series which will eventually cover the history of the House of Lords from medieval times, looking in detail at the House of Lords as a parliamentary institution, and at all those who have sat there over the centuries.

Here we have a survey of the Lords during one of the most important and fascinating periods in its history – the years between 1660, the restoration of Charles II, and 1715, the year of the first Jacobite Rebellion against the first of the Hanoverians, George I. It was not merely the monarchy that was restored in 1660; so was the House of Lords itself following its abolition as 'useless and dangerous' after the deposition and execution of Charles I.

This brief volume looks, chronologically, at the development of the Lords from its Restoration; at the crucial part its members played during the often turbulent, but almost entirely peaceful, revolution which followed the fall of James II and the accession of William and Mary in 1688–89; and at the passing of the legislation which laid the foundations for our constitutional monarchy.

It is a volume remarkable not only for the period it encompasses, but for the lively biographical sketches of so many of the leading figures in this seminal period of English history, seminal not least for the relations between the monarch and Parliament and between the two Houses.

This short but comprehensive survey will be followed by a series of detailed volumes on the House of Lords – volumes which, like their counterparts in the history of the House of Commons, will include more detailed historical surveys together with biographies of all who played a part in the deliberations of the upper House.

No one can fully understand the history of our country without having a reasonable knowledge of the development and evolution of our great institutions, and central to such an understanding is a knowledge of the history of Parliament. I very much hope that this volume will awaken a new interest in the House of Lords during one of the most fascinating and formative periods of that history.

The Trustees are particularly grateful to Dr Paul Seaward, Director of the History of Parliament and one of the editors of this volume, to his co-editor, Ruth Paley, and to the others who have contributed to the text. We are also very much in the debt of Professor Paul Langford, Chairman of the Editorial Board, and his colleagues.

Sir Patrick Cormack FSA

Contents

List of illustrations

Preface

The House of Lords may never have been more interesting or more politically significant than in the period between its restoration, along with the monarchy, in 1660, and the accession of George I in 1714. Its re-establishment itself represented a remarkable reversal of events. The House had been abolished in 1649 as 'useless and dangerous' in the revolution that also deposed and executed King Charles I. The almost casual decision in 1660 to reinstate it was an indication of the nearly universal desire to return to old and familiar institutions – 'the ancient landmarks' – which would also bring back Charles II from exile, and result in the recreation of an episcopal Church of England. Yet despite the conservative tide of 1660, such institutions could no longer take their existence, and their importance, as much for granted as they did before the Civil War. For the Lords, that knowledge made the body, and its members, assertive of their role and defensive about their privileges.

It was not just its assertiveness that characterised the Lords in this period. Politics changed irrevocably over the five and a half decades discussed here. With memories of its divisions fresh in the mind, political battles quickly turned into debates on the causes and consequences of the Civil War. Half-suppressed for twenty years, those divisions would be revived and reinterpreted with a vengeance in the early 1680s over the question of the exclusion of the king's brother, the Catholic James, duke of York, from the throne.

James's self-destructive determination to pursue his policy of reintroducing Catholicism to England after he became king in 1685, and the legacy of the Revolution that followed in 1688–89, confused and disrupted them. Nevertheless, the split between two political traditions, founded in the Civil War and named 'Whig' and 'Tory', would settle to become the organising principle of English, and then British, politics for more than a century and a half. They were an essential ingredient in the politics of the House of Lords, where sat the principal government ministers and some of the most able politicians of their day.

Politics in the upper House, though, was about much more than party rivalries. It was profoundly complicated by the connections and rivalries between individual peers and their families, for the House of Lords mingled family politics and private interests with public life and national concerns to a degree that is deeply alien to most modern legislatures. Members could and did use it to promote their own businesses, solving their disputes by exploiting their privileges or by obtaining private legislation. They were as interested in issues that sustained and developed the local and regional dominance of their families as in subjects of national concern, such as the health of the Church, the inheritance of the throne, or the likelihood of war and peace.

This book aims to provide some idea of the way in which the House of Lords operated from the Restoration to the Hanoverian succession, and a sense of the interplay of family affairs and national politics, of individual ambition and collective privilege, which were always involved in its proceedings. The research on which it rests has been carried out by the History of Parliament Trust for its project on The House of Lords, 1660–1832. The first instalments of that project, the biographies of Members of the House of Lords from 1660–1715 and an account of the House of Lords as an institution over the whole period, are planned for publication in 2013–14. This book introduces in advance of that publication some of the highlights of that research and suggests some of the issues and questions that may be addressed more fully when the work is completed. It makes no claim to be a comprehensive treatment of its subject: *The History of Parliament: the House of Lords 1660–1715*, however, will be a more comprehensive account than anything previously attempted on the House of Lords.

The research for this book has been undertaken by Ruth Paley, Beverly Adams, Robin Eagles and Charles Littleton, and the book edited by Ruth Paley and Paul Seaward. Stuart Handley, who joined the Section during the project, has also contributed information and suggestions. The section on the chamber in chapter 6 is based substantially on work by Dr Clyve Jones. The section on the Scottish representative peers is based substantially on work by Dr Graham Townend. Dr Nicholas Holland provided advice on translation and iconography. Picture research was undertaken by Jo Walton and Julia Harris-Voss. The Section has also benefited greatly from the support and advice of Sir John Sainty and Dr Colin Brooks, and the chairman of the Editorial Board of the History, Professor Paul Langford, who have read and commented on drafts of some or all of the text. We are greatly indebted to them. The Section is also, as usual, grateful to the owners and custodians of archive and library collections used in the compilation of this book and the bigger project on which it is based. Sources quoted in this book have come from just a few of the collections we have consulted, and we are particularly grateful to the marquess of Bath, the duke of Bedford, the duke of Beaufort, the Berkeley Will Trust, Sir Richard Carew Pole, the Governing Body of Christ Church, Oxford, the duke of Devonshire, the Trustees of the Goodwood Collections and West Sussex Record Office and the county archivist, Trustees of the Lowther estate and the marquess of Salisbury, for access to and permission to quote from their collections.

Editorial styles and conventions

The way in which peerage titles are used in this book requires some explanation. Peers could accumulate and shed a bewildering variety of names during their lives. Fundamentally, a title would be passed down within a family by the rules of inheritance, so that between 1660 and 1715 there were, for example, two Barons Wharton, the 4th and 5th Barons. If the family line, and therefore the title, died out, however, the same title could be used again for another peerage: William Savile, 2nd marquess of Halifax, died in September 1700 with no male heir; three months later the Halifax title was used again as a barony for Charles Montagu. Many individuals were promoted in the peerage and thus were known at different times by different titles. Sir Thomas Osborne, for instance, was successively Viscount Latimer, earl of Danby, marquess of Carmarthen and duke of Leeds.

Further complications can arise where an individual peer held two or more titles at the same time. In such cases, the next most senior title could be used by his heir as a matter of courtesy, a 'courtesy title', though it did not confer the right to sit in the House of Lords. Robert Montagu, for example, heir to the earldom of Manchester and known as ('styled') Viscount Mandeville, was thus eligible for election to the Commons and represented Huntingdonshire for fourteen years. On the other hand, some heirs to peerages were summoned to the House of Lords during their fathers' lifetimes under a writ of acceleration. In such cases they would use one of their father's more junior titles. Henry Howard was styled earl of Arundel until he succeeded as 7th duke of Norfolk in 1684, but he sat in the House of Lords from 1678 under a writ of acceleration in his father's junior barony as Lord Mowbray.

Further confusion can be caused by the possession of titles in other peerages. The three separate kingdoms of the British Isles (England and Wales; Scotland; Ireland) each had its own peerage but until 1707 only those with a title in the English peerage could sit in the House of Lords at Westminster. Men who held titles in the Scots or Irish peerage, but held none in the English peerage, might be elected to the House of Commons. A number of peers who held titles in the Irish or Scottish peerages also held titles in the English peerage. They were then commonly known by the highest ranking of their titles, irrespective of the peerage to which it belonged, but in the House of Lords they were referred to by their highest English title. James Butler, created duke of Ormond in the Irish peerage in 1661, sat in the House of Lords from 1660 to 1682 as the earl of Brecknock.

Similar confusion can occur when referring to bishops, who frequently moved from one see to another. One name in particular illustrates the point, since there were two William Lloyds in this period sitting as bishops in the House of Lords, one of whom was successively bishop of St Asaph, of Lichfield and Coventry and of Worcester; the other was bishop of Llandaff, Peterborough and finally of Norwich.

In order to avoid confusion, in each chapter individual peers are given their full name and title at first mention, for example Philip Wharton, 4th Baron Wharton or Thomas Wharton, 5th Baron Wharton. Subsequent mentions are by title only unless more than one holder of the same peerage is mentioned within the chapter, in which case the individual is given his number, rank and title (e.g. the 4th Baron Wharton). No numeral is given to the first holder of a newly created peerage. In the case of courtesy titles the individual concerned is described as *styled* – thus before 1669 (when he became 2nd earl of Berkshire) Charles Howard was *styled* Lord Andover although he sat in the House of Lords as Baron Howard of Charleton. Bishops are given their full name and see at first mention, thus William Lloyd of St Asaph, but subsequent references are by surname and see (Lloyd of St Asaph).

Amounts of money that would have seemed astronomical to contemporaries, but are commonplace today, are frequently mentioned throughout this book. Attempts to convert such sums into modern values are fraught with difficulty. Simple arithmetical conversions (say, multiplication by 100) sometimes roughly catch the meaning of a sum in modern terms, but often, because inflation has affected different commodities in different ways, they give a poor idea of its real purchasing power. Some sense of their real value may be provided by some comparative figures. In the late seventeenth century an unskilled labourer might be lucky to earn 1s. a day in the distant provinces or up to 2s. a day in the high wage economy of London; he would also face regular seasonal unemployment. In 1672, the rectory of Burrough Green in Cambridgeshire, near Newmarket, was one of the most valuable livings in the country, providing its rector (Thomas Watson, later a bishop) with an income of £128 a year (more senior clergymen would be able to accumulate a number of livings and positions with stipends to increase their income). Samuel Pepys, a relatively senior civil servant as clerk of the acts in the Navy, received an annual salary of £350.

Finally, in this work, references have been provided only for direct quotations from contemporary sources and these can be found at the end of the book. Full supporting references will be published with the relevant articles in *The History of Parliament: the House of Lords 1660–1715*. The spelling and punctuation of all quotations have been modernised, as have the conventions concerning dating.

FIG. 1 *A catalogue of the noblemen and peers of the kingdom of England, according to their birth and creation, in the reign of Charles the Second* (1662).

The House of Lords restored, 1660–61

At the beginning of 1660, the House of Lords did not exist. At the climax of the English Revolution, less than a week after the execution of King Charles I in January 1649, the House of Commons had resolved 'That the House of Peers in Parliament is useless and dangerous, and ought to be abolished'.[1] On 19 March, two days after it had formally dismantled the monarchy, the new Commonwealth abolished the House of Lords and the parliamentary privileges of the peerage.

The revival of the House was part of the bewildering and, to royalist partisans, miraculous, series of events that led to the Restoration of the monarchy in May 1660. Four years after abolishing the monarchy and the Lords, the Commonwealth had itself been dismissed by its discontented army under the charismatic leadership of Oliver Cromwell. After Cromwell's death in September 1658 it proved impossible to recreate the balancing act by which he had managed to retain the loyalty of the army while trying to establish a legitimate civilian administration. While the army leadership battled with a restored Parliament, General George Monck, the commander of the army in Scotland, precipitated the final crisis (see below, p. 8). His dramatic march to London at the beginning of 1660 split the army and forced the civilian politicians of the Long Parliament, originally elected in 1640, to agree to hold elections for a new Parliament. On Friday 16 March, at almost the last moment before Parliament was dissolved, they asserted:

> that the single actings of this House, enforced by the pressing necessities of the present times, are not intended, in the least, to infringe, much less take away, that ancient native right, which the House of Peers, consisting of those lords who did engage in the cause of the Parliament, against the forces raised in the name of the late king, and so continued until 1648, had, and have, to be a part of the Parliament of England.[2]

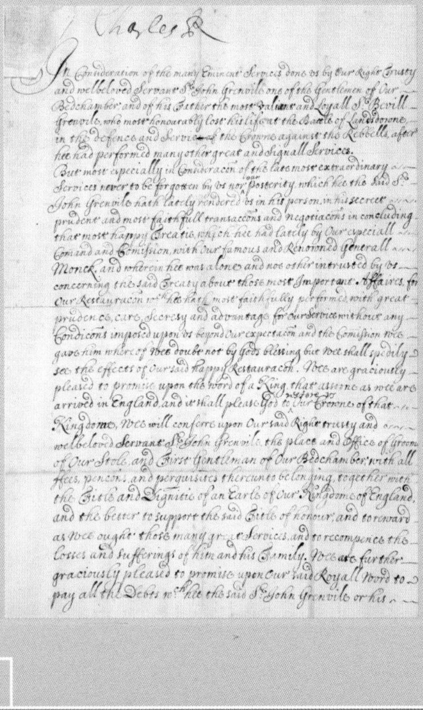

Charles R

In Consideration of the many Eminent Services done us by Our Right Trusty and welbeloved Servant Sr John Grenvile one of the Gentlemen of Our Bedchamber and of his Father the most valiant and Loyall Sr Bevill Grenvile, who most honourably lost his life at the Battle of Lansdowne in the defence and Service of the Crowne against the Rebells, after hee had performed many other great and signall Services.
But most especially in Consideracon of the late most extraordinary Services never to be forgotten by us nor our Posterity, which hee the said Sr John Grenvile hath lately rendered us in his person, in his secreet prudent and most faithfull transaccons and negociacons in concluding that most happy Treatie, which hee had lately by Our especiall Comand and Comission, with Our famous and Renowned Generall Monck, and wherein hee was alone and noe other intrusted by us concerning the said Treaty about those most Important Affaires, for Our Restauracon wch hee hath most faithfully performed, with great prudence, care, secresy and advantage for Our Service without any Condicons imposed upon us beyond Our expectacon and the Comission wee gave him whereof wee doubt not by Gods blessing but wee shall speedily see the effects of Our said happy Restauracon. Wee are graciously pleased to promise upon the word of a King that assoone as wee are arrived in England and it shall please God to restore us to Our Crowne of that Kingdome, wee will conferre upon Our said Right trusty and welbeloved Servant Sr John Grenvile the place and Office of Groome of Our Stole, and First Gentleman of Our Bedchamber, with all ffees, pencons and perquisites thereunto belonging, together with the Title and Dignitie of an Earle of Our Kingdome of England, and the better to support the said Title of honour, and to reward as wee ought those many great Services, and to recompence the Losses and Sufferings of him and his Family, Wee are further graciously pleased to promise upon Our said Royall word to pay all the Debts wch hee the said Sr John Grenvile or his

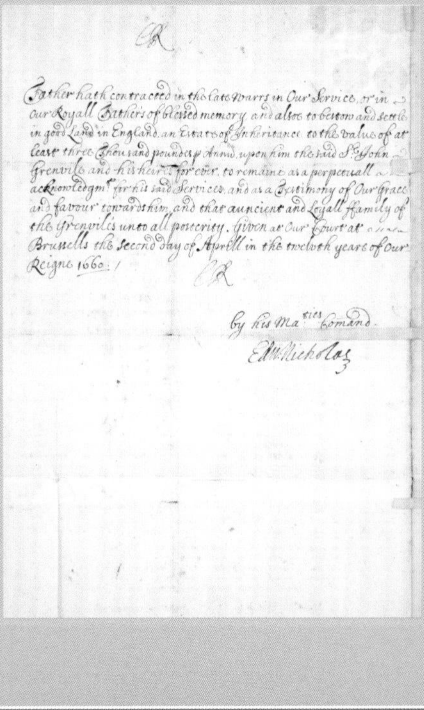

CR

Father hath contracted in the late warrs in Our Service, or in Our Royall Father's of blessed memory, and alsoe to bestow and settle in good Land in England an Estate of Inheritance to the value of at least three Thousand pounds p Annu upon him the said Sr John Grenvile and his heires for ever, to remaine as a perpetuall acknowledgmt for his said Services, and as a Testimony of Our Grace and favour towards him, and that auncient and Loyall ffamily of the Grenviles unto all posterity. Given at Our Court at Brussells the second day of Aprill in the twelveth yeare of Our Reigne 1660.

CR

by his Maties Comand.

Edw: Nicholas

FIG. 2 *Warrant of Charles II to John Granville, 2 April 1660. Granville acted as the king's go-between with Monck in the negotiations leading up to the Restoration: here he is promised an earldom, a post in the bedchamber and an estate of £3,000 after the Restoration.*

This left the peers who had fought on behalf of the king still excluded; the bishops were too, by virtue of an act of Parliament passed in 1642. But a House of Lords would be part of the new Convention Parliament. Around six weeks later, on 25 April, the Convention Parliament met at Westminster. That morning ten peers took their seats in their old chamber. Simeon Ashe, a puritan minister who had long been close to Edward Montagu, 2nd earl of Manchester, preached a sermon; the House chose Manchester as its Speaker (there being no lord chancellor or lord keeper to take the chair); it demanded that its records be returned to the custody of John Browne, who had been appointed clerk of the Parliaments in 1638. It sent letters to six more peers asking them to attend. The House of Lords, which had not met since 6 February 1649, was again in being.

It was almost inevitable that the new Parliament would call Charles I's son, Charles II, back from exile to take power. It was far from obvious how much power he would be allowed to take. For almost two weeks, supporters of different visions of the restored monarchy struggled to turn the odds in their favour, while royal courtiers watched anxiously from the continent. An election aftergame was played in the Commons, as each side challenged the polls in an attempt to unseat its opponents. In the Lords the crucial battle was whether all peers would be allowed to take their seats, or only those who had supported the parliamentary cause.

When it first met in 1660, the House of Lords was dominated by the men who had opposed Charles I in the civil wars and had then struggled against the religious and social radicalism of the army.

FIG. 3 *Charles landed at Dover on 25 May: he waited until his birthday, four days later, to arrive in London. This painting by Isaac Fuller shows him en route to the Banqueting House in Whitehall, where he was presented with addresses by both Houses of Parliament.*

Among these 'presbyterians' were the earl of Manchester and Algernon Percy, 4th earl of Northumberland. Manchester was a veteran parliamentarian, a civil war general who had led the presbyterian group in the 1640s. Northumberland, a central figure in the parliamentary leadership in the early 1640s, had desperately attempted to negotiate with Charles I in 1648. Both still hoped for limitations on the power of the restored king. Northumberland wrote in mid-April that 'some there are that would have [the king] restored to all, without any condition, ... but the soberer people will I believe expect terms of more security for themselves and advantage for the nation'.[3] Cast aside in 1647 by Cromwell and the Army, the 'soberer people' were now submerged by the royalist tide. The military did nothing to prevent young royalist peers, including some Catholics, from taking their seats, negating the influence of the presbyterian peers. A well-judged statement by the king, the Declaration of Breda, which left the details of the political and religious settlement to be determined by Parliament, secured a resolution in both Houses 'that, according to the ancient and fundamental laws of this kingdom, the government is, and ought to be, by king, Lords, and Commons'. On 25 May 1660 Charles II landed at Dover; on 29 May (his 30th birthday) he rode into Whitehall Palace. There, in the Banqueting House, it

FIG. 4 The most magnificent riding of Charles the IId to the Parliament, *etching by Richard Gaywood, 1661: Charles is accompanied on the right of the picture by his brother, James, duke of York, George Villiers, duke of Buckingham, and his lord chancellor, Edward Hyde, earl of Clarendon. To the left, leading the horse of state is George Monck, duke of Albemarle.*

was Manchester who acted as the Lords' spokesman, to 'express their lordships' great joy for his Majesty's safe return to his throne'.[4]

The political struggle moved to the religious settlement. The nature of the Church, its institutions, its clergy and its worship, had been at the heart of the confrontations which had brought civil war in 1642. During the 1640s, the Church of England had been dismantled. The bishops had been expelled from Parliament in 1642; episcopacy itself was formally abolished in 1646. An attempt to create a new Church, closer to the Presbyterian churches of continental Europe, had foundered. Informal religious sects, regarded by churchmen as schismatic and sinful and by the social elite as dangerously rootless, had flourished. Royalists – and even most Presbyterians – wanted to restore a national Church with an episcopal structure. Their visions of this restored national Church, however, were very different. Presbyterians in both Houses struggled to prevent a straightforward restoration of the pre-war Church of England. Two days after the celebration in the Banqueting House, when the king removed the remaining restrictions on royalist peers, presbyterian influence in the Lords was overwhelmed. Royalists in the upper House collaborated with the restored regime to block the presbyterian majority in the Commons from securing a settlement on the religious question. Once the army was disbanded, an Act of Indemnity and Oblivion covering the events of the Revolution had been passed and an apparently substantial annual revenue voted for the crown. The king dissolved the Convention to prepare the way for a new Parliament – one which,

Charles and his advisers hoped, would offer a more secure basis for the rebuilding of royal power in Church and state.

The Commons in the 'Cavalier Parliament', elected in April 1661, was, as the government had hoped, a far more royalist and pro-Church body than its predecessor. The Lords was, in theory at least, an even more reliable partner of the restored monarchy. At his coronation on 20 April 1661, the king created new peers, and promoted others, rewarding royalist families and individuals (Arthur Capell and Edward Hyde as earls of Essex and Clarendon) as well as former parliamentarians and presbyterians (Arthur Annesley and Charles Howard as earls of Anglesey and Carlisle; Denzil Holles, Anthony Ashley Cooper, George Booth and John Crew as Barons Holles, Ashley, Delamer and Crew). The latter were successful and experienced parliamentarians who would become powerful forces in national political life. In terms of numbers, though, they made little difference to the temper of the House. One of the first acts of the Cavalier Parliament was to restore the bishops to the House of Lords. When it reconvened after a short recess in November 1661, the votes of the thirty or so parliamentarian and presbyterian peers were balanced by those of the twenty-six bishops, almost all of whom supported the court. When Northumberland agreed to hold the proxy vote of his brother-in-law, old friend and political ally Robert Sydney, 2nd earl of Leicester, he ruefully remarked that 'there will not be much use made of proxies in the House, for all things are likely to pass there very unanimously.'[5]

Chapter 1

'The ancient land mark': the House of Lords in the constitutional landscape

The power of the peerage: the House of Lords before the Restoration

Abolished together and restored together, the relationship between the House of Lords and the monarchy was a close and ancient one. The House of Lords had grown out of the councils of the principal magnates of the kingdom, summoned by early medieval kings to give them advice and support. Most peers still assumed themselves to be the monarchy's natural provider of both, and looked in turn to the crown for the flow of offices and pensions which helped to maintain their political power and social status. As, from the late thirteenth and fourteenth centuries, representatives of the county gentry and urban communities collected together in the House of Commons, these meetings of leading magnates developed into one of the trio of institutions which were collectively regarded as constituting Parliament – the king, the Lords and the Commons. Parliament would become an institution whose principal aim was to represent the grievances of the people and to assent, on their behalf, to taxation. In these activities, the Commons was unquestionably the centre of attention. Yet peers were dominant figures in political life, because of their local power, the influence they could exercise over Members of the House of Commons, and their close relationship with the monarch. Their competition with each other for honour, wealth and power was played out at the royal court, in the House of Lords, and often, by proxy, in the House of Commons.

    Collectively, they might also deploy their power against the crown. If the nobility regarded themselves as the monarchy's greatest resource, the power and influence of the greatest magnates could equally be its most potent threat. It was common in the late sixteenth and early seventeenth centuries to overlay onto the medieval structures of Parliament the classical distinction of the one, the few and the many, with the monarch as the one, the House of Lords as the few, and the House of Commons as the many. According to ancient political theory, the perfect constitution would balance those elements. If one of them became predominant, the state might degenerate into tyranny, oligarchy or a crude democracy. Seventeenth century politicians and political theorists closely examined the histories of Greece and Rome to understand how monarchies could slip into tyrannies, and how aristocracies might challenge monarchies and descend into chaos and civil war. They looked even more closely at the many examples from England's medieval history of confrontations between the king and his magnates.

As recently as 1601, Robert Devereux, 2nd earl of Essex, had led a desperate rebellion against the administration headed by Queen Elizabeth I's principal minister, Robert Cecil. In early Stuart England a successful aristocratic coup seemed, on the face of it, unlikely. Compared to some continental aristocracies, the English nobility seemed harmless. They had significant privileges, but were not exempt from taxation and did not have exclusive access to certain offices as was the case in other European countries. By creating large numbers of new peerages, James I and Charles I had encouraged the link between noble status and loyal service to the king. Many of the new peers – men like Robert Carr, earl of Somerset; George Villiers, duke of Buckingham; Thomas Wentworth, earl of Strafford – had risen to enormous wealth and power almost entirely through royal favour.

The crisis of the 1640s, however, was to prove that the peerage of the seventeenth century was collectively powerful still and that it was far from simply dependent on the monarchy. Robert Devereux, 3rd earl of Essex, Algernon Percy, 4th earl of Northumberland, Robert Rich, 2nd earl of Warwick, Philip Herbert, 4th earl of Pembroke, and William Fiennes, Viscount Saye and Sele were among the central figures who took Parliament to war against the king. Imbued with classical humanist ideas, they were keenly aware of the status of the peerage as the king's counsellors and as the source of an independent power to check and control misgovernment. Parliament's *Nineteen Propositions* of June 1642 were initiated in the Lords and echoed some of the demands of the baronial reform movements of the middle ages. The king's *Answer*, drafted by two of his reformist advisers, both of them Members of the House of

FIG. 5 *Toilet mirror, c. 1665, diamond-point engraved glass, with ebony-veneered wood frame. George Villiers, 2nd duke of Buckingham, obtained a patent in 1660 for the manufacture of mirrors at Vauxhall. This example includes the arms of the City of London, and vignettes of the king and queen; the queen mother (Queen Henrietta Maria), the duke of York, and the duke of Albemarle, General Monck.*

Commons, Lucius Carey, 2nd Viscount Falkland (in the Scottish peerage) and Sir John Colepepper, almost casually conceded an equality of status between the king, the Lords and the Commons, a position from which the crown spent the next half-century trying to recover. It also warned the Lords against an attempt to dominate the monarchy, emphasising that their role was to balance the centrifugal forces within the constitution. The Lords, it said, 'being trusted with a judicatory power, are an excellent screen and bank between the prince and people, to assist each against any incroachments of the other, and by just judgements to preserve that law, which ought to be the rule of every one of the three'. The *Answer* sketched out its vision of the consequences of the failure of the peerage to perform its task: it would be treated by the Commons in the same way as the

Saviour of the nation: George Monck, duke of Albemarle (1608–70)

George Monck, the younger son of an impoverished country gentleman, killed his first man, a Devon under-sheriff who had arrested his father for debt, in 1626 when he was 18. To escape prosecution he fled the country and became a professional soldier. From 1641 to 1644 he fought against the Irish rebellion under the command of James Butler, then earl of Ormond, an Irish peer. Transferred to England, he was captured by the parliamentarians in 1644. In 1646, with the royalist cause in ruins, he accepted employment under Parliament, fighting again in Ireland. Successes there, at sea against the Dutch, and against the Scots made him one of the army's most successful commanders by the time of the death of Cromwell in 1658. Monck, in command of an isolated army of occupation in Scotland, became a key figure in the political negotiations of 1659–60. His dramatic march on London in early 1660 sealed the fate of the English republic. When he became committed to a restoration of the monarchy is no clearer now than it was in 1660. His agenda, as far as it can be determined, was set out in an eight point paper presented to the House of Commons in May 1660. Three of the points related to the land settlement. Another stipulated that he was to be commander of the army for life. One point referred to the vexed question of religion, calling for 'an assembly of divines' rather than a convocation (which would be dominated by supporters of an episcopal Church of England) to settle the Church.

Initially at least, Charles II was highly wary of the general and his army. There was an awkward moment when, a few days after the king's arrival in Canterbury, on his way to London, Monck 'without any preamble or apology, as he was not a man of a graceful elocution', handed the king a long list of names, implying that they – almost all of them former parliamentarians – should be provided with senior positions in his administration. Monck, though, never pressed home his advantage: these, he told the king subsequently, were all people whom he had promised to recommend to the king without any expectation that he would accept them.[1] Monck was heaped with flattery, honours and gifts: on the way to London,

FIG. 6 (ABOVE) *Thomas Simon's gold medal of Monck, struck in 1660.*
FIG. 7 (OPPOSITE) *Albemarle was still the subject of popular representation in 1680, ten years after his death, on this tin-glazed earthenware dish, possibly made to commemorate a marriage in London that year.*

though still a mere commoner, he sat with the king and his brothers in the royal coach while the 2nd duke of Buckingham was consigned to the boot; when the royal party swapped to horses, the king was flanked on his right by his brothers and on his left by Monck. He was appointed to the new privy council, made master of the horse, captain general of the forces in all three kingdoms, a gentleman of the bedchamber and lord lieutenant of Devon and was tipped as a possible lord treasurer. In July 1660 he became one of only three non-royal dukes in the English peerage, choosing the title of Albemarle in a deliberate reference to his supposed Plantagenet origins.

Albemarle never did become a threat to the stability of the regime. Instead he became its reliable spokesman, go-between and trouble-shooter, whose multiple public lives – as military commander, as a key figure in maintaining law and order and as a member of the privy council as well as of the House of Lords – put him at the centre of the policy making process for nearly every aspect of Restoration government. In June 1660, for example, before he became a peer, and during the acrimonious debates in the Commons on the Act of Indemnity and Oblivion, he 'told 'em that he knew His Majesty's mind (and had come to declare it)'.[2] Although he had significant parliamentary influence in both Houses, he never tried to create a personal political following. His contribution

to the business of the House of Lords was unremarkable. He largely distanced himself from the presbyterians, who hoped that he would back their proposals for a moderate settlement of the Church. The one area in which Monck's influence was clearly visible was the Restoration land settlement. Confirming titles to land lawfully sold during the Interregnum – even when the sales had been the direct result of the fines imposed on royalists – was central to securing the support of former parliamentarians as well as the loyalty of the army. In May 1660, when the Commons had discussed the restitution of lands to the marquess of Winchester (having already made a similar order for Buckingham and others) Monck

forestalled debate by saying that 'it would give rise to discontent in the army'.[3] As a major beneficiary of Interregnum land sales Albemarle also had a strong personal interest in ensuring they were not overturned.

Albemarle's main role was to maintain order. In the autumn of 1660 he arranged for military patrols to protect Londoners from highwaymen and when fears about highway robberies again became acute in 1667, it was to him that the Commons turned for advice. In July 1662 he was appointed lord lieutenant of Middlesex and Southwark, thereby assuming responsibility for suppressing any disorder that might arise during the ejection of Presbyterian ministers

FIG. 8 *Albemarle's funeral cortège, from* The order and ceremonies used for, and at the most solemn interment of the most high, mighty and most noble prince George, duke of Albemarle *(1670). Francis Sandford's lavish volume describes the lying-in-state of the body at Somerset House, with an effigy of the duke lying on the coffin 'in a buff coat, and over that complete azure armour with gilt nails, a cravat about his neck, his ducal coronet and cap turned up with ermine on his head, invested in his ducal robe of crimson velvet'. The funeral, the costs of which were borne by the crown, cost more than £5,000, with a further £300 spent on embalming the body.*

from their livings under the Act of Uniformity. After the Great Fire of London, the king and the privy council turned to Albemarle as the only man who could keep a grip on the capital. Once again he was seen as the saviour of the nation, able 'to give the king his kingdom a second time.'[4] He helped the king deal with his quarrelsome courtiers, acting as messenger when one was banned from court and preventing several duels. Despite his failing health, faith in his military abilities remained extraordinarily high so that his appointment as general at sea in 1666 was regarded as a virtual guarantee of victory, prompting lenders to open their purses: 'Money comes in freely … upon easier terms than before,' remarked William Sancroft, later archbishop of Canterbury, 'upon the great reputation of that good man'.[5]

Towards the end of 1668 Albemarle's health collapsed. By February 1669 his condition had become public knowledge, and for the remaining months of his life, in telling confirmation of his almost talismanic status as the saviour of the monarchy, newsletters and private correspondents provided regular accounts of his condition. His last major act was to secure the future of his dynasty: negotiations for the marriage of his son, Christopher Monck, to the daughter of Lord Ogle (later the 2nd duke of Newcastle) secured a portion of almost royal size (£20,000) and resulted in a wedding that took place on the penultimate day of 1669. Albemarle died just four days later: his body was laid in state at Somerset House and the king footed the bill for his lavish funeral.

two Houses had treated the king. In the end the common people would collectively

> discover this *Arcanum Imperii*, that all this was done by them, but not for them, grow weary of journey-work, and set up for themselves, call parity and independence, liberty; devour that estate which had devoured the rest; destroy all rights and proprieties, all distinctions of families and merit; and by this means this splendid and excellently distinguished form of government [will] end in a dark equall chaos of confusion, and the long line of our many noble ancestors in a Jack Cade, or a Wat Tyler.[1]

In some respects, the *Answer* was prophetic. In the seven years after its publication the House of Lords was edged into insignificance and then summarily abolished. The lords spiritual had already been excluded from the Lords by statute in February 1642, in one of the last acts of Parliament to receive the royal assent before the outbreak of the civil war. In May and June Parliament had demanded the removal of Catholic peers from the House of Lords, although by then they had already withdrawn themselves voluntarily. A steady trickle of prominent peers obeyed the king's summons to join his council at York.

In 1646 both Houses of Parliament agreed an ordinance to nullify all peerage creations made since 20 May 1642. By then the peers sitting at Westminster had dwindled from 142 to 29. Apologists for the Commons became increasingly dismissive of the relevance and importance of the Lords. Parliament's most active propagandist, Henry Parker, argued in *Jus Populi* of 1644, that

> the truth is, both monarchy, and aristocracy, are derivative forms, and [owe] a dependance upon democracy, which though it be not the best, and most exact form for all nations and empires at all times, yet it is ever the most natural, and primarily authentical; and for some times and places, the most beneficial.[2]

After the king's defeat, the remaining peers struggled ineffectually to combat the religious and political radicalism of the army leadership, earning the condemnation of Levellers like Richard Overton for their attempts to use their judicial powers against them. Overton emphasised the peers' association with the crown when he complained bitterly of the 'unlimited' jurisdiction of the House of Lords and the 'barbarous unheard of inhumanities (such as never were acted by their *Norman* progenitors, since the *prerogative foundation* of that Norman house was ever laid, or ever since they bore the name of an House of Peers)'.[3] Following the refusal of the House of Lords to participate in setting up the high court of justice to try the king, what was left of the Commons – the 'Rump' Parliament – declared in early 1649

> that the people are, under God, the original of all just power and ... the Commons of England, in Parliament assembled, being chosen by, and representing the people, have the supreme power in this nation and ... that whatever is enacted, or declared for law, by the Commons, in Parliament assembled, hath the force of law; and all the people of this nation are concluded thereby, although the consent and concurrence of king, or House of Peers, be not had thereunto.[4]

The king's execution and the abolition of the House of Lords followed soon afterwards.

Removed from political power, the peerage looked set to decay. Royalist aristocrats followed their king into exile or retreated to their estates, proscribed from playing their ancient role in government and replaced as governors of their local communities by county committees and professional soldiers. Even their estates were under threat, hit by fines and sequestration by the parliamentary authorities. The English republic and its propagandists, such as Marchamont Nedham, insisted over the next few years on the dangers of a 'standing aristocracy' and dismissed, at least implicitly, the argument for any separate body to balance the power of a single chamber. Regular elections would ensure, they claimed, that the system did not become moribund or corrupt.

Aristocracy in some form or other, though, was difficult to forget. The Rump's attempt to legislate for new elections exposed the ideological and political faultlines between the republic and the army. Cromwell dismissed it in April 1653 and established the Protectorate. The Protectorate's constitution, the Instrument of Government of December 1653, settled the 'supreme legislative authority' in 'one person [the lord protector] and the people assembled in parliament' – a unicameral assembly which met for the first time in 1654. Over the next five years the constitution was debated more intensively than before or for many years afterwards. Central to the debate was the relationship between executive and legislature and the maintenance of a balance between them. The greatest single contribution to it was James Harrington's *Oceana*, published in 1656. In a sophisticated analysis of the forces at work in English society,

Harrington pronounced dead what he called the 'gothic balance' between a military nobility and the king. Henry VII's suppression of the independent military power of the nobility had left the crown without a support against anyone else. The result had been the monarchy's collapse and the rise of the army and its general. Harrington proposed to replace the feudal nobility with a new type of aristocracy, compatible with an essentially republican constitution. Qualification for membership would be based on property, rather than on heredity, but its members would be popularly elected. His senate and popular assembly would fulfil different functions: the one would propose solutions, the other would decide on them. The basic principle of how to ensure that two separate interests cooperate satisfactorily was, said Harrington, well known enough,

> even unto girls ...for example, two of them have a cake yet undivided, which was given between them. That each of them therefore may have that which is due, 'Divide', says one unto the other, 'and I will choose; or let me divide, and you shall choose.' If this be but once agreed upon, it is enough; for the divident dividing unequally loses, in regard that the other takes the better half; wherefore she divides equally, and so both have right.[5]

Harrington's tract revived and revised the notion of a balance of institutional forces as a means of tempering unchecked power. The subject was at the centre of political debate in 1656 because of Parliament's controversial decision to try the Quaker James Nayler for blasphemy. In late February 1657 a proposition emerged, probably from the protector's court, for re-establishing the essential elements of the old constitution – a 'king, a House of Lords and a lower House'.[6] A few days later Cromwell argued that

> it is time to come to a settlement and lay aside arbitrary proceedings, so unacceptable to the nation. And by the proceedings of this Parliament, you see they stand in need of a check or balancing power (meaning the House of Lords or a House so constituted) for the case of James Nayler might happen to be your own case. By their judicial power, they fall upon life and member.[7]

The scheme proposed the creation of an 'Other House' with 40 to 70 members nominated by the protector, subject to approval by the Commons; this 'Other House' would have criminal jurisdiction but only on impeachment from the Commons; the crown would be offered to the protector. The package, known as the Humble Petition and Advice, was

'There is no pleasure in the memory of the past': William Fiennes, Viscount Saye and Sele (1582–1662)

William Fines Vifcount Sey and Seale, Lord Sey and Seale,

FIG. 9

he historian and statesman Edward Hyde, earl of Clarendon, described Viscount Saye and Sele as 'a man who had the deepest hand in the original contrivance of all the calamities which befell [this] unhappy kingdom', 'the pilot that steered all those vessels which were freighted with sedition to destroy the government'.[1] A libel circulated in 1641 dubbed him the 'Anabaptist' leader of 'a pack of half witted lords' who should be 'torn in pieces' for their actions.[2] It was scarcely surprising that by the time of the Restoration, Saye and Sele had had inscribed over the arch in the oak drawing room of his house at Broughton the words: *Quod olim fuit, meminisse minime iuvat* (There is no pleasure in the memory of the past).[3]

Sayle and Sele had been a prominent critic of both James I and Charles I before the Civil War, deeply involved in the puritan circles in which the parliamentary leaders John Pym and John Hampden were also active. His loyalty to the court had been briefly bought by promotion to a viscountcy through Buckingham's influence in 1624. Within two years he had again deserted it. Throughout the Civil War he was committed to the parliamentary cause: after it, he opposed the king's execution and refused to take any part in Cromwell's government. The proposed 'Other House' he treated with contempt as a 'stalking horse and vizard to carry on the design of overthrowing the House of Peers'. Cautioning his friend, Philip Wharton, 4th Lord Wharton, against accepting Cromwell's offer of a place in it, he described the ancient peerage as 'the beam keeping both scales, king and people, in an even posture, without encroachments one upon another to the hurt and damage of both'.[4] He resolved that 'if a writ be sent me I will lay it by me and sit still'.[5]

By the time of Cromwell's death in 1658, Saye and Sele was cautiously in favour of a Restoration of the monarchy, albeit one based on the conditions under negotiation with Charles I in 1648. He warily entered into correspondence with royalist activists. He may have been more inclined to a Restoration because of his alarm at the growth in the dangerously anti-hierarchical Quaker movement. Despite his antipathy to the episcopal Church of England, Saye and Sele reserved his most vehement distaste for the Quakers, whom he attacked in two pamphlets, *Folly and Madness made manifest* (1659) [Fig.10] and *The Quakers reply manifested to be railing* (1660) [Fig.11]. During the 1650s he harshly persecuted members of the sect. Two Quakers resident within his own manor were ejected from their homes, along with their wives and children, and left in the streets for three weeks, while he had two more imprisoned for 10 months for failing to doff their caps to him.

Although he delayed travelling to London in the spring of 1660, convinced that 'he would be of greater use in his own neighbourhood for the election',[6] he undertook to be present in advance of the new Parliament and was among the first to re-enter the restored House. In the frenzied first month of the Convention, he was deeply involved in its committees preparing for the king's return. His early proposal to draw up an act of indemnity which would pardon some of those involved in the regicide, was angrily rejected by General Monck, and his hopes of a negotiated Restoration were swept aside, as little was allowed to stand in the way of Charles II's return. According to some sources he was rewarded with the privy seal, though there is some doubt as to whether he was ever appointed to the office. If he were, no patent survives, and he had relinquished the post by 1661 when it was granted to Lord Robartes. He was, however, confirmed in office as lord warden of the cinque ports, though he was unsuccessful in his efforts to secure the restoration of the court of wards, of which he had previously been the master. Saye and Sele lived for only two years after the Restoration.

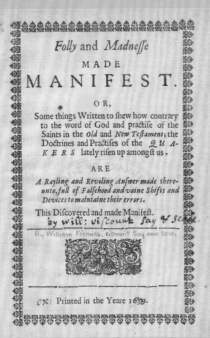

1639
F465

Folly and *Madnesse*
MADE
MANIFEST.
OR,

Some things Written to shew how contrary
to the word of God and practise of the
Saints in the *old* and *New Testament*; the
Doctrines and Practises of the Q U A-
K E R S lately risen up amongst us,

ARE

*A Rayling and Reviling Answer made there-
unto, full of Falsehood and vaine Shifts and
Devices to maintaine their errors.*

This Discovered and made Manifest.

by will: viscount say & sea.

By William Fiennes, Viscount Say and Sele.

OX: Printed in the Yeare 1659.

F465

(1)

*An account of the Devils changing his
device from Ranting to Quaking, yet still
carrying on the same malicious Design a-
gainst the souls of men: together with the
rise and progress of this latter Delusion;
as also a Declaration of their rotten
Principles, wherein their Foundations
are shaken, and their folly made manifest to all.*

He seduced People whom they call Quakers, not
without cause, because the Devil first began with
them, with that trick of his, to make people believe there was something extraordinary in the
Work, they out of a railing spirit, which shew-
eth what that spirit is which they are led by, for
good Angels and Spirits will not give railing tearms, no not to
Devils: They call me a Persecutor, a whited Wall, a painted
Sepulchre, one that keeps Swearers and Drunkards in my house:
The Devil is the Father of lies and liars; let any one of them

B make

FIG. 10

THE
QVAKERS
REPLY

manifested to be railing;

OR

A pursuance of those by the light of
of the Scriptures, who through their darke
imaginations would evade the Truth;

WHEREIN

*Not only the unsoundness of their prin-
ciples, but their weakness in mantaining
of them, is farther discovered*

by will: viscount say & seah.

Ox: Printed in the yeare 1660.

(61)

*The Quakers reply herein manifested to be
(like the Jesuits sophistry) only shifting
evasions, which rather darkens, than
clears the truth in hand; as also to be but
as sparks of railing, streaming out of
their hearts, burning with wrath, not only
against the defender of truth, but a-
gainst the truth it selfe.*

R. *Bray Doyly* you being a sober & discreet Gentleman, and a neighbour of mine, whom in both
those respects, I had cause to value; It grieved
me when I heard that you were wrought upon
by these seduced, and seducing people, which
caused me to desire, that you would read a few
things, which I had written to prevent my neighbours from being led into their erroneous waies, and also (if it might be) to
reduce those who had been turned out of the way of truth by
their subtile devises, which they have from him who turnes himselfe into an Angel of light, that he may deceive. I received lately from you an answer thereunto; from some of the Leaders of
that unhappy company, & I find it such as I alwaies see their wri-

I 3 tings

FIG. 11

The Oxford antiquary Anthony Wood perpetuated
the myth that he had been well rewarded, writing bitterly that while others who had sided with the monarchy and had 'been reduced to a bit of bread for his
Majesty's cause' had 'little or nothing given to relieve
them', Saye, who 'had acted as a grand rebel for his
own ends almost 20 years' had been rewarded, and
died 'quietly in his bed'.[7]

15

accepted by Cromwell (though without the title of king and with the Other House as a purely nominated Chamber) at the end of June 1657.

The 'Other House' first sat in January 1658 when it ran into the determined opposition of a tactical coalition of republicans and royalists in the Commons who argued that it threatened the power of the Commons: 'You have settled them only as a high court of justice; but if you make them a co-ordinate power with you, you give them the power of your purses, of peace and war, of making laws'.[8] They claimed that the Other House could not act as a balance because its members were not sufficiently wealthy: 'they have not interest, not the forty-thousandth part of England'.[9] Cromwell dissolved Parliament less than a month after the session had begun, bitterly insisting that he had made it a condition of the new constitution that there should be 'some other body that might interpose between you and me, on the behalf of the Commonwealth, to prevent a tumultuary and popular spirit'.[10] A year later, shortly after Oliver Cromwell's death, a new Parliament met and returned to the same debate. The opponents of the Other House again insisted that it had no foundation which would justify its power and support its position:

> there are forty knights in this House that represent more than the property of all the other House. The House of Lords, heretofore, could draw to the field half the nation. They had great dependencies. They had a foundation, a propriety [i.e., property], which was sufficient to support a third estate. The old lords did stand in balance by their propriety . . . All government is built upon propriety, else the poor must rule it.[11]

The Other House was an artificial construction designed to bolster the Protector and his government. Silius Titus argued in a pamphlet of 1659 that

> if in the former government, encrease of nobility was a grievance, because the new nobility, having fresh obligation to the crown, were the easilier led to compliance with it: and if one of the main reasons for exclusion of the bishops out of the House of Lords, was because that they being of the king's making, were in effect so many certain votes for whatever the king had a mind to carry in that House: how much more assured will that inconvenience now be, when the protector, that wants nothing of the king, but, in every sense the title, shall not only make and nominate a part, but of himself constitute the whole House? In a word (Sir) if our liberty was endangered by the former House, we may give it lost in the Other House.[12]

FIG. 12
A celebration of the restoration of the old regime: the king on the throne of the House of Lords; the House of Commons with its Speaker; the bishops and the Book of Common Prayer; traitors rewarded and 'sectaries rejected'. The Latin text is adapted from Virgil, referring to the return of the goddess Astraea, meant to usher in a new golden age.

The House of Lords at the Restoration

A year after Titus wrote these words, the Lords had been restored. Would they endanger liberty through their closeness to monarchy, or engender chaos again by challenging the crown's power? Or would they, as the theorists believed they should, act as a buffer between the crown and the Commons to guarantee stability? The idea of the peers as a balance had, if anything, been strengthened by the events of the past twenty years. They were, it was said in a 1675 debate,

> by birth-right the counsellors of the kingdom ... whose interest and business is to keep the balance of the government steady, that the favourites and great officers exceed not their bounds, and oppress the people, that justice be duly administered, and that all parts of the government be preserved entire ... [they are] the council, the wisdom and judgement of the nation, to which their birth, education, and constant employment, being the same in every Parliament, prepares and fits them.[13]

Despite such apparent confidence in their role, and their fitness for it, the abolition of the House of Lords in 1649 had sharpened the political anxieties of the peerage. Some perceived a subtle strand of anti-aristocratic feeling which they identified as the persistence of civil war republicanism. Thomas Wriothesley, 4th earl of Southampton, the first lord treasurer after the Restoration, complained in 1663 that

> the genius of the nation tends too much to democracy and ... the balance of all wealth and election of burgesses (the persons that can only in Parliament give the crown a support) belongs most to merchants, traders and yeomanry and that revenue or supply is seldom given, but that some regalia or prerogatives are the price of it.[14]

It was the commoners, according to one disgruntled politician writing in 1698, who held the 'strength of England in their hands'.[15] Algernon Sydney, the younger son of Robert Sydney, 2nd earl of Leicester, nephew of Algernon Percy, 4th earl of Northumberland, and a central supporter of the republic of 1649–53, wrote in Harringtonian fashion in his prolix *Discourses concerning Government* that the death of feudalism had wrecked the ancient foundations of government and

> tis as impossible to restore it, as for most of those who at this day go under the names of noblemen, to perform the duties required from the ancient nobility of England... they have neither the interest nor the

'The most proper mediators and interposers to the king': Edward Hyde on the House of Lords, December 1660

'Your lordships will easily recover that estimation and reverence that is due to your high condition, by the exercise and practice of that virtue from whence your honours first sprang; the example of your justice and piety will inflame the hearts of the people towards you; and from your practice they will make a judgement of the king himself. They know very well, that you are not only admitted to his presence, but to his conversation, and even in a degree to his friendship; for you are his great council. By your example they will form their own manners, and by yours they will make a guess at the king's. Therefore, under that obligation, you will cause your piety, your justice, your affability, and your charity, to shine as bright as is possible before them. They are too much in love with England, too partial to it, who believe it the best country in the world; there is better earth, and a better air, and a better, that is, a warmer, sun in other countries: but we are no more than just, when we say that England is an inclosure of the best people in the world, when they are well informed and instructed; a people in sobriety of conscience the most devoted to God almighty; in the integrity of their affections, the most dutiful to the king; in their good-manners and inclinations, most regardful and loving to the nobility; no nobility in Europe so entirely loved by the people; there may be more awe, and fear, and terror of them, but no such love towards them as in England. I beseech your lordships, do not undervalue this love. They have looked upon your lordships, and they will look upon your lordships again, as the greatest examples and patterns of duty to the king, as the greatest security and protection from injury and injustice, and for their enjoying whatsoever is due to them by the law, and as the most proper mediators and interposers to the king, if, by any failure of justice, they should be exposed to any oppression and violence.'

Lord Chancellor Hyde (later the earl of Clarendon), speaking to the House of Lords at the close of the Convention Parliament, 29 December 1660, LJ, xi, 238.

FIG. 13 *Edward Hyde, earl of Clarendon (1609–74), by Sir Peter Lely: Charles II's principal minister is shown wearing his robes as lord chancellor, with the purse for the Great Seal. Hyde had been a prominent member of the House of Commons at the beginning of the Long Parliament of 1640, before he joined the king in 1642 and became one of the most influential royalist propagandists and politicians.*

estates required for so great a work. Those who have estates at a rack rent, have no dependants. Their tenants, when they have paid what is agreed, owe them nothing; and knowing they shall be turn'd out of their tenements, as soon as any other will give a little more, they look upon their lords as men who receive more from them than they confer upon them. This dependence being lost, the lords have only more money to spend or lay up than others, but no command of men; and can therefore neither protect the weak, nor curb the insolent.[16]

The nobility may not have been quite what it was in the Middle Ages, but the idea that the wealth and power of the aristocracy was ebbing away was much overstated. It is true that an increase in the wealth of gentry families made the peerage look less exceptional than previously; true, too, that England would experience over the half a century after the Restoration a massive financial and commercial expansion which would further enrich businessmen and gentry. Yet in many ways the position of the peerage would improve after 1660. The formal abolition of the court of wards that year removed an institution that had jeopardised the survival of many noble estates during minorities. Economic expansion benefitted the peerage just as much as it did the gentry, and many aristocratic families would consolidate and improve their estates substantially in the century after 1660. The peerage collectively and individually possessed a substantial slice of the wealth of the country; how much is not easy to establish. Gregory King, the pioneering late seventeenth-century political economist, estimated that in 1688 the 160 or so noble families between them had an annual income of about £448,000, which he reckoned to be about one per cent of the total national income. But his estimate is widely regarded as much too low. Much aristocratic wealth was held in land, and the most elaborate attempt to calculate their holdings suggests that the percentage of cultivated land possessed by the aristocracy was between 15 and 20 per cent in 1688 and that it rose slightly in the eighteenth century.

At the Restoration peers regained their prominent, even dominant, role in government, politics and society. They regarded it as axiomatic that they should receive important offices in central and local government. Edward Hyde, earl of Clarendon, objected to the appointment of a proposed treasury commission made up of commoners: a peer was nominated as its leader. Peers expected to exercise political leadership both through their places in Parliament and outside it. The most powerful political leaders would spend most of their political careers in the House of Lords.

They dealt with and influenced the king, the Commons, their colleagues and clients; they led and articulated opinion at court and in the country; some aspired to control or influence friends, allies and relatives in the lower House whose elections they had procured. The peers' places in Parliament enabled them to mount an aggressive assertion of their status and their privileges as individual peers. They insisted, much more strongly than before the Civil War, on the importance of their corporate role within Parliament. They even aspired to expand it.

In doing so, they would irritate and provoke their partners in the lower House. The Lords' vigorous reassertion of the judicial role of their House became an issue of exceptional sensitivity when it seemed to clash with the privileges of the Commons. Three cases dealt with by the Lords on appeal from the lower courts – *Thomas Skinner v. the East India Company* in 1668–70 (see below, p.24), *Sherley v. Fagg* in 1675, and *Ashby v. White* in 1704 – caused rows between the two Houses that put an end to progress on any other significant business until they could be resolved or suppressed. For the Commons, they raised questions about the interference of the upper House with the freedom of their proceedings and the politicisation of justice. For the Lords, a threat to their judicature was a threat to their constitutional significance. Anthony Ashley Cooper, earl of Shaftesbury, commented on the Sherley case that,

> this matter is no less than your whole judicature; and your judicature is the life and soul of the dignity of the peerage of England. You will quickly grow burdensome if you grow useless. You have now the greatest and most useful end of Parliaments principally in you, which is not to make new laws, but to redress grievances and to maintain the old landmarks. The House of Commons' business is to complain, your lordships to redress, not only the complaints from them that are the eyes of the nation, but all other particular persons that address you.[17]

Underlying these skirmishes was the resumption of confrontational and increasingly ideological politics. The origins of many of the most controversial issues of the Restoration lay in the unresolved divisions of the civil wars, especially over the character of the national Church and the assumption that religious freedom was in conflict with public order. Onto these divisions during the 1670s were imposed new anxieties: suspicions about the commitment of Charles II, his brother James and the court to Protestantism (confirmed by James's acknowledged reception into the Roman Catholic Church) together with a national panic about the ambi-

tion of France to become the premier international power and the government's reluctance to oppose it. By the early 1680s this mixture had resulted in the formation of the vaguely defined but ideologically powerful parties, Tory and Whig. The first inherited some of the principles of royalism: steadfast adherence to the crown, support for the Church of England against Protestant nonconformity and a claim to stand by law against disorder and demagoguery. The second represented something of the old spirit of parliamentarianism: a stand for liberty and property against arbitrary government, a call for liberty of conscience, anti-popery and the defence of Protestantism against the encroaching threat of international Catholicism. The role of party in politics was never simple. There were many other factors which influenced political argument at Westminster and across the country, and the parties themselves were a long way from being the sophisticated electoral machines of later years. Nevertheless, once party had emerged as the new organising principle of politics, though it might sometimes be obscured, it would never fully disappear.

The existence of two Houses moulded the way the partisan politics at Westminster developed. One of the tactics politicians found most useful was to stimulate confrontations between the Houses. It occasionally achieved spectacular success. The vehemence with which the Lords pursued *Skinner v. the East India Company* owed a great deal to the leadership of peers opposed to a government-backed conventicle bill. The dispute over *Shirley v Fagg* was orchestrated to block an attempt to prevent religious nonconformists from holding public office. Usually, the crown continued to expect the House of Lords to act as a buffer between it and the people, rejecting the Commons' unacceptable demands so that the king did not have to do so himself. In March 1670 when Charles II revived what he claimed to be an ancient practice of attending the debates in the Lords in person, he was underlining his conviction that when they understood his views, peers ought to follow them. When the House of Commons demanded in 1673 that the king should withdraw his Declaration of Indulgence – an attempt to dispense with the laws governing religious worship – the government appealed to the Lords to defend the prerogatives of the Crown and to stimulate an inter-cameral row, albeit unsuccessfully in this instance. In 1680 the Lords' rejection of the Commons' proposals to prevent the duke of York (the future James II) from succeeding as king roused fury against the Lords (and especially the

FIG. 14 (OPPOSITE PAGE) *Anthony Ashley Cooper, earl of Shaftesbury (1621–83), after John Greenhill: one of the generation of smart young politicians who had risen to prominence during the Protectorate, Shaftesbury was regarded with deep suspicion by those with a royalist background. He was thought to be ambitious, scheming and unscrupulous, especially after he became identified with the Whig movement of the Exclusion Crisis. He is shown here during his tenure of the lord chancellorship, in 1672–73, wearing his robes and with the chancellor's purse.*

Skinner v. the East India Company

A dispute between the Houses which started in the spring of 1668 brought Parliament to a virtual standstill for nearly two years. At the centre of it was Thomas Skinner, a merchant from a London commercial dynasty, and one of his brothers, Frederick, who worked as a factor for the East India Company at Bantam in western Java (part of modern day Indonesia). The company forbade its employees from trading on their own account but during the Interregnum it had been difficult to enforce such a regulation. As a consequence, Frederick Skinner had amassed a considerable stock of goods. In 1657 Thomas Skinner sailed to Java to help him bring them back. A series of verbal, legal and physical confrontations followed with the company. In the end, Thomas Skinner had to surrender his ship and return by land, empty handed.

He arrived back in England shortly after the Restoration, and began a campaign for compensation of £40,000 from the East India Company. He had no case under English law, as the actions in question had taken place abroad. No doubt it was his family's connection, via their patron the countess of Peterborough, with James, duke of York, that give him some hope of redress, and, as a series of hearings before privy councillors established, made him refuse any compromise. Charles II finally gave up trying to resolve the dispute and referred the matter to the House of Lords.

The Lords took up the case on the grounds that there was no other way in which Skinner could get redress. He met with a remarkably sympathetic reception from Members of the House who heard it in spring 1668. A committee recommended damages of just over £28,000, although that was reduced by a vote of the full House to £5,000. At that point the East India Company decided to fight back in the Commons, arguing that because some of the directors of the company were Members of the Commons, the Lords had infringed Commons' privilege. The Commons agreed with them: they also challenged the extension of the upper House's claim to be a judicature to cases in original jurisdiction, especially one that was more proper for a foreign, than an English court of law, and pointed out that the Lords had no procedures by which it could evaluate the truth of the evidence it was offered.

The ensuing confrontation was deliberately encouraged by George Villiers, 2nd duke of Buckingham and his acolytes in the Commons in order to prevent the passage of the Conventicle Bill, and was not helped by the fact that, following the fall of the earl of Clarendon the previous year, several ministers were competing to establish their control over Parliament. The king, irritated by Parliament's failure to make progress on the business that mattered to him, required both Houses to adjourn on 9 May 1668. When they finally reconvened in the autumn of 1669, the whole affair was reopened, helped by the anonymous publication by the senior Presbyterian politician, Denzil Holles, Baron Holles, of his own highly partisan account of the dispute, *The grand question concerning the judicature of the House of Peers stated and argued*. The Lords affected to be conciliatory, offering the Commons a bill concerning the privilege of both Houses in November. It annoyed, rather than placated, the Commons: 'The Commons are as well the Great Council as the Lords; give them their way of tryal, and you may give them all' complained one Member: 'By their bill they would insinuate into the people, that by taking away Privilege the Lords are the only men – The Rump took away the Lords Privilege, and the Lords would take away ours.'[1]

The issue was resolved only when Charles II took a grip on parliamentary management in the Commons, and in February 1670 effected a compromise in which the record of the dispute, including the Lords' judgements on the case, were erased from the Journals of both Houses. Neither side had formally backed down, although the Lords never again attempted to hear a case in original jurisdiction. Thomas Skinner fought on, obsessively trying to revive his case until his death in 1695.

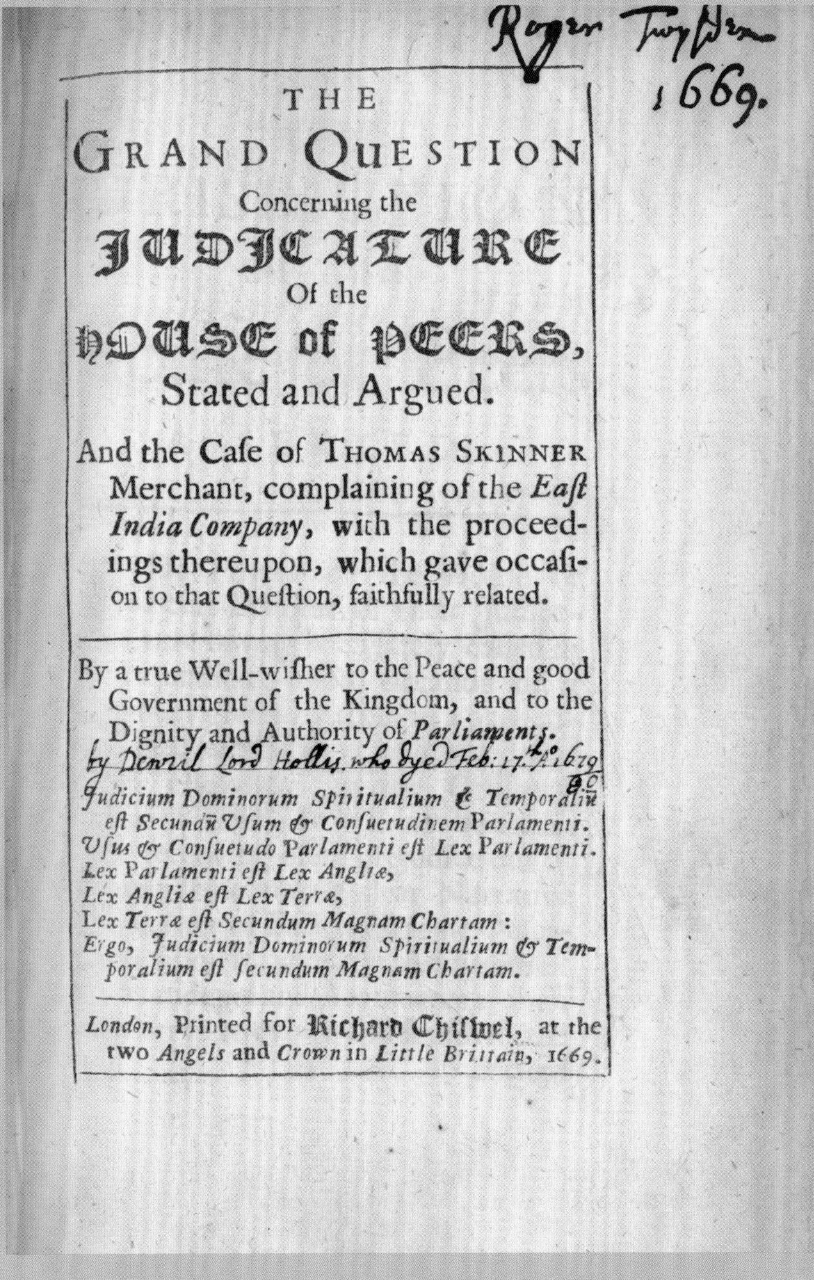

THE
GRAND QUESTION
Concerning the
JUDICATURE
Of the
HOUSE OF PEERS,
Stated and Argued.

And the Case of Thomas Skinner Merchant, complaining of the *East India Company*, with the proceedings thereupon, which gave occasion to that Question, faithfully related.

By a true Well-wisher to the Peace and good Government of the Kingdom, and to the Dignity and Authority of *Parliaments.*

by Denzil Lord Hollis, who dyed Feb: 17.th 1679

Judicium Dominorum Spiritualium & Temporaliū est Secundū Usum & Consuetudinem Parlamenti.
Usus & Consuetudo Parlamenti est Lex Parlamenti.
Lex Parlamenti est Lex Angliæ,
Lex Angliæ est Lex Terræ,
Lex Terræ est Secundum Magnam Chartam :
Ergo, Judicium Dominorum Spiritualium & Temporalium est secundum Magnam Chartam.

London, Printed for **Richard Chiswel**, at the two *Angels* and *Crown* in *Little Brittain*, 1669.

FIG. 15 *Denzil Holles, Baron Holles, timed the publication of this skewed version of the legal arguments in the case of* Thomas Skinner v. The East India Company *very carefully. As intended, it re-ignited the controversy and disrupted parliamentary business.*

25

bishops). It was reminiscent of that caused by the peers' resistance to the impeachment of Thomas Wentworth, earl of Strafford in 1641.

As a result, the Lords sometimes risked being seen as a mere tool of royal government. It was probably the philosopher John Locke or perhaps his patron, the 'country' politician the earl of Shaftesbury, who argued in 1675 that the reason for 'so much pains taken by the Court to debase, and bring low the House of Peers' was a desire to introduce a military government: 'the power of *peerage*, and a *standing army* are like two buckets, the proportion that one goes down, the other exactly goes up'.[18] Algernon Sydney would explain the peers' frustration of the will of the Commons as the result of political manipulation and corruption by a Tory government. Echoing what had been said about the 'Other House' in the 1650s, he questioned the superiority of the qualifications of recently ennobled Tories against those of families which had provided prominent parliamentarians in the Civil War, and expressed his contempt of a peerage that no longer, to his mind, possessed the ancient virtues he thought should animate the nobility.

> Nothing can be more absurd, than to give a prerogative of birth to Craven, Tufton, Hyde, Bennet, Osborn and others, before the Cliftons, Hampdens, Courtneys, Pelhams, St Johns, Baintons, Wilbrahams, Hungerfords and many others. And if the tenures of their estates be considered, they have the same, and as ancient as any of those who go under the names of duke, or marquess. I forbear to mention the sordid ways of attaining to titles in our days; but whoever will take the pains to examine them, shall find that they rather defile than ennoble the possessors. And whereas men are truly ennobled only by virtue, and respect is due to such as are descended from those who have bravely serv'd their country, because it is presumed (till they shew the contrary) that they will resemble their ancestors, these modern courtiers, by their names and titles, frequently oblige us to call to mind such things as are not to be mentioned without blushing. Whatever the ancient noblemen of *England* were, we are sure they were not such as these.[19]

The House of Commons could also be seen as increasingly corrupted by the crown. Parliament was central to the politics of Restoration England in a way that it had never quite been before the Civil War. A large navy, a permanent army, and regular interventions in European politics required finance on a scale previously unknown to royal government, achievable only by securing the assent of the House of Commons. Ministers directed a corresponding amount of effort to managing and controlling the lower

House. From the 1670s ministers such as Henry Bennet, earl of Arlington, and Thomas Osborne, earl of Danby, began to build lists of supporters in the Commons on a more systematic basis than before, deliberately distributing office and royal favour to their allies in both Houses. Alarm at these new ways of managing Parliament was evident for the remainder of the period: Andrew Marvell alleged in 1678 that it 'is too notorious to be concealed, that near a third part of the House [of Commons] have beneficial offices under his majesty, in the privy council, the army, the navy, the law, the household, the revenue both in England and Ireland, or in attendance on his majesties person'.[20] The concern was exacerbated by the extraordinary longevity of the Cavalier Parliament. Elected in 1661, it survived until 1678 – kept in being by Charles II who calculated that it was better to retain the devil he knew than to summon a new and unpredictable one.

This could affect the way the House of Lords was perceived. It could be argued in the 1670s that the House of Lords was the only way to protect the integrity of the constitution against a Commons majority created either by the corruption of governments or the new corruption of party politics. George Villiers, 2nd duke of Buckingham, complained that a House of Commons that was more or less permanent was becoming much more in character like the House of Lords:

> I have often wondered how it should come to pass, that this House of
> Commons, in which are so many worthy gentlemen, should ... be less
> respectful to your lordships (as certainly they have been) than any
> House of Commons that ever were chosen in England. And yet if the
> matter be a little enquired into, the reason of it will plainly appear, for
> my lords the very nature of the House of Commons is changed: they do
> not now think they are an assembly that are to return to their own
> homes, and become private men again, as by the laws of the land and
> the ancient constitution of Parliaments they ought to do, but they look
> upon themselves as a standing senate and as a number of men pick'd
> out to be legislators for the rest of their whole lives: and if that be the
> case my lords they have reason to believe themselves our equals.[21]

Shaftesbury and Buckingham both tried to articulate an alternative vision of the role of the House of Lords. Instead of a support for the crown, it could become a bastion against executive dominance of a supine and corrupted House of Commons. This dovetailed easily into the rhetoric about aristocratic independence and liberty; it flattered the peers, too, by promoting their House as the equivalent of the Roman senate standing against the corruption of imperial Rome – so many Ciceros combating the might of Caesar. The reality was very different, for the House of Lords rarely wavered from support for the government of Charles II or James II. But the Revolution of 1688 ushered in a much more complex political world in which the idea that the peerage might act to uphold liberty and the constitution against the encroachment of the lower House became rather more plausible.

In the aftermath of the Revolution, English politics underwent a rapid and remarkable transformation. Most obvious was the regularity with which Parliament met. Before the Revolution, Parliament had been an occasional event. That it met every year afterwards was due in part to the aspirations of many Whigs to make it into a permanent feature of government, but rather more to the necessities of the new and fragile regime. William III's main purpose in invading had been to secure England as an ally against the French. For the next twenty-five years, with only a brief intermission after the Peace of Ryswick, signed in September 1697, England was engaged in full-scale continental war of a greater intensity and expense than any it had ever experienced. The government's financial demands were unprecedented. The solutions involved a revolution in public finance – the creation of lotteries, the Bank of England, and a national debt – which was dependent on statute and new principles of parliamentary control. The financial role of the House of Commons made it the focus of a new system of state finance and, with so much at stake, its membership, and hence the outcome of each election, became crucial to the success of governments.

The Commons also became more difficult to manage. The Triennial Act (reluctantly allowed to pass by William III in 1694) mandated general elections every three years. The Act of Settlement of 1701 prohibited members of the Commons from holding offices of profit under the crown. Together with the Triennial Act, it was intended significantly to reduce the ability of the crown and its ministers to control the Commons. A series of 'place bills' attempted to extend the prohibition on office holding more widely. Under the 1706 Act for the Security of her Majesty's Person (sometimes known as the Regency Act) any Member who took one of several named minor offices during a session was required to resign his seat and undergo re-election.

From the Revolution to the Hanoverian Succession, the House of

GEORGE VILLERS DUKE OF BUCKINGHAM.

FIG. 16 *George Villiers, 2nd duke of Buckingham (1628–87), by Sir Peter Lely, c. 1675: Charles II's ubiquitous companion was also a man of serious political ambition, who played a large, if often opaque, role in English politics in the 1670s.*

Commons was highly volatile and closely responsive to the opinion of the electorate. Its politics continued to be dominated by the Tory and Whig party labels of the 1680s. Yet the 1680s' association of Toryism with loyal support for the king's government, and Whiggism with opposition to it, was upset and confused. The great majority of Whigs had little difficulty with adjusting to the deposition of James II and the new king's plunge into an international coalition against Louis XIV. Many Tories were more slowly reconciled to the removal of the rightful heir to the throne, far from enthusiastic about continental entanglements and highly suspicious about the security of their cherished Church of England in the hands of William III and his increasingly Whig-dominated governments. Even so, there remained Whigs who were still determined to control and modify the powers of royal government and Tories who still felt the tug of loyal support for the king's government. The result was that party affiliations were complicated by an older distinction of the 1670s between the 'court' – the pliant, perhaps bought, supporters of the executive – and the 'country' – steadfastly independent incorruptible Members. There were 'court Tories' and 'court Whigs'; 'country Tories' and 'country Whigs' – not to mention a bewildering array of personal factions and splits within parties and factions over specific issues.

The hothouse world of Revolution politics would subtly alter the way the House of Lords was used. Within this kaleidoscope of party and faction, advantage could be seized by the groups who were best able to marshal their forces, and those who were outnumbered in one House could fight back in the other. In the Restoration the Lords had been a last line of defence for the crown; after the Revolution it could still function in that way, but it became also a redoubt from which either party, as well as the government, would resist plans formulated by their opponents in the Commons. The Whigs were the usual beneficiaries, if only because the majorities in the Commons were usually Tory ones. From 1702–5 they fought the Tories over the imposition of restrictions on occasional conformity (the practice, common among dissenters, of occasionally taking communion in Church of England services in order to qualify for public office under the Test Acts). In a series of crises in 1711–14 the Lords threatened the stability of the government of Robert Harley, earl of Oxford, and his determination to conclude peace with France and Spain.

Such contests were bound, from time to time, to result in confrontations between the two Houses about their roles and their powers.

FIG. 17 *The frontispiece to* Argumentum anti-normanicum, *a 1682 tract by the Whig lawyer and polemicist William Atwood, which contests the view that William the Conqueror had taken England by conquest. The issue was keenly debated in the 1680s because if the kings of England owed their throne to the Norman Conquest, the rights and liberties of the English people appeared to be only a concession from an absolute ruler, rather than accepted by their rulers as a condition for taking the throne. The picture shows William, following the battle of Hastings, swearing to keep the laws of his English predecessor, Edward the Confessor. Atwood later went to New York, where he fell foul of the governor there, the Tory Lord Cornbury (see below, p. 228).*

Frustrated by the opposition in the Lords, the Commons would taunt the peers with their inability to amend financial legislation, 'tacking' non-financial provisions unlikely to pass the Lords onto supply bills, as when a provision to renew the commission of accounts in 1692 was added into the poll tax bill, offering them a choice between acceptance, or losing the bill and jeopardising the war effort and the stability of the government. The Commons were often provocative. Although the peers generally accepted

'Apt to go forward and backward in public affairs': Charles Howard, earl of Carlisle (1628–85)

Heir to a cadet branch of the powerful Howard family established in Cumberland and Northumberland, throughout his life Charles Howard, earl of Carlisle, trimmed his sails to the prevailing political winds in order to retain his local and national prominence. The bishop and historian Gilbert Burnet wrote of him that during the Interregnum he had 'run into a high profession of religion, to the pitch of praying and preaching in their meetings. But after the Restoration he shook that off, and run into a course of vice. He loved to be popular, and yet to keep up an interest at court; and so was apt to go forward and backward in public affairs'.[1] As a young man he was a leading figure in Protector Oliver Cromwell's coterie of supporters, acting as captain of Cromwell's personal bodyguards and as his principal administrator and agent in the north. For this service the protector in 1657 bestowed on him a hereditary peerage as Viscount Howard of Morpeth, under which title Howard sat in the short-lived 'Other House'.

After the fall of the Protectorate, Howard established contact with Charles II. George Monck, on his march from Scotland, appointed him governor of Carlisle in order to watch his back in the north as he headed to London for his showdown with the Rump Parliament. Howard was down in London himself for the Convention and there this former officer of the Protectorate army and known supporter of 'enthusiastic' preachers declared that, 'As monarchy had been so long interrupted by rebellion and faction, so had episcopacy by schism and heresy, and that no one that spoke against episcopacy offered anything better'.[2] In June 1660, most likely on the recommendation of Monck, he was one of four former Cromwellians sworn to the new privy council and was later appointed lord lieutenant of Cumberland and Westmorland. At Charles II's coronation in April 1661 he was rewarded with the title of earl of Carlisle.

Over the next few years, Carlisle represented Charles II on diplomatic missions to Russia in 1663–5 (where he fell out with the Tsar to such an extent as to refuse the gifts given for the king and to sound out the Swedes about an anti-Russian coalition) and to Sweden in 1668–9. In the north of England he ruthlessly harrassed the 'mosstroopers' on the lawless northern borders and helped to defend Newcastle and the north against Dutch attack in the Second Dutch War of 1664–7. In London, his interventions were not always quite so helpful to the government. With fellow former Cromwellians Anthony Ashley Cooper, Baron Ashley (later earl of Shaftesbury), Philip Wharton, 4th Baron Wharton and Thomas Belasyse, 2nd Viscount Fauconberg (who had sat with Carlisle in Cromwell's 'Other House' back in the late 1650s), he was a key figure in the 'country' and 'presbyterian' groups which collaborated on the impeachment of the earl of Clarendon in 1667, plotted against the king's Catholic brother, James, duke of York and worked to support Protestant nonconformists against the Church establishment. To block James's succession to the throne he tried to advance the claims of Charles II's Protestant but bastard son James Scott, duke of Monmouth. According to York, in 1674 Carlisle and Shaftesbury assured Charles II that, despite the king's constant denials of ever having married Monmouth's mother, 'let him but say it, they should find such as would swear it'.[3] He helped to sponsor the ultimately abortive negotiations in early 1675 between the Presbyterians and the bishops in order to develop a bill to 'comprehend' the Presbyterians within the Church, formulated between dissenters including the popular theologian Richard Baxter, and the Church moderates John Tillotson (later archbishop of Canterbury) and Edward Stillingfleet (later bishop of Worcester) (see below, p. 170).

Once the court began to dangle the offer of the governorship of Jamaica before him he abandoned his allies. Shaftesbury, who had earlier addressed an important political manifesto to Carlisle in early 1675, marked him down as 'doubly vile' in his 1677 political black list. Carlisle's record in Jamaica was not a success: trying to please both the court and the colonists, he ended up making enemies of both. By the time he returned to England in 1680 he was seriously afflicted with gout – James Butler, duke of Ormond (admittedly not the most sympathetic witness) described him as 'the decripidest man

The Right Hon:^ble Charles, Earle of Carlisle, Vicount Howard of Morpeth, Baron Dacre of Gilsland. Lord Lieutenant in the Counties of Cumberland, and Westmoreland, and one of the Lords of his Majesties most Honourable Privy Councell, etc:

that ever I saw out of bed' in July 1683[4] – and he died in 1685, shortly after the king, having never recovered his former prominence in politics. He was buried in York Minster.

FIG. 18 *Charles Howard, earl of Carlisle, by William Faithorne, 1669.*

the right of the Commons to legislate for taxation, they expected such legislation to pay due attention to their privileges, providing for the peers to be assessed by their fellow peers and not by commoners. When in 1693 the Lords were faced with a land tax bill that contained no such provision they were forced to choose between rejecting the bill altogether or attempting to amend it. The decision to try to amend it infuriated the Commons; a rejection of the bill would have infuriated both king and Commons.

In disputes over taxation the Lords generally had to give way under pressure from the crown to ensure the passage of taxation. Nevertheless, the success of what was often only a small number of peers in the Lords in battling majorities in the Commons said something about the political talent available in the Lords. The Whig churchman, historian and politician Gilbert Burnet, bishop of Salisbury, remarked in his *History of my own time* that the House of Lords had become a much more impressive place than before: he had seen 'in our time four or five lords, by their knowledge, good judgment, and integrity, raise the house of peers to a pitch of reputation and credit, that seemed once beyond the expectation or belief of those who now see it'. Burnet – the most partisan of bishops – meant Whig talent, for it was the Whig peers who had adopted an increasingly confrontational and political attitude as they dealt with an expanding Tory presence in the House of Commons. Burnet demanded that the peers

> ought more particularly to protect the oppressed, to mortify insolence and injustice, and to enter into the true grievances of their country; that they may represent these, where it may be proper; and shew at least a tender care of those who ought to be protected by them, if they cannot effectually procure a redress of their grievances.[22]

In doing so, he was echoing what Buckingham had said a quarter of a century before, implying that a Tory-dominated Commons could no longer properly fulfil its proper representative function: the Lords would have to do so instead.

It was a polemical and rhetorical point, rather than a practical one. Because peers sat in their House by right, rather than election, they were in some sense more independent from popular pressure and party politics than were members of the Commons. But they were still subject to political pressure. After the Revolution, as before, the peers and the monarch remained natural allies: the House of Lords was still likely to submit to a clear steer from the crown. The relationship, already strong in constitutional theory, was made closer still by the benefits which many peers received at the hands of the king. A shift in the ideological complexion of the government could, however, create considerable problems. Not all peers were as happy serving the king in a Tory administration as they were in a Whig one, or vice versa. As a result, governments recognised the need to manage the Lords just as they managed the Commons: offering posts and pensions in exchange for political support. The introduction into the Lords in 1707 of the sixteen representative peers of Scotland created a block of peers whose relative poverty and distance from London meant that they required a subsidy to participate in parliamentary life. The ministry took full advantage. Even so, after 1712 Robert Harley, the newly ennobled earl of Oxford, had great difficulty in constructing sufficient support for his new ministry in the House of Lords and began to offer inducements to a group of peers – the 'poor lords' – in order to ensure their attendance and loyalty to his ministry.

When all else had failed, the crown's ability to create new peers could shift the political balance. There was a narrow line between using peerages to reward favourites and ministers and using them to shore up the government's political position in the House of Lords. Creations could cause deep unease among the existing aristocracy. Algernon Sydney's anger at the ennoblement of Tories during Charles II's reign was echoed in 1701 by William Cavendish, duke of Devonshire, and Henry Yelverton, Viscount Longueville. In 1703 Anne created five new peers and promoted two existing peers, all but one of whom were Tories who would help shift the party political balance in the House. Most blatant of all was the addition to the House, under the Oxford's direction, of twelve peers all at once – 'Harley's dozen' – during the political crisis in the winter of 1711–12 in order to save the ministry's carefully negotiated peace with France (see below, pp. 337-8). The genesis of the crisis of 1712 was a token of the vigour and effectiveness of the House of Lords as it negotiated the new realities of British politics. Determined in asserting its rights and privileges and creative in expanding its judicial role, regularly refreshed with new Members, many of whom had had a long apprenticeship in the House of Commons, the Lords were changing from the feudal aristocracy despised by Harrington into a more politically sophisticated body.

Religion and faction, 1661–73

The religious settlement dominated the politics of the Cavalier Parliament. From 1661 to 1665 supporters of the Church in the House of Commons sponsored a series of Acts – known inaccurately as the 'Clarendon Code' – which excluded Presbyterians from the Church of England's ministry and tried to close down alternative forms of worship. They were discreetly encouraged from the Lords by the bishops, and particularly by the effective clerical politician, Gilbert Sheldon, bishop of London.

By late 1661 and early 1662 the government had became alarmed enough at the political consequences of the assault on Presbyterianism to try to moderate it in the Lords. The greatest battles took place over the new Act of Uniformity, which arrived in the Lords in January, later accompanied by a revised Book of Common Prayer, in which no significant concessions were made on the Anglican liturgy. Presbyterians looked to 'the Lord's House'[1] for relief.

Despite the efforts of the rich old Parliamentarian, Philip Wharton, 4th Lord Wharton, to coordinate opposition, of Algernon Percy, 4th earl of Northumberland to resist the new liturgy, of Charles II's principal minister, Edward Hyde, earl of Clarendon, to persuade the bishops to agree concessions, and of the Catholic George Digby, 2nd earl of Bristol to give the king a power to permit individuals not to comply with religious legislation, the bitter arguments in both Houses in February and March 1662 left the Act of Uniformity an uncompromising measure. It came into force on 24 August 1662, 'Black St Bartholomew's day', when some two thousand clergy unable to give the required 'unfeigned assent and consent' to the new Book of Common Prayer were removed from their livings.

There was an attempt to reverse the Act by a royal Declaration of Indulgence in December 1662. It was followed up by a bill presented in the House of Lords in February 1663 by a presbyterian peer, John

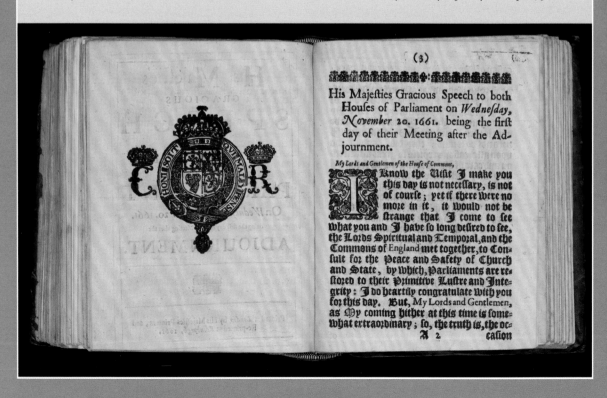

FIG. 19 (OPPOSITE) *The king made a formal appearance in Parliament on 20 November 1661 to mark the return of the bishops to the House of Lords. His speech on that occasion was drafted by his chief minister, Edward Hyde, earl of Clarendon.*

FIG. 20 (RIGHT) *Clarendon's draft of the speech.*

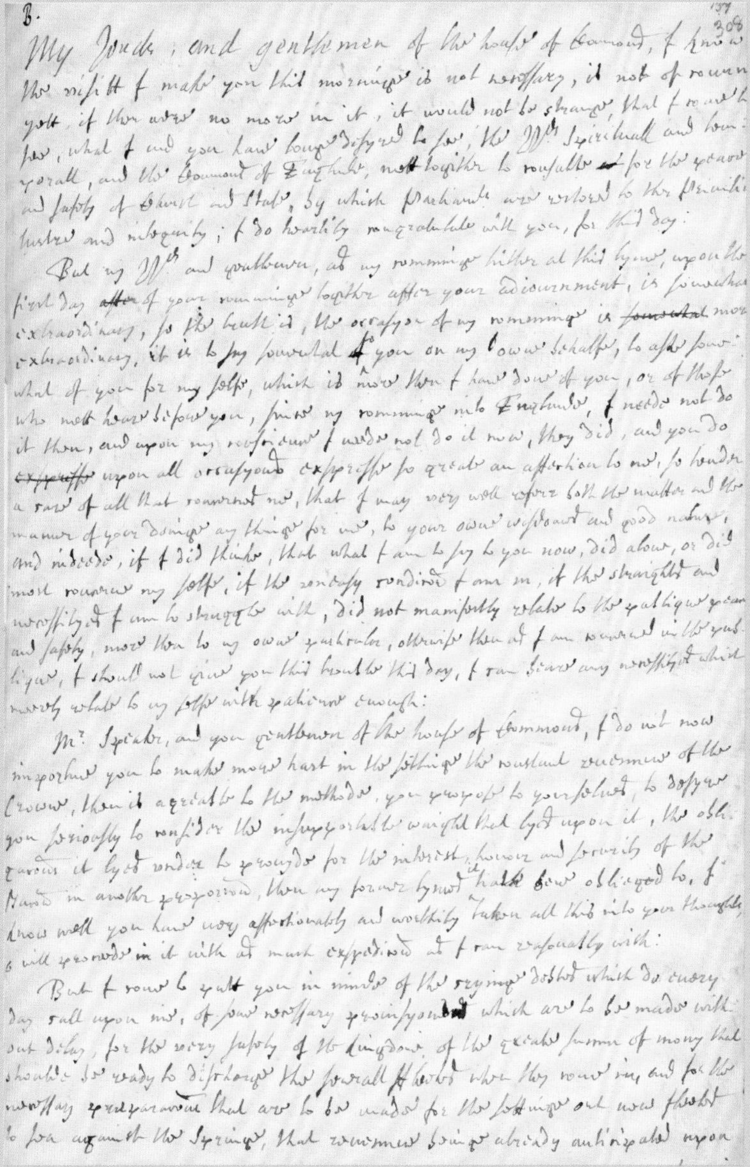

Robartes, 2nd Baron Robartes (later earl of Radnor), designed to give the king 'such a power of indulgence, to use upon occasions, as might needlessly force [dissenters] out of the kingdom, or, staying here, give them cause to conspire against the peace of it'.[2] The potential breadth of the powers proposed to be given to the king shocked Clarendon, although it was the reaction in the Commons – perhaps orchestrated by Gilbert Sheldon, now archbishop of Canterbury – that forced the bill's abandonment.

As had always been likely, an act to create uni-form worship in England and Wales instead encouraged nonconformity. Many of those unwilling to conform to the requirements of the Act of Uniformity had taken their congregations with them, setting up alternative meetings – 'conventicles' – for their worship. Church supporters regarded them as hotbeds of political, as well as religious, dissent. Parliament became increasingly preoccupied with the regulation and suppression of nonconformity. The 1664 Conventicle Act was aimed at stopping nonconformist assemblies. In the Lords, presbyterian peers protested ineffectually against it: a proviso from Lord Ashley to compensate those unlawfully arrested was rejected; George Booth, Baron Delamer, begged that legislation would be 'merciful to us Presbyterians and at least give us leave to play innocently at bowls';[3] Wharton condemned the 'exorbitant power' that allowed justices of the peace to convict without a jury.[4] Six weeks after the act came into force, eight Quakers from Hertford were the first to be sentenced to deportation under the act. The following year a new bill required the ejected clergy to swear that they would not support 'change or alteration in Church or State' on pain of banishment from within five miles of corporations. The debate in the Lords saw the unimpeachably royalist Thomas Wriothesley, 4th earl of Southampton, voice forceful objections to the oath as a breach of political liberty. The bill, though, was 'strongly carried on' by the duke of York and the bishops,[5] and the so-called 'Five Mile Act' completed the suite of legislation designed to force dissenters back into the Church.

Two things complicated the debates on religion in the Cavalier Parliament. The first was Charles II's interest in lifting the disabilities imposed on Roman Catholics. Anti-popery had been strongly embedded within English politics and culture since at least the 1580s, but English Catholics were few in number and relatively marginalised (although a number of peers did continue, quietly, to exercise the old religion). They had already attempted to capitalise on the king's sympathy, unsuccessfully petitioning the House of Lords in 1661 for relief. The earl of Bristol masterminded a strategy for Catholics of allying with the Presbyterians. In the debates of 1662 he had vigorously promoted the idea of a royal power to permit individual exemptions from the religious laws; he subsequently tried to drum up support for a general toleration. One reason why the 1663 bill to allow the king to relieve dissenters was received with such hostility was that it was viewed as a Trojan horse for the toleration of Catholics.

The second complication was the destructive factionalism of the royal court. Clarendon, who took a perverse pride in his contempt for courtly values, was especially vulnerable. Bristol thought that Clarendon's opposition to Robartes's bill had ruined his credit with the King; but Bristol's own attempt to force himself into Charles's inner counsels through an impeachment of the lord chancellor in July 1663 rebounded on himself. He was forced to go into hiding for more than a year and most peers refused to touch a petition which his wife tried to have presented to the House of Lords in early 1664 (William Brydges, 7th Baron Chandos 'leapt back swore he would [not] touch the paper for forty pound; believed it not the part of a kinswoman to offer such a thing to him').[6] Clarendon, though, had many other enemies, including the ambitious and cultured secretary of state, Henry Bennet, earl of Arlington, the king's striking but manipulative mistress, Barbara Villiers, Lady Castlemaine, and his close friend, George Villiers, 2nd duke of Buckingham.

At the end of August 1667, in the wake of England's defeat in the disastrous Anglo-Dutch war of 1664–7, his enemies finally secured Clarendon's dismissal. Turning his longest-serving minister into a scapegoat for the disaster, Charles supported Clarendon's impeachment on dubious charges of treason and corruption (see below, p. 104). The impeachment turned into a confrontation between the two Houses, made dangerous because the chief of Clarendon's supporters in the House of Lords was his son in law, Charles's brother, the duke of York. Clarendon's opponents failed to get the House of Lords to commit him to the Tower of London and the impeachment started to fall apart. As the rows looked likely to produce a bitter split between the king and his brother and their respective camps, and as Charles hinted at a more brutal proceeding against him by bill of attainder, Clarendon slipped away into exile for ever at the beginning of December.

Clarendon's fall made the political landscape suddenly less familiar. His rivals, particularly Ashley and Buckingham, were regarded as hostile to the Church and were now freed from his restraint. Presbyterians sensed a new opportunity to moderate the religious laws. But their efforts in early 1668 to promote 'comprehension' – a relaxation of some of the requirements of the Act of Uniformity to enable

FIG. 21 *Thomas Wriothesley, 4th earl of Southampton (1608–67), after Sir Peter Lely (c. 1661). Appointed as lord treasurer in September 1660, Southampton was an important moderating voice in the restored regime.*

Presbyterians to return to the Church of England – were blocked in the Commons, again with the support of the Anglican hierarchy and Archbishop Sheldon. Instead, for two years after 1668 argument centred on the renewal of the 1664 Conventicle Act which expired at the end of the 1667–8 session. The Commons passed a replacement in April 1668. Its passage through the Lords was deliberately thwarted, and all other significant business in both Houses blocked, by a furious dispute between the two Houses on a matter of privilege (Skinner v. the East India Company, see above, p. 24). The government was only able to move ahead with its own business when in spring 1670, the king agreed to accept the Conventicle Bill and to quash attempts by Buckingham and others to defeat it. In March the king took to coming into the Lords to watch the proceedings on the bill, perhaps because of his interest in an ultimately unsuccessful proviso confirming his power in ecclesiastical affairs, regarded by the Commons as an extraordinary extension of the royal prerogative.

The proviso to the Conventicle Bill showed that the king had not abandoned his interests in a radical alteration of the religious laws. But after 1670 religious policy became inextricably entangled with foreign affairs. The war of 1664–7 against the Dutch – a misconceived piece of political adventurism motivated by commercial interests, ideological obsessions and political aggrandisement – had succeeded only in awakening the territorial ambitions of France's youthful and belligerent monarch, Louis XIV. English politicians turned to fretting that the French threatened the balance of power in Europe and the stability of the Dutch republic – one of the few other Protestant powers in Europe. Far from sharing their

fears, while Charles II entered a popular alliance to resist French plans in 1668, he began secret negotiations for an accord with Louis. In May 1670 he agreed to the secret articles of the notorious Treaty of Dover – known only to himself, his brother the duke of York, secretary of state Arlington, the crypto-Catholic politician Sir Thomas Clifford and the Catholic Henry Arundell, 3rd Baron Arundell of Wardour. The agreement committed Charles II to a military alliance with France against the Dutch and, extraordinarily, to the Catholicization of England and his own eventual confession of adherence to the Roman Church. It remained secret for years to come. A few people, though, guessed something of it. The conversion to Catholicism in or about 1669 of York, the heir apparent to the throne, was widely suspected and caused deep anxiety in England and elsewhere, for it implied a seismic shift in the confessional politics of Europe.

In 1670 Charles told Parliament that he was seeking finance for war against France when he intended war against the Dutch. He did not meet Parliament again before he launched a joint offensive with the French on the Netherlands in March 1672. At the same time, he issued a second Declaration of Indulgence in which he acknowledged that the 'sad experience' of the previous twelve years had shown that 'forcible courses' against dissenters were useless.[7] Closely supported within government by a combination of Clifford (shortly afterwards made Baron Clifford of Chudleigh and lord treasurer) and the thoroughly Protestant Ashley (soon to become earl of Shaftesbury and lord chancellor), the Declaration was ostensibly designed to keep nonconformists politically loyal at a time of war. It permitted the king to dispense with the legislation relating to religious conformity and effectively legalised conventicles by introducing a system of licensing.

When Parliament finally met in the spring of 1673, the king anticipated that the Declaration would be subjected to severe attack. He insisted to both Houses that it was not meant in 'any way prejudice the Church' but, he went on, 'I shall take it very, very ill, to receive contradiction in what I have done: And

I will deal plainly with you, I am resolved to stick to my Declaration'.[8] The Commons nevertheless voted that it was beyond his power to suspend the law in this way. Ministers looked to the Lords to support it against the Commons. Ashley was spoiling for a fight: 'rather lose money, than lose rights … state the point to the House of Lords and engage them in it, who will certainly determine otherwise'.[9] He was wrong: the Lords gave polite support to the crown but were not prepared to provoke another inter-cameral dispute on an issue in which the majority of their members agreed with the Commons. The king was forced to back down and withdraw the Declaration.

The anger and alarm at the direction of royal policy since 1670 was all too obvious in the Parliament of 1673. In addition to sinking the Declaration of Indulgence and failing to provide adequate finance for another year of war, the Commons acted to prevent 'dangers which may happen from popish recusants', constructing a test that would root Catholics out of public office by requiring office holders to take the Anglican communion annually and to subscribe to a declaration against transubstantiation, a cornerstone of Catholic theology. The Lords agreed. On 15 March the bill was intemperately denounced

FIG. 23 *The Bishop's Chapel, at Farnham Castle. Farnham Castle was the home of successive bishops of Winchester and the administrative centre of their diocese. Bishop Morley spent £8,000 on remodelling the castle after the Restoration, including refurbishing the chapel: raising the money required involved a private act of Parliament in 1663.*

by Clifford in a speech which infuriated many peers, including his ministerial colleague Shaftesbury, and encouraged suspicions about a Catholic cabal at the centre of government. He narrowly escaped removal to the Tower, and the bill became law as the Test Act. It would introduce a new phase in Restoration politics.

Chapter 2

The peerage: recruitment, extinction and the inflation of honours

Letters patent and the laws of descent

A peerage was a hereditary honour given by the monarch. It conferred a distinction on a family for posterity rather than simply rewarding an individual. The point was made explicit in the letters patent that turned William Russell from earl to duke of Bedford. The new title was to be a perpetual memorial to his son, the Whig martyr William, Lord Russell, executed in the 'Tory Reaction' in 1683. Russell, the patent said, was

> the ornament of our age … whose superlative merits we think it not
> sufficient should be transmitted to all future generations upon the
> credit of public annals; but will have them inserted in these our royal
> letters patents, as a monument consecrated to the most accomplished,
> and consummate virtue in the said family.[1]

Although Charles II did occasionally create life peerages, the only recipients of such honours were women, who had no right to sit in the House of Lords. One of them was the widow of Sir Henry Belasyse, 'a woman of much life and great vivacity, but of a very small proportion of beauty', created Baroness Belasyse of Osgodby for life in 1674, largely as recompense for not insisting on the signed promise of marriage allegedly given her by the heir to the throne, James, duke of York.[2] It would be a century and a half before the crown tried to create a male life peer, when it precipitated a conflict with the House.

Peers were usually created by issuing letters patent. A peerage created in this way usually descended in the direct male line from father to eldest legitimate son. Occasionally, because of particular family circumstances, the patent specified a different descent, known as a special remainder. For example, the celebrated general Frederick Hermann von

Schomberg, second-in-command to William of Orange in the invasion of England in 1688, reversed the normal order of succession to favour his younger sons. Created duke of Schomberg in recognition of his services to William III, he specified that his honours be inherited by his youngest rather than his eldest son and in default of male heirs they would descend to the next youngest son. The peerage was inherited successively by his sons Charles and Meinhard, but there were no sons in the next generation and it was extinguished at the death of Meinhard in 1719.

In some cases the special remainder was deliberately intended to broaden the inheritance in order to render extinction of the peerage less likely. The earldom of Coventry granted in 1697 to Thomas Coventry, 5th Baron Coventry, for example, specified that in the case of the failure of his own male heirs the earldom would pass to the male heirs of his grandfather and then to those of his great uncle, thus bringing quite distant cousins into the line of inheritance. A unique set of conditions was included in the letters patent granted to the daughter of Lord Lucas. Sir John Lucas had been created Baron Lucas of Shenfield in 1645. The terms of the creation allowed the title to be inherited by his younger brother Sir Charles and then by his older, but illegitimate, brother Sir Thomas. Lucas himself had only one surviving child, a daughter, and he outlived his brothers: Sir Charles died unmarried in 1648, shot by the parliamentarians after the surrender of Colchester; Sir Thomas died before 1650, leaving two sons, Charles and Robert. By 1663 it was probably already apparent that the peerage would become extinct: the younger Charles Lucas's marriage had produced two daughters but no sons; Robert Lucas remained a bachelor. Lord Lucas therefore obtained a fresh patent of nobility creating his daughter Mary (who had become countess of Kent meanwhile) Baroness Lucas of Crudwell, but with a complex and unprecedented clause specifying that the new peerage would pass by the common law rules of inheritance. This meant that in the absence of a male heir it would never go into abeyance but pass through the female line and survive to remind posterity of the achievements of the Lucas family. The calculation proved to be correct. The peerage of Lucas of Shenfield became extinct on the death of Robert Lucas in 1705; the peerage of Lucas of Crudwell survives to this day.

Although letters patent had become the normal mechanism for creating a peerage, other methods had been used in the distant past. The receipt of a writ summoning a commoner to the House of Lords was

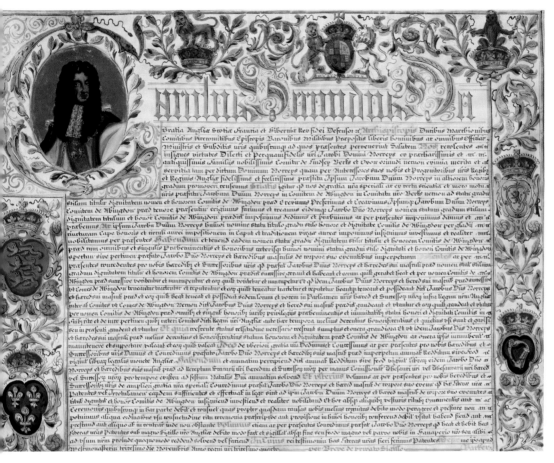

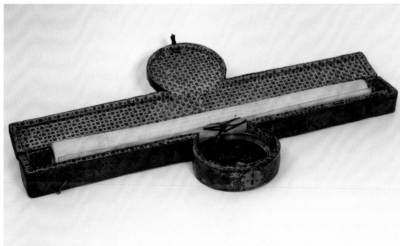

FIG. 24 *James Bertie, Baron Norreys (1653–99), was created earl of Abingdon in November 1682, after his care in ensuring the successful prosecution in Oxford of the Whig propagandist Stephen College. His letters patent were carefully preserved in a specially-made case.*

Baronies by writ:
the Clifford barony

The development in the seventeenth century of the idea that a writ of summons to Parliament conferred on the individual receiving it a barony that could be inherited by his male and female heirs – 'heirs general' – complicated the entire peerage system. Medieval kings had often issued writs to their supporters summoning them to the upper house of Parliament without intending to ennoble the recipient's descendants in perpetuity. As membership of Parliament's upper house became more closely associated with a hereditary peerage it began to be assumed that such men had automatically acquired a heritable barony. Some people took advantage of the ambiguity surrounding such 'baronies by writ' to press their claims to a prestigious medieval title.

John Frescheville, for example, had been created a baron by royal patent in 1665. In 1677, however, he argued before the House that his barony really dated back to 1297, when a distant ancestor, Ralph de Frescheville, had received a writ of summons to Parliament from Edward I. It was pointed out that no other member of the family had received a writ of summons in the interim, and the petition was defeated. Yet Frescheville's attempt indicates both the peers' obsession with the antiquity of their titles and the murkiness of the law surrounding medieval titles and baronies by writ. Two cases in the 1690s helped to clarify the question: the claim of Richard Verney to the barony of Willoughby of Broke, created (supposedly) by a writ of summons of 1497, and the dying embers of the half-century-long conflict between two of the most powerful families in the country over the ancient barony of Clifford.

The central character in the latter story was Lady Anne Clifford (as she was generally known). Her claim to the title rested on a writ of summons directed to Robert de Clifford in 1299. She argued that, because the title descended through heirs general, it had come to her after the death of her father George Clifford, 13th Baron Clifford and 3rd earl of Cumberland, rather than to his brother, the 4th earl. Her cousin Elizabeth Clifford also claimed the title: she argued that she had it by descent through the heir

male, her father, the 4th earl's son, Henry Clifford, 5th earl of Cumberland. It strengthened Elizabeth's claim that her father had been summoned to Parliament in 1628 as 'Lord Clifford' on the assumption that that was a junior barony of his own father. To make matters even more confusing, in 1644 Charles I had bestowed on Elizabeth's husband, the Irish peer Richard Boyle, 2nd earl of Cork, the English title of Baron Clifford of Lanesborough. The competing Lady Cliffords, Anne and Elizabeth, had tried to effect a reconciliation in 1664 through the marriage of Elizabeth's daughter, also called Elizabeth, to Lady Anne's grandson, Nicholas Tufton, who shortly thereafter became 3rd earl of Thanet.

Despite the marriage, the tensions over the Clifford title remained, creating a row in 1665 over the use in a private bill of the title 'Lord Clifford' for Lord Clifford of Lanesborough, to which Lady Anne Clifford took exception. The Boyles reluctantly agreed to retain the 'of Lanesborough', no doubt helped by the fact that they obtained a promotion in the English peerage, to earl of Burlington. Relations were not improved when in 1671–2 the eccentric Thanet was suspected of having tried to poison Burlington's daughter, and perhaps even Burlington himself, through the agency of a servant. Burlington agreed to preserve him from public ignominy only because his daughter insisted on continuing to live with him.

The death of Lady Anne in 1676, followed by 1678 by the deaths of her two daughters and a granddaughter (among whom the title had briefly been 'in abeyance'), left Thomas Tufton, 6th earl of Thanet, grandson of Lady Anne Clifford, as the inheritor of her claim to the title. In November 1690, perhaps provoked by the summons to the House of Lords of Burlington's heir in his father's barony of Clifford of Lanesborough, Thanet petitioned the House claiming the Clifford title as the heir general of Robert de Clifford. Elizabeth, the countess of Burlington, submitted a counter-petition to Thanet's claim, rehashing the arguments that the title should descend through the heir male. Her death in January 1691, before the case could be heard fully at the bar, may have enabled

FIG. 25 *Lady Anne Clifford (Anne, countess of Pembroke) (1590–1676), after Sir Peter Lely.*

the issue to be resolved. Thanet had cultivated Lord Clifford of Lanesborough, offering his 'interest' at Appleby in 1690 to secure the election of Clifford's son to the House of Commons. Clifford of Lanesborough, expecting to inherit the Burlington title, decided not to continue his mother's squabble, and promised not to obstruct Thanet's claim.

There was, though, another challenge to Thanet's barony of Clifford. In January 1695 the House rejected the petition of Richard Verney to sit in Parliament as Baron Willoughby de Broke. Verney's claim was based on an ancestor's writ of summons of 1497. The House objected that the title had passed through the female line and that for a period it had been held in abeyance between three female coheirs – just as the Clifford barony had been between 1676 and 1678. Under pressure from

Thanet, just two months later the House reversed its decision – though not without a protest signed by ten peers – and resolved that a barony by writ could indeed be inherited through the female line as well as the male and that if, after being held in abeyance by female coheirs for a time, it came to rest again in a single surviving male heir, that heir could rightfully demand a writ of summons.

Ironically when Thanet died in 1729 without leaving a son, his earldom, created by patent, descended quite easily to the male heir, his nephew Sackville Tufton, but the barony of Clifford, whose descent through the female line Thanet had worked so hard to have recognized, now fell into abeyance yet again – and this time between his five daughters and coheirs.

recognised as creating a hereditary peerage (known as a barony by writ). Although this method was rarely used in the period 1660 to 1715, it could be a way of covering up errors, as for example when the wrong heir to the barony of Willoughby of Parham was summoned to the House of Lords in 1680. Even when there was no error, such cases led to considerable confusion in the law of descent.

Under modern peerage law, the inheritance of a peerage created by writ of summons is governed by different rules than one created by letters patent. Instead of normally passing only from father to eldest son, it is assumed to descend through the female line (to 'heirs general') in the absence of a direct male heir. The peerage can therefore pass to a single daughter and hence to her heirs. Because the honour is indivisible, however, it is blocked ('abeyant') if the peer concerned leaves two or more female heirs. It remains abeyant until only one of the female lines survives. Then the peerage emerges again, unless in the meantime the crown has exercised its right to terminate the abeyance by conferring the title on a particular heir. In the seventeenth century, however, these principles were still being developed, and the practice was flexible and inconsistent (see above, p. 46).

Recruitment

In the sixteenth century the peerage consisted of only about 40 peers. During her long reign Elizabeth I kept creations to a minimum; at her death there were still only about 50 peers. Her successor, James I, had no inhibitions about the size of the peerage, nor scruples about exploiting peerages to gratify courtiers and gentlemen and to provide an additional source of income for his courtiers. Courtiers, including James's favourite, George Villiers, duke of Buckingham, accepted money to intercede with the king to secure peerages for honour-hungry gentry. Sir Robert Dormer (created Baron Dormer in 1615) paid £10,000 for his; Sir John Roper (Baron Teynham) and Sir John Holles (Baron Haughton) paid the same amount for theirs in 1616, giving rise to the witticism that Teynham (a title actually taken from the name of Roper's manor in Kent) really stood for Ten Ms (referring to the roman numeral for 1,000). Promotions in the peerage could be obtained in the same way. £10,000 bought earldoms for Lord Cavendish (as earl of Devonshire) and Lord Rich (as earl of Warwick); the relatively new baron, Lord Haughton, parted with perhaps

FIG. 26
John Bushnell's elaborate funeral monument for John Mordaunt, Viscount Mordaunt (1626–75), was said to have cost £250. Mordaunt is shown in semi-classical garb, holding a marshal's baton. The statue is flanked by oval tablets bearing details of Mordaunt's genealogy, suggesting that he was as anxious as his brother, Henry Mordaunt, 2nd earl of Peterborough, to emphasise the family's ancient lineage (see below, pp. 71-2). The pedestals (out of this picture) are surmounted by a pair of gauntlets and a viscount's coronet. The ensemble conveys the impression that Mordaunt was at once a senator, chivalric knight and nobleman.

half that sum in order to become earl of Clare. In the process the peerage grew rapidly. By 1628 there were nearly 130 peers.

The Civil War produced further pressure for marks of favour and the recognition of the services of loyal followers of the crown; peerages could also help to attract funds for the cash-starved royalist war effort. The peculiar circumstances of the civil war and interregnum meant that royal promises became a cheap way of raising funds and support. Twenty years after Thomas Brudenell had paid £6,000 for his barony in 1628, Charles I, then a prisoner in Carisbrooke Castle on the Isle of Wight, promised him an earldom in return for a mere £1,000 to help fund an escape attempt. Brudenell had to wait until 1661 for his earldom (of Cardigan). Charles II was himself lavish with offers of ennoblement. Early in March 1659 he sent a blank warrant for the creation of a viscountcy to Elizabeth, wife of the royalist plotter, John Mordaunt, telling her to bestow it upon 'the person you think fittest to oblige'. She bestowed it on her husband.[3] Some wartime and Interregnum peerages were regarded as deeply dubious. In May 1660 Allen Brodrick, secretary of the royalist Sealed Knot, wrote to Edward Hyde (later earl of Clarendon) to suggest that all grants of peerage made since 1642 should be annulled, as many were given to those of little merit, 'such as the marquess of Dorchester, who is not fit to be groom to an honest man'.[4] (Brodrick was not the only person to be suspicious of the Catholic Henry Pierrepont, marquess of Dorchester, 'a person so firm to the doctrine and discipline of the Church of Rome, that he is even in the highest degree Jesuited, so that the many and subtlest Papists have not only by way of civility a free admittance to his table, but to him they come, as a wise and close favourite for advice in their cause'.)[5] In 1660 the House of Lords discovered that there were two claimants to the title of duke of Somerset, both men who had distinguished themselves in the service of the crown during the civil wars. William Seymour, marquess of Hertford, was the great-grandson of Edward Seymour, Protector Somerset, who had been attainted in 1552. In 1660 he tried to overturn this attainder, thus enabling himself to succeed as duke of Somerset. To his consternation he discovered that Edward Somerset, 2nd marquess of Worcester, claimed to have in his possession several documents by which Charles I had granted *him* the dukedom of Somerset. When the House of Lords began an investigation, Worcester withdrew his claim, explaining that the grant was a conditional one and that he had not fulfilled the relevant conditions. Others suspected that the investigation would reveal the documents to be forgeries. The episode caused so much concern about the possible existence of otherwise unknown and unrecorded patents of nobility and grants of office that the Lords passed a bill 'for preventing inconveniencies which may arise by patents and grants, made, or pretended to be made, during the late troubles' and to impose an expiry date on them, though the bill was lost in the Commons.

From the Restoration in 1660 to the death of Queen Anne in 1714 well over 100 individuals were added to the English (after 1707 the British) peerage. There was intense pressure to obtain peerages, and – since the expansion of the peerage involved a certain devaluation of the honour – once a man had obtained one, to obtain a better one. One of the most ambitious was the politician who had helped to ignite the political crisis of 1678–81 by revealing diplomatic correspondence in the House of Commons, Ralph Montagu. Having inherited his father's barony in 1684, he was promoted to an earldom in 1689 in recognition of his support for William III's invasion. In 1694 he wrote to the king requesting a dukedom, arguing that he was the head of a family far more distinguished than others which enjoyed that distinction, that his marriage to the eldest daughter of the duke of Newcastle entitled him to it, and that his service to the king had not yet been sufficiently rewarded:

> I may add another pretension, which is the same for which you have
> given a dukedom to the Bedford family, the having been one of the first
> and held out to the last in that cause which for the happiness of
> England brought you to the crown. I hope it will not be thought a less
> merit to be alive and ready in all occasions to venture all again for your
> service, than if I had lost my head when my Lord Russell did; I could
> not then have had the opportunity of doing the nation the service I did
> when there was such opposition made by the Jacobite party in bringing
> my Lord Huntingdon, the bishop of Durham and my Lord Ashley
> [Astley] to vote against the Regency and your having the crown, which
> was passed but by those three voices and my own.[6]

Montagu had to wait for his dukedom until 1705 when his son married a daughter of John Churchill, duke of Marlborough.

Those wanting a peerage had to be determined and persistent. Henry Paget, son and heir of William, 7th Baron Paget, was given a peerage of his own in 1712, as Baron Burton, one of 'Harley's dozen'. The Paget family had been angling for an earldom since 1705 and the new Lord Burton, believing that Oxford had promised to help him to one, constantly pestered him about it, until by 1714 he had gained the distinct (and not uncommon) impression that Oxford was fobbing him off:

> Your lordship having told me eight or nine months ago, that her
> Majesty had been pleased to consent to grant me the favour I had (by
> your kind promise) desired for myself ... I hope you'll allow me to be
> surprised that I should ... have any occasion to solicit for what I

Henry St John, Viscount Bolingbroke (1678–1751)

'Adorned', according to Jonathan Swift, 'with the choicest gifts that God hath yet thought fit to bestow upon the children of men' – though another Tory clergyman remarked 'of how little use the greatest parts are to one void of all sense of honour and religion' – Henry St John was elected to the Commons at the age of 22 in 1701.[1] Three years later the young Tory firebrand was secretary at war; by 1710 he was secretary of state, the closest confidant and fellow intriguer of the man who was virtually prime minster, Robert Harley. As part of the price for his support, he expected a peerage.

St John wanted a peerage in part because he considered it his due as the cadet member of a noble family: the St Johns were a prominent Wiltshire family, a branch of the family which had been Barons Saint John of Bletso since 1559, and earls of Bolingbroke since 1624. It may also have been a way to achieve parity with his patron, colleague and rival, Robert Harley, who had been promoted to the Lords in May 1711 as earl of Oxford. St John's elevation to an earldom had been mooted in December of that year when 'Harley's dozen' ensured the defeat of the Whig opposition in the House of Lords to the ministry's peace policy (see below, p. 337). At that time, he was considered to be of more value to the ministry as a manager in the lower House. The treaty safely negotiated, the question of St John's elevation arose again. Following the death of his kinsman Paulet St John, 3rd earl of Bolingbroke, without direct heirs, the barony of St John had descended to another cousin. The earldom was extinct. St John wanted the senior title to be revived for him.

There was, however, a problem: the queen's disapproval. For all his charm and ability, St John had a sulphurous reputation as a rake and a libertine, and as a man who climbed to power over the bodies of his friends. Oxford succeeded in persuading the queen to grant St John a peerage in July 1712, but she baulked at raising him to an earldom. He was instead offered the lesser title of Viscount Bolingbroke. St John contemplated rejecting the peerage altogether. Jonathan Swift advised him to adopt an alternative title to

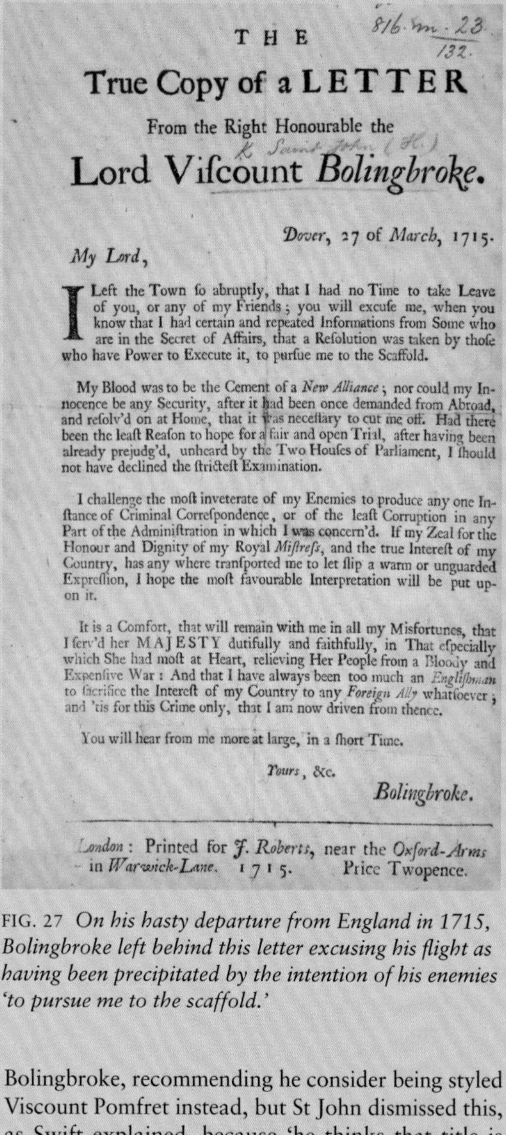

THE

True Copy of a LETTER

From the Right Honourable the

Lord Viſcount *Bolingbroke*.

Dover, 27 of *March*, 1715.

My Lord,

I Left the Town ſo abruptly, that I had no Time to take Leave of you, or any of my Friends; you will excuſe me, when you know that I had certain and repeated Informations from Some who are in the Secret of Affairs, that a Reſolution was taken by thoſe who have Power to Execute it, to purſue me to the Scaffold.

My Blood was to be the Cement of a *New Alliance*; nor could my Innocence be any Security, after it had been once demanded from Abroad, and reſolv'd on at Home, that it was neceſſary to cut me off. Had there been the leaſt Reaſon to hope for a fair and open Trial, after having been already prejudg'd, unheard by the Two Houſes of Parliament, I ſhould not have declined the ſtricteſt Examination.

I challenge the moſt inveterate of my Enemies to produce any one Inſtance of Criminal Correſpondence, or of the leaſt Corruption in any Part of the Adminiſtration in which I was concern'd. If my Zeal for the Honour and Dignity of my Royal *Miſtreſs*, and the true Intereſt of my Country, has any where tranſported me to let ſlip a warm or unguarded Expreſſion, I hope the moſt favourable Interpretation will be put upon it.

It is a Comfort, that will remain with me in all my Misfortunes, that I ſerv'd her MAJESTY dutifully and faithfully, in That eſpecially which She had moſt at Heart, relieving Her People from a Bloody and Expenſive War: And that I have always been too much an *Engliſhman* to ſacrifice the Intereſt of my Country to any *Foreign Ally* whatſoever; and 'tis for this Crime only, that I am now driven from thence.

You will hear from me more at large, in a ſhort Time.

Yours, &c.

Bolingbroke.

London: Printed for *J. Roberts*, near the *Oxford-Arms* in *Warwick-Lane*. 1715. Price Twopence.

FIG. 27 *On his hasty departure from England in 1715, Bolingbroke left behind this letter excusing his flight as having been precipitated by the intention of his enemies 'to pursue me to the scaffold.'*

Bolingbroke, recommending he consider being styled Viscount Pomfret instead, but St John dismissed this, as Swift explained, because 'he thinks that title is already in some other family, and besides he objects that it is in Yorkshire where he has no estate'.[2] Eventually, he accepted the proffered title, but made no secret of his irritation that he had been so shabbily treated:

> In the House of Commons… I was at the head of business, and I must have continued so, whether I had been in court or out of court. There was therefore nothing to flatter my ambition in removing me from thence, but giving me the title which had been many years in my family…

FIG. 28 *In this picture, attributed to Alexis Simon Belle, Bolingbroke is portrayed in the robes worn for the coronation of October 1714. The scattered papers on the table proclaim him to be a man of business as well as rank. In his outstretched hand he holds, perhaps a little disdainfully, his viscount's coronet.*

To make me a peer was no great compliment, when so many others were forced to be made to gain a strength in parliament; and since the Queen wanted me below stairs in the last session, she could do no less than make me a viscount, or I must have come in the rear of several whom I was not born to follow.[3]

Bolingbroke finally realized his other ambition, of succeeding Oxford at the head of the ministry, a few days before the death of Queen Anne. Talk of being made a knight of the garter and of finally being promoted to his coveted earldom was halted by the queen's demise. Promptly put out of office by the new regime, in 1715, and believing that the Whigs were preparing to put him on trial for his life, he fled to the continent disguised as the servant of a French diplomat. Once he got there, he compounded his difficulties by agreeing to serve James II's son, the Pretender, as his secretary of state. His reward was the coveted earldom of Bolingbroke in the Jacobite peerage. He did eventually make his peace with the Hanoverians and was granted leave to return to England in 1725. The terms of his pardon stipulated that he was to be restored to his title but barred from admission to the Lords.

From an inferior title, Bolingbroke had progressed to an unrecognized honour and ultimately to an empty one.

thought would some time ago have been finished. But your lordship saying very little upon that subject to me when I saw you last at Windsor, and saying nothing about it since my coming to town, I cannot but think myself treated with great unkindness.[7]

He was finally given his earldom, the earldom of Uxbridge, after the accession of George I, one of 14 coronation peerages.

Peerages were routinely given to members of the royal family, such as Charles II's brothers, James, duke of York (later James II), and Henry, duke of Gloucester, who died within months of the Restoration, and his uncle, the renowned cavalry commander Prince Rupert, who as duke of Cumberland exercised an occasional influence in English politics. Of the monarchs of the period only James had a legitimate son who survived to adulthood, and he lived and died in exile after the Revolution, referred to as the Pretender. James's several other legitimate sons were given dukedoms, but all died in infancy. James's illegitimate son, James FitzJames, was made duke of Berwick, but was too young to attend the House before the Revolution and would in any case have been barred by his Catholicism. At the Revolution he joined his father in exile and (holding French and Spanish dukedoms as well) became a distinguished military commander, leading Franco-Spanish troops to victory in 1707 against the Anglo-Dutch forces at Almanza. Charles II – pestered mercilessly by his mistresses on the subject – conferred peerages on several of his illegitimate sons (five became dukes) and on the husbands of his illegitimate daughters. The eldest and most favoured was James Crofts, later known as James Scott, who became duke of Monmouth in 1663 and took his seat in the House of Lords in 1670.

Peerages were often used to reward ministers and courtiers and to sweeten potential enemies. In the early years of the Restoration, peerages flattered the men who had made the return of Charles II possible, General George Monck (duke of Albemarle), and the naval commander, Edward Montagu (earl of Sandwich), as well as those pillars of the parliamentary and Cromwellian regimes who were believed to be still capable of helping or hindering the new regime: Denzil Holles (Baron Holles), Anthony Ashley Cooper (Baron Ashley, later earl of Shaftesbury), Charles Howard (earl of Carlisle) and Arthur Annesley (earl of Anglesey). Staunch royalists were also rewarded: Arthur Capell, 2nd Baron Capell of Hadham, was promoted to an earldom (Essex) in memory of his father's Civil War services. Peerages were also used to dignify senior ministers: Sir Henry Bennet,

The Effigies of his highnes Henrye,
Duke of Glocester.

Ob. Sept. 1660.

FIG. 29 *According to Edward Hyde, earl of Clarendon, Henry, duke of Gloucester (1640–60), the youngest brother of Charles II, was 'a prince of extraordinary hopes'. Despite his youth he had a reputation for wisdom and gallantry. In May 1660 he shared in the triumph of the Restoration, and began regularly to attend the House of Lords; six months later he died of small pox, barely 21 years old.*

secretary of state, was made Baron Arlington in 1665, and earl of Arlington in 1672; Sir Thomas Clifford became Baron Clifford shortly before he became lord treasurer in 1672; Sir Thomas Osborne acquired a Scottish viscountcy in 1673; an English viscountcy (Latimer) followed his appointment as Lord Treasurer later that year, with promotion to an earldom (Danby) a year later. Danby's support for William of Orange later brought him a marquessate (Carmarthen in 1689) and then a dukedom (Leeds in 1694). Like Charles II at the Restoration, William III after the Revolution made good use of his ability to create new peers or promote existing ones to honour his closest allies or those he needed to conciliate. In April 1689 he created four new peers and promoted another seven. Another three creations followed in May. The recipients included his

FIG. 30 *James, duke of York (1633–1701), by Henri Gascard, shown as lord high admiral. Charles II's failure to produce a legitimate heir meant that it was increasingly obvious that his younger brother, James duke of York, would succeed to the throne. York's conversion to Catholicism spawned an increasingly virulent campaign to exclude him from the throne.*

brother-in-law Prince George (duke of Cumberland), his English ally Henry Sydney (Viscount Sydney), his Dutch friend and adviser Hans Willem Bentinck (earl of Portland), prominent English military men like John Churchill (promoted from a barony to be earl of Marlborough), the naval commander Arthur Herbert (earl of Torrington) and Schomberg. Another substantial round of creations took place in 1694: only two commoners were raised to the peerage but eight existing peers were promoted, five of them to dukedoms. Anne similarly rewarded friends and political allies, among them John Churchill, husband of her close friend Sarah, who was transformed from earl to duke of Marlborough.

Peerages were also given for more everyday political services. Francis Newport's promotion from a barony to a viscountcy in 1675 was meant to detach him from 'country' politicians and bring him more firmly within the ambit of the court. Christopher Hatton was promoted from a barony to a viscountcy in January 1683 in recognition of his solid support for the court during the exclusion crisis. Ralph Stawell was rewarded with a barony the same year for his part in keeping political and military control over Somerset and the South West during the Popish Plot and Exclusion Crisis and for his robust efforts to repress dissenters there. Early in 1688, when James II's agents were hard at work in an attempt to pack the Commons with supporters of the king's policies, it was rumoured that James intended to pack the Lords too by conferring English peerages on Irish Catholic peers. The survival of two writs of summons dated 1685 and 1688 directed to the Catholic Thomas Petre (who succeeded as 6th Baron Petre in January 1685) raises suspicions of an attempt to force the House to accept Catholic peers as well (see below, p. 126). Examples of political creations multiplied in the reign of Anne, when Tories found themselves frequently under pressure in the Lords. In March 1703 five commoners were elevated to the upper house and two earls (including Ralph Montagu) became dukes as part of a concerted effort to bolster the ranks of the Tories. A further round of creations and promotions followed in 1706. Most notorious of all was the creation of the ten new Tory peers (who, together with two heirs to peerages summoned by writs of acceleration, were dubbed 'Harley's dozen') on 31 December 1711 and 1 January 1712 in order to provide the House of Lords with a majority in favour of peace with France (see below, p. 337).

Many peerages were favours not to the recipient, but to a powerful courtier or politician who stood as his patron. Men like James, duke of

Married to the king's daughter: Edward Henry Lee, earl of Lichfield (1663–1716)

Sir Edward Henry Lee owed his peerage to his marriage in 1677, at the age of fourteen, to Charlotte Fitzroy, the thirteen-year-old daughter of Charles II and his mistress, Barbara Villiers, duchess of Cleveland. His creation as earl of Lichfield, one of the subsidiary titles of the recently deceased duke of Lennox and Richmond, may have been intended by the king as a slight on the surviving dowager duchess of Richmond, Frances Stuart, who had spurned his advances. The king bestowed on the new countess of Lichfield, his favourite daughter, a portion of £20,000 (from which the earl received an annual pension of £2,000), a further £600 for 'house keeping' and the rangership of Woodstock Park, the profits of which were estimated to be worth approximately £800 per annum. The Lichfields also received a house on Downing Street, the kernel of the present No. 10.

Lichfield, whose family home was at Ditchley Park, on the edge of the Cotswolds, was related to much of the Oxfordshire aristocracy and gentry, especially to the Bertie earls of Abingdon. Still only just of age on James's accession, he was unusually compliant with the king's plans to repeal the Test Act. Lichfield's influence in the county made him, in theory at least, a key ally. His cousin, James Bertie, earl of Abingdon, was removed from the office of lord lieutenant of Oxfordshire when he refused to put to local officials the king's 'three questions' – an attempt to uncover attitudes to the king's policy of religious toleration for Catholics. Lichfield replaced him. It was Lichfield's regiment of foot that James chose to canvass to gauge the army's attitude to his plans. The countess of Lichfield was one of those who was present at the birth of James's son, James Edward, Prince of Wales – denounced as a fraud by large numbers of Protestants desperate that there should not be a Catholic heir. She vouched for the genuineness of the birth; her husband announced it to the deputies in his Oxfordshire lieutenancy.

At the Revolution, Lichfield could do nothing to rally the county to the king. Abingdon, who had kept his colonel's position in the militia, was able to gather a force swiftly and join William of Orange at Exeter.

After James's departure from England, Lichfield attended the Convention. He rejected the idea that the king had abdicated, that the throne was vacant, or that William and Mary be voted king and queen. He was put out of all of his offices. The lord lieutenancy returned to Abingdon, and the rangership of Woodstock to the Whig peer, John Lovelace, 3rd Baron Lovelace, whom he had displaced in 1679. Lichfield (who had never been much of an attender anyway) never sat in Parliament again. For the rest of his life he remained a 'non-juror', refusing to take the new oaths of allegiance. Like most non-jurors, he was regularly assumed to be involved in Jacobite plotting. In 1690 and again in 1691 Lichfield was arrested, but although he was heavily implicated in the conspiracy headed by Viscount Preston in 1691, for which he was 'clapped up' in the Tower,[1] he escaped trial and was permitted to retire to his estates. The Lichfields had already sold their lease of the house in Downing Street in 1690.

Although as a non-juror Lichfield had lost all of his offices, he retained a significant interest in the counties where he held land. In 1695 he informed his agent Cary that he would not meddle in the imminent elections in Oxfordshire, but in December of the following year, in response to an application from Sir John Verney for his support in the by-election for Buckinghamshire, Lichfield undertook to do what he could on his behalf. In the event Verney was unsuccessful, but Lichfield was pleased with how close he had come to securing one of the seats and encouraged him to stand again at the next election. In 1710, Verney (since promoted to the Irish peerage as Viscount Fermanagh) was successful and Lichfield wrote to congratulate him and assure him of the part he had played in securing the seat for him.

Described by John Moore, bishop of Norwich, as 'a very sober good tempered gent',[2] Lichfield and his wife were said to have enjoyed a remarkably harmonious marriage, which produced eighteen children. His daughters caused him some anguish: in 1699 he was shaken by the 'sour accident' of one of them 'turning papist'; and another, Charlotte, separated from her husband, Benedict Leonard Calvert, 4th

Baron Baltimore, on account of her affairs. In 1696 while travelling to Epsom, Lichfield was seriously injured when he fell from his coach and the wheels ran over his hip, but he lived long enough to see the Hanoverian succession and the defeat of the Jacobite rebellion of 1715, and died the following year, 'much grieved', according to the Oxford Jacobite Thomas Hearne, 'at the iniquity and distraction of the times'.[3] He was succeeded in the peerage by his son, the builder of the present Ditchley Park.

FIG. 31 *Whitehall Palace viewed from the west, painted c. 1676–80 by Hendrick Danckerts, at around the time the Lichfields acquired the building on Downing Street, which can be seen to the right of the picture.*

York, brokered the conferment of peerages on their own friends and relations. The earldom of Feversham given in April 1676 to Sir George Sondes with a special remainder to his son-in-law, Louis de Duras, Baron Duras, was an oblique method of conferring an earldom on one of York's close associates. It was presumably intended to avoid the controversy that might be engendered by outright conferral of an earldom on a Frenchman. Sir Charles North became Lord Grey of Rolleston in October 1673 (by a writ of summons, rather than letters patent), even though he stood to inherit the barony of North in due course. The grant was related to his marriage six years earlier to the daughter of William Grey, Baron Grey of Warke, a former parliamentarian and an ally of the then lord chancellor, Anthony Ashley Cooper, earl of Shaftesbury. Significantly Sir Charles North's new title did not celebrate his own family name or estates but was, in effect, an indirect ennoblement of the old baron's daughter, whose jointure estates lay in Rolleston, Staffordshire. It is possible that Shaftesbury, who was by then in open opposition to the duke of York and was consequently an object of suspicion at court (he was dismissed from office barely two weeks later), had secured the peerage from the king as a way of bolstering his own support in Parliament. Grey of Rolleston (who became 5th Baron North in 1677) was later a prominent and vociferous supporter of Titus Oates and ultimately of the Revolution of 1688. Another peer, William Fermor, owed his title of Baron Leominster, conferred in April 1692, not to his own merits, but to his marriage a month earlier to Lady Sophia Osborne, the daughter of Thomas Osborne, the then marquess of Carmarthen.

It was commonly believed that peerages were sold as they had been before the Civil War, although the evidence is unreliable. Bishop Fell of Oxford was said to have received a patent for an earldom worth £1,000 from the king, so that he could sell it on in aid of completing the great gate at Christ Church. Baptist Noel, 3rd Viscount Campden, was believed to have parted with £4,000 in 1682 in an attempt to secure an earldom; he was still a viscount when he died in October 1682, but his son Edward was promoted earl of Gainsborough four and a half weeks later. Edward Conway, Viscount Conway, was rumoured to have paid £10,000 to Charles II's mistress, Louise de Kéroualle, duchess of Portsmouth, for his advancement to an earldom in 1679, although he protested that he had not sought the honour. In 1711 it was rumoured that Sir Richard Child, one of the sons of the phenomenally wealthy merchant Sir Josiah Child and a member of the Commons, was planning to buy a peerage for

FIG. 32 *Charles North, 5th Baron North and Baron Grey of Rolleston (c. 1636–1691), by Edmund Ashfield, c. 1670–80.*

£10,000; the rumour reminded Thomas Windsor (Viscount Windsor in the Irish peerage and shortly afterwards Baron Mountjoy in the British), of the duchess of Marlborough, who, he alleged, would 'do anything for money, making a man that's no gentleman a lord'.[8] The maligned duchess herself claimed that the only time she used her influence to secure a peerage was in 1703 when John Hervey was made Baron Hervey of Ickworth, at the request of his father-in-law, Sir Thomas Felton. Hervey's elevation was certainly odd: he was the only Whig amongst the five commoners who received peerages that year and his creation was said to have been achieved in the teeth of vigorous opposition.

The case of the Childs showed that wealth alone was not enough to secure a peerage. Sir Richard Child failed in his bid, although he did obtain a less prestigious Irish peerage in 1718 – granting Irish rather than

English peerages enabled successive governments to reward individual commoners without inflating the size of the English peerage. The Child family managed instead to buy an *entrée* to the English peerage through the substantial dowries Sir Josiah bestowed on his daughters, who as a result were able to marry into the highest ranks of the aristocracy. Sir Richard's sister married Charles Somerset, styled marquess of Worcester, who would have become 2nd duke of Beaufort had he lived; his niece married Wriothesley Russell, 2nd duke of Bedford; his stepsister married James Brydges, heir to the barony of Chandos and later duke of Chandos.

Child's case also hints at some of the unspoken conventions that underlay the grant of a peerage. Peers were expected to have sufficient wealth, social standing or political weight and to have significance and respectability in their own counties in order to justify being raised in status above the local gentry. Those reckoned to be of relatively humble origin risked the contempt of their fellow peers. In 1685 the news that a mere lawyer, the lord chief justice, George Jeffreys, was to be raised to the peerage raised eyebrows. Jeffreys had a special remainder included in the letters patent creating him a baron that was designed to ensure that his heirs would be sufficiently wealthy to support the dignity: the honour was to descend to his sons by his second (rich) wife, reverting to his eldest son only if that line failed (as it did). There could be opposition to the gift of new peerages on the grounds of respectability. In 1665 the duke of York's recommendation of a peerage for George Savile was thwarted by objections from Charles II's chief minister, Edward Hyde, earl of Clarendon, who suspected Savile of atheism, and Savile's peerage (as Viscount Halifax) only materialised in January 1668 after Clarendon's fall from power. John Frescheville's hopes for a barony with a special remainder to his two daughters were thwarted when the younger one eloped with a penniless soldier and engineer. His patent as Baron Frescheville finally passed the great seal in 1665 without the special remainder that would have ensured its transmission to the next generation. James II's grant of peerages to several insignificant political figures simply because they were Catholics – and not even prominent or wealthy ones – flew in the face of convention too, although contemporaries also objected to them because they were further evidence of the king's campaign to remove the civil disabilities on Catholics.

There were perennial complaints that new peerages were expanding the size of the peerage and diluting its prestige. In 1668 the House asked the committee for privileges to consider precedents for writs of acceleration and the consequent multiplication of titles of honour. During the debate in 1701 on what was to become the Act of Settlement, the duke of Devonshire suggested the addition of a clause to prevent what he deemed to be the irresponsible creation of peerages, declaring it to be ridiculous that the son of a tailor could become a peer. Viscount Longueville weighed in with a motion to add a clause to the bill specifying a property qualification for peerages, graded by rank. He thought that even the lowest rank of the peerage should possess £3,000 in landed property and that this should be inalienable. Neither proposition passed into law. The creation of 'Harley's dozen' in 1712 brought new concerns. Most critics had to accept that most of those created were perfectly respectable. The exception was Samuel Masham, a nonentity who was married to the queen's household servant and close friend (and also cousin and ally of chief minister Robert Harley, earl of Oxford), Abigail Hill. Masham's social and economic qualifications to become a peer were defended in print with a translation of his letters patent, which explained how he was 'sprung from an equestrian family of the superior order'.[9] A creation the following year, that of Robert Benson as Baron Bingley, attracted more odium. Bingley's Yorkshire neighbour, Thomas Wentworth, earl of Strafford, wrote that he was

> of no extraction. His father was an attorney and no great character for an honest man, and I think concerned in the affairs of Oliver Cromwell. He left him a good estate in Yorkshire of about £1,500 a year, and an old seat just by Wakefield. This gentleman has been a very good manager and has saved 5 or 6,000 pounds or more. He has lived very handsomely in the country without being a drinker, though very gallant amongst the ladies.[10]

Sir John Reresby, another Yorkshireman, reckoned that Benson's father had been

> the most notable and formidable man for business of his time, one of no birth, and that had raised himself from being clerk to a country attorney to be clerk of the peace at the Old Bailiff, to clerk of assize of the northern circuit, and to an estate of £2,500 p.a., but not without suspicion of great frauds and oppressions.[11]

The speed of Benson's rise, his willingness to flaunt his wealth and his talent for putting his neighbours' noses out of joint added to the irritation at his elevation. After his elevation on 21 July 1713, the acid Oxford Tory,

Dr Stratford, complained that while 'it was justly alleged in the late creation [Harley's dozen] that all of them were of ancient families; no one I have met with is much acquainted with the new lord's pedigree'.[12] William Berkeley, 4th Baron Berkeley of Stratton, considered that Benson's elevation was further proof that 'every year that House [of Lords] receives some great blow, that I am persuaded ... it is the interest of the public to have the dignity kept up'.[13]

Status and the inflation of honours

Much of the pressure for new peerages came not from men like Benson, but from those who were peers already and anxious to be elevated further. The result was a growth in the highest ranks of the peerage. In 1660 when George Monck became duke of Albemarle he became one of only three non-royal dukes in the kingdom. Over the next 25 years Charles II went on to bestow dukedoms on three other non-royal individuals (Newcastle, Ormond, Beaufort); all the other dukedoms that he created were for his own illegitimate sons or for the infant sons of his brother. James II created only one duke – his own illegitimate son James FitzJames, duke of Berwick. By contrast, during the first five years of his reign, William III created one royal duke (Prince George of Denmark) and seven non-royal ones. Queen Anne created seven non-royal dukes as well as conferring an eighth on the future George II. As dukedoms became more common, some peers came to see the honour as not only desirable but attainable. Within three months of the death of his father-in-law, the last Cavendish duke of Newcastle, in 1691, John Holles, earl of Clare, was threatening to resign his offices because of his disappointment that the king had not yet bestowed the dukedom on him. He became duke of Newcastle in 1694. Rank within the peerage was a matter of obsessive concern for peers. One effect of 'Harley's dozen' in 1712 was to create further demands from those peers who now found that their relative ranking within the peerage had altered. Queen Anne told Robert Harley, earl of Oxford, that promotions in the peerage should be done by degrees. Accordingly she insisted that Thomas Pelham-Holles, 2nd Baron Pelham, ought to be promoted to an earl before he could become a duke. Oxford agreed that 'the gradation of titles is the best and truly honourable way [for] the other creates heart burning in the other Lords'.[14] There are many examples of heart burning. In December 1706 Thomas Wentworth, 2nd Baron Raby,

FIG. 33
Robert Benson, Baron Bingley (1676–1731), by Andreas von Behn, 1704. This portrait miniature was probably created when Benson was travelling on the continent.

suddenly found himself outranked by the former Barons Cholmondeley and Godolphin, both created earls, who had previously been junior to him. Raby himself desperately wanted a recreated earldom of Strafford, extinguished at the death of his cousin, William Wentworth. Peers could be reluctant to receive their peerages at the same time as other men, when invidious comparisons might be made. When John Sheffield, 3rd earl of Mulgrave was hoping for a marquessate he made it clear that 'he valued it chiefly, because he thought he should have it alone, for to be

The great experiment:
John Wilkins (1614–72),
natural philosophy and
toleration

Son of an Oxford goldsmith with interests in engineering, himself a natural philosopher who wrote on space travel and habitation on the moon, John Wilkins, consecrated bishop of Chester in November 1668, was an unconventional clergyman. During the Interregnum he hosted at Wadham College, Oxford, of which he was warden, an 'experimental club' which attracted, amongst others, Sir Christopher Wren. After the Restoration he helped to found the Royal Society. Brought up by his grandfather, a puri-

tan divine known as 'Decalogue Dod', he had been placed in his wardenship at Wadham by the parliamentary visitation of the University in 1648, had become chaplain to the puritan-minded William Fiennes, Viscount Saye and Sele (see above, p. 14) and married a sister of Oliver Cromwell.

After the Restoration a man like Wilkins might have found preferment difficult. But his sermons, delivered in a plain and accessible style as moral or philosophical lectures, appealed to an easily-bored Charles II. He found an ally at court in George

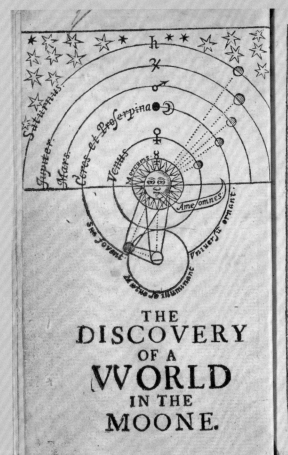

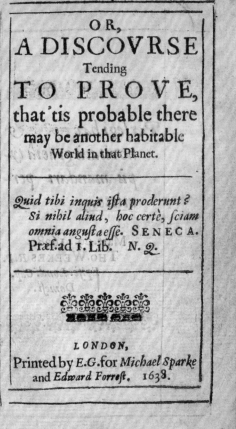

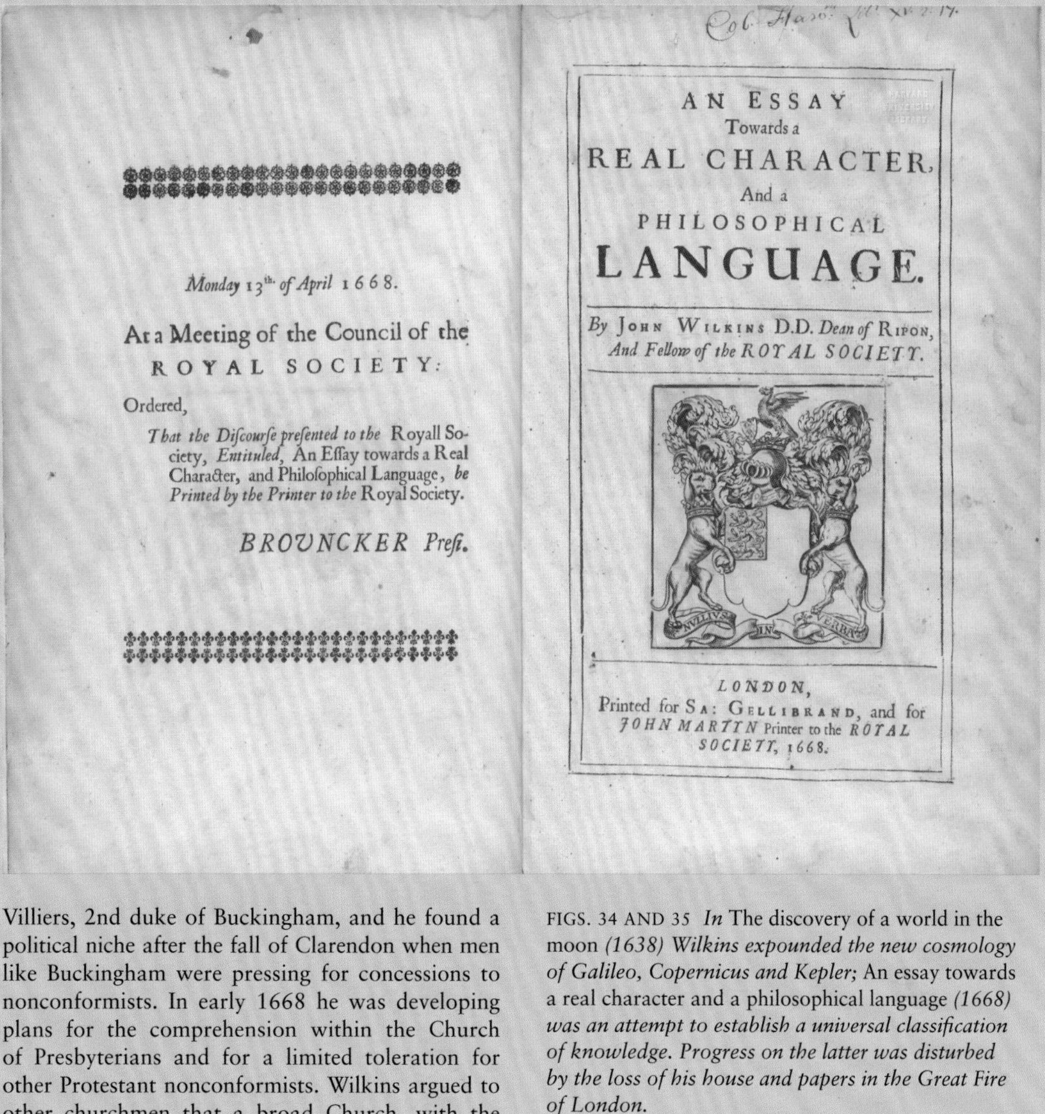

Monday 13th of April 1668.

At a Meeting of the Council of the
ROYAL SOCIETY:

Ordered,

That the Discourse presented to the Royall Society, Entituled, An Essay towards a Real Character, and Philosophical Language, be Printed by the Printer to the Royal Society.

BROUNCKER Presi.

AN ESSAY
Towards a
REAL CHARACTER,
And a
PHILOSOPHICAL
LANGUAGE.

By JOHN WILKINS D.D. Dean of RIPON,
And Fellow of the ROYAL SOCIETY.

LONDON,
Printed for SA: GELLIBRAND, and for
JOHN MARTIN Printer to the ROYAL
SOCIETY, 1668.

Villiers, 2nd duke of Buckingham, and he found a political niche after the fall of Clarendon when men like Buckingham were pressing for concessions to nonconformists. In early 1668 he was developing plans for the comprehension within the Church of Presbyterians and for a limited toleration for other Protestant nonconformists. Wilkins argued to other churchmen that a broad Church, with the Presbyterians 'comprehended' within it, would be a stronger one. Naively, he told another bishop, Seth Ward, of Salisbury, about the proposals; Ward told Archbishop Sheldon; Sheldon was able to mobilize opposition and the bill was easily sunk in the Commons. Despite his indiscretion, when Bishop George Hall died after having accidentally stabbed himself with his own pocket knife in August 1668, Wilkins stepped into his bishopric of Chester. With the duke of Buckingham in the ascendant, further preferment seemed inevitable and in early February 1669 many thought Wilkins was destined for high office: Samuel Pepys called him 'a mighty rising man'.[1] In 1670, however, Charles, for the moment,

FIGS. 34 AND 35 *In* The discovery of a world in the moon *(1638)* Wilkins expounded the new cosmology of Galileo, Copernicus and Kepler; An essay towards a real character and a philosophical language *(1668) was an attempt to establish a universal classification of knowledge. Progress on the latter was disturbed by the loss of his house and papers in the Great Fire of London.*

abandoned efforts to build a comprehensive Church. In a deal with the enemies of dissent in the Cavalier Parliament, he agreed to accept the renewal of the conventicle bill, which outlawed attendance at religious worship outside the structure of the Church. Wilkins regarded it as 'an ill thing both in conscience and policy'. Charles II instructed him to stay away from the House during the passage of the bill, but Wilkins defied him, asserting that he had a constitutional right to debate and vote 'and was neither afraid nor ashamed to own his opinion...and to act pursuant to it'.[2]

Wilkins died in November 1672 after developing kidney stones. On his death bed he declared him-

IOAN:WILKINS PRIMUS SOCIETATIS REG:SECRET:ET BENEFACTOR WADHAMENSIS
GARDIANUS DEC:RIPON:MAGISTER COL:TRIN:CANT:EPISCOPUS CESTRIENSIS OBIIT

FIG. 36 *John Wilkins by Mary Beale.*

self 'ready for the Great Experiment'.[3] His interests in natural philosophy, coupled to support for the parliamentary divorce of Lord Roos and his views on 'natural' religion had led some colleagues to suspect him of 'rational atheism'. To the intense suspicion of many of them (one of whom dubbed Wilkins his 'brother in evil'),[4] Wilkins had helped to create a tradition of moderate Restoration churchmanship, which would later be dubbed 'latitudinarianism'. Two of its exponents, John Tillotson, Wilkins' son-in-law, and Edward Stillingfleet, mentioned in Wilkins' will, would go on to be key thinkers behind the 1689 Toleration Act and the post-Revolution church settlement (see below, p. 170).

Creations and promotions in the peerage from the Restoration to the death of Anne (excluding females and royal minors who died in infancy)

YEAR	BARONS	VISCOUNTS	EARLS	MARQUESSES	DUKES*	DUKES**
Charles II 1660–85	28	7	38	1	4	6
James II 1685–8	4	0	3	1	0	1
William and Mary 1689–1694	6	4	10	2	7	1
William III 1695–1702	5	1	7	0	0	0
Anne 1702–1714	20	1	10	3	7	1

*(excluding royal bastards and other royals) **(royal bastards and other royals)

made a marquess when others are made dukes, he had rather be, as he is.' Working hard to keep Mulgrave loyal, Robert Spencer, 2nd earl of Sunderland (see below, p. 134), confided to Portland the significance of his support:

> I hope the king will agree to the whole, and not put him [Mulgrave] off to a promotion, for if he does, he is lost, and you know it is then to no purpose to manage the House of Lords, for though a great deal more is necessary all the rest will be insignificant without him.[15]

Mulgrave became marquess of Normanby in 1694 and duke of Buckingham in 1703.

Within each degree, peerages were ranked by their date of creation, although the grant of a peerage was occasionally accompanied by a special provision making it more senior than it would naturally be. Such special treatment was bitterly resented by those over whom the new peer jumped. When William Knollys was created earl of Banbury in 1626 with precedence as if he were the first such creation of the reign, the House was appalled. The king's wish was reluctantly obeyed when it was pointed out that the effect would be temporary, the new earl being elderly (he was nearly 80 years old) and childless. The precedence attached to the earldom may well have been a factor in the House's reluctance to accept the claim of Nicholas Knollys to the earldom after the Restoration (see below, p. 127). William Howard, Viscount Stafford, owed his viscountcy to a similar row over precedence. In 1640 Charles I created him Baron Stafford with enhanced precedence. When he realised the opposition it would provoke in the House of Lords he decided to make Howard a viscount instead. So important was precedence within the peerage that at the time of Harley's mass creation in 1711–12, nine of the letters patent issued on the same day (1 Jan. 1712) were not merely dated but timed, at hourly intervals, so that no disputes about precedence would be possible. A campaign to heap further honours on John Churchill, duke of Marlborough, in 1708 did invoke the power of Parliament by suggesting that a statute be passed to give him formal precedence over all other dukes. The suggestion frightened even his own allies for it

> would raise more envy and hatred in our ancient nobles than the thing would be worth. For none are so jealous of their dignities and pre-eminence as those that have nothing else to value themselves upon and I am afraid the number of those is great. And the ill humour and resentment of those peers that would be disobliged by it would run through all their families and relations.[16]

Peers with royal blood did form a special category; but the idea that some peers might be elevated above the rest by their kinship with the monarch was equally resented by other peers. The worst example – and one that carried major political implications – was that of the king's illegitimate son, the duke of Monmouth. Pepys reported on 8 February 1663 that 'The little duke of Monmouth, it seems, is ordered to take place of all dukes, and so doth follow Prince Robert [Rupert] now, before the duke of Buckingham or anyone else.'[17] A year later he described the 'great offence' given when Monmouth wore deep mourning at the death of the duchess of Savoy 'so that he mourns as a prince of the blood, while the duke of York doth no more and all the nobles of the land not so much'.[18] The phrase 'prince of the blood' was itself disliked. When in 1678 Prince Rupert, duke of Cumberland, was described as a 'prince of the blood' in the declaration announcing the new Privy Council, Gilbert Holles, 3rd earl of Clare, objected that the term was unknown in English law. He was supported by William Wentworth, earl of Strafford, who declared the phrase to be 'a French term of art, and of a large extent there; and that already the King's natural sons did greatly encroach on the ancient nobility by placing themselves above all others of the same classes'.[19]

Particular prestige attached to ancient titles and lineage, in part because the more ancient the title, the greater the precedence. In February

1678 Lord Frescheville petitioned the king for precedence as a peer with a title stretching back to the thirteenth century on the basis of a writ of summons issued to an ancestor in 1297. The king referred the matter to the House which reported in March 1678 that they 'do not find sufficient ground to advise his Majesty to allow the claim of the petitioner'.[20] But ancient origins, real or imagined, were valued for their own sake, and peers' search for them was egged on by the antiquarian interests of heralds such as Sir William Dugdale and Gregory King. George Monck, one of the least socially elevated of peers, chose Albemarle (an anglicized form of Aumale, a small town in Normandy) as his title. The name had been used more than two hundred years earlier for Henry V's cousin, Edward, duke of York, and emphasised Albemarle's claim of links to the Plantagenet royal family. The Feilding family claimed descent from the Habsburgs, a fiction that Basil Feilding, 2nd earl of Denbigh, was eager to perpetuate, and which masked the recent rise to prominence of a Warwickshire family of solid gentry origin. Denbigh also secured a grant of the barony of St Liz in 1665, which emphasised his family's links with the St Liz or Seyton earls of Huntingdon and Northampton in the 12th century, though it gave him no honours beyond those he already enjoyed. When Charles Smyth was given a barony in 1643 he chose the title of Carrington, a reference to the supposed foundation of his family by Sir Michael de Carington, standard bearer to Richard I during the crusades. John Ashburnham, created Baron Ashburnham in 1689 claimed that his family enjoyed high status even before the Conquest. His wife also claimed pre-Norman descent: her family traced their ancestry to the sixth century Welsh king Brychan Brycheiniog. Henry Mordaunt, 2nd earl of Peterborough, whose titled ancestors went back only to the reign of Henry VIII, compiled, with the help of his chaplain, a work that combined fictitious family history with personal memoir and published it under a pseudonym as *Succinct genealogies of the noble and ancient house of… Mordaunt of Turvey* (fig. 37).

Inheritance and extinction

Peers worked, above all, to ensure that their family name, wealth and honour would be passed down to posterity. They were often defeated by death, disease and the laws of inheritance. As a result, despite the large number of fresh creations, once the pent-up demand for peerages was met

FIG. 37 *Henry Mordaunt, earl of Peterborough's* Succinct genealogies of the noble and ancient houses of Alno or de Alneto, Broc of Stephale, Latimer of Duntish, Drayton of Drayton, Mauduit of Westminster, Green of Drayton, Vere of Addington, Fitz-Lewes of Westhornedon, Howard of Effingham and Mordaunt of Turvey justified by publick records, ancient and extant charters, histories and other authentick proofs, and enriched with divers sculptures of tombs, images, seals, and other curiosities *(1685). This engraving shows the tomb of one of Peterborough's relatively recent ancestors. See also fig. 26.*

The TOMB of JOHN *the Second Lord* Mordaunt, *as it is* Extant *in the Church of* Turvey, *in the County of* Bedford.

in the decade immediately after the Restoration, the size of the House of Lords grew slowly until the later years of Anne's reign. The extinction of a peerage could happen remarkably suddenly. In 1670, while on a continental tour with his wife, the wealthy 26-year-old 5th earl of Northumberland, Joceline Percy, took ill at Turin and died 'of fever caused by travelling in the great heat'. His body, accompanied by his 'disconsolate lady', was brought back to England for burial.[21] When he had written his will before his departure, he had a young son Henry and two daughters. Within a few months of his death only one daughter, Elizabeth, remained, then about three years old, and the ancient earldom of Northumberland was extinct. Like many others, the barony of Crew, created in 1661 for John Crew, barely lasted two generations, becoming extinct at the death of his youngest surviving son, Nathaniel (bishop of Durham) in 1721. Some peerages did not even make it that far. John Holles, descendant and namesake of the Holles who had bought the barony of Haughton and the earldom of Clare from James I, married one of the co-heiresses to the estates of the Cavendish dukes of Newcastle, extinguished at the death of the second duke without male heirs in 1691. He was himself created duke of Newcastle in 1694 but his only child was a daughter; the peerage was once again extinguished when he died after a fall from his horse in 1711.

High levels of infant mortality jeopardised the survival of many aristocratic families. Of sixteen children born to John Granville, earl of Bath, only five outlived him. Although he raised two sons to adulthood, his grandson, William Henry Granville, the 3rd earl, died of smallpox aged just nineteen, and the earldom died with him. Smallpox claimed the lives of many others; but there were plenty of other diseases which claimed the lives of aristocratic heirs. Charles, the sickly only son of the rakish poet John Wilmot, earl of Rochester, succeeded to the earldom aged just nine. The young boy had already displayed symptoms believed at the time to be the king's evil (scrofula) for which he was touched by Charles II, but which now seem more likely to have been congenital syphilis. Regarded in his father's circle as 'a fair-haired brilliant boy' and though 'scarce ten years old... of parts beyond twenty',[22] he died not long after his father, in 1681, and on his death the earldom became extinct and the Wilmot estates passed to his three sisters.

The need to produce heirs was therefore uppermost in aristocratic minds. The 27 children of Robert Shirley, earl Ferrers, by his long-suffering two wives were probably not a breathtakingly single-minded strategy

'Faithful services'?
Christopher, Baron Hatton
(1605–70)

Christopher Hatton became Baron Hatton in Civil War Oxford. A remote cousin of the courtier of Queen Elizabeth I, Hatton had sat in the House of Commons, but migrated to the royalist camp where he became comptroller of the household and received his peerage. After the king's defeat, Hatton went to live in exile in France, partly to avoid the consequences of his debts, exacerbated by the £4,000 he was fined by the parliamentary regime. Although he became close to the king's chief adviser, Edward Hyde (later earl of Clarendon) in the 1650s, he was for the most part only on the fringe of the royalist court and council, proposing a number of impractical and fanciful schemes to promote Charles II's restoration, one of which involved marrying the daughter of John Lambert, a senior soldier in Cromwell's army, to the king. By 1656 he had become sufficiently disgruntled with being ignored to make his peace with the Commonwealth and return to England. He nevertheless remained in close contact with the exiled court, and as the Restoration became more likely he started to submit his demands for recognition for his role in the king's cause.

The result was disappointment. He was annoyed at his failure to be advanced in the peerage to a viscountcy, which he claimed he had been promised during the Interregnum for his 'faithful services'.[1] His requests for office were as audacious as they were unrealistic. Unsuccessful in his petition to be appointed treasurer of the household, he pushed hard for the office of lord privy seal. In the end he got the governorship of Guernsey. Hatton made no haste to take up the job. Appointed in May 1662, it was two years before he eventually set out for the island. Quickly disabusing those who had written in anticipation of his arrival of their 'future happiness' under his governance,[2] he contrived from the outset to alienate the whole island. He harangued the islanders at the quayside for their factiousness; he imprisoned the lieutenant governor and controversially supported the dissenters against the Anglican justices (the jurats). Reporting back to Clarendon that Guernsey was 'the magazine of all contraband trade from England'[3] he nevertheless started selling arms to the French. To make matters worse, his younger son, Charles, ran off with the daughter of his prisoner, Colonel Lambert: the very person Hatton had originally proposed as a bride for the king.

Within a few months of his arrival, Hatton was summoned home to answer the long list of complaints which had reached London's ears. He ignored the command. It was not until the spring of 1665 that he was prevailed upon to return to England, despite his insistence that the journey would probably kill him. Once there, he was quick to launch a campaign to clear his name. It got off to a bad start with his petition to the king. He wrote to Clarendon how he had 'just crawled from the jaws of death' but was dismayed that while dictating his petition from his sickbed, 'by some slip of the tongue or pen some unwarrantable expression was added', as a result of which Hatton craved Clarendon's advice as to how he could 'restore himself to the king's favour' and make up for this mysterious *faux pas*.[4] Although rumours circulated in April 1667 that he was shortly to return to his government of Guernsey and although he remained, nominally, governor until his death five years later, he never returned to the island. Hatton died in 1670. His heir, another Christopher Hatton, succeeded to the reversion of the governorship of Guernsey and proved to be a markedly more competent holder of the office.

to ensure the survival of his line (he was also said to have fathered 30 illegitimate children by his various mistresses) although it certainly achieved that aim. Impoverished younger brothers might deliberately refrain from marriage and the procreation of legitimate heirs, but if they inherited, they would embark on determined attempts to secure the family line. Charles Rich, 4th earl of Warwick, was in his early forties when he succeeded to the peerage unexpectedly. His wife's memoirs imply that as he was a younger brother with limited expectations, they had kept their family small, although after the illness and death in 1664 of his son and heir, the pious couple tried unsuccessfully for more children, hoping that the earldom, so long associated with 'the owning and countenancing of good people' would not descend to Warwick's much disapproved-of younger brother, Hatton Rich.[23] Thomas Petre was over 50 years old and still unmarried when he succeeded as 6th Baron Petre in 1685 following the deaths of both of his older brothers. Within months of his succession, he had married, though it was nearly five years before his wife produced an heir. In a few cases peers were prevented from having heirs because their marriages had broken down and divorce was not (as yet) easily available to them. The specific reason advanced by John Manners, styled Lord Roos (the future 9th earl and duke of Rutland), for his divorce by act of Parliament in 1670 was that he wanted to contract a second legal marriage and produce a legitimate heir to his peerage. The same argument was used by Henry Howard, 7th duke of Norfolk, and Charles Gerard, 2nd earl of Macclesfield, when they too sought to divorce their wives (see below, pp. 88, 260).

The transmission of a peerage to posterity was not just a matter of ensuring the continuation of the line. It was also about maintaining the dignity and standing of the family. The possession of a peerage implied a long-term commitment to a high, even ruinous, standard of living, not just for the peer but also for his immediate family. When the earl of Bedford was first offered a dukedom in 1689 he turned it down 'because he had many sons that would then all be lords, and he had not a sufficient estate to support their honour'.[24] Getting money, keeping it, and transmitting it to the next generation were just as great preoccupations as the pursuit of social distinction, and ones which were just as interwoven with the politics and the business of the House of Lords.

'Livy and sickness has a little inclined me to policy': country and court, 1673–78

The passage of the Test Act produced a sensation. The king's brother, James, duke of York, resigned from his office as lord admiral in open acknowledgement of his Catholicism. Two days later Clifford resigned as lord treasurer for the same reason. York's decision to take as his second wife a young Italian Catholic, Mary of Modena, looked like a bid to secure a Catholic succession to the throne. Lord Chancellor Shaftesbury, a man whom contemporaries found hard to read but whose distaste for Catholicism and all forms of clerical influence was well-known, made no secret of his hostility to York. After a bad-tempered nine-day long session of Parliament in October and November, in which the king failed to get the supply he needed to carry on the war, Shaftesbury was dismissed. Out of office, he led an attack early in 1674 against the ministers he held to be responsible for the war, Henry Bennet, earl of Arlington and George Villiers, 2nd duke of Buckingham in particular. Buckingham defected, joining Shaftesbury and the opposition veteran, Denzil, Baron Holles (see below, p. 130), to form the nucleus of a determined and effective opposition grouping – the 'country lords', who kept up a constant barrage against the king's brother. Shaftesbury presented alarmist reports to the House of imminent Catholic rebellions. Charles Howard, earl of Carlisle, another of Cromwell's old allies, proposed that any member of the royal family who married a Catholic without Parliament's consent should be excluded from the throne (see above, p.32).

In the aftermath of the 1674 session Charles turned decisively against the supporters of dissent. Instead he looked to a competent, pushy and rising minister, Thomas Osborne, created Viscount Latimer the previous year. Now promoted as earl of Danby, he tried to revive the royal alliance with the Church and its friends. He also tried – with much less success – to persuade Charles to a fundamental realignment of his foreign policy: to abandon the unpopular French and support the Dutch and Prince William of Orange, the king's nephew and leader of a country which, though a republic, still looked to a royal family to lead its executive government.

Before the parliamentary session opened in April 1675 Shaftesbury made public his intention to resist the court. As it began, Danby introduced his test bill designed to cement his pact with the Church. All office-holders were to be required to swear not to attempt to alter the government in Church or state. The debates in the Lords – on one day lasting from nine in the morning until almost midnight – identified the themes which would dominate Danby's period in power. He was accused of creating a tyranny in partnership with the Church, one which would ensure that 'priest and prince' were worshipped together 'in the same temple'.[1] The test bill would have passed the Lords but for a judiciously orchestrated dispute with the Commons over two cases (*Sherley v. Fagg* and *Crispe v. Dalmahoy*) that raised questions about the right of the Lords to hear appeals from Chancery in cases involving members of the lower House.

In the autumn the opposition or 'country' peers stepped up their challenge to Danby when they demanded the dissolution of the Cavalier Parliament. To them, the Parliament, which had sat for more than fourteen years, symbolized the entrenched relationship between the Church and state as well as a corrupt pact between a government distributing rewards to its parliamentary supporters and a Commons keen to enjoy the benefits for as long as it could. On 20 November 1675 they lost their motion, but by a mere two votes, only achieved through counting proxies. They caused a sensation with a protest against the rejection of their proposed address which amounted to a transparent condemnation of Danby, his methods and his policies:

> It seems not reasonable, that any particular
> number of men should for many years
> engross so great a trust of the people, as to
> be their representatives in the House of
> Commons; and that all other the gentry
> and the members of corporations of the
> same degree and quality with them should
> be so long excluded: neither, as we humbly
> conceive, is it advantageous to the
> government, that the counties, cities,

FIG. 38 *Thomas Clifford, Baron Clifford (1630–72) after Sir Peter Lely, c. 1672, shortly before his conversion to Catholicism and subsequent loss of office. Only recently ennobled and dead 13 years before the coronation of James II, he is nevertheless depicted in coronation robes.*

and boroughs, should be confined for so long a time to such Members as they have once chosen to serve for them ... The long continuance of any such as are intrusted for others, and who have so great a power over the purse of the nation, must ... naturally endanger the producing of factions and parties, and the carrying on of particular interests and designs, rather than the public good.[2]

Two days afterwards, the king prorogued Parliament. It did not meet again until February 1677.

Over the long prorogation, the country lords tried to maintain the pressure for a new Parliament. Works attributed to Holles put forward the claim that the prorogation breached a statute of Edward III (hitherto considered obsolete) that required Parliament to meet annually. The most striking of the opposition polemics was *A letter to a person of*

quality, a sensational and highly partisan account of the debate in the Lords on the test bill, probably ghosted by the philosopher John Locke, a close associate of Shaftesbury. It painted a picture of a conspiracy between Danby and his episcopal allies, who aimed:

To make a distinct party from the rest of the nation of the high episcopal man, and the old cavalier, who are to swallow the hopes of enjoying all the power and office of the kingdom, being also tempted by the advantage they may receive from overthrowing the Act of Oblivion ... next they design to have the government of the Church sworn to as unalterable, and so tacitly owned to be of divine right ... Then in requital to the crown, they declare the government absolute and arbitrary, and allow monarchy as well as episcopacy to

be *jure divino*, and not to be bounded, or
limited by human laws. And to secure all
this they resolve to take away the power,
and opportunity of Parliaments to alter
any thing in Church or state, only leave
them as an instrument to raise money, and
to pass such laws, as the court, and
Church shall have a mind to.[3]

Because Danby's political bribery had neutralised the
House of Commons, the Lords, it boasted, was the
last bastion of liberty and property against this clerical and ministerial assault. Even the indolent and
scandalous John Wilmot, 2nd earl of Rochester,
pricked up his ears: 'I would be glad to know if the
Parliament be like to sit any time', he wrote to his
friend Henry Sydney, 'for the peers of England being
grown of late years very considerable in the government, I would make one at the session. Livy and
sickness has a little inclined me to policy'.[4] When
Parliament did reconvene, on 15 February 1677, the
lord chancellor, Heneage Finch, Baron Finch (later
earl of Nottingham) talked about 'the strange diffi-
dence and distrust, which, like a general infection,
begins to spread itself into almost all the corners of
the land'.[5]

Danby's political strategy in the new session was
to rebuild parliamentary confidence around measures
against 'popery' and France. The 'country' opposition
planned to coordinate a demand from both Houses
for a dissolution and new elections. Four peers –
Shaftesbury, Buckingham, Wharton and William
Cecil, 3rd earl of Salisbury – held the House in debate
for several hours, but the boldness of their arguments
and the whiff of a conspiracy to subvert the government handed Danby an opportunity. The four lords
were summoned to the bar and, refusing to request
the pardon of the House or the king for
their 'contempt of the authority and being of the present Parliament' were committed to the Tower.
Buckingham and Shaftesbury demanded that they
should take their own cooks with them – which the
king took to imply that they feared an attempt to poison them.

With the country lords out of the way, Danby
made some headway with his plans to neutralise the
issue of York's succession, presenting a set of bills
providing safeguards against a Catholic monarch. It
took months, however, before Charles finally, and
reluctantly, accepted Danby's case for an alliance with
the Dutch against France. By January 1678, it had
been agreed. William of Orange asked for, and got,
the hand in marriage of the king's niece Mary, the
heiress presumptive to the throne after her father
York. The marriage bolstered his own interest in the
succession to the English, Scottish and Irish thrones.
It gave him Charles's reluctant agreement to support
his continuing war with France, and a licence to
involve himself in British politics. Charles asked
Parliament for funding to intervene in the continental
war on the side of the Netherlands. The country lords,
finally released from the Tower on making their
apologies to the king, tried to insist on a declaration
of war before any money was given. Their scepticism
was justified. In May Charles offered Louis XIV his
neutrality in return for a large subsidy which would
allow him to hold Parliament in abeyance. He never
got his money: the Treaty of Nijmegen, agreed at the
beginning of August, ended the war between France
and the Netherlands before England could become
involved, leaving Charles in a mess: with troops
raised, but no money to pay them. When Parliament
reassembled in October 1678, the government tried
again to get the Commons to agree taxes. By then,
though, the political crisis had deepened dramatically.

Chapter 3

Getting and spending

Getting and keeping

Many of the peers were well able to maintain the standards of conspicuous expenditure expected of them, for the peerage included the great majority of the wealthiest men in the country. Their power and influence was founded on the possession of huge landed estates, yielding fabulous incomes and an opportunity to play a leading role in local and national political life. Contemporaries normally formed their impressions of aristocratic wealth by estimates of their annual income from land. The political economist Gregory King initially estimated the average annual income of the 160 aristocratic families at £2,800, although he later revised it to £3,200. Even the latter figure seems much too low: Viscount Longueville thought that £3,000 a year was the basic minimum required to maintain the dignity of a peerage, and the popular almanac *Angliae Notitia* in 1669 put its guess at the average income of peers at £10,000.

For a few peers, all of these estimates were way short of the mark. John Montagu, who became 2nd duke of Montagu in 1709, was said to have inherited £30,000 a year, and was also calculated to possess a personal estate valued at £200,000. George Monck, duke of Albemarle, was reputed to have been worth more than £20,000 a year, with estates stretching across at least twelve English counties and supplemented by extensive landholdings in Ireland and America. He lived in ostentatious splendour at his principal house, New Hall in Essex, a former royal palace. Fulke Greville, 5th Baron Brooke, was believed to be worth nearly £16,000 a year. His niece married William Pierrepont, 4th earl of Kingston, whose income was some £12,000 a year. Estates of between £7,000 and £4,000 a year were more typical, such as those of John Holles, 2nd earl of Clare (between £6,000 and £7,000 a year); the Jacobite James

Radclyffe, 3rd earl of Derwentwater (just over £6,000) and John Poulett, 3rd baron Poulett (nearly £5,000).

Although agricultural land remained the crucial measure of wealth, peers and bishops were as eager as anyone else to exploit the mineral and industrial possibilities it provided. In many cases they used their position as legislators to promote private bills to facilitate huge capital projects on their estates. Thomas Windsor, 7th Baron Windsor (later earl of Plymouth), was just one of many peers to take an interest in navigation schemes, in his case a project to make the Avon navigable from Evesham to Stratford. An extraordinarily wide range of peers also had interests in drainage projects. Arthur Annesley, earl of Anglesey, John Belasyse, Baron Belasyse, John Berkeley, Baron Berkeley of Stratton, John Manners, 9th earl of Rutland, John Ashburnham, Baron Ashburnham, and Arthur Herbert, earl of Torrington, all had some involvement in projects in Deeping Fen or the Bedford Level or both, and promoted legislation to safeguard their interests there. The Cavendish dukes of Newcastle possessed iron works in Sherwood Forest. William Widdrington, 4th Baron Widdrington, acquired interests in the coal rich manor of Stella in Durham along with his wife in 1700. Other peers had interests in salt production and fishing rights.

There was money to be made from financial schemes too. John Bennet (later Baron Ossulston) joined a consortium in 1671 to farm the customs and between 1672 and 1674 he purchased fee farm rents in East Anglia, Gloucestershire, Derbyshire and Yorkshire. Several peers became involved in speculative building ventures. Thomas Wriotheseley, 4th earl of Southampton, was responsible for the early transformation of Bloomsbury in London into a residential area; Henry Jermyn, Baron Jermyn (later earl of St Albans), turned St James's Fields into the aristocratic enclave of St James's Square. Jermyn, whose plans for the area were modelled on the Palais Royal in Paris, was determined to create houses that were 'fit for the dwelling of persons of quality'.[1] He reserved the most important sites for his close acquaintances, Belasyse and Henry Bennet, earl of Arlington. It was apparently at his instigation, and in an attempt to preserve his monopoly, that a bill to prevent the erection of any new buildings in London was introduced into the House of Commons in 1677.

Peers also invested in the big commercial undertakings, the East India and South Sea Companies. George Berkeley, 9th Baron (later Earl) Berkeley, who took great pride in his status as one of England's premier

FIG. 39 *These sconces, made by John Bodington in 1710–11, bear the arms of William Herbert, 2nd marquess of Powis (1667–1745), with a duke's coronet. Powis's father, William Herbert, created a marquess in 1687, was made duke of Powis and marquess of Montgomery by James II in January 1689, very shortly after he had lost his throne.*

barons, nevertheless married the daughter of a prosperous London merchant and then became not merely an investor but an active member of the East India Company and governor of the Levant Company. The Royal African Company, heavily engaged in the expansion of the slave trade and the shift from free to slave labour that took place in American and West Indian colonies during this period, also attracted titled investors: its members included Anthony Ashley Cooper, earl of Shaftesbury (despite his association with the cause of political liberty in England), his later enemy James, duke of York, Prince Rupert, duke of Cumberland, the 1st duke of Albemarle, Jermyn, and Ralph Grey, 2nd Baron Grey of Warke. James Butler, duke of Ormond, possessed an extraordinary estate in Ireland. A number of peers acquired colonial estates. Albemarle, Edward Hyde, earl of Clarendon, and William Craven, earl of Craven, were all among the first proprietors of the Carolinas in North America – a vast tract of land extending from Virginia southwards to Spanish Florida.

Some dabbled in less orthodox schemes. Christopher Monck, 2nd duke of Albemarle, invested £800 in an operation to salvage treasure from a shipwreck near Hispaniola, securing a return of more than £40,000. He was so convinced of the riches of the West Indies that when he left England to take up the governorship of Jamaica he took miners and mining equipment with him to search for silver. Prince Rupert and Shaftesbury were involved in a business venture concerned with a new process in gun

'All trade is a kind of warfare': the 1669 committee on the decay of trade

To a landowning aristocracy, the decline in the return on agricultural land – the 'fall of rents' – was the cause of great anxiety during the later 1660s. Concern about it was one reason for the hostility to the imports of Irish cattle at the time (see below, p. 254). The House of Lords rarely set up committees of inquiry, but it did establish one in October 1669, to 'consider of the causes and grounds of the fall of rents and decay of trade within this kingdom'.[1] As its title suggests, the inquiry ranged much more broadly than agricultural problems into issues of foreign trade as well.

That may have been because part of the impetus behind the inquiry came from the re-establishment of a royal council of trade in October 1668, probably at the instigation of Anthony Ashley Cooper, Baron Ashley (subsequently the earl of Shaftesbury), well known for his contacts with the City of London and with important economically-minded intellectuals and merchants such as Benjamin Worsley, Josiah Child and Thomas Papillon, all of whom were appointed to the council. When the Lords committee met it resolved at its first meeting to summon these and others of the council's chief luminaries.

The debates and evidence of the committee were diligently (if sometimes illegibly) recorded by its clerk,

FIG. 40 *Sir Josiah Child (1631–99), attributed to John Riley.*

FIG. 41 *Thomas Papillon (1623–1702), by Sir Godfrey Kneller.*

and present a fascinating mixture of homespun agricultural wisdom, the straightforward practical knowledge of farmers and businessmen, and the contradictory prognostications of economists.[2] Less than two years after the end of a disastrous naval confrontation with the Dutch republic based, largely, on commercial competition, Child – the dominant voice among the witnesses – told the committee that 'all trade [is] a kind of warfare'. Constant reference was made to Dutch commercial success. Child eulogised the republic and its inhabitants: the value placed on innovation, education and alleviating poverty through employment; 'their thrifty way of living'; their banks; their liberty of religion. When Worsley was examined by the committee he condemned shoddy English workmanship, 'the negligence of manufacturers, whereby the nation has lost their repute abroad'. The

committee made strenuous attempts to obtain information from the customs farmers (the commercial operation which ran the customs) concerning the balance of payments, but the farmers protested that they did not know what the balance of trade meant and had no idea how long it would take to compile the information. The committee eventually, exasperated, ordered them to produce the return; two days later it received a scrappy and inadequate list of the value of imports and exports.

The issue on which the committee spent most time was high interest rates. Child was well-known as an advocate of reduced interest rates, and the exotic traveller, freethinker and teetotaller (or 'water-drinker', as John Evelyn called him) Sir Henry Blount, backed him up: 'the chief thing is matter of interest being so high'. One committee member, John Lucas,

FIG. 42 *Sir Henry Blount (1602–82), by Sir Peter Lely.*

Baron Lucas, objected that a statutory regulation of interest rates would be unjust, because there were no plans to provide compensation and because it would lead to a shortage of credit, discouraging investment for the rebuilding of London after the Fire, and for all types of 'industrious men'. Child replied that lower interest rates would lead to higher land values and encourage trade, because 'no man trades but [unless] he promiseth himself a greater benefit than 6 per cent'. The committee backed Child, voting eleven to one that a bill should be prepared to lower interest rates to 4 per cent.

One of the other issues occupying the committee was immigration: many witnesses argued that the influx of skilled workers from abroad, tempted by the country's religious tolerance, was a critical factor in the success of the Dutch economy. Child and Papillon – the grandson of a refugee who fled religious persecution in France in 1588 – set out the case that free-

dom of religion was essential to promote trade, and the committee took further evidence from the secretary of the council of trade – Pierre du Moulin, another Huguenot, the son of a minister of the reformed French church. The committee resolved by eight votes to one that 'some ease and relaxation in ecclesiastical matters be a means of improving the trade of this nation', and their resolution was reported to the House the following day.

Despite the near-unanimity of the committee on these points, however, they failed to convince the House. Although in the next session of Parliament the House of Lords did pass a bill for a general naturalisation of foreign residents, it was not taken up by the Commons. No progress was made on the plea for toleration, which was perhaps the key aim for Ashley. A year later, instead, Parliament revived the act designed to suppress worship outside the Church, by banning nonconformist conventicles (see above, p. 41).

FIG. 43 *Christopher Monck, 2nd duke of Albemarle (1653–88), by John Smith, after Thomas Murray: an alcoholic who spent his life in the shadow of his more famous father, Albemarle's reckless and extravagant style of living rapidly dissipated the family fortune.*

manufacture, for which they sought an act of Parliament in 1675 granting them exclusive rights over the technique; Shaftesbury himself chaired the committee in the Lords.

Debt and consumption

Income, however, was not the whole story. In their responses to a circular requiring them to assess their estates for taxation in 1689, a number of peers and bishops claimed that their income was swallowed up by debt. 'I never yet knew what it was to be out of debt since I came to my estate' wrote Charles Fane, 3rd earl of Westmorland;[2] John Cecil, 5th earl of Exeter, insisted that 'My father left me in debt, and I have all the world to judge whether I have since lived like a man that designed to lessen it';[3] Ralph Montagu, then earl of Montagu, declared that he owed more than £20,000. Assuming that these statements were correct – and given the association between the possession of a peerage and honour it would have been a very serious matter to dispute it – it seems that in many cases the wealth of the peerage was more apparent than real. After the Restoration William Paget, 6th baron Paget, supposedly enjoyed an income of £3,000 a year. He claimed that after payment of debts and annuities he had only £23 left. One cause was the English custom of leaving an estate intact to a single male heir, which made it necessary to develop additional or alternative streams of income to ensure that widows, daughters and younger sons could continue to live in appropriate style. Often, the only way to achieve this was by mortgaging land. The way in which estates were tied up with debt, annuities and jointures could create problems of labyrinthine complexity. George Neville, 13th Baron Abergavenny, expected to inherit lands in six English counties and an annual income of almost £2,700; but in order to obtain his inheritance he had to initiate a series of legal proceedings, deal with thirteen different stewards and bailiffs and negotiate with two dowager baronesses (the mother and wife of his predecessor) both of whom were determined to retain lands they claimed as jointures. Some families were engaged in litigation over such arrangements for many years.

Sometimes debt was due to factors beyond peers' control. The earls of Derby blamed theirs on forced sales of land and damage to their estates during the Civil War, and harboured a grudge well into the eighteenth century against the failure of the Restoration regime to help re-instate their earlier grandeur (see below, p. 250). Charles Goring, 2nd earl of Norwich, declared that, because of his loyalty in the war, his father had been reduced to an estate of £450 a year by the time of his death in 1663 and predicted ruin unless the king took compassion for 'a family of loyalty and passionate affection for him'.[4] In the immediate aftermath of the Restoration, the problems of recovery were compounded by unfavourable agricultural conditions. The 'fall of rents' compounded Harringtonian perceptions of an aristocracy under siege and was frequently discussed in both Houses of Parliament in the first decades of the Restoration (see above, pp. 12-13, 82). In a famous speech in the House of Lords in 1671 another disillusioned royalist John Lucas, Baron Lucas, complained about the decline in agricultural prices and rent values and argued that many royalists had actually been better off under the Cromwellian regime:

as our burthens are increased so our strength also is diminished and we
are less able to support them for in the time of the late usurping powers
though great taxes were exacted from us we had then means to pay.
We could let our lands and sell our corn and cattle and there was
plenty of money through the nation. Now there is nothing of this, for
brick is required of us and we have no straw allowed us to make it,
wherefore our lands are thrown into our hands and corn and cattle are
of little value.[5]

Much aristocratic debt, though, was attributable to the cost of keeping
up the dignity of the peerage. 'I do not know' wrote William Wentworth,
earl of Strafford, in 1687, 'how to live decently, with less expence than
three thousand pound a year, or near it.'[6] Living 'decently' was a major
preoccupation. Peers were expected to impress by their hospitality, luxury
and ostentation. Even bishops were prone to it: 'I cannot live here to such
a conspicuity of hospitableness and charity, yea of gratitude, as becomes
the kings service' wrote John Gauden, shortly after his appointment as
bishop of the unglittering diocese of Exeter.[7] Money was poured into out-
ward displays of wealth. Large retinues were *de rigueur* for the grandest.
In 1666 sightings of a group of 50 horsemen caused alarm until the men
explained that they were the retinue of Charles Stuart, 3rd duke of
Richmond. On his way to imprisonment in the Tower of London in 1677,
George Villiers, 2nd duke of Buckingham, travelled with two coaches 'and
a great retinue of his footmen all in gallant new liveries and six hackney
coaches following them.'[8] Owning and maintaining houses of appropriate
grandeur was a permanent drain on resources. William Craven, earl of
Craven, owned six houses. The earl of Scarsdale's principal seat, Sutton
Hall in Derbyshire, assessed for the purposes of the hearth tax at 26
hearths in 1670, was dwarfed by the dowager Lady Southampton's town
house in Bloomsbury (50 hearths), let alone by Thorndon Hall, the Essex
home of the Barons Petre (72 hearths) or the earl of Devonshire's houses,
Hardwick Hall and Chatsworth, assessed at 114 and 79 hearths respectively (and this was before the construction of the present house at
Chatsworth, begun in 1686). George Digby, 2nd earl of Bristol claimed
to be a poor man, yet he not only kept an impressive livery, he also lived,
from 1674, in a grand mansion in Chelsea, later known as Beaufort House
(figs. 46, 48). Peers spent lavishly, often ruinously, on building projects.
Some of the most expensive were constructed to express political and
dynastic ambitions. Clarendon House, built for Edward Hyde, earl of

The Macclesfield inheritance

he system of primogeniture and the device of the strict settlement were designed to ensure that an aristocratic estate would pass down in a straight line in a family from father to son for generations. Reality was rarely so simple, and some noble families of late seventeenth and early eighteenth century England frequently went to law over the inheritance of their estates. The battles over the Cheshire estate of Gawsworth was one of the worst examples, involving forgery, divorce and adultery, the wilful, almost malicious, diversion of an inheritance, and an infamous duel which killed one of the most talented Tory politicians of the reign of Queen Anne.

In his will of 1641 the childless Sir Edward Fitton had left the Gawsworth estate to a distant Irish cousin, William Fitton, in order to keep the family name attached to the property, rather than to his nephew, the royalist officer, Colonel Charles Gerard. After the Restoration, Gerard, now Baron Gerard of Brandon, contested the will, claiming that Sir Edward on his death bed had invalidated his 1641 will and in a later will of 1643 (only recently 'discovered') had bequeathed the property to himself. Gerard and his associates threatened and cajoled a notorious forger, Abraham Granger, to testify that he had forged the 1641 will on the Fitton family's orders. Granger played his part well, the jury found in Gerard's favour and Chancery decreed the property to Gerard. An outraged Alexander Fitton, to whom the estate had descended, arranged for the publication of a short work, *A true narrative of the proceedings ... between Charles Lord Gerard of Brandon and Alexander Fitton, esq*, describing how Granger had perjured himself and how Gerard had got him to do so. Gerard demanded that the House of Lords take action, and the unequal struggle ended with Fitton fined £500 and imprisoned until he could find sureties to guarantee his good behaviour for life. He was a prisoner for the next twenty years.

Gerard, on the other hand, was granted the earldom of Macclesfield in 1679. His son and heir Charles, who inherited the title in 1694, was as unpleasant a character as his father, notorious for his violent and dissolute life (he received a pardon for the drunken and unprovoked murder of a footboy in St James's Park in May 1676) and the unscrupulous promotion of the Whig cause in Lancashire and Cheshire. A major-general in William III's army, he associated with a set of debauched and violent officers, most notably Charles Mohun, 4th Baron Mohun, who was married to Macclesfield's niece Charlotte (see below, p. 182). Both men had separated from their respective wives, something that may have drawn them closer together. Macclesfield's marriage was ended in 1698 by an Act of Parliament. The proceedings on the bill exposed both Macclesfield's cruelty and his wife's adultery, generally assumed to be with Macclesfield's Cheshire neighbour and fellow army officer Richard Savage, 4th Earl Rivers. The Act made the children of the union illegitimate, and prevented them from succeeding to the Macclesfield title or estates. It left Macclesfield's younger brother Fitton Gerard (named after the Fitton family) the heir to both.

Yet when Macclesfield died unexpectedly in November 1701, he left almost the whole of his personal and real estate to Mohun, bypassing Fitton completely. The will, a shock to everyone, may have been designed to punish Fitton, who had tried to obstruct the divorce bill. Fitton died about a year later, upon which the Macclesfield earldom became extinct, and Mohun moved into full possession of the Gerard estate. There was one more obstacle: the rival claims of the prominent Scottish peer James Hamilton, 4th duke of Hamilton, who in 1698 had married another niece of the 2nd earl of Macclesfield, Elizabeth Gerard. Mohun inherited a dispute over Lady Hamilton's marriage settlement, which came to a tragic head when, after an angry altercation in a lawyer's chambers, the two rivals met in a duel in November 1712, during which both were mortally wounded.

Hamilton had only recently been appointed British ambassador to France at a time when peace negotiations were in a delicate stage and the suspicion that the duel was a Whig plot to assassinate the Tory (and suspected Jacobite) Hamilton added fuel to the controversy surrounding the two deaths. Nor was it

FIG. 44 *Macclesfield introduced a bill to divorce his wife in 1698, on the grounds of her adultery with Richard Savage, 4th Earl Rivers: this brief pamphlet would have been produced to explain and support the case for the bill. The poet Richard Savage (c.1697–1743) later claimed to be one of the children of Lady Macclesfield's affair; although many of his contemporaries believed him, she declared that her children had died young and denounced him as an impostor.*

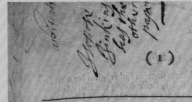

(1)

REASONS

FOR THE

Earl of Maclesfeld's

Bill in Parliament,

For Diffolving the Marriage between Him and his Wife, and Illegitimating her Spurious Iffue.

THE Bill by way of Petition, according to the ufual Form in like Cafes, recites the Lady's notorious open Adultery, having had Children begotten on her Body in Adultery, and ufing vile Practices to have her fpurious Iffue impofed and obtruded upon him; therefore it enacts and adjudges, That the Bond of Marriage being notorioufly and fcandaloufly violated by her Adultery, be from henceforth diffolved, annulled, vacated, and made void.

That it be lawful for the Earl to Marry again; and that the Wife and Children of any other Marriage fhall enjoy all advantages as if he had never been Married to this Lady, or that fhe had no Iffue.

It illegitimates and difinherits the Iffue begotten, or to be begotten on her Body; and enacts, that all the Eftate of the Earl, and of his Father, fhall be in the fame plight and condition, and Perfons inheritable to it, as if fhe had no Child.

Preferves the Settlement of the Eftate, which moved from the Earl's Father, in all the Limitations other than to her and her Iffue.

As

the end of the fallout from Macclesfield's unusual bequest. The feud conducted in the courts between the Gerard heirs and descendants and those of Mohun continued for many years after the deaths of the two protagonists. The Mohun family, however, kept Gawsworth.

Clarendon, in London's Piccadilly from 1665–67, was reputed to have cost more than £40,000. Clarendon perceived it as marking the status conferred upon his family by his daughter's marriage to James, duke of York; others saw it as evidence of his corruption and presumption (see below, p. 104). It helped to bring about his downfall the same year as its completion, and its second owner, the 2nd duke of Albemarle, was forced to sell it in 1683 to a group of speculative builders who demolished it and redeveloped the site. Daniel Finch, 2nd earl of Nottingham, laid out some £80,000 to build his fine Palladian house at Burley. Chatsworth was rebuilt for the 4th earl (later duke) of Devonshire. Castle Howard, commenced in 1699 for Charles Howard, 3rd earl of Carlisle, set new standards of extravagance, signalling Carlisle's boundless (and unfulfilled) political ambition. Castle Howard, in its turn, was eclipsed by Blenheim Palace, built for John Churchill, duke of Marlborough, (although not completed until after his death) at a cost of around £300,000. Enormous houses were not just expensive to build, but also to maintain: they furthermore created an expectation that their owners would use them for lavish entertaining. During the summer of 1703 when Thomas Thynne, Viscount Weymouth (see below, p. 312), learned of the queen's progress towards Bath, he was torn between his wish to invite her to stay at Longleat and his fear that he would be unable to provide a sufficiently magnificent entertainment for the royal party.

Like monumental houses, funerary monuments contributed to the perpetuation of the renown of a family, as much as an individual. The earldom of Bristol was extinguished when the 3rd earl, John Digby, died without a direct male heir in 1698: he and both his wives were commemorated for posterity in an impressive marble memorial in Sherborne Abbey (fig. 46). Henry Somerset, duke of Beaufort, was celebrated by a magnificent funerary monument, originally erected in St George's Chapel, Windsor, but now in the church at Great Badminton, depicting the duke in his garter robes with full length female figures depicting truth and justice, and reciting his virtues and many high offices (see below, p. 298).

The costs of such conspicuous consumption were sometimes borne by the tradesmen who all too often found it difficult to persuade noblemen to pay their bills. In 1669 work on Cobham Hall, the duke of Richmond's country house in Kent, had to be stopped through inability to pay the workmen's wages. In 1691 Peregrine Osborne, the future 2nd duke of Leeds, had to borrow £150 to pay for liveries and fourteen gold badges

for his watermen so that they would appear 'according to his quality'. The unfortunate individual who loaned the money was only able to do so because he in turn borrowed from a money lender. His £150 and the accrued interest were still unpaid twenty years later. By 1709 the bill for work at Chatsworth came to £12,000; the mason, deciding that he had nothing more to lose, took Devonshire to court. The building of Blenheim Palace also collapsed into debt and litigation after the Marlboroughs fell out of royal favour.

An equally effective way of dissipating a fortune was to spend time at court. The ambitious hoped to attract royal favour and its fruits – an office, a new title or a pension. But those in the grip of hope locked

FIG. 45 *John Churchill, duke of Marlborough, looks out over Blenheim Palace, a building that was meant to be as much a national monument as a stately home. Begun in 1705, it was not completed until 1724, two years after Marlborough's death.*

FIG. 46 *John Digby, 3rd earl of Bristol (1634–98) had no son to inherit his earldom which was extinguished at his death in 1698. He chose instead to immortalise himself and his two wives (Alice Bourne, d. 1658, and Rachel Wyndham, d. 1709), by means of this funeral monument, which stands in the south transept of Sherborne Abbey.*

themselves into the daily extravagance of court life. In 1667 Penelope, wife of Henry Mordaunt, 2nd earl of Peterborough, confessed to Samuel Pepys that 'her plate and jewels are at pawn for money, and how they are forced to live beyond their estate, and do get nothing by his being a courtier'.[9] In October 1665 Edward Conway, Viscount Conway, reported that he had been invited to visit Lady Castlemaine, the king's mistress, every night 'which I shall frequently embrace as an opportunity of the king's conversation which is very desirable'.[10] What was not so desirable was the gambling that went with it. The same month Castlemaine lost £580 in a single night. A few, though, thrived on it: Robert Greville, 4th Baron Brooke, allegedly won £4,800 in one night. Big sums were lost on the racetrack as well, thanks to Charles II's interests in horse racing. John Lovelace, 2nd Baron Lovelace, lost £600 on one race at Newmarket in 1668. He died two years later in poverty in the gatehouse of Woodstock

FIG. 47 *The funeral monument to John Cecil, 5th earl of Exeter (c. 1648–1700), in the church of St Martin, Stamford, designed by Pierre Monnot. A patron of the arts, spending lavishly on his nearby home Burghley House, Exeter rarely attended the House of Lords, and after the Revolution ceased to do so altogether.*

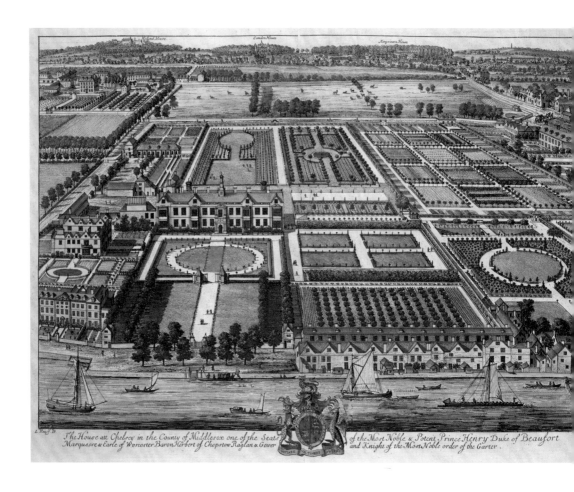

The House att Chelsey in the County of Middlesex one of the Seats of the Most Noble & Potent Prince Henry Duke of Beaufort Marquesse & Earle of Worcester Baron Herbert of Chepstow Raglan & Gower and Knight of the Most Noble order of the Garter.

FIG. 48 *In the early eighteenth century this, the largest and most impressive house in Chelsea, was owned by Henry Somerset, duke of Beaufort. It had earlier belonged to George Digby, 2nd earl of Bristol; earlier still it was the home of Sir Thomas More.*

Park. Gambling probably contributed to the indebtedness of Charles Fane, 3rd earl of Westmorland, who according to his nephew, Thomas Fane the 6th earl, left only about half of what he had inherited. In 1681 the 3rd earl wrote to the fantastically rich 2nd duke of Albemarle, attributing his recent losses to 'being so highly elevated with your wine' and pleading with the duke to accept the £500 already paid, presumably in lieu of whatever greater debts he truly owed.[11]

The financial hazards of a life at court were well appreciated. The 6th earl of Westmorland also condemned his father's folly in expecting rewards from the court that never materialised, 'which I would have to be a warning to all not to spend their estates to serve a court in expectation of being afterwards repaid or rewarded. Tis an action all courtiers smile at.'[12] But many did it nevertheless, and even those who were suc-

cessful in extracting something from the court found the returns failed to match their outlay. The attempts of the 3rd duke of Richmond to cut a figure at court and live up to his dignity landed him further and further in debt, despite receiving valuable lands and offices from the crown. As early as 1662 his debts amounted to more than £50,000, and his household expenses alone amounted to more than £5,000. By 1699 – more than 25 years after his death – his debts still totalled more than £24,000.

The search for office

For those whose attendance at court was rewarded, there were some rich pickings. The salary of the prestigious office of lord treasurer was £8,000 a year and it carried enormous potential for further profit, although Thomas Wriothesley, 4th earl of Southampton, treasurer from 1660 to 1667 and a byword for integrity (if not for efficiency) was said, remarkably, to have made no money out of it. The appointments in 1711 of

FIG. 49
Horse racing flourished after the Restoration and Charles II's passion for it turned Newmarket into a fashionable centre for socialising and gambling. Charles II himself instituted the Newmarket Town Plate in 1664. This 1687 engraving by Francis Barlow shows a race at Dorset Ferry near Windsor Castle in August 1684, the last held before the death of the king.

'Cecil the Wise': James Cecil, 4th earl of Salisbury (1664–94)

orn in 1666 into one of the most politically significant families of England, James Cecil was connected to its foremost aristocratic dynasties, and was heir to an estate in six counties worth nearly £11,000 a year. By the time of his death only 28 years later, the family's financial security and political fortunes were in decline, and he was the butt of satire; by the nineteenth century he was remembered merely as a bloated buffoon.

It was not all his own fault. When he inherited the earldom from his father, not yet seventeen years old, in May 1683, he was obliged to provide for four brothers and five sisters, and was saddled with debts and legacies of over £135,000. But lacking in maturity and deliberation, he made his problems much worse. Two months after he inherited, he rushed into marriage with the thirteen year old Frances Bennet. The match should have brought him a dowry of £20,000 plus £1,800 a year in land. According to Cecil family tradition, Frances's astute brother in law, John Bennet of Abington, halved the dowry by ensuring the wedding took place before the girl's 16th birthday, helped by her mother's desperation to conclude the marriage out of 'daily fear and apprehension' that her daughter would be abducted and carried off 'to some inferior match'.[1] Salisbury entered into lengthy litigation with his brother Robert Cecil over the provisions of their father's will, and swanned off to Europe for the remainder of his minority. Fretting about his exorbitant lifestyle, his agents asked him to return to England to quash rumours that he had been kidnapped by Turks and had lost £40,000 by gambling at the French court.

Salisbury eventually came back when he came of age in 1687, by which time his conversion to Catholicism, obesity and adventuring were well known, caricatured in a popular lampoon, Cecil the Wise. Entering into the Jacobean regime with enthusiasm, he built a Catholic chapel at Hatfield and encouraged the public celebration of mass. During anti-Catholic riots in June 1688, Salisbury's house was targeted: his servants, firing from the house to protect it from the rioters, killed the parish beadle. He geared up to resist the Prince of Orange's impending invasion by equipping a troop of horse with smart uniforms and parading them before the king in October. After William's landing, however, Salisbury was in deep trouble. By Christmas Eve he was in the Tower on a charge of high treason. He was accused of removing his young brothers (who were also his heirs) from Eton and sending them to James II's court in France: the House of Lords took drastic action to recover the boys. When he appeared at the bar of the House to respond to his impeachment, his arrogant bearing did little to aid his cause and his estate managers feared that this 'unhappy self-willed man has put fair to undo himself, his relations, friends', leaving them all in a 'ruinous' condition.[2] In October 1690 he eventually secured release from the Tower on bail of £10,000, only to face his siblings' private bill, designed to take administration of the estate out of his hands on the grounds of his 'continuing a Papist and persisting in his zeal for that party'.[3] It became law on 20 December 1690. The entire legislative effort was wasted, however, when Salisbury's wife gave birth to a son and heir the following June. By the following spring, his pessimistic managers concluded that 'the trust lands will unavoidably go to pot' and that they had better 'look after good bargains' to ensure their own financial security.[4]

Salisbury remained loyal to the exiled James II, drawing his sword in a coffee house to defend the reputation of the exiled king. On another occasion, he fell into a heated argument with a dinner guest whilst discussing James II's hunting prowess, and both men had to be confined by their friends to prevent a duel. In May 1692 he was again arrested on suspicion of high treason for Jacobite activity. Salisbury fell ill with 'black jaundice'[5] and died on 24 October 1694. Invitations were sent to a list of peers to send a mourning coach and six horses each to accompany his corpse from Soho to Hatfield, where it was buried in the family vault.

The R.ᵗ Hon.ᵇˡᵉ James Earl of Salisbury &c

G. Kneller Eques pinx   I. Smith fe. et exc.

FIG. 50 *The birth of a son, James Cecil (1691–1728), to the 4th earl of Salisbury and his wife in 1691 upset the preparations made by his brother to take over the estate. James inherited the title, estates and debts of his father in 1695, becoming the 5th earl. Unlike his father, he became a staunch Anglican, though interested in Protestant and Catholic theology.*

Arthur Annesley, 5th earl of Anglesey, as vice-treasurer of Ireland and receiver general and paymaster of the forces in Ireland were said to be worth £6,000. A gentleman of the bedchamber received £1,000 a year for a post with no executive function. At the accession of James II in 1685 the Peterboroughs finally reaped the rewards of loyal service: the earl became groom of the stole with a salary of £1,000 a year as well as high steward and chief bailiff to the queen; his countess became groom of the stole to the queen. In January 1661 at York's behest, John Berkeley, Baron Berkeley of Stratton, was appointed to the lucrative office of lord president (or governor) of Connaught in Ireland for life, with a salary of £1,200 and a sizeable income from rents. Beyond the salary, there were plenty of incidental benefits from such jobs. As comptroller of the household, William Maynard, 2nd Baron Maynard, was handling around £58,000 a year. Like all those who held money on behalf of the Crown, he was able to invest it in the meantime for his own benefit. Such positions also attracted considerable perquisites. At the death of William III in 1702 the lord chamberlain, Edward Villiers, earl of Jersey, quickly laid claim to a sizeable proportion of the late king's furniture. Discovering that his counterpart in the Netherlands was going to demand what was left in the king's Dutch houses, Jersey swiftly claimed these too. At the death of Queen Anne's husband, Prince George, in 1708, John West, 6th Baron de la Warr, his groom of the stole, claimed the prince's plate whilst Scroop Egerton, 4th earl of Bridgwater, his master of the horse, claimed his coaches and horses.

Such posts were not costless: new appointees might have to buy out their predecessors, negotiating a price which seems commonly to have been about six or seven times the annual salary of the office, making the post into something like an annuity. In 1674 Robert Bertie, 3rd earl of Lindsey, purchased a place as gentleman of the bedchamber from Buckingham for a reputed £6,000. In February 1685 it was rumoured that Henry Jermyn, Baron Dover, was to purchase the office of master of the horse – a post described in 1702 as one 'of great profit . . . as well as honour'[13] – for £20,000 (£10,000 of which was to be paid by the king), although this failed to materialise. Not all offices were attractive. Some required ability and hard work; some were politically dangerous. When Ford Grey, earl of Tankerville (see below, p.238), was offered the post of first commissioner of the admiralty in May 1699, he was reported to have responded that 'he would be drawn through a horse pond before he would take that employment'.[14] Some, like distant colonial governorships, exposed the holder to the risks of travel and disease, as well as distancing the holder from further opportunities at home. Others, though lucrative in theory, might involve heavy expenditure which would be difficult to reclaim. Embassies were particularly problematic. Robert Spencer, 2nd earl of Sunderland, ambassador extraordinary to Paris in 1672, reputedly ran up debts in excess of £4,000 maintaining a lavish lifestyle, although he did secure recompense from the government for it. In 1699 Charles Berkeley, 2nd earl of Berkeley was appointed one of the lords justices of Ireland. In an unusual arrangement, the allowance of almost £7,000 a year for the post was shared between the three justices. Within six months he was complaining from Dublin Castle that:

> besides difficulties in public matters, which I fear will every day
> increase, as things are between England and Ireland, the great business
> I designed by this employment was to pay my debts; but the expenses
> are so great and the profits so small that it's well if I don't increase
> them here.[15]

Further benefits could be had from the crown in the form of contracts, licences and patents. In 1685, Peterborough, Henry Hyde, 2nd earl of Clarendon, and Henry Howard, 7th duke of Norfolk, were granted the right to licence pedlars and petty chapmen, which the three peers planned to sub-contract for £10,000 a year. The patent, however, was cancelled shortly afterwards, perhaps when it was recognised how controversial it might be. In 1661 Parliament awarded the revenues for wine licensing to York, which he contracted out in return for an annuity of £16,000. In 1663 the contractor, the steward of his household, John Berkeley, Baron Berkeley of Stratton, boasted he had already made £50,000 out of the deal. Gifts from the crown could provide significant windfalls, such as the grant in 1669 to the countess of Suffolk and the 2nd earl of Peterborough of £5,000 from the proceeds of the prize goods of the captured ship *Sancta Maria*. Favourites of the king and the royal family were well placed to benefit from a stream of financial and other advantages. Charles Sackville, styled Lord Buckhurst, son and heir of Richard Sackville, 5th earl of Dorset, not yet a peer in his own right, but a close companion of the king, was awarded a pension for life in 1670 and a free gift of £4,400 in 1673. Four months after being created earl of Middlesex in February 1675, he was granted the lease on 35 houses on the Strand, worth an estimated

A poor lord? George Booth, 2nd earl of Warrington (1675–1758) votes on the malt tax

George Booth, 2nd earl of Warrington, was one of the many peers who inherited a fractured estate overcharged with debt, in his case from his father, the radical Whig leader Henry Booth, earl of Warrington. When he succeeded to an estate worth barely £2,000 a year in 1694, the debts amounted to almost £25,000. His problems were compounded by the discovery of the first earl's unrealistic will three weeks after his death in a box of scrap paper tucked away in a corner of a room at Dunham Massey Hall in Cheshire, including bequests based on assumptions about gifts and legacies he had expected to receive but which had not, in the end, materialised. The new earl of Warrington tried, but failed, to conceal its existence from his siblings, who challenged him in the courts to produce it. When the prerogative court of Canterbury found the will valid in July 1698 Warrington reluctantly attempted to execute it.

Convinced that his forebears' involvement in national and local politics had caused them to neglect the estate and to run up excessive expenses, Warrington was determined to avoid doing the same, despite the pleas of his younger brother Henry that he should live more extravagantly to make himself 'popular' in the county. In two letters of 1715 and 1722 he recounted to Henry in detail the privations he had undergone as a young boy. Warrington remembered how 'I have seen my father several times the year before the Revolution fall aweeping at the greatness of his debts' and recalled in horror the dingy outmoded furniture in the family house of Dunham Massey Hall, all very much in contrast to his father's public image.[1] (After 1691 the first earl ceased keeping open house for his tenants and would go to the nearest taverns to meet his followers, rather than undergo the expense of hosting them in his own house.)

Despite his lack of desire for public office, the 2nd earl did attend the House of Lords quite regularly, where he acted as an independent 'country' peer. But during the Tory ministry of 1710–14, as the earl of Oxford looked desperately for votes to shore up his permanently faltering majorities in the Lords, the constantly cash-strapped Warrington seemed a likely target. His go-between was Warrington's brother-in-law Russell Robartes, younger brother of the 2nd earl of Radnor. Robartes, like Warrington, was constantly in financial difficulties, partly because Warrington himself had never paid in full the portion of £12,000 promised to Robartes on his marriage to the earl's sister. Though a Whig, he had gone over to the Tories when it helped him to succeed to his uncle's lucrative office of teller of the exchequer in October 1710. Warrington himself was reeled in just before the vote on the controversial malt tax in June 1713, when Oxford offered to pay him the long-standing arrears of a pension due to his father, amounting to £6,500, in exchange for Warrington's vote for the tax. The bill squeaked by thanks to Warrington's vote, 76 to 74 (see below, p. 304-5).

Warrington thought he had fulfilled his part of the bargain and expected immediate payment of the arrears. Oxford, as he often did, hoped to use the promise of payment as a way of keeping Warrington dependent on the ministry. It backfired badly with Warrington, who withdrew his support for the ministry and fired off increasingly angry letters to the lord treasurer, at first appealing to his sense 'of conscience and honour', later bitterly reflecting on the cynicism and desperation of Oxford's tactics. In June 1714 he found out that the queen herself had known nothing of the promises long made to him in her name and haughtily brought his long correspondence with Oxford on the matter to an end: 'I did not ask it [the arrears] of your Lordship, nor do I want it to buy my bread. Your Lordship promising it was a great surprise to me, and the conclusion is no less so, for I can't guess why you are pleased to treat me thus, or of what use it can be to yourself'.[2]

The Rt. Hon.ble Henry Booth Ld. De la Mer of Dunham Massey in the County Pal: of Chester, Ld. Lieutent. of the said County, One of the Lds. of their Ma.ties most hon.ble Privy Council, and One of the Lds. Com.rs. of the Treasury &c.

G Kneller pinx: I Smith fe: & exc:

FIG. 51 *Henry Booth, 1st earl of Warrington, by John Smith, after Sir Godfrey Kneller: father of the second earl, Henry Booth was regarded as a 'modish zealot' by the Tory poet and politician Arthur Maynwaring, who also sketched him as 'Of a dark spirit, turbulent and proud / Rude to superiors, fawning to the crowd; / Prompt to revenge, and treacherously base / Plotting when in private, blustering when in place'. His unrealistic will left his son with an insoluble problem.*

annual rental of £1,220. It was the same month in which, in company with Henry Savile and John Wilmot, 2nd earl of Rochester, he defaced the sundial in the king's garden at Whitehall.

The profits of office were not restricted to salaries and pensions. Privileged access to the crown, or to the crown's ministers, provided opportunities to beg favours for friends, neighbours and acquaintances and to solicit gifts for the services thus rendered. There were many allegations that courtiers accepted bribes to secure peerages on others' behalf (see above, pp. 60-1). The 1st duke of Albemarle probably amassed part of his fortune by accepting presents in return for his help in obtaining advancement. George Legge, Baron Dartmouth, high in the favour of James II, was also accused of accepting money for his assistance; Edward Noel, earl of Gainsborough, allegedly paid him £5,000 to become governor of Portsmouth and keeper of the New Forest. The benefits of commanding such interest were political as well as financial. Thomas Osborne, when earl of Danby in the 1670s, used his command of royal patronage to reward his relatives as well as to cement his political support. John Frescheville, Baron Frescheville, was Danby's uncle and one of his most reliable henchmen in the Lords. A sheet among Danby's papers, headed 'Lord Frescheville's grants and payments' shows that during 1675–6 Frescheville received the reversion of several valuable properties and, in the meantime, a pension of £152 a year for life and fee farm rents in Yorkshire totalling £120 a year. During 1677 Frescheville was given an additional £1,200 out of the secret service fund.

Many peers saw royal office and privileges as almost a birthright. The astonishingly self-promoting Ralph Montagu, duke of Montagu, drove the duchess of Marlborough – whose daughter had married Montagu's son – to exasperation in his pursuit of more and more offices for his family. On one occasion she explained that 'there is so few employments, and so many to be gratified for the Queen's service, that I can't think of asking the captain of the yeomen of the guard for my son-in-law [John Montagu, later 2nd duke], who has (in reversion) one of the best things the Queen has to give, and for his life'.[16] Montagu responded that:

> The queen's mind is much altered in not allowing of two great offices in one family. My lord treasurer [Godolphin] his son and daughter-in-law have three, my Lord Devonshire and his son had two, my Lord Sunderland and my lady have two, the duke and duchess of Ormond the same, also the duke and duchess of Somerset. The duke of Bolton is

warden of the New Forest, vice admiral in those seas and governor of
the Isle of Wight: all places of great honour and profit. These examples
will I hope in some measure make my excuse with your grace and show
you madam that I am not unreasonable in my pretensions for my son
as you may perhaps judge me to be.[17]

There were plenty of other disgruntled peers. In 1711 when the court Tory
Charles Finch, 4th earl of Winchilsea, heard that he was not to be lord
admiral, he grumbled that he could scarcely afford his journeys to London
to attend the queen and the House. On becoming first lord of trade a few
months later he still complained that his expenses were greater than the
salary and that his post was 'inferior . . . both in profit and honour to
those employments I had before.' George Goring, earl of Norwich, desperate to silence his creditors, petitioned his old antagonist, Edward Hyde,
now earl of Clarendon, for the restitution of the lucrative offices and
privileges he had enjoyed before the civil war. In 1663, as he lay dying at
an inn at Brentford he dictated a brief will (entirely concerned with the
settlement of debts) and composed an angry letter to Clarendon's son,
complaining that he had received by the hands of his father 'the most fatal
blow' to his fortune.[18]

Peers often claimed that it was prestige rather than income that
mattered to them, for office denoted royal favour. The Whig Charles
Lennox, duke of Richmond, wrote in 1708 to Charles Spencer, 3rd earl
of Sunderland:

> Your lordship knows I have received so many rebukes from the court
> that I am a little shy of being refused again therefore will not ask any
> body's favour till I have some encouragement first from you ... I hope
> your lordship is sensible that it is not the salary of a place makes me
> ambitious of one but being the only man of our party that yet has
> never been countenanced I think I have reason to desire my friends to
> show themselves so.[19]

The crown certainly accepted some obligation to enable senior royal ministers and peers to live in appropriate style. The 1st earl of Clarendon was
given £20,000 by Charles II with his earldom when his prominence in the
government was matched by his new status as the father of the duchess
of York in 1660. Lord Clifford was given a peerage and an estate in
Somerset worth £2,000 per year when he became lord treasurer in 1672,
although his salary of £8,000 a year and the customary New Year gifts
gave him an income greater than all but the greatest landowners. One of

'Jove the fulminant': Edward Hyde, earl of Clarendon (1609–74) and corruption

y the time of his fall from power and exile in 1667, Edward Hyde, first earl of Clarendon, had become a byword for ambition and corruption. In part it was because of the clandestine marriage, a few months after the Restoration, of his clever and precocious daughter, Anne Hyde, to the king's dull brother, the duke of York. In an age when royalty expected to marry royalty, the marriage put him in an extraordinary position for a commoner, of being, potentially at least, father-in-law and grandfather to English monarchs. He was well aware that it was a very risky one. In the memoir he composed after he was forced into exile, he described the panic which had gripped him after he found out about the engagement: 'he looked upon himself as a ruined person, and that the king's indignation ought to fall upon him as the contriver of that indignity to the crown, which as himself from his soul abhorred, and would have had the presumption of his daughter to be punished with the utmost severity, so he believed the whole kingdom would be inflamed to the punishment of it, and to prevent the dishonour which might result from it'.[1]

Hyde, born near Salisbury in 1609, was a Wiltshire gentleman of no great means but valuable connections. He used them, as well as his considerable intelligence and self-confidence, to build himself a career in the law in the 1630s, in Parliament in the 1640-2, and as propagandist, civil servant and adviser to the king during the Civil War and Interregnum. By 1660 he was the ubiquitous and indispensable chief adviser to Charles II, the king's eyes, ears and mind. According to Clarendon's own account, the crisis over Anne Hyde's marriage saw Charles II at his best: the king treated his histrionics as ridiculous, and got on calmly with sorting out the consequences of a family *mésalliance*. Far from ruining Hyde and his family, the marriage did create one of the political powerhouses of late Stuart politics – the Hyde-York connection. York proved a loyal, if sometimes awkward, son-in-law, trying to shield Clarendon from impeachment in 1667. After his exile, the relationship between

FIG. 52 *Prospect of Albemarle [Clarendon] House, by William Skillman after John Spilberg, 1683. After Clarendon fell from power Clarendon House was sold to Christopher Monck, 2nd duke of Albemarle, whose extravagant lifestyle left him unable to service the mortgage. He sold it to a syndicate of speculative builders who demolished the house and developed the area. Modern-day Albemarle Street marks the centre of the site.*

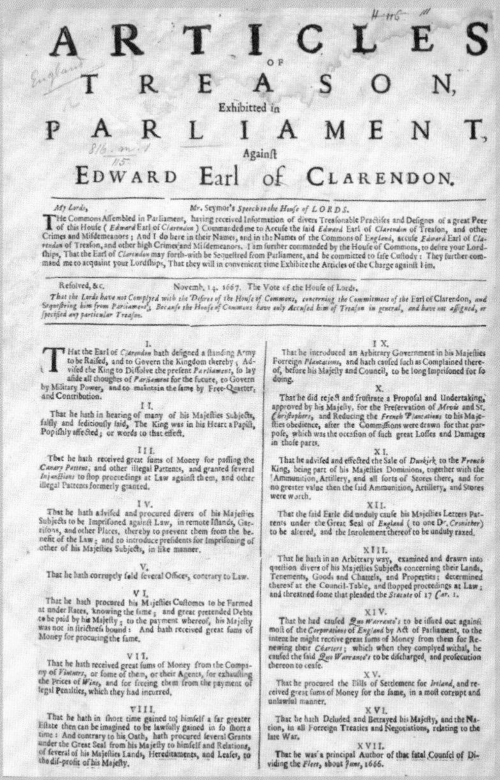

ARTICLES OF TREASON, Exhibitted in PARLIAMENT, Againſt EDWARD Earl of CLARENDON.

My Lords, Mr. Seymor's *Speech to the Houſe of LORDS.*

THe Commons Aſſembled in Parliament, having received Information of divers Treaſonable Practiſes and Deſignes of a great Peer of this Houſe (*Edward* Earl of *Clarendon*) Commanded me to Accuſe the ſaid *Edward* Earl of *Clarendon* of Treaſon, and other Crimes and Miſdemeanors ; And I do here in their Names, and in the Names of the Commons of *England*, accuſe *Edward* Earl of *Clarendon* of Treaſon, and other high Crimes and Miſdemeanors. I am further commanded by the Houſe of Commons, to deſire your Lordſhips, That the Earl of *Clarendon* may forth-with be Sequeſtred from Parliament, and be committed to ſafe Cuſtody : They further command me to acquaint your Lordſhips, That they will in convenient time Exhibite the Articles of the Charge againſt Him.

Reſolved, &c. Novemb. 14. 1667. The Vote of the Houſe of Lords.

That the Lords have not Complyed with the Deſires of the Houſe of Commons, concerning the Commitment of the Earl of Clarendon, *and Sequeſtring him from Parliament; Becauſe the Houſe of Commons have only Accuſed him of Treaſon in general, and have not aſſigned, or ſpecified any particular Treaſon.*

I.

THat the Earl of *Clarendon* hath deſigned a ſtanding Army to be Raiſed, and to Govern the Kingdom thereby ; Adviſed the King to Diſſolve the preſent *Parliament*, ſo lay aſide all thoughts of *Parliament* for the future, to Govern by Military Power, and to maintain the ſame by Free-Quarter, and Contribution.

II.

That he hath in hearing of many of his Majeſties Subjects, falſly and ſeditiouſly ſaid, The King was in his Heart a Papiſt, Popiſhly affected ; or words to that effect.

III.

That he hath received great ſums of Money for paſſing the *Canary Pattent*, and other illegal Pattents, and granted ſeveral *Injunctions* to ſtop proceedings at Law againſt them, and other illegal Pattents formerly granted.

IV.

That he hath adviſed and procured divers of his Majeſties Subjects to be Impriſoned againſt Law, in remote Iſlands, Garriſons, and other Places, thereby to prevent them from the benefit of the Law ; and to introduce preſidents for Impriſoning of other of his Majeſties Subjects, in like manner.

V.

That he hath corruptly ſold ſeveral Offices, contrary to Law.

VI.

That he hath procured his Majeſties Cuſtomes to be Farmed at under Rates, knowing the ſame ; and great pretended Debts to be paid by his Majeſty ; to the payment whereof, his Majeſty was not in ſtrictneſs bound : And hath received great ſums of Money for procuring the ſame.

VII.

That he hath received great ſums of Money from the Company of *Vintners*, or ſome of them, or their Agents, for exhauſting the Prices of *Wine*, and for freeing them from the payment of legal Penalties, which they had incurred.

VIII.

That he hath in ſhort time gained to himſelf a far greater Eſtate then can be imagined to be lawfully gained in ſo ſhort a time : And contrary to his Oath, hath procured ſeveral Grants under the Great Seal from his Majeſty to himſelf and Relations, of ſeveral of his Majeſties Lands, Hereditaments, and Leaſes, to the diſ-profit of his Majeſty.

IX.

That he introduced an Arbitrary Government in his Majeſties Forreign *Plantations*, and hath cauſed ſuch as Complained thereof, before his Majeſty and Council, to be long Impriſoned for ſo doing.

X.

That he did reject and fruſtrate a Propoſal and Undertaking, approved by his Majeſty, for the Preſervation of *Mevis* and St. *Chriſtophers*, and Reducing the *French Plantations* to his Majeſties obedience, after the Commiſſions were drawn for that purpoſe, which was the occaſion of ſuch great Loſſes and Damages in thoſe parts.

XI.

That he adviſed and effected the Sale of *Dunkirk* to the *French* King, being part of his Majeſties Dominions, together with the Ammunition, Artillery, and all ſorts of Stores there, and for no greater value then the ſaid Ammunition, Artillery, and Stores were worth.

XII.

That the ſaid Earle did unduly cauſe his Majeſties Letters Pattents under the Great Seal of *England* (to one Dr. *Cronither*) to be altered, and the Inrolement thereof to be unduly raxed.

XIII.

That he hath in an Arbitrary way, examined and drawn into queſtion divers of his Majeſties Subjects concerning their Lands, Tenements, Goods and Chattels, and Properties ; determined thereof at the Council-Table, and ſtopped proceedings at Law ; and threatned ſome that pleaded the *Statute* of 17 *Car.* 1.

XIV.

That he had cauſed *Quo Warranto's* to be iſſued out againſt moſt of the *Corporations* of *England* by Act of Parliament, to the intent he might receive great ſums of Money from them for Renewing their *Charters* ; which when they complyed withal, he cauſed the ſaid *Quo Warranto's* to be diſcharged, and proſecution thereon to ceaſe.

XV.

That he procured the Bills of Settlement for *Ireland*, and received great ſums of Money for the ſame, in a moſt corrupt and unlawful manner.

XVI.

That he hath Deluded and Betrayed his Majeſty, and the Nation, in all Forreign Treaties and Negotiations, relating to the late War.

XVII.

That he was a principal Author of that fatal Counſel of Dividing the *Fleet*, about *June*, 1666.

FIG. 53 *Articles of treason exhibited in Parliament against Edward, earl of Clarendon, 1667. The impeachment of Clarendon was inspired by his enemies at court: the Lords' refusal to commit him to the Tower indicated the amount of support he enjoyed in the upper House.*

the Yorks and Clarendon's two sons – Henry (earl of Clarendon from his father's death in 1674) and Laurence (earl of Rochester from 1682) – was one of the most important relationships of English politics: they remained among the closest advisers of James II until James's determination to surround himself with Catholics broke the link.

The first earl himself derived enormous profit from his relationship with the royal family. Holding on to his office of lord chancellor (he rejected with temerity a suggestion that he should relinquish it for the more shadowy and informal and very French role of *premier ministre*) he was created Baron Hyde of Hindon in 1660 and earl of Clarendon in 1661, and provided with a substantial estate to maintain the dignity. He was right, though, about the marriage exposing him to jealousy. Like one of his heroes, Francis Bacon, a lord chancellor before him, Clarendon may have too readily enjoyed wealth and power. The small number of allegations that he was bribed as a judge, which were part of the impeachment proceedings against him in 1667, do not invite confidence, but there were plenty of other ways instead of outright bribery of making money as a lord chancellor, such as exploiting the fees required for sealing numerous legal instruments. Clarendon must have enjoyed them to the full. He freely admitted that his palatial new house on Piccadilly, Clarendon House, so visible a demonstration of his wealth and power, was a serious mistake. It made him an easy target for the satirist Andrew Marvell, who, in his *Last Instructions to a Painter* created an enduring image of Clarendon as the *major domo* of a corrupt court, an elderly and incompetent but still malevolent force, trying to control everything while the state falls apart around him:

> See how he Reigns in his new Palace
> *culminant*,
> And sits in State Divine like *Jove* the
> *fulminant*![2]

In some ways it was ironic, for Clarendon professed to be shocked when in the 1640s he first experienced the court merry-go-round of favours and offices, and, according to his memoir, tried to shield both Charles I and Charles II from the importunity of petitioners. Clarendon resisted the casual assumption of the aristocracy and others that the crown should be the source of profit. His rejection of it cost him dearly. For – apart from his alliance with the duke of York – Clarendon had done little to build up his own following within the court and Parliament. When the king turned against him in November 1667 he lost the one remaining source of his power, and fled abroad to spend his last few years in France, returning to the enormous *History of the Rebellion*, an account of the Civil War, which he had begun twenty years before in exile.

Charles II's more impecunious illegitimate sons, Charles Beauclerk, duke of St Albans, was granted an annuity of £2,000 in 1694 'for the better support of his dignity'.[20] When William III turned his favourite, William Henry Nassau de Zuylestein, into the earl of Rochford, he also provided him with an annual pension of £1,000. The largest and most notorious grants came in the reign of Queen Anne. When John Churchill was promoted from earl to duke of Marlborough, he was given £5,000 a year, followed two years later by a grant of the lands on which he would build Blenheim Palace.

The need to bestow prestigious and lucrative positions on politically powerful, but not necessarily competent, individuals did not always produce the best results in terms of government. The choice of John Berkeley, Baron Berkeley of Stratton, to be a navy commissioner in July 1660 reflected, as Pepys later commented, a 'want of other ways of gratification'.[21] Seeing Berkeley in action at a meeting of a committee of the Royal Fishing Company in 1664, Pepys remarked that he 'is the most hot, fiery man in discourse, without any cause, that I ever saw'.[22] It was little surprise that Berkeley stayed in Ireland after his appointment as president of Connaught only long enough to lease the office at a 'good yearly rent'.[23]

Aristocratic poverty

Royal handouts prevented some peers from sinking below the standard of living which would be recognised as appropriate for their status. They were not above exaggerating their plight. In September 1664 Charles Howard, styled Lord Andover (later 2nd earl of Berkshire), petitioned the crown for payment of his pension, claiming that he was so hard up that he was 'upon the uttermost confines of starving'.[24] Another aristocrat heavily reliant on royal largesse, even before he inherited his title, was Edward Hyde, styled Lord Cornbury until he succeeded as 3rd earl of Clarendon (see below, p. 228). By 1697 he had fallen out with his father and uncle, key figures among the Tories and, like Andover thirty years earlier, was reported to be 'starving'.[25] In 1701 he was appointed as governor of New York and given an annual pension of £600. He was recalled in 1707 after a series of allegations against him, including cross-dressing. Before he could return he was gaoled at the suit of several creditors. He complained bitterly that the level of his debts had been exaggerated and that he would be solvent if his own debtors paid up.

After inheriting the earldom in October 1709 he was able to claim privilege as a peer (which evidently reached as far as America) and secure his release from gaol. When he finally returned to England, Queen Anne (his cousin) provided him with shelter in Somerset House and annual gifts of between £200 and £2,000.[26]

Aristocratic poverty was often the result of small estates heavily encumbered by provision for children, or titles and estates parting company and going to different families. William Ley, 4th earl of Marlborough, inherited his title and little else after the death of his nephew at the battle of Lowestoft in 1665. His father, James Ley, the 1st earl, had left only a small estate, subject to dowries for his eight daughters and provision for his widow. The 4th earl claimed to possess only a small tenement from which he raised £50 a year and to live in what he described as little more than 'a poor thatched house' and which on another occasion he likened to a 'poor enchanted hermitage'.[27] He was so desperate that in 1677 he came up with a scheme to use the proceeds from selling his earldom 'to repurchase part of the estate that my relations sold away' and thus enable him to support his lesser title as Baron Ley.[28] Thomas Willoughby became 11th Baron Willoughby of Parham in 1680 at the death of his distant kinsman, Charles, 10th Baron Willoughby. The relationship was so distant that the 10th baron had no idea that another branch of the family existed and, assuming that his peerage would be extinguished at his death, left the bulk of his estate to his niece. Thomas Willoughby was transformed overnight from a moderately prosperous yeoman farmer to an impoverished peer. An annual pension of £200 with the addition of an occasional 'free gift' from the crown enabled him to make some attempt to live up to the dignity of his new honour. At his death his personal estate – which had to be divided between his widow and six children – was worth less than £200. Most inventories of aristocratic estates of this period include items such as paintings, tapestries, furniture, jewellery and sometimes even that most valuable of luxury items of the day, foot carpets. Willoughby's most valuable possessions were his oxen, cows and horses, worth in total only £70. His eldest son Hugh inherited the title and five shillings, but little else. Hugh was in turn succeeded by his younger brother Francis – a mere tenant farmer.

Some peers were driven to desperate straits to keep their heads above water. When John Lovelace, 3rd Baron Lovelace, tried to sell one Oxfordshire estate to his son-in-law, Sir Henry Johnson, his mother, the dowager Lady Lovelace, insisted that the tenants continue to pay rent to her (when one of them refused, Lady Lovelace and a posse of retainers forced their way into the house, pistols and blunderbusses in hand, and committed the tenant's servants to Oxford gaol). Eventually, he mortgaged the estate to Richard Boyle, earl of Burlington, at the same time as he sold the reversion to it to Johnson without informing him of the mortgage. Privilege of peerage theoretically protected him from the bailiffs, but his creditors nevertheless seem to have found a way of closing in: his house in Suffolk Street in London was 'in manifest danger of being seized'.[29] His executor was still receiving letters from creditors demanding payment years after Lovelace's death. After the Restoration, Thomas Howard, the 70-year-old earl of Berkshire, devoted most of his efforts to overcoming his mounting burden of debt. It was the need to secure himself from his creditors, rather than enthusiasm to serve the king, which led him to take his seat in the Lords at the first opportunity in May 1660. Over the next few years, despite receiving handouts from the crown and selling Berkshire House to the king for £8,000, he was alleged to have resorted to extorting money from Jewish merchants whom he threatened with expulsion; receiving stolen goods (though he invoked privilege against the merchant who accused him); and sharp practice in exercising the right, granted to him in 1662, of levying court fines. In 1666 he was beaten up in his own house, probably by two of his creditors, and took shelter in his coach which was then standing in the courtyard. His assailants drove it and the earl out into the street and left them there. He found refuge for the night only through the charity of a woman who had once been his mother-in-law's servant. The Catholic barons Stourton had been in financial difficulty even before the Restoration. After it, they plunged deeper and deeper into debt. Edward Stourton, 13th Baron Stourton, who succeeded in 1685, nevertheless continued to live up to his aristocratic status. Barred from office by the Test Acts, he survived by the simple expedient of refusing to pay his debts. He sacked a succession of stewards and bailiffs without settling any accounts, thus effectively transferring the deficit in his finances from himself to them. Those who tried to pursue him for payment found that he could be an implacable opponent, able and willing to harass his creditors. The strategy eventually unravelled. Despite Stourton's desperate attempts to maintain a façade of solvency, he was increasingly unable to service the interest on his debts, let alone pay off the capital. In 1714 he sold his estate to Sir Thomas

Meres for a theoretical £19,400; the property was already mortgaged to the hilt to Meres, and Stourton actually received only £775 from the sale.

Recovery and consolidation

In order to transform their finances, impoverished peers (as well as politically, socially and financially ambitious ones) looked to marriage. The injection of wealth brought by a rich heiress could have spectacular results. All too frequently, though, it went to the already rich, rather than the desperate poor. The wife of the wealthy 2nd duke of Albemarle brought with her a dowry of £20,000 and lands worth £12,000 a year. The most notable catch of all was Elizabeth Percy, heiress to the vast fortune of her father, Joceline Percy, 5th earl of Northumberland, and 'the richest match in this nation'.[30] Her father died in 1670 (see above, p. 73). The following year, when she was still only about four, William Cavendish, duke of Newcastle, proposed that she marry his grandson, Henry Cavendish, later styled Lord Ogle. Elizabeth's grandmother, the dowager countess of Northumberland, fought off this and other proposals, insisting that her granddaughter's 'tender years are not yet capable of distinguishing what may conduce most to her future happiness. And when she is of age to judge I must be so just as to give her the choice of all those who shall then offer themselves'.[31] Elizabeth married Ogle in April 1679 at the age of twelve. When he died eighteen months later the competition for her hand broke out all over again. Within less than a year she had remarried, this time clandestinely to Thomas Thynne of Longleat. Thynne, at 38 vastly older than his bride and said to be of dissolute habits, had bribed someone (variously alleged to have been her apparently solicitous grandmother or a Mr Bret) with £10,000 to facilitate the marriage, which may well have been carried out forcibly. Lady Elizabeth soon ran away to Flanders, apparently aided by Henry Sydney, younger brother of Algernon and the future earl of Romney. The ensuing scandal made 'so great a noise in town' it was reported, 'that my Lord Shaftesbury's trial' – the great political event of the year – 'is hardly spoke of'.[32] In February 1682 Thynne was murdered at the instigation of yet another of Lady Elizabeth's suitors, the German-born Count Karl Johann Königsmark. Lady Elizabeth herself was widely suspected of complicity in the crime: her third marriage, three months later, to Charles Seymour, 6th duke of Somerset, brought her a powerful protector from any of the

FIGS. 54 AND 55
The killers of Thomas Thynne in 1682 were arrested, tried and executed; the man who probably hired them, Count Königsmark, was charged only as an accessory. He was in any case found not guilty. Thynne's death resulted in the reuniting of two branches of the Thynne family and the creation of a vast new estate (see below, p. 312).

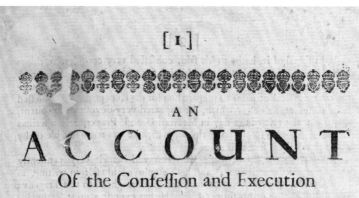

[1]

AN

ACCOUNT

Of the Confeſſion and Execution

OF

Captain *Vratz*,
Geo. *Boraski*,
AND
John Sterne, } Who were this preſent Friday, being the Tenth of *March*, Executed at *Pell-mall*, for the Barbarous Murther of *Thomas Thynne* Eſquire.

TOGETHER

With a particular Relation of their Behaviour in *Newgate* ſince their Condemnation, and manner of their paſſing to the place of Execution.

SInce the Condemnation of theſe Notorious Criminals, they have been conſtantly Viſited by many eminent Divines, who have Religiouſly endeavoured to prepare them for their ſpeedy End, and to make them have a due ſenſe of the State they are going to enter into, by preſſing ſeveral Pious and Religious Diſcourſes to them, importing the horridneſs of Bloud-guiltineſs, and how hainous a thing it is in the ſight of God to ſhed Innocent Bloud; endeavouring thereby to bring them to a true ſenſibleneſs of their approaching death.

On Sunday laſt the Reverend Doctor *Burnet* Preached to them, and the other Priſoners, and made a moſt excellent Sermon, ſetting forth the nature of Sin, and the dreadfulneſs of Hell and Damnation, ſhewing them their danger of being irrecoverably and eternally loſt and undone; exhorting them to repent and mourn heartily for their ſins. As for their Behaviour ſince their Condemnation, the Captain appeared for ſome days after his being Sentenced, with no kind of ſeeming Concern, but onely at the Manner of his Death; declaring, He had many times in Battel hazarded his Life with abſolute Unconcernedneſs; but his dying this Ignominious Death, would leave a Stain upon his Poſterity. But upon hearing the Doctor preach, it pleaſed God to ſet his ſin ſo home upon his Conſcience, that he began to be ſomewhat more concerned than before; whereupon the Doctor took the opportunity of his ſeeming Concernedneſs, by farther inſtructing and directing him in the Work of Repentance and Faith; ſo that it is hoped he is become a true Penitent; and

LONDON: Printed for S. T. 1682.

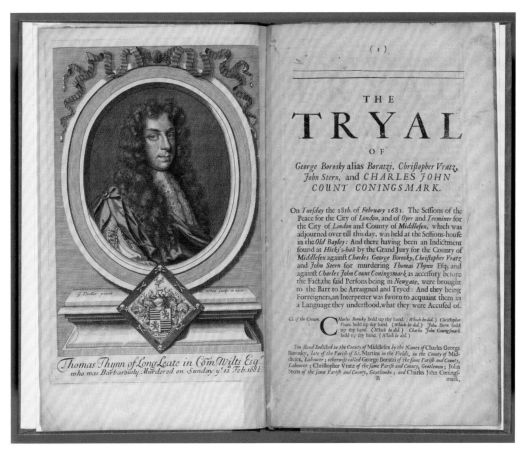

FIG. 55

consequences, though not the happiness her grandmother had proposed twelve years before.

Those who succeeded in marrying an heiress might anyway discover that the expected financial benefits did not materialise. Marriage portions sometimes went unpaid and heiresses were not always what they seemed. Aubrey de Vere, the impoverished 20th earl of Oxford, tried to repair his fortunes by marrying Anne Bayning, one of the two daughters and co-heiresses of Paul Bayning, 2nd Viscount Bayning in 1647. The marriage should have netted him a legacy of £20,000, but it was never paid: the Bayning estates were entangled in a web of debt and conflicting claims. In the event Oxford's own rights to the estates were jeopardised by his wife's premature death (aged only 22) in 1659, and all he gained from the venture – apart from involvement in a series of complex and expensive legal actions – was the Bayning mansion in Essex which he

FIG. 56 *Aubrey de Vere, 20th earl of Oxford (1626–1703), by Sir Godfrey Kneller. Holder of one the most prestigious and ancient titles in the English peerage, Oxford was also one of the poorest of the peers. Dependent on the court for favour and hand outs he was nevertheless one of the first to abandon James II for the Prince of Orange in 1688.*

subsequently demolished to sell for building materials. The duke of Richmond similarly found that marriage to an heiress failed to solve his financial difficulties. In 1662 he took as his second wife Margaret Lewis, a widow worth £38,000: her marriage settlement, however, tied up her estate so that at her death, five years later, it descended to her son by a previous marriage rather than to her husband.

For rebuilding shattered aristocratic finances and consolidating great estates the best answer was low spending and good administration. The inheritance of the peerage and estates by a peer who was underage could help enormously. The Restoration made it possible for a minority to become a period of consolidation in great estates, rather than ruin. Before the Civil War the estate of an underage peer was at the mercy of the court of wards, which might grant control during the minority to those who had no long-term interest in maintaining it or enhancing its value. The abolition of feudal tenures and hence also of the court of wards in 1646, confirmed by the Convention Parliament in 1660, enabled families to retain control of their lands and to administer them for the benefit of the heir. At the same time they were relieved of the need for the sort of ostentatious consumption that commonly underlined and undermined the status of the peerage: retrenchment, in the case of a minor, was socially acceptable in a way that it was not for an adult. It worked for the Catholic barons Petre. At the Restoration their estates were in disarray. William Petre, 4th Baron Petre, spent much of the rest of his life rebuilding the family fortunes. The Test Act (and his subsequent arrest over suspicions of involvement in the Popish Plot) cut him and his successors off from advancement at court – apart from the brief period of James II's reign when a distant cousin, Edward Petre SJ ('Father Petre'), was in high favour. Robert Petre, 7th Baron Petre, succeeded as a minor in 1707. His marriage to an heiress, Catherine Walmsley, enriched the estate: his untimely death from smallpox in 1713, followed by the posthumous birth of a son, ushered in another long minority during which the family's fortunes were consolidated.

The case of Henry Clinton showed what might be achieved through a combination of luck, marriage and a minority. About seven years old when he became 7th earl of Lincoln at his father's death in September 1693, Clinton inherited little else apart from his title. Left without sufficient landed income to maintain the dignity of the peerage, Lincoln's mother received a pension of around £200 a year 'as royal bounty towards the support and maintenance' of her son until he came of age.[33] Early in Anne's reign, the earl of Ailesbury, noting that Lincoln lived 'in an obscure manner for want of what to support him in his dignity',[34] proposed a pension for him. Even though he was dependent on a Tory-dominated court for financial support, once Lincoln came of age and began to sit in the Lords in 1708, he made his allegiance to the Whigs clear. After the accession of George I he received as his reward lucrative offices in the king's household. He also had an extraordinary stroke of luck. Having no male heirs, the admiral Arthur Herbert, earl of Torrington, left much of his estate, including the manor house of Oatlands in Weybridge, Surrey, and 10,000 acres in the Bedford Level, to the impecunious Whig stalwart. An anecdote found in the papers of Jacobite family of Oliphant recounts that 'Lord Torrington, one day at table with his heir at law, whom he hated, the conversation turned upon the poor Quality in England'. One of the party mentioned the worthiness and poverty of Lincoln, 'a noble family, with only £500 per annum', after which Torrington, 'though he never saw Lord Lincoln, left him his estate of £6,000 per annum at his death, which happened a few days after'.[35] Lincoln's fortunes were transformed. They were further enhanced by his marriage in May 1717 to Lucy Pelham, sister to the fabulously rich Thomas, duke of Newcastle, and the brilliant politician Henry Pelham.

The Newcastle estate was another example of the effects of marriage, good luck and prudent management. John Holles, 4th earl of Clare, inherited lands worth about £10,000 a year at the death in 1691 of his eccentric father-in-law, Henry Cavendish, 2nd duke of Newcastle, although it required a three-year legal battle (and a duel) to secure his title to the estate. With it came debts estimated at £72,580 and annual interest charges of £4,000. Another windfall, worth between £5,000 and £6,000 a year, followed the death in January 1694 of his kinsman Denzil Holles, 3rd Baron Holles. This, too, was heavily mortgaged but, now promoted to be duke of Newcastle, Clare began to redeem the lands, using a private bill in 1697 to confirm the settlement. He also bought additional properties, spending some £200,000 over many years in the process. At the accession of Anne, he was said by Gilbert Burnet, bishop of Salisbury, to be 'the richest subject that had been in England for some ages', with an estate estimated, plausibly, at above £40,000 a year.[36]

The prosperity and survival of aristocratic families and their estates were not just matters of private concern. They preoccupied monarchs and their governments, and they took up much of the time of the House of Lords. For although the Lords dealt with the public business of the nation through its role, with the House of Commons, in making the law and through its separate role as a court, it was deeply involved in the individual concerns of the peerage: their rights and privileges as peers; their schemes for the enrichment of themselves and their families; and the inheritance of their titles and their estates. It acted, too, to try to preserve the integrity and quality of the peerage. Although nobility was conferred by the crown, the peerage itself, through the role of the House of Lords in settling disputed claims, played a major part in regulating its transmission through the generations; and although a peerage conveyed a title and certain rights, it did not necessarily confer participation in the English and British legislature.

'I pray God restrain the minds of unquiet and tumultuous men': exclusion and reaction, 1678–88

The allegations made in August 1678 by the fantasist Israel Tonge and his clever, exotic yet poisonous associate, Titus Oates, about a plot by Catholics to kill the king in order to hasten the accession of James, duke of York, were implausible. Cast into an already over-excited political world, and given some veracity by the subsequent murder of one of the magistrates initially involved in investigating them, they were nevertheless explosive. An immediate fear of resurgent and fanatical Catholicism spread over English political life. Despite the tiny number of Catholic peers, Charles Yelverton, 14th Baron Grey of Ruthin, rushed up to London, excitedly telling a friend that 'I do not love to neglect the House in this crisis, especially when I have seen at first ourselves outnumbered by the popish lords'.[1]

When Parliament opened in October, the government lost control of its proceedings altogether. Both Houses investigated the plot in minute detail; in the Lords, Anthony Ashley Cooper, earl of Shaftesbury, made allegations about Catholic troops in the army and their dependence on York, while the king's illegitimate son, James Scott, duke of Monmouth, hotly called for the removal of Catholics from around his father. The Commons sought the arrest of five Catholic peers who were allegedly involved in the conspiracy: Henry Arundell, 3rd Baron Arundell of Wardour; John Belasyse, Baron Belasyse; William Petre, 4th Baron Petre; William Herbert, earl (later marquess) of Powis; and William Howard, Viscount Stafford. They also passed a bill to exclude all Catholics from the House of Lords. In the Lords Shaftesbury highlighted evidence that seemed to implicate York himself. On 4 November he demanded that York be removed from the King's presence and counsels. When the bill to prevent Catholics from sitting in Parliament came to the Lords, York, in tears, moved for a provision specifically to exempt himself on the grounds that his religion was 'a private thing between God and his own soul'.[2] What was interpreted as a veiled threat about what he might do if his proviso were rejected conveyed a more sinister impression. The 'test' bill was passed, and although York's proviso was accepted, it was by only two votes. Faced with taking not only the oaths of allegiance and supremacy but also a declaration against transubstantiation, most Catholic peers ceased to attend the Lords. Henry Howard, later 7th duke of Norfolk, who sat in the House as Lord Mowbray, resumed his seat six months later after converting to the Church of England. Henry Pierrepont, marquess of Dorchester, suspected of being a Catholic, was among the first to take the oaths, but was seen to have said only some of the words. Peers insisted he take it again the following day.

In December 1678, the crisis deepened further. The former ambassador to Paris, Ralph Montagu, annoyed by his treatment by the king and Thomas Osborne, earl of Danby, over his affair with one of Charles' illegitimate daughters and by his failure to obtain the secretaryship of state, took his revenge by revealing Danby's correspondence of May with the French offering (on behalf of the king) to prorogue Parliament in return for a French subsidy. The Commons voted to impeach Danby on 19 December. The majority in the Lords refused to commit their colleague to the Tower, arguing that the charges against him did not amount to treason. Faced with a complete paralysis of government, Charles prorogued Parliament on 30 December, losing a bill to raise money to disband the army. Towards the end of January 1679 he dissolved the Cavalier Parliament – after almost eighteen years – and called new elections.

One of the objectives of the country peers had at last been achieved: a new House of Commons was likely to have very different attitudes to religious nonconformity. It had just the same suspicions of the King and his government. When it opened on 6 March 1679 it ignored the king's offer of a cooperative relationship and the pardon he had provided for Danby and continued its predecessor's prosecution of the former lord treasurer. Encouraged by the king, the Lords tenaciously defended Danby's rights and their own privileges. They rejected the Commons' argument that the bishops, whose votes might tip the balance in Danby's favour, were not entitled to participate in the trial. A deadlock between the two Houses was debated in print by Denzil Holles, Baron Holles, by

FIG. 57 *This broadside by Francis Barlow sets out the main allegations made by Titus Oates and others, starting with the murder of the magistrate, Edmund Berry Godfrey, and suggesting a plan to impose the authority of the pope in England with armies from Spain and Ireland.*

Thomas Barlow, bishop of Lincoln, and by Edward Stillingfleet, later bishop of Worcester (see below, pp. 130, 170).

In April, Charles attempted a new strategy, to bring into the privy council the 'country' leaders Shaftesbury, George Savile, Viscount Halifax, Arthur Capel, earl of Essex and William Cavendish, then styled Lord Cavendish (later 4th earl and duke of Devonshire). It worked in so far as Parliament voted money to disband the troops, but it failed to overcome the crisis. Divided by the venomous personal hostility between Shaftesbury and Halifax, split between the advocates of a vigorous pro-Dutch and anti-French foreign policy (including Halifax, Essex and Robert Spencer, 2nd earl of Sunderland) and those whose focus was on the domestic crisis (Shaftesbury, James Scott, duke of Monmouth and William, Lord Russell, the son and heir of the 5th earl of Bedford), and hamstrung by the King's patent lack of commitment to it, the new council was bound to fail.

By 1679 the central question for politicians was how to neutralise the threat that a Catholic on the throne might try to destroy Protestantism in the

FIG. 58 *Silver medal, commemorating a London jury's rejection on 24 November 1681 of a government indictment for high treason of Anthony Ashley Cooper, earl of Shaftesbury. The verdict was greeted with bonfires and other celebrations in London, including the striking of this medal.*

country. Halifax and his faction demanded 'limitations' or 'expedients' which would protect the liberties of the subject and the Protestant religion. Once it emerged into the open, a proposal to exclude James from the succession altogether attracted much greater support. It may have originated in a group of militant members of the Commons; but when Shaftesbury decided to jump onto the bandwagon it started to roll much faster. An exclusion bill was introduced into the Commons in May 1679. The king, advised by Halifax, stopped it by proroguing Parliament, and in July, hoping that public excitement over the popish plot was diminishing, he dissolved it and called a new one.

The elections proved him wrong. Charles accepted York's advice not to allow the new Parliament to meet. The council was bypassed and fell apart. A furious Shaftesbury was dismissed in October, marking the end of the king's attempt to appease the opposition. A formidable petitioning campaign, designed to push him into allowing Parliament to meet as scheduled in January 1680, only increased his resolve to resist: it was postponed to October. A new determination emerged at court, with the king increasingly relying on the cool nerves and considerable abilities of an emerging triumvirate, 'the chits': Laurence Hyde (younger son of the 1st earl of Clarendon, and later earl of Rochester), Sidney Godolphin (later earl of Godolphin) and Robert Spencer, earl of Sunderland, who carefully prepared the political ground for the next session, resting their hopes on an anti-French foreign policy.

When Parliament did finally meet, more than a year after it was originally elected, their carefully developed strategy fell apart, partly because the death of Holles in February 1680 had removed one of the more moderate opposition leaders. Some interpreted the king's willingness to allow Parliament to sit in October as acceptance of his brother's exclusion. Charles again promised 'any remedies which shall be proposed that may consist with the preserving of the crown in its due and legal course of descent' but the options had significantly narrowed. Splits developed among the chits themselves: Sunderland advocated a deal with Shaftesbury accepting exclusion; Hyde stuck firmly to York. The Commons passed an exclusion bill, although one that left open the identity of the successor. Carried up to the Lords, it was considered immediately in a dramatic and tense twelve-hour debate attended by the king himself. Some saw it as an oratorical duel between Shaftesbury and Halifax (who was said to have spoken sixteen times), but others spoke too. Philip Stanhope, 2nd earl of Chesterfield invoked 'the blood of the last king', which had left 'an eternal stain upon this kingdom'.[3] Henry Mordaunt, 2nd earl of Peterborough, described the campaign against exclusion as 'a cause in which every man in England was obliged to draw his sword' and sent the House into disorder when he laid his hand on the hilt of his sword as if he intended to use it.[4] The bill was rejected by a majority of thirty-four votes. All fourteen bishops present in the House voted against it. Bishop Fell wrote the next day to his friend Lady Hatton that 'We are not far from breaking out into hostility. I pray God restrain the minds of unquiet and tumultuous men.'[5]

The Lords' vote marked the real start of the 'Exclusion Crisis'. For a moment it seemed to have taken the Commons' breath away – evidence of how far everyone (including Sunderland, who had voted for the bill (see below, p. 134)) had persuaded themselves that Charles would cave in. The reaction raised uncomfortable echoes of the descent into the Civil War in the early 1640s. Lists of the peers who had voted against exclusion were stuck up in the Westminster coffee houses. With the king a frequent

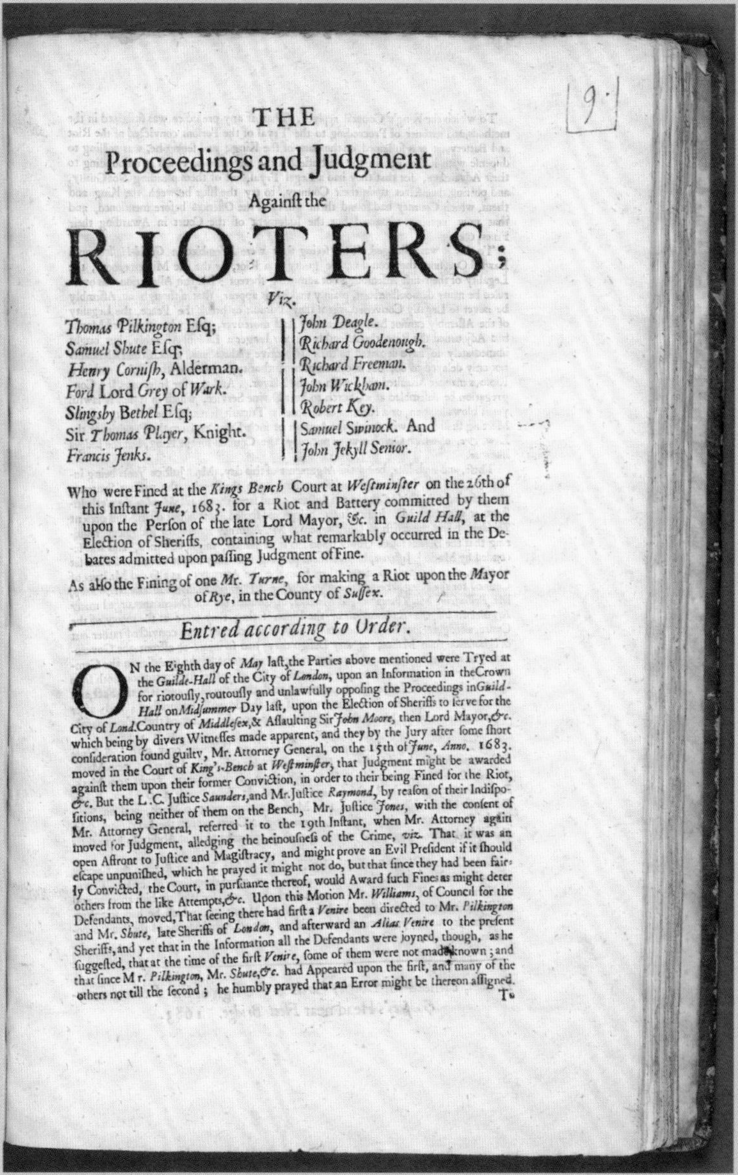

THE
Proceedings and Judgment
Against the
RIOTERS;
Viz.

Thomas Pilkington Esq;	*John Deagle.*
Samuel Shute Esq;	*Richard Goodenough.*
Henry Cornish, Alderman.	*Richard Freeman.*
Ford Lord *Grey* of *Wark.*	*John Wickham.*
Slingsby Bethel Esq;	*Robert Key.*
Sir *Thomas Player*, Knight.	*Samuel Swinock.* And
Francis Jenks.	*John Jekyll Senior.*

Who were Fined at the *Kings Bench* Court at *Westminster* on the 26th of this Instant *June*, 1683. for a Riot and Battery committed by them upon the Person of the late Lord Mayor, &c. in *Guild Hall*, at the Election of Sheriffs, containing what remarkably occurred in the Debates admitted upon passing Judgment of Fine.

As also the Fining of one *Mr. Turne*, for making a Riot upon the *Mayor* of *Rye*, in the County of *Sussex.*

Entred according to Order.

ON the Eighth day of *May* last, the Parties above mentioned were Tryed at
the *Guilde-Hall* of the City of *London*, upon an Information in the Crown
for riotously, routously and unlawfully opposing the Proceedings in *Guild-*
Hall on *Midsummer* Day last, upon the Election of Sheriffs to serve for the
City of *Lond.* Country of *Middlesex*, & Assaulting Sir *John Moore*, then Lord Mayor, &c.
which being by divers Witnesses made apparent, and they by the Jury after some short
consideration found guilty, Mr. Attorney General, on the 15th of *June*, *Anno.* 1683.
moved in the Court of *King's-Bench* at *Westminster*, that Judgment might be awarded
against them upon their former Conviction, in order to their being Fined for the Riot,
&c. But the L. C. Justice *Saunders*, and Mr. Justice *Raymond*, by reason of their Indispo-
sitions, being neither of them on the Bench, Mr. Justice *Jones*, with the consent of
Mr. Attorney General, referred it to the 19th Instant, when Mr. Attorney again
moved for Judgment, alledging the heinousness of the Crime, *viz.* That it was an
open Affront to Justice and Magistracy, and might prove an Evil President if it should
escape unpunished, which he prayed it might not do, but that since they had been fairly Convicted, the Court, in pursuance thereof, would Award such Fines as might deter
others from the like Attempts, &c. Upon this Motion Mr. *Williams*, of Council for the
Defendants, moved, That seeing there had first a *Venire* been directed to Mr. *Pilkington*
and Mr. *Shute*, late Sheriffs of *London*, and afterward an *Alias Venire* to the present
Sheriffs, and yet that in the Information all the Defendants were joyned, though, as he
suggested, that at the time of the first *Venire*, some of them were not made known; and
that since Mr. *Pilkington*, Mr. *Shute*, &c. had Appeared upon the first, and many of the
others not till the second; he humbly prayed that an Error might be thereon assigned.
To

FIG. 59 *When the desperate struggle for political control of the City of London erupted into physical violence at the long-drawn out election of the City's sheriffs in 1682, it enabled the government to prosecute the Whig ringleaders in 1683.*

and intimidatory presence, the Lords earnestly discussed alternatives that would provide the necessary guarantees for the Protestant religion. Charles abandoned any attempt to come to terms with Parliament in January 1681, dissolving it and dismissing those of his ministers – especially Sunderland and Essex – who had supported exclusion. In a bid to disrupt the alliance between opposition leaders and those prominent in City of London politics he summoned a new Parliament to meet at Oxford. And indeed, amid the elections in February there were repeated reports of pre-revolutionary moves in London, as well as rumours that the king planned to seize the opposition leaders at Oxford.

Nothing of the kind happened, although Shaftesbury thought it necessary to appear in Oxford with a protective cavalcade of armed men. When he met the new Parliament on 21 March, the king offered a regency during James's reign. In an extraordinary conversation on 24 March Shaftesbury proposed to Charles that the crown be given to Monmouth. The government arranged for Charles's

By the King.
A PROCLAMATION
For the Apprehending of *James* Duke of *Monmouth*, Ford Lord *Gray*, Sir *Thomas Armestrong* Knight, and *Robert Fergusou*.

CHARLES R.

Hereas We have received Information upon Oath, That *James* Duke of *Monmouth*, Ford Lord *Gray*, Sir *Thomas Armestrong* Knight, and *Robert Fergusou*, have Traiterously Confpired together, and with divers other ill affected and defperate Perfons of this Our Kingdom, to compafs the Death and Deftruction of Our Royal Perfon, and of Our deareft Brother *James* Duke of *York*: And to effect the fame, have held feveral Treafonable Confultations to Levy Men, and to make an Infurrection within this Our Kingdom, And being given to underftand that the faid Criminals are fled , and left their Habitation to avoid the Juftice of Our Laws : We have therefore thought fit, by and with the Advice of Our Privy Council, to Publifh Our Royal Pleafure , And We do hereby ftrictly Charge and Command the faid *James* Duke of *Monmouth*, Ford Lord *Gray*, Sir *Thomas Armestrong*, and *Robert Fergusou*, and every of them, forthwith to render themfelves to fome of Our Judges or Juftices of the Peace, in order to their Profecution according to Law. And We do hereby Require and Command, as well all and fingular Our Judges, Juftices of the Peace, Mayors, Sheriffs, Conftables, and Headboroughs, as alfo the Officers and Minifters of Our Ports, and all other Our Subjects, whatfoever, within Our Realms of *England*, *Scotland*, *Ireland*, or Dominion of *Wales*, and all other Our Dominions and Territories, to be diligent in Enquiring and Searching for the faid Offenders in all Places whatfoever, as well within Liberties as without ; And if they fhall happen to take any of them, or that they fhall render themfelves, Our further Will and Pleafure is, That they caufe him or them fo Apprehended, to be fafely carried before the next Juftice of the Peace to the Place where he or they fhall be Arrefted, whom VVe ftrictly Charge to commit to Prifon, and prefently inform Us or Our Privy Council of fuch Apprehenfion. And VVe do hereby further Declare and Publifh, That if any Perfon or Perfons, after this Our Proclamation, fhall directly or indirectly, Conceal, Harbour, Keep, Retain or Maintain the faid Offender, or any of them , or fhall Contrive or Connive at any Means whereby they or any of them may efcape from being Taken or Arrefted, or fhall not ufe their beft Endeavours for the Apprehenfion of them, as well by giving due Advertifement thereof to Our Officers, as by all other good Means, We will (as there is juft caufe) proceed againft them that fhall fo neglect this Our Commandment with all Severity. And We do alfo Declare, That whofoever fhall Difcover the faid Offenders, or any of them, either within Our Kingdoms of *England*, *Scotland*, *Ireland*, or Dominion of *Wales*, or in any other Our Dominions and Territories, or elfewhere beyond the Seas, and fhall caufe them, or any of them, to be Apprehended and brought in as aforefaid, fhall have a Reward of Five hundred pounds for each of the faid Perfons, to be paid unto him in Recompence of fuch his Service.

Given at Our Court at Whitehall *this Twenty eighth day of* June, 1683. *In the Five and thirtieth Year of Our Reign.*

GOD fave the KING.

Edinburgh, Printed by the Heir of *Andrew Anderson*, Printer to His moft Sacred Majefty. 1683.

FIG. 60 *Charles II's illegitimate son, James, duke of Monmouth, was regarded by the Rye House plotters as their figurehead: on the betrayal of the plot, the government issued this proclamation in 1683 requiring his apprehension along with associates including Ford Grey, 3rd Baron Grey of Warke (see below, p. 238). He and his fellow conspirators went into hiding. Indicted for treason, he nevertheless managed a temporary reconciliation with his father before leaving for the continent early in 1684.*

magisterial put-down to be published the following day: 'I would much sooner lose this life, of which you pretend to be so watchful preservers, than ever part with any of my prerogative, or betray this place, the laws, or the religion, or alter the true succession of the crown, it being repugnant both to conscience and law'. Shaftesbury was supposed to have responded that the law could be changed, to which the king was said to have replied: 'My lord, if this is your conscience, it is far from being mine: for this cannot be done without overthrowing all religion and all law'.[6] Five days later Charles attended the Lords, as was now normal, but on leaving the chamber he donned his robes, which had been brought to him secretly, summoned the Commons and dissolved the Parliament without further ceremony, entirely disrupting Shaftesbury's plans to create some form of demonstration. A couple of weeks later he published a declaration in defence of his actions. It firmly associated the current crisis with that of 1642, appealing to

> all those who consider the rise and progress of the late troubles and confessions, and desire to preserve their country from a relapse, and who cannot but remember that religion, liberty and property were all lost and gone when the monarchy was shaken off, and could never be revived till that was restored.[7]

The strains of loyalty

The dissolution of March 1681 crystallized the polrization of the political world, refashioning and perpetuating divisions that dated back to the 1640s. Supporters of exclusion were nicknamed Whigs, implying both criminality and descent from the

FIG. 61 *Shortly after the accession of James II, the instigator of the Popish Plot, Titus Oates, was convicted of perjury. Part of his punishment was to be pilloried outside Westminster Hall, shown here in a painting of 1687; he was also whipped through the streets of London.*

Scottish Presbyterianism that their opponents blamed for the Civil War. Their opponents, partisans of the rights of kings and the Anglican Church, were labelled Tories, linking them to Irish Catholic cutthroats. In the wake of the dissolution Charles committed himself to his hitherto none-too enthusiastic alliance with the Tories, against what he regarded as the anti-monarchical principles of Whiggism. Tories enthusiastically set about the repression of religious dissent and the destruction of the Whigs. The duke of York was firmly re-established at the centre of government, and Tories, in particular Laurence Hyde, now earl of Rochester, dominated it. George Savile, promoted to earl of Halifax, returned to office as a token of a broader administration; Sunderland also slid back in, indispensable though untrusted. One of the second rank opposition leaders, Theophilus Hastings, 7th earl of Huntingdon, abandoned his former friends: to his intense embarrassment, an alleged confession in

October 1681 that he 'had by experience found, that they who promoted the bill of exclusion were for the subversion of monarchy itself', was widely publicised in the Tory press.[8] Whigs remained influential beyond the court, and especially in the metropolis. An attempt to put Shaftesbury on trial for treason there in November 1681 failed when the jury, carefully packed by London's Whig sheriffs, threw out the case. The king's illegitimate son, Monmouth, rallied Whig support in the provinces. He was given a rapturous welcome in Chester in September 1682 by Charles Gerard, earl of Macclesfield, and local Whigs.

121

That same month the Tories seized political control of London in a highly controversial and bitterly-fought election for the City's sheriffs. Shaftesbury went into hiding before fleeing to the Netherlands, where he died in early 1683. Evidence of a real, if half-formed, Whig conspiracy – the Rye House Plot – involving the assassination of the king and his brother, was discovered in summer 1683. It gave the government what it needed to remove the Whig leadership. The testimony of William Howard, 3rd Baron Howard of Escrick (caught trying to hide in, or escape up a chimney, and described by the king, ironically in the event, as 'so ill a man that he would not hang the worst dog he had on his evidence'),[9] led to the execution of the Whig leader, William, Lord Russell, and the theorist, Algernon Sydney. A third Whig 'martyr', the earl of Essex, slit his own throat whilst imprisoned in the Tower, although he was widely suspected to have been murdered. Shaftesbury's right-hand man, Ford Grey, 3rd Baron Grey of Warke (later earl of Tankerville) escaped to Germany where, outlawed for treason and his lands confiscated, he spent the next two years eking out his existence on donations from his younger brother Ralph and his spurned wife Mary (see below, p. 238). Monmouth was also forced into exile.

Chased from national politics and purged from local office, the Whigs were powerless to contest James's accession after Charles's unexpected death in February 1685. James's first (and only) Parliament, which met in May 1685, was dominated by Tories, their loyalty confirmed by James's strenuous denials that he represented any threat to the Church or the laws of England. Monmouth's rebellion the following month – an ill-planned attempt by Charles's bastard son to capitalise on his following in the west country, which ended in a rout for his ragtag army at Sedgmoor – consolidated support for the crown. Several Whig peers were implicated: Henry Booth, 2nd Baron Delamer and Thomas Grey, 2nd earl of Stamford, were arrested. Grey of Warke, back from Germany, saved his life with a confession that was used (unsuccessfully) against Delamer and Charles Gerard, then styled Viscount Brandon (later 2nd earl

of Macclesfield). Monmouth himself, captured on 8th July, was executed a week later without a trial, under an act of attainder passed by Parliament in June.

Monmouth's defeat encouraged James to go ahead with his plans to overturn anti-Catholic legislation, and prepared the ground to do so when Parliament met again in November 1685. The earl of Huntingdon drafted a speech in support of the repeal of the 1678 Test Act which, he claimed, 'was a bill hurried into a law sent you by the then House of Commons to deprive your Lordships of the most essential point of peerage, limitations to your seats in Parliament, by imposing oaths and tests which [neither] we nor our fathers ever knew before'.[10] But opposition was already mobilising. Halifax tried to persuade Philip Stanhope, 2nd earl of Chesterfield, to attend the House, assuring him that even some previously obedient court lords were now willing to defend 'the strongest bulwarks of all that is left us'.[11] The first clash came over the commissions issued to Catholic army officers over the summer in direct contravention of the Test Act. A debate on the issue in the Lords on 19 November held in the king's presence probably led to James's decision to prorogue Parliament the following day. It was the king's final meeting with Parliament, although it was not formally dissolved for another two years.

Frustrated in achieving his aims through Parliament, James searched for another means of doing so. With the encouragement of his closest minister, Sunderland – the former exclusionist – he abandoned the Tories and the Church, and with them the Anglican loyalty and support that had been his inheritance. His Tory ministers, the Hyde brothers, Rochester and Henry Hyde, 2nd earl of Clarendon, were dismissed in early 1687. Catholic advisers became prominent in his inner counsels, including Henry Arundell, 3rd Baron Arundell of Wardour, John Belasyse, Baron Belasyse, and William Herbert, promoted from earl to marquess of Powis, three of the Catholic peers imprisoned during the Popish Plot, and James's close ally, the Irish Catholic Richard Talbot, Viscount Tyrconnell, who had also been implicated in the Popish Plot. James brooked little

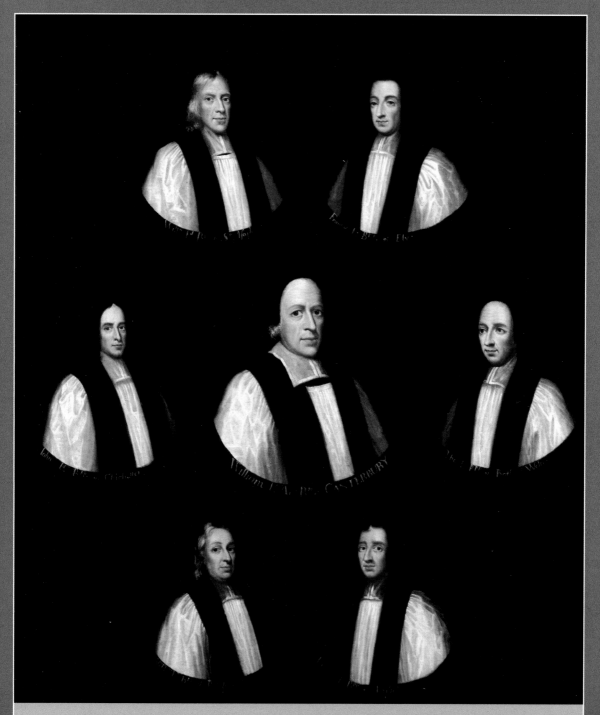

FIG. 62 *The seven bishops committed to the Tower in 1688, painted by an unknown artist: William Sancroft, archbishop of Canterbury in the middle, with clockwise from top right: Francis Turner, bishop of Ely; Thomas Ken, bishop of Bath and Wells; Jonathan Trelawny, bishop of Bristol; Thomas White, bishop of Peterborough; John Lake, bishop of Chichester; and William Lloyd, bishop of St Asaph.*

opposition. Bishop Henry Compton of London was suspended from office in 1686 for failing to stop anti-Catholic sermons; William Cavendish, 4th earl of Devonshire (one of the leaders of the debate on the Catholic officers in the Lords in 1685) was fined £30,000 for a minor breach of the peace. James's appointments to the episcopate of Thomas Cartwright (Chester) and Thomas Watson (St. David's) – 'scabby sheep' who had 'no reputation or interest, so they are despised by those they court' – evidenced his determination to browbeat the Church.[12] From late 1686 to mid 1687 James ran what became known as a 'closeting campaign', inviting members of both Houses into his private study at Whitehall to probe their attitudes and pressurise them into compliance. His first Declaration of Indulgence, issued on 4 April 1687, formally suspended the execution of the penalties for religious nonconformity. In July he dissolved Parliament, and began to make preparations for a new one which would, he hoped, repeal the Test Acts. In October he required the lords lieutenant to submit three questions to local office holders and gentlemen in order to identify those who would or would not support the repeal of anti-Catholic legislation. Those whose answers were deemed to be unsatisfactory were removed from their lieutenancies. Henry Howard, now 7th duke of Norfolk, wrote plaintively to his cousin Francis, 5th Baron Howard of Effingham, in Virginia, that 'you could never have found a more seasonable time to be where you are'.[13] A list compiled in May 1687 detailing the attitude of 161 peers recorded 85 among the opposition to James, 19 of uncertain designation, 22 Catholics or suspected Catholics and 35 Protestant peers who were either ministers or of such doubtful views that their opposition to the court was suspect.[14]

At the end of April 1688 James re-issued his Declaration, together with a statement of his resolve to call Parliament. When he ordered the clergy to read it to their congregations on two successive Sundays he precipitated a head-on collision with the Church. Actively supported by Clarendon, seven bishops – Sancroft (Canterbury), Lloyd (St Asaph), Turner (Ely), Ken (Bath & Wells), White (Peterborough), Trelawny (Bristol) and Lake (Chichester) – formally requested that the order be rescinded. They were arrested, imprisoned in the Tower and tried for seditious libel. Sunderland, who had tried strenuously to prevent it, attended the trial in June; he was kicked on the way in and threatened on the way out. Despite James's efforts to secure a complaisant bench of judges, on 30 June the bishops were acquitted. General public rejoicing underlined the isolation of king and court. But the birth of a son to the king and queen, earlier the same month, produced what was for most of the country a nightmarish vision of an entrenched Catholic monarchy. On the day that the bishops were acquitted, seven politicians sent an invitation to James's son in law, Prince William of Orange. It begged him to intervene.

Chapter 4

The Lords in Parliament

Writs of summons and disputed peerages

When, in the summer of 1665, the duke and duchess of York were travelling through Northamptonshire, one of those anxious for the honour of meeting and entertaining them was Nicholas Knollys. The Yorks had declined his invitation to breakfast; but when Knollys spotted their coach, he stopped it and repeated the invitation. A second refusal led him to clutch the duke's foot so hard 'he had almost drawn off his shoe.'[1] Knollys' persistence won the day; the royal couple agreed to a brief visit and were entertained with sweetmeats and fruit. His desperation to meet the king's brother and his wife was related to his campaign to prove that he was a member of the nobility, entitled to sit in the House of Lords. In the Convention Parliament Knollys had taken his seat as 3rd earl of Banbury. He had not, though, been summoned to the Cavalier Parliament that replaced it in May 1661.

Except in the unusual circumstances of the 1660 Convention, peers and bishops could not simply turn up to the House of Lords and expect to be admitted. They were supposed to receive a writ of summons, issued by the lord chancellor in the name of the crown. Writs were never refused to peers with a proper title; but nor were they issued automatically. Queen Anne's well-known antipathy to having her Hanoverian heirs in England meant that the future George II did not receive one after his creation as duke of Cambridge in 1706. When the Hanoverian envoy Baron Schutz demanded one on his behalf in April 1714, Lord Chancellor Harcourt tried to avoid giving him a response. When Schutz insisted, Harcourt 'told him the writ had never been denied, or to my knowledge, demanded.'[2] Other failures to issue a writ could be caused by ignorance. William Ley succeeded as 4th earl of Marlborough in June 1665, but did not receive a

FIG. 63 *This writ of summons (to attend Parliament on 19 May 1685) is puzzling. It is addressed to Thomas Petre, 6th Baron Petre, a Catholic who was barred from the House by the Test Act. Whether he was summoned as a matter of course or whether James II was hoping Catholic peers might be admitted is not known.*

writ of summons until March 1670, some six months after he drew attention to his existence (and his poverty) by petitioning for payment of arrears owed by the crown.

Such cases were unusual. The social world of the nobility was a small and intimate one and in most cases there was no difficulty in establishing who was the proper heir to a peerage. When Sir Dudley North became 4th Baron North in 1666, he sent his son Francis (later Baron Guilford) to make enquiries and discovered that the writ 'might be obtained of my lord chancellor … and he has taken order in it'.[3] In 1678 when William Howard succeeded as 3rd Baron Howard of Escrick he simply turned up at the door of the House and asked to be admitted. The House ordered a writ to be issued and Howard took his seat the next day. The speed with which writs of summons could be issued is remarkable and suggests that very little proof was required. The writ of summons to Robert Carey, 6th Baron Hunsdon, was issued on Saturday 26 May 1677, the very day that he inherited the title from his cousin; he attended the House the following Monday. In these cases it must have been easy to identify the rightful heir. A side effect of the abolition of the court of wards, though, was the removal of the centuries-old requirement for formal inquiries (known as inquisitions *post mortem*) into the ownership and descent of lands. As a result it became more difficult to keep track of aristocratic pedigrees. The heralds of the college of arms attempted and failed on at least two occasions to obtain a bill from Parliament for what was in effect an early form of civil registration. The 1678 bill required noble and gentry families to provide a sworn certificate of the death and burial of members of their families 'together with their respective marriages and issues and the respective ages of every one of them according to the several seniorities of such issues'.[4] Similar information was to be provided retrospectively for the previous twenty years. Peers objected to the invasion of their privileges inherent in the requirement that they take an oath before commoners, as well as the imposition of a new set of administrative fees and fines.

There were, inevitably, occasional disputes over the identity of the correct heir to a peerage. In such cases the lord chancellor could exercise his discretion and refuse to issue a writ of summons, leaving it open to the aggrieved individual to petition the crown for his writ. There was no fixed way in which such claims were resolved. They had once been referred to the court of chivalry, but that court had fallen into disuse and was not revived until 1687 (after a gap of nearly fifty years) by James II. It rarely sat thereafter. Claims had also been referred to the privy council or, when Parliament was in session, to the House of Lords. When Henry Mildmay and Robert Cheek both petitioned the crown in August 1660 to recognize them as Baron Fitzwalter, Charles II referred them to the House of Lords. The House never got round to formally hearing the claim during the Convention. After Henry Mildmay's death, his brother William renewed it, and it was again referred to the House. This time it was heard, but no decision was reached.[5] When Mildmay revived his petition in 1670, Parliament was no longer sitting. As a result, the case was eventually determined in the privy council.

The case of Nicholas Knollys, the man so determined to invite the duke of York to breakfast, and his heirs, was never satisfactorily resolved. Knollys received no writ of summons to the Cavalier Parliament because it was widely suspected that his real father was his mother's lover, not her husband. The House of Lords, to which his petition was referred in 1661, failed to take any decision on the subject, even though he made another attempt to ask for his writ in 1670. His son, Charles Knollys, made a third attempt in 1685; still no decision had been taken when, in 1692, he was indicted in the court of king's bench for murder after killing his brother-in-law in a duel. His claim to privilege of peerage was dismissed in the House of Lords by a narrow margin. The judges, however, ruled that Knollys *was* a peer and refused to try him. Since neither the House nor the ordinary courts would accept jurisdiction, Knollys escaped scot-free. Five years later Knollys again petitioned for a writ and the House returned to the case, questioning the lord chief justice, Sir John Holt, about his decision: Holt told them that 'he [ought] not to be questioned for his opinion in any cause that came before him in Westminster Hall'.[6] The House backed off, and there the case rested. According to one account Knollys

FIG. 64 *The peers who met in the House of Lords on 25 December 1688 asked William of Orange to send out circular letters for the calling of a Convention Parliament. A meeting of the members of the House of Commons in Charles II's last three Parliaments made the same request the following day. William agreed to do so on the 28th, and the circular was printed, and despatched the next day. Writs of summons were not sent, as in the absence of the king there was no authority to send them. This one is directed to Charles Talbot, earl (later duke) of Shrewsbury (see below, p. 212).*

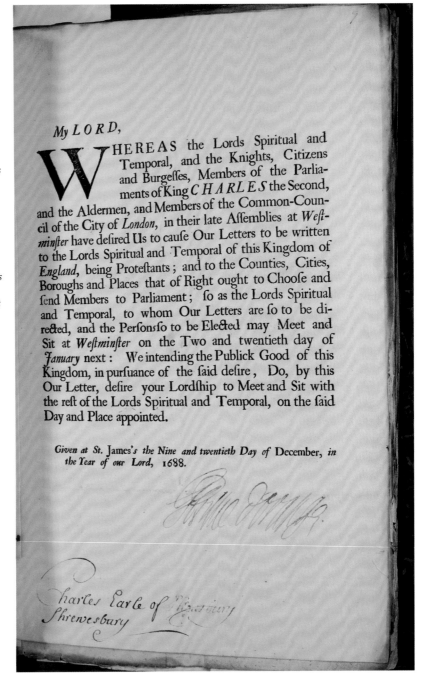

My *LORD*,

WHEREAS the Lords Spiritual and Temporal, and the Knights, Citizens and Burgeſſes, Members of the Parliaments of King *CHARLES* the Second, and the Aldermen, and Members of the Common-Council of the City of *London*, in their late Aſſemblies at *Weſtminſter* have deſired Us to cauſe Our Letters to be written to the Lords Spiritual and Temporal of this Kingdom of *England*, being Proteſtants; and to the Counties, Cities, Boroughs and Places that of Right ought to Chooſe and ſend Members to Parliament; ſo as the Lords Spiritual and Temporal, to whom Our Letters are ſo to be directed, and the Perſons ſo to be Elected may Meet and Sit at *Weſtminſter* on the Two and twentieth day of *January* next: We intending the Publick Good of this Kingdom, in purſuance of the ſaid deſire, Do, by this Our Letter, deſire your Lordſhip to Meet and Sit with the reſt of the Lords Spiritual and Temporal, on the ſaid Day and Place appointed.

Given at St. James's *the Nine and twentieth Day of* December, *in the Year of our Lord,* 1688.

Charles Earle of Shrewesbury

told Queen Anne that the solution was for her to make him a marquess. He complained that 'the hardship of having my place in Parliament undetermined, has been the chief source of my misfortune and hindrance of my preferment which if fairly represented to her Majesty might incline her to take me into her consideration'.[7] Knollys revived his petition for a writ of summons in 1712 but to no avail. His descendants were still pursuing the claim a century later.

Some heirs to peerages were summoned in their fathers' lifetimes by what was known as a writ of acceleration. It provided a convenient way for the government to secure the presence of younger, more active peers in the House. Issuing the writ was at the discretion of the crown. It naturally chose individuals who would bolster the government's support. The unwritten rules required the writ to be issued only in cases where the father held two or more peerage titles, one of them ranked at earl or above. A misunderstanding of these rules seems to have been behind the promotion in the peerage of Conyers Darcy in 1682. Conyers Darcy was both the 5th Baron Conyers and the 6th Baron Darcy. In 1680 his son, a loyal government supporter also named Conyers Darcy, was summoned to the House as Lord Conyers to boost support for the court at the height of the exclusion crisis. It was probably belated anxiety over the use of the writ that led to the promotion to an earldom (Holdernesse) of Conyers Darcy senior, who was 83 years old and had not attended the House since 1661.

Rules of membership

Not all peers were entitled to receive a writ of summons and sit in the House of Lords. By convention, a woman who was a peer in her own right could not take a seat in the House; nor could a peer who was under 21 years old, or at least very close to it. Occasional exceptions were made: James, duke of York, was only 10 when he was summoned in the extraordinary wartime circumstances of the Oxford Parliament in January 1644; Charles II's other younger brother, Henry, duke of Gloucester, took his seat in May 1660, aged 19. Robert Spencer, 2nd earl of Sunderland, was 20 when he took his seat a year later, apparently without controversy.

There was a row, though, when in 1667 Charles II summoned the 20 year old John Wilmot, 2nd earl of Rochester, who took his seat immediately, and shortly afterwards John Sheffield, 3rd earl of Mulgrave (later

'The soul of an old stubborn Roman': Denzil Holles, Baron Holles (1598–1680)

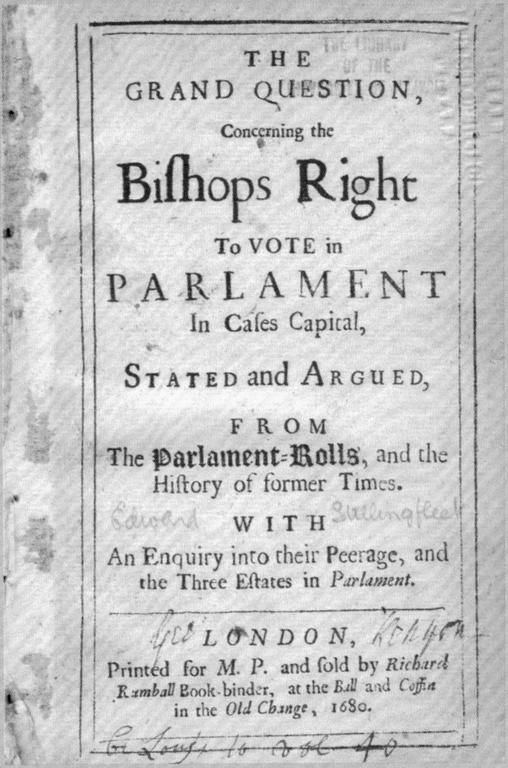
THE
GRAND QUESTION,
Concerning the
Bishops Right
To VOTE in
PARLAMENT
In Cases Capital,
STATED and ARGUED,
FROM
The Parlament-Rolls, and the
History of former Times.
WITH
An Enquiry into their Peerage, and
the Three Estates in *Parlament.*

LONDON,
Printed for M. P. and sold by *Richard Ramball* Book-binder, at the *Ball* and *Coffin* in the *Old Change*, 1680.

FIG. 65 *Holles was a prominent contributor to the debate on whether the bishops should be allowed to vote in the impeachment of the lord treasurer, Thomas Osborne, earl of Danby. He was answered in this pamphlet by Edward Stillingfleet, before he became a bishop (see below, p. 170), who argued that the bishops were bound to play a full role in civil affairs.*

As they struggled with Charles II over the exclusion from the throne of James, duke of York, the parliamentarians of 1679 had a tangible link to the parliamentary resistance to Charles I half a century before in the person of Denzil Holles, Baron Holles. First elected to the Commons in 1624, Holles was one of the men who had caused uproar in the chamber in 1629 as they held the Speaker in his chair while the House passed a series of motions critical of the government. Holles had been one of the five Members whom the king had attempted to arrest in 1642, and he had led the presbyterians in the late 1640s as they battled with the army for political control in the aftermath of the king's defeat.

In early 1660 Holles was among former parliamentarians who met at Suffolk House, the London residence of Algernon Percy, 4th earl of Northumberland, aiming to impose conditions on a Restoration. They failed, but Holles was respected enough by the new regime to be provided with a peerage in April 1661 and a prestigious post as ambassador to France (where he met his second wife, a wealthy Huguenot widow from Normandy). He returned to England in the autumn of 1667, and from thenceforward was one of the most active members of the House of Lords and one of the most vigorous defenders of its rights and privileges. He was at the forefront of the defence of the House's judicature in the case of *Skinner v. the East India Company* in 1668–9 (see above, p.24). He collected and published his research into medieval precedents, together with a strongly partisan case for the Lords' judicial rights to hear cases and appeals in the first instance, as *The grand question concerning the judicature of the House of Peers stated and argued*. The king and his ministers were not happy with the attempt to keep the controversy going, and the council ordered copies of the anonymous and unlicensed book to be seized. For the first week of the following session the Commons, too, spent an inordinate amount of time trying to ascertain the author.

Although he had supported the re-establishment of an episcopal Church of England, Holles was profoundly opposed to one that excluded Presbyterians or persecuted moderate nonconformists. At least part of his purpose in publishing *The grand question*, and his later discussions of the subject in 1675, was to stoke up a dispute which he hoped would prevent the passage of the bill against nonconformist conventicles, force the dissolution of the Cavalier Parliament, and ensure its replacement with a body that would produce a more moderate settlement of the Church. During the 1670s he was one of the principal opponents of the Catholic James, duke of York, of the 'Anglican' policies of Thomas Osborne, earl of Danby and of Charles II's alliance with Louis XIV. From 1674 his house in Covent Garden had become the central meeting place for his colleagues Anthony Ashley Cooper, earl of Shaftesbury, George Villiers, 2nd duke of Buckingham, George Savile, Viscount Halifax and others to plan their campaigns against Danby's test bill and for the dissolution of Parliament

after the fifteen-month prorogation in 1675–77 (see above, p. 77). Holles was widely regarded as the author of three anonymous pamphlets arguing that the long prorogation had automatically resulted in dissolution.

Holles, though, stood slightly apart from his colleagues. In 1678 and 1679 he was seen by the French ambassador Barillon as the leader of a group of presbyterians on whose behalf he negotiated, independently of Shaftesbury, with Danby and the French to overcome the political crisis. In early January 1679 Holles was in contact with Danby via the court physician and patron of nonconformists Sir John Baber, and Danby himself turned up at Holles's house late one night to thrash out the details of a deal. The lord treasurer agreed that he would convince the king to disband the army, dissolve Parliament, summon a new one and make a formal declaration that no Parliament in the future would last for less than six months nor longer than three years, in exchange for supply in the new Parliament. Holles's ally Roger Morrice recorded the details of these negotiations in his 'Ent'ring book' in secretive shorthand, noting that this business 'was carried on and transacted solely by his Majesty, the lord treasurer, the Lord Holles, Sir John Baber and Sir Thomas Littleton and Mr Morrice was privy to it all

FIG. 66 *The funeral monument for Holles, in St Peter's church, Dorchester, Dorset.*

along from the beginning to the end and no man else'.[1] Morrice did not know, however, that Holles also kept the French ambassador, Barillon, informed of the negotiations.

The deal failed to stick in the increasingly polarized atmosphere of the 1679 Parliament, and Holles found himself alone among the opposition in defending Danby. Nevertheless, even as late as December 1679 Barrillon still felt that Holles, then turned 81, was 'the one man in all England for whom all the different cabals have a great regard'.[2] Holles died in February 1680, and was buried in Dorchester in a ceremony in which, as Morrice reported, 'as great respects and honour [were] paid to his memory by the town and country as hath ever been known, and more coaches and horsemen attended his corpse out of the city than (as it's said) has ever been seen'.[3] Another ally, Gilbert Burnet, later sketched the character of his friend: 'He had the soul of an old stubborn Roman in him. He was a faithful but rough friend, and a severe but fair enemy.'[4]

131

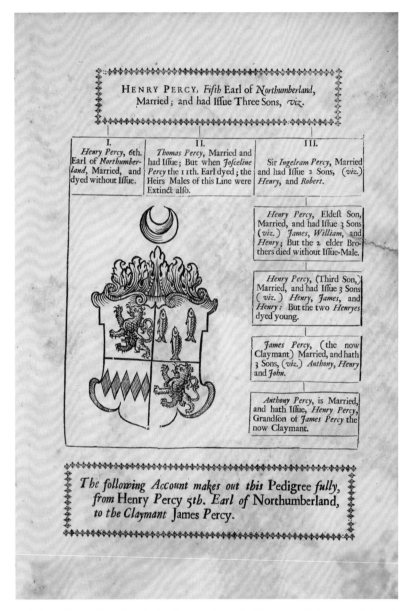

FIG. 67 *The earldom of Northumberland was extinguished by the death in 1670 of the 5th earl, Joceline Percy, without male heirs. The claim subsequently advanced by James Percy (1619–c1690), a modestly affluent trunkmaker, was dismissed by the Lords in 1673. Undeterred, Percy devoted the rest of his life to fighting a claim that most people considered to be groundless, if not downright risible: this pamphlet represents another attempt, of 1685. On 11 June 1689 the House declared his claim to be 'groundless, false, and scandalous' and ordered the old man to appear in Westminster Hall wearing a paper describing him as the 'false and impudent pretender to the earldom of Northumberland'. Whether it was ever carried out is as yet unknown.*

duke of Buckingham and Normanby). Mulgrave was barely 19. A motion that the king should 'be sparing of writs of this nature for the future' was immediately referred to the committee for privileges.[8] The king sent a message saying that he 'did not know that the earl of Mulgrave was much under age; and therefore did grant him his writ of summons to Parliament: and now, having granted such a writ unto him, his majesty desires that he may be admitted to sit in Parliament' and assuring the House that 'he will be careful to prevent any inconveniencies of the like nature that may be for the future.'[9] It was no coincidence that the two young men had been summoned just as the enemies of the recently dismissed lord chancellor, Edward Hyde, earl of Clarendon, were finding their plans for his impeachment obstructed in the House of Lords. The subsequent discussions in the committee for privileges chaired by one of Clarendon's enemies, George Villiers, 2nd duke of Buckingham, concentrated on the question of whether the involvement of minors in the judicial activities of the House – such as impeachment – might make any judgment invalid. In December the House agreed that 'minors ought not to sit nor vote in parliament'.[10] Mulgrave tactfully waited two years before taking his seat. In 1670 Christopher Monck, aged 16, succeeded his father as 2nd duke of Albemarle. Having already spent three years in the Commons as knight of the shire for Devon, he now found himself barred from both Houses: from the Commons because he was a peer, and from the Lords because he was a minor. He finally took his seat in 1675. It was a further ten years before the convention on underage peers was made into a standing order, the result, probably, of a further attempt by a group of peers, including James Butler, Baron Butler of Moore Park (the future 2nd duke of Ormond), to take their seats before reaching their majority.

Two English peerages created before 1660 did not confer the right to sit in the Lords, possibly because the recipients were foreigners. James Hay (later earl of Carlisle), born in Scotland but naturalised in 1604, was created Lord Hay in 1606, but was not entitled to sit in the House until he received a second English peerage in 1615; the patent for the Dutchman Johan van Reede's creation as Baron Reede (1645) omits the usual formula about sitting in Parliament so presumably neither he, nor his grandson Frederik, 2nd Baron Reede, who succeeded in 1682, would have been able to take their seats in the House even if they had wished to (both were resident abroad). Nevertheless, after the Restoration a handful of foreigners, including James Butler, the Irish duke of Ormond, James Maitland,

'The subtillest, workingest villain that is on the face of the earth': Robert Spencer, 2nd earl of Sunderland (1641–1702)

The first earl of Sunderland was killed in 1643 at the siege of Gloucester, two months after he had received the title. His tortured decision at the beginning of the Civil War to throw in his lot with the king betrayed the complexity of his political views. His son, only two years old at his father's death, was less tortured, but just as complex. His family and political connections were politically eclectic. He married into the Catholic Digby family (though his wife became a firm and pious Anglican); he was related by marriage to the future Whig leader, Anthony Ashley Cooper, earl of Shaftesbury, and to the 'trimmer', George Savile, marquess of Halifax; he served his political apprenticeship with the leader of the Anglican royalist revival of the mid-1670s, Thomas Osborne, earl of Danby. Sunderland grew up with a gambling habit and a keen sense of fine things: but what he was mainly interested in was power and government.

Sunderland's careful cultivation in the late 1670s of the king's mistress, Louise de Kéroualle, duchess of Portsmouth, helped him to capitalize on the fall of his patron, Danby, and the Popish Plot crisis. Brought into government as one of the secretaries of state in 1679, Sunderland used his connections to try to negotiate with Danby's enemies. He succeeded in bringing his brother-in-law, Halifax, back to court (with whom he was otherwise on permanently poor terms) and was even poised to reintroduce Shaftesbury to favour. Convinced that Charles II would have to give way on the exclusion from the throne of James, duke of York, and that the only viable alternative was James's son-in-law, William, Prince of Orange, in the dramatic Lords debate of 15 November 1680 Sunderland chose to vote for exclusion. It was as difficult a decision as his father's, nearly forty years before. The personal consequences, if not fatal, appeared to have wrecked his career. His wife wrote that 'the king acts as if he were mad. The bill was yesterday cast out of the Lords' House, and [Sunderland] is in great disgrace for giving his vote for the bill … I have no more to say but that Lord Sunderland has gained immortal fame, which is better than anything he can lose'.[1] Sunderland's mother, the dowager countess, was less sympathetic: 'it cannot be as I would have it so long as my son is well with Lord Shaftesbury.'[2] Sunderland, 'as ill with the king as it is possible',[3] was put out of office.

Extraordinarily, within two years he was back, and reappointed to the secretaryship, thanks in part to Portsmouth's interposition.[4] Even more surprisingly, he survived the accession of James II, adroitly outmanoeuvring the Hyde brothers by forging alliances with James's Irish ally Richard Talbot, Viscount Tyrconnel in the Irish peerage, and moderate Catholics at court. For the next three years, Sunderland was deeply implicated in the development of James's pro-Catholic policies, although he struggled to keep the expectations of the king and his more zealous advisers in touch with reality. On the birth of an heir to the throne in June 1688, Sunderland took the plunge and firmly identified with the regime by converting to Rome. It reduced his countess, who first heard about it from her brother, to tears: she retired to their house at Althorp in Northamptonshire to pray for his return to his religion and his senses. No-one (save possibly James II) was convinced by it: Gilbert Burnet wrote that it 'looked too like a man who, having no religion, took up one rather to serve a turn, than that he was truly changed'.[5] Like his vote on exclusion, it was another career-ending mistake. Over the next three months James's regime imploded. Sunderland, under severe stress himself, desperately advised the king to reverse all of his policies of the past three years. On 29 October, a few days before the Prince of Orange landed in Devon, the king sacked him. Some time in the middle of December he took flight for Rotterdam.

Sunderland's justification of his actions under the previous regime was brought back to London by his countess and printed as *The earl of Sunderland's letter to a friend in London*. Received as a cynical piece of propaganda, it did him little good. A period of exile was inevitable: his political asylum in the Netherlands, with the agreement of William III, owed much to his wife's tireless advocacy. His return to England in 1690 owed more to the king's memory of how Sunderland had advanced him as an alternative

FIG. 68 *This unusual portrait of Sunderland from the collection at Althorp was painted by the Roman artist, Carlo Maratta, during his visit to Rome in 1664. The piece of masonry on which he leans features a bas-relief sculpture of 'love conquering time'. The reference is to Sunderland's engagement to Lady Anne Digby, the daughter of George Digby, 2nd earl of Bristol, arranged in 1663: Sunderland broke off the engagement in a panic in June that year, probably a reaction to her father's loss of royal favour which ended in his misconceived effort to impeach the earl of Clarendon. The match was renewed, however, on his return.*

to James back in 1680. He began a third career as the king's unofficial adviser 'behind the curtain', negotiator and power broker, the king's eyes and ears. 'The subtillest, workingest villain that is on the face of the earth', as the then Princess Anne wrote in 1688,[6] he was still loathed by many contemporaries for the way he had seemed to cling to power by his fingertips; they were also irritated by his characteristic drawl and sneering manner. He only briefly, and very reluctantly,

held formal office again for a few months in 1697, as lord chamberlain. But Sunderland, perhaps because he virtually ruled himself out of a formal political role, was the one man capable of bringing and holding together the complicated coalitions of men that government in the 1690s required, and one of the few men whose advice William regarded as untainted by party or personal interest.

the Scots earl of Lauderdale, and the Frenchman, Louis de Duras (Baron Duras) received English peerages and sat in the House of Lords, and William III, to the considerable annoyance of his new subjects, conferred English peerages on several of his Dutch favourites and, less controversially, turned Prince George of Denmark into the duke of Cumberland. His actions were so unpopular that a clause was added to the Act of Settlement of 1701 to prevent the Hanoverians from doing the same thing. After the death of Anne, no one, apart from royal dukes, born outside the British Isles or in a crown colony, unless to English parents, would be permitted to sit in either House.

Far more significant was the exclusion of peers through the administration of oaths. In 1606, in the aftermath of the gunpowder plot, a new oath of allegiance was devised in an attempt to identify Catholic opponents of the crown. It forced Catholics to distinguish between their civil obligation to obey the king and their religious obligation to obey the Pope. After the assassination of Henry IV of France in May 1610 the king made it clear that he expected the peers to take the oath. In 1626 the House itself passed a standing order requiring its members to take the oath once in every parliament. Many Catholics complied. Despite this, very shortly after the king was restored, in June 1660, an order requiring members to take the oath of allegiance was referred to the committee for privileges, which discussed whether a peer could be deprived of his inherent right to be summoned to Parliament.[11] In subsequent years the House occasionally imposed the oath, but it never threatened to expel those who did not take it. In 1673, however, spurred by renewed fears of Catholic subversion and the revelation that James, duke of York had converted to Rome, Parliament passed a statute (the first Test Act) requiring all office holders to take the oaths of allegiance and supremacy (see above, p. 42). The act also imposed on them a declaration against transubstantiation and a requirement to take the Anglican sacrament – conditions that were impossible for Catholics to accept. Though it resulted in the resignation of the duke of York and Thomas Clifford, Baron Clifford from their offices, it did not affect membership of the House.

It was not long before an attempt was made to impose the same requirement on Members of the House of Lords. In 1675 a bill to prevent dangers from 'disaffected persons' which provided for the imposition of a religious test – an oath not to endeavour any alteration of the government in Church or State – on the Members of both Houses, was promoted as part of the earl of Danby's bid to form a close political association with the Church of England and its supporters. It was bitterly resisted in the Lords by 'country' peers, who recognized it as a scheme to remove permanently the supporters of dissent from the House, as well as a direct assault on peers' birthright and their freedom of speech. On 30 April 1675 after a fierce debate in a committee of the whole House acceptance of the bill was accompanied by an order that 'no oath shall be imposed by any bill, or otherwise, upon the peers, with a penalty in case of refusal, to lose their places and votes in parliament', although, as was pointed out in a protest by a number of peers a few days later, it was negated by the House's subsequent acceptance of key elements of the bill.[12] Its opponents succeeded in stifling it by diverting attention to a privilege dispute between the Houses over the case of *Sherley v. Fagg*.

Three years later, at the height of panic about the Popish Plot, the House accepted a bill that would exclude those who would not take the oaths of allegiance and supremacy and the declaration against transubstantiation. It effectively excluded all Catholics, although an exception was made for the duke of York himself (see above, p. 116). Most Catholics left the House, though a few, such as Thomas Parker, 14th Baron Morley, took the oaths and remained. Morley continued to sit in the House until his death in 1697. His motive was almost certainly financial (see below, p. 179). Another Catholic who deserted the faith was Henry Howard, the future 7th duke of Norfolk, who sat in the Lords as Lord Mowbray: although he withdrew from Parliament with the other Catholic peers on 30 November 1678, six months later he changed his mind and took the Anglican sacraments. A variety of appointments to important local offices soon followed.

The oath of allegiance was revised after the Revolution of 1689 and the acceptance of the throne at Parliament's request by William and Mary. No issue was more sensitive to Tories who had reluctantly accepted the effective deposition and replacement of the king. The new oaths were carefully framed to avoid referring to the new king and queen as lawful and rightful monarchs; instead they simply required a commitment to bear true allegiance to them. Most found it possible to comply. A small number – the non-jurors – refused. Prominent among the handful of lay non-jurors was James II's former brother in law, the 2nd earl of Clarendon. There were many more bishops, who were, eventually, deprived of both their places in Parliament, and their bishoprics (see below, p. 152).

FIG. 69 *High spirited, spoiled and extravagant, the erratic behaviour of James Hamilton, 4th duke of Hamilton in the Scottish peerage was a trial both to his family and to his political followers. His Jacobite sympathies and opposition to the Union of England and Scotland underwent a drastic about turn in 1708 when he defected to the Whigs. He turned his coat again in 1710 and joined the Tories. His involvement in the long-running series of law suits over the Macclesfield inheritance led in 1712 to a duel with Charles Mohun, 4th Baron Mohun in which both men died (see below, pp. 182, 294-5).*

The Scottish peers

The Act of Union of 1707 merged the English and the Scottish peerages into the peerage of Great Britain. It was not a merger of equals. In terms of precedence, Scots peers were placed below English ones of the same rank, and only 16 of them, elected by their fellow Scots peers to serve for the life of each parliament, were to sit in the House of Lords. The relevant clauses in the Act of Union were carefully drawn to ensure that the elections would not become a focus for Jacobite unrest. They were much less clear about the procedures to be followed. Given the complicated intrigues in Scotland surrounding the passage of the Union treaty, and the recriminations which followed it, disputes over the results were inevitable, the first of which resulted in a decision in January 1709 that peers of Scotland who became peers of Great Britain after the Union could not vote in elections for Scottish representative peers (see below, p. 295).

Of more concern to English peers was the possibility that a large number of Scots peers would become British peers. Scots peers, generally far poorer than English ones, were believed to be susceptible to corruption by unscrupulous ministers, and the English constantly suspected the existence of plans to expand their numbers. Their fears were confirmed when in 1711 it was rumoured that the duke of Hamilton would be granted a British peerage as duke of Brandon. The vehemence of the reaction took ministers by surprise: there had been no objection raised to the dukedom earlier given to Queensberry, only to his participation in the elections in 1708; moreover, it was acknowledged to be entirely within the prerogative of the crown to confer British titles on those who already held either Scots or English peerages (although the queen's presence in the Lords when Hamilton's peerage was debated suggests that she thought her rights were being impugned). The opponents of the Hamilton peerage stressed that 'nobody could deny but the queen might create him duke of Brandon', but they claimed that the terms of the Act of Union precluded any Scots peers sitting and voting in the House except for the sixteen representative peers.[13] The House resolved 'that no patent of honour granted to any peer of Great Britain, who was peer of Scotland at the time of the Union, can entitle such peer to sit and vote in parliament, or to sit upon the trial of peers'.[14] Within weeks of the resolution, there was talk of abandoning the representative election system for a permanent Scottish nobility with the right to sit in the upper House – that 'out of the 116 or 120 Scots peers,

FIG. 70 (OPPOSITE)
Thomas Sprat,
bishop of Rochester
(1635–1713), with
his son, the
archdeacon of
Rochester,
mezzotint by John
Smith after Michael
Dahl, 1712. Sprat,
associated with
John Wilkins (see
above, p. 66) was
chaplain to George
Villiers, 2nd duke of
Buckingham and
appointed as
one of the trustees
to oversee the
payments of
Buckingham's
enormous debts.
He became a
leading
propagandist for
the crown, and
enjoyed extensive
favour, culminating
in appointment as
bishop of Rochester
in 1684. He
continued to find
favour under James
II, although as the
king's pro-Catholic
policies became
more pronounced,
his support was
increasingly
equivocal. At the
Revolution he
advocated a
regency, rather
than a change of
monarch. For the
rest of his life he
was under constant
suspicion as a
Jacobite agent.

30 of their number or so, should be pitched upon, and set up as the sole peers in Scotland.'[15] Although nothing came of these proposals in 1712, similar ones would eventually come before the House in the form of the 1719 peerage bill (see below, p. 342-3).

The lords spiritual

The bishops – the 'lords spiritual' – were summoned to sit in the House of Lords in the same way as their secular counterparts – the 'lords temporal' – although they were not peers. They owed their positions, and their places in the Lords, not to inheritance or creation, but to appointment by the crown. Bishoprics were the highest preferments in the Church and were much sought after by prominent and well-connected clergymen. As they had important roles in the administration of the Church, and, in many places, influence in local affairs and municipal elections, they were of great importance in ecclesiastical and secular government alike; and because they formed a phalanx of 26 votes within the Lords, they were of great interest to any faction, including the court, anxious to dominate the upper House for whatever purpose. Episcopal nominations provided one of the most bitterly fought political battlegrounds in the struggle to control policy towards the Church and nonconformity.

The bishops had been excluded from the House of Lords by an act of parliament passed in 1642, and in 1646 episcopacy itself had been abolished by a parliamentary ordinance. Although the royal court did not recognise the validity of the ordinance, no episcopal appointments had been made since 1644 and by 1660 17 of the 26 bishoprics were vacant. The appointment of bishops to most of these vacancies between August and November 1660, organised by the king and his lord chancellor, Edward Hyde (shortly afterwards made earl of Clarendon), was an indication of the likely direction of the settlement of the Church. Key appointments of politically effective clergymen who were set on a thorough re-establishment of the Church were George Morley (Worcester), Humphrey Henchman (Salisbury) and Gilbert Sheldon (London). In an attempt to draw Presbyterians into the episcopate, three of them were offered bishoprics, although only Edward Reynolds (Norwich) accepted.

As with all appointments, personal connection was of critical importance in securing an episcopate. Nicholas Monck of Hereford and Alexander Hyde of Salisbury were both thought to owe their elevations

to their kinsmen (the duke of Albemarle and the earl of Clarendon). Links
to the right people at court could even overcome otherwise disadvant-
ageous personal qualities. Henry Glemham of St Asaph was great-uncle
to Lady Castlemaine, one of the king's more powerful mistresses; Samuel
Pepys professed astonishment that she had used her influence to make a
bishop of 'a drunken, swearing rascal and a scandal to the Church'.[16]
William Talbot, elevated in 1699, was related to Charles Talbot, duke of
Shrewsbury, although his candidacy was assisted by his thoroughly
Whiggish allegiances. Marriage to the daughter of Thomas Osborne, duke

The bishops restored

t the Restoration, there were a mere nine bishops left of the pre-Civil War episcopate. No new bishops had been created since 1644. The survivors, deprived of their episcopal pomp, had managed through the Interregnum on private incomes or the kindness of others. They included the 71-year-old Brian Duppa, a bishop since 1638. Duppa had survived 'as the tortoise doth, by not going out of [his] shell', relishing in correspondence with his friend Sir Giles Isham, if not poverty, the idea of living like one of the early Christians. To Duppa, the Restoration was a miracle. He told Isham that he was in 'in such a dream as David mentions when God turned away the captivity of Sion' at the extraordinary reversal of fortune.[1] Translated to Winchester after the Restoration, he enthusiastically presided over a cultural revolution in the worship of the court. It was too much for some observers: Samuel Pepys complained about Duppa's 'overdone' ceremonies.[2] But the formidable task of re-establishing the Church in his diocese left Duppa overwhelmed with 'multiplicity of business' and 'wea-

ried out with impertinencies'.[3] Nevertheless he earned £50,000 by renegotiating leases in his dioceses before he died in 1662. He was visited on his deathbed by Charles II, who knelt for his blessing, and his body lay in state for four weeks at York House in London before he was given a solemn funeral.

John Warner, at 79, was Duppa's senior. Also a bishop since 1638, he had been a firm favourite of Charles I. He was less popular with the Restoration establishment. 'Wily Warner of Rochester'[4] had narrowly escaped impeachment in 1641 and had strenu-

FIG. 71 (OPPOSITE) *John Gauden, bishop of Worcester, published this tract celebrating the readmission of the bishops to the House of Lords in 1661. The pillar represents gratitude, a traditional Christian virtue. It stands on a plinth decorated with figures symbolising the Church, knightly or perhaps noble virtues, and workers on land and sea; it also carries words celebrating the return of the rule of law under God. The pillar itself honours king and parliament for instigating the benefits conferred by the return of episcopacy and is surmounted by three crowns representing the three kingdoms of the British Isles. The woodcuts on the title page refer, on the left, to the Old Testament story in which Aaron's rod miraculously budded as a token against rebels and, on the right, to the New Testament story of the fig tree cursed by Jesus and rendered barren. Further scriptural references are placed below including a reference to Christ's healing of the ten lepers: 'When he saw them he said to them "Go show yourselves to the priests" and as they went they were cleansed' (Luke 17.14).*

ously resisted the exclusion of the bishops from the Lords, defending 'the antiquity and justice of the bishops' votes in parliament'.[5] He spent a nomadic existence during the Interregnum, and was quick at the Restoration to petition the House of Lords for the restoration of his episcopal income.[6] Unlike Duppa, he was not translated to a more lucrative see. Smarting from a sense of injustice, that he was 'utterly forgotten in all',[7] he refused to petition for promotion at the age of 80, when he was 'going out of this world,'[8] but took up where he had left off, his sermons as feisty and partisan as before the civil wars. He grumbled continually about the task of restoration: since the bishops' power had been 'utterly taken away' it was 'no marvel...that the bishop hath work enough to set all in order'.[9] By the time of his death in 1666 he was said to have recovered his financial position 'chiefly by his narrow manner of life' and he bequeathed in excess of £18,000.[10]

These 'leftover' bishops were augmented over the summer and autumn of 1660 by new consecrations. Among them was Brian Walton, a target for the opponents of the pre-Civil War episcopate because of his 'unquiet and unpeaceable carriage', and his 'lowly incurvation and bowing towards the altar'.[11] Accused of bringing Catholic practices into the Church, he had been deprived of his livings in 1642. In forced retirement, Walton began work on his celebrated Polyglot Bible, remarkably supported by Cromwell, who allowed the paper for printing to be imported duty-free. It was not merely an achievement of scholarship, but physically impressive. When one reader's bookshelves holding the Polyglot collapsed over his head, he confessed it 'a wonder' that the weight 'had not beaten out [his] brains'.[12] In 1660, in recognition of his 'virtues...sufferings, and indefatigable industry', Walton was elevated to Chester. The *Public Intelligence* reported that on his arrival in his see 'many thousands' conducted Walton to his palace, and he was saluted with 'several volleys of shot'. The ensuing cathedral service was followed by a secular entertainment. Walton was 'highly caressed and entertained' by the local gentry and nobility; but the celebrations were marred by the 'rascally faction and crop-eared

BRIANVS WALTONVS. S.T.D. CANTAB.COLL.S PET
E CLEVELANDIA IN COMITAT. EBORAC
BIBLIA POLYGLOTTA INCHOAVIT A: DOM.
LIII. ABSOLVIT A: M.DCLVII. A: ÆTATIS SVÆ. LVII.

whelps … who did their endeavours to make it a maygame and a piece of foppery'. Walton had sat in the Lords for only three days when he died on 29 November 1661, and was 'attended to his grave by three heralds of arms in their formalities'. Despite his early death, he had helped to shape the style, policies and prejudices of the re-established Church which, his epitaph claimed, he had purified from the 'foul… aspersions cast upon her pure and spotless innocence by those illiterate and clergy-trampling schismatics'.[13]

FIG. 72 *Brian Walton's massive Polyglot Bible, published in 1657, set new standards in biblical criticism. Nine languages were used in the work which was not only a great intellectual achievement but also a commercial success.*

of Leeds, was similarly essential in the elevation of Philip Bisse to Hereford (see p. 154).

Episcopal appointments were also related to moves in the political and factional struggles for control of the Church and ecclesiastical policy. The elevation in 1667 to Exeter of Anthony Sparrow (see below, p. 316) enabled Gilbert Sheldon, by then archbishop of Canterbury, to assert episcopal control over a see where Sparrow's predecessor, Seth Ward, and successive local magnates had done little to combat the growth of non-conformity. The change of political and religious direction at court after the fall of Clarendon in 1667 was signalled by the elevation two years later of John Wilkins, one of the key thinkers behind comprehension schemes (see above, p. 66), whilst the emergence of a political reaction against nonconformity and towards the Church in the 1680s was mirrored in appointments like that of Laurence Womock, one of the most out-spoken Anglican propagandists. The manipulation of episcopal appoint-ments for political purposes was even more obvious during the reign of James II, when a commitment to toleration and passive obedience seemed to be the only qualification necessary for preferment.

After 1688 it was a Tory, the devout Anglican secretary of state, Daniel Finch, 2nd earl of Nottingham, who had the greatest initial influ-ence in moulding the post-Revolution episcopate. The episcopate lost a cohort of Tories through the defection of the non-jurors, and Nottingham's replacements were a politically balanced group, ranging from the radical Whig John Tillotson (Canterbury) to the conservative Edward Stillingfleet (Worcester). William III's bishops were remarkably flexible in their party affiliation. John Moore, bishop of Norwich from 1691, for example, often perceived as moving towards the Whig camp, is more accurately described as politically independent.

When they took a personal interest, monarchs were a decisive fac-tor in appointments. Tillotson, promoted from dean to archbishop of Canterbury in place of the non-juror Sancroft in May 1691, was a favourite with the new king and queen, and became a key member of the Orange propaganda machine. In the reign of Queen Anne, however, when episcopal appointments were placed in the pot of the complex negotia-tions required to maintain the support of the Junto Whigs for the admin-istration of the duumvirs, Godolphin and Marlborough, the queen's insistence on the appointment of the Tory Offspring Blackall to the bish-opric of Exeter sparked a political crisis in 1707 (see below, p. 288). After

FIG. 73 (OPPOSITE)
Although he became a conforming Anglican clergyman, John Tillotson (1630–94, archbishop of Canterbury from 1691 to his death) had been brought up in a dissenting household, and retained a life-long sympathy for those Protestants who remained outside the Anglican church. His sermons were renowned for their simple and direct style – an effect achieved through considerable effort and much re-writing. They were published and re-published long after his death and became a staple of eighteenth century libraries.

the formation of a Tory ministry in 1710, however, episcopal appointments swung towards the Tories with the appointment in 1713 of Adam Ottley to St. David's and Francis Atterbury, the acknowledged leader of the highflying Tory clerics, to Rochester in the same year.

Ceasing to be a Member

There were medieval precedents for disclaiming English peerages, but by the mid-seventeenth century the practice was frowned upon. In 1639 Charles I forced Roger Stafford to surrender the barony of Stafford on the grounds that he was too poor to sustain the dignity and regranted it to William Howard, with its original precedence among the barons. There was an outcry, which the king sidestepped by promoting Howard to a viscountcy. As a result of the case, in 1640 the House added a statement about the inalienability of peerage honours to its decision on another peerage claim. It confirmed this in 1678 after considering the complicated case of Robert Wright, also known as Robert Howard, Danvers or Villiers. When Wright had succeeded as Viscount Purbeck in 1658 he disclaimed the peerage, claiming that he was unable to support the dignity. Like Nicholas Knollys, however, his true paternity was in doubt. In July 1660 he paid a substantial fine to the crown in order to confirm the disclaimer, and the issue was never discussed in the House in his lifetime. In 1678, when his son, Robert Villiers, attained his majority, he petitioned for a writ of summons, alleging that his father had no right to renounce the peerage. The committee of privileges agreed and the House resolved 'That no fine now levied to the king, can bar such title of honour, or the right of any person claiming such title under him that levied or shall levy such fine.'[17] As far as Villiers was concerned the practical effect of the decision was nullified by the House's refusal to entertain his claim because of his father's alleged illegitimacy (which may have been influenced by the fear that a decision in his favour would have allowed him to inherit what was left of the estates of George Villiers, 2nd duke of Buckingham, and his lesser title as earl of Buckingham). No writ of summons was ever issued to Villiers or to his heirs.

In Scotland before the Union, it had been possible for Scots peers to resign their peerages. The duke of Queensberry himself did so in 1706 in order to ensure the transmission of his honours to his second surviving son, Charles, rather than his eldest, mentally incapacitated son, James

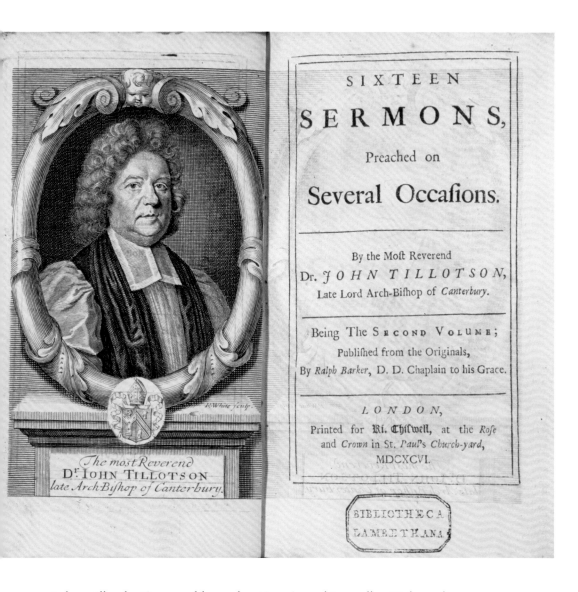

SIXTEEN

SERMONS,

Preached on

Several Occasions.

By the Most Reverend
Dr. *JOHN TILLOTSON*,
Late Lord Arch-Bishop of *Canterbury*.

Being The Second Volume;
Published from the Originals,
By *Ralph Barker*, D. D. Chaplain to his Grace.

LONDON,
Printed for Ri. Chiswell, at the *Rose*
and *Crown* in St. *Paul's Church-yard*,
MDCXCVI.

The most Reverend
Dr IOHN TILLOTSON
late Arch-Bishop of Canterbury.

(who, still only 10 years old, was kept imprisoned in a cell at Holyrood). After the Union, however, the practice was ended, to the dismay of Thomas Hay, 7th earl of Kinnoull, in 1711, who persuaded the young James Drummond, 3rd viscount of Strathallan, dying of consumption, to renounce his peerage on his deathbed to enable it to be regranted to his own second son, who was set to inherit Strathallan's estates, but not his title.

Effectively therefore there were only two ways for a peer to be

FIG. 74
John Lake, bishop of Chichester (1624–89) was one of the seven bishops prosecuted by James II. Despite his opposition to James II's policies he became a non-juror after the Revolution of 1688. His sudden death just a year later meant that he escaped actual deprivation.

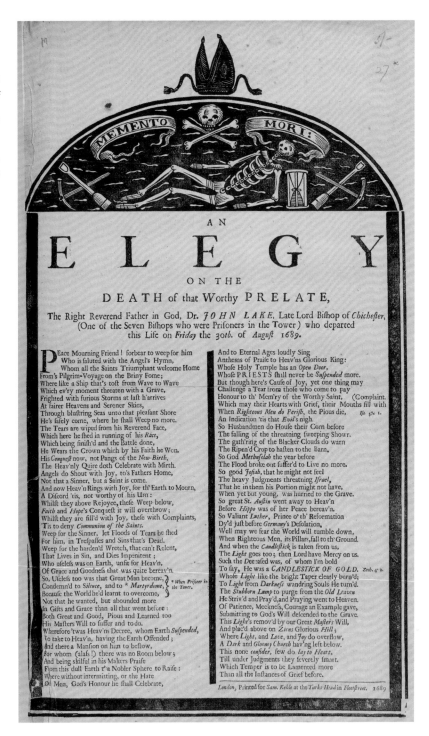

FIG. 75 *Another of the seven bishops who became a non-juror, Thomas White, bishop of Peterborough (1628–98), was suspended from his see in August 1689 and subsequently deprived. He attended Sir John Fenwick (see below, p. 216) to the scaffold. This piece of silver jewellery, containing a coloured engraving of White, shows how some held the non-jurors in veneration.*

divested of membership: death, or attainder. On a peer's death the peerage would pass as a matter of course to the heir (if there were one). A conviction for treason or an act of attainder barred not only the individual from his title and right to a seat in the House, but also his successors. Attainders could be reversed. Thomas Wentworth, earl of Strafford, was attainted and executed in May 1641, but his titles were recreated for his son, William Wentworth, the following December. When in May 1662 Parliament reversed the attainder, Wentworth inherited his father's peerages and regained the precedency that attached to the original creations rather than to the creations of 1641. Worries about the effect of attainder influenced the drafting of the letters patent creating the dukedom of Bedford in 1694. These included a special remainder to safeguard its descent to the duke's grandson, Wriothesley Russell, son of William, Lord Russell, who had been executed for his part in the Rye House Plot. Without the special remainder it could have been held that the dukedom should pass to Lord Russell's younger brother rather than to his son. Scottish peerage law, in this respect slightly different to that in England, was brought into line with it following the Union.

Bishops, as they were members of the House only by virtue of their office, lost their places in Parliament if they were deprived of their office.

A non-juring bishop:
Thomas Ken (1637–1711)

Raised in the sociable household of his brother-in-law, the 'compleat angler' Izaak Walton, Thomas Ken was familiar with many of the most eminent clergymen of the Church of England. Even the family dog was named after Brian Duppa, the bishop of Winchester (see above, p. 142). At Oxford in the late 1650s he attended secret readings of the banned Book of Common Prayer with several other men who would become future bishops. After the Restoration, through Walton's ecclesiastical connections, he became chaplain to George Morley, bishop of Winchester. After her marriage to William, Prince of Orange, he accompanied Princess Mary to The Hague as her Anglican chaplain, where he irritated William by attempting to intervene in a love affair between William Henry Nassau de Zuylestein, later earl of Rochford, and Jane Wroth, and dismissed a plan to unite the Dutch Reformed churches with the Church of England. At home, his refusal to share his lodgings with the king's mistress Nell Gwyn during a royal progress to Winchester seems to have done him no harm with Charles II. He was elevated to Bath and Wells at the beginning of 1685, donating £100 towards the rebuilding of St Paul's instead of holding the customary celebratory banquet.

Ken was closely associated with James II, and had been suspected of leaning towards Catholicism. He would, however, become a trenchant critic of the king's promotion of it. Ken wrote to the king to protest about the heavy reprisals for the Monmouth Rebellion throughout his diocese. When preaching at court he pulled no punches in his criticism of royal policy. 'There are times', he thundered in one particularly antagonistic sermon, 'when prophets cannot ... keep silence'.[1] In June 1688, Ken was one of the seven bishops put on trial by James after they presented him with a petition against the legality of the king's new Declaration of Indulgence.

Ken might protest, but he drew the line at participating in acts of formal resistance to the king. In November he fled from the advancing Dutch invasion force, wanting there to be no doubt that he was 'in a firm loyalty to the king'.[2] The requirement to take the oaths to William and Mary sent him into agonies of indecision as he weighed up on the one hand the risks of causing a schism in the Church if he and others refused to take them, and on the other the danger of condoning what he regarded as an irreligious and illegal deposition. In the end, he decided he had to refuse, and so became one of the non-juring bishops. Protesting from his episcopal chair in Wells Cathedral that he was still the rightful and canonical bishop, he was formally deprived of his see in February 1690.

After his deprivation, Ken lived with various friends and relatives. Most often, he stayed at Longleat with his friend from his time as an Oxford undergraduate, Thomas Thynne, Viscount Weymouth (see below, p. 312). Obstinate in his opposition to the new regime, he was suspected of Jacobitism, and was arrested and interrogated in 1692 and 1696. In 1695, he emphasized his belief that his deprivation was illegitimate and that he was still the bishop of Bath and Wells by taking a funeral service dressed in his full episcopal robes. After the death of William he became more willing to compromise. When his friend George Hooper was appointed to his former diocese – an appointment for which he claimed responsibility – he finally accepted his displacement. He died on 19 March 1711.

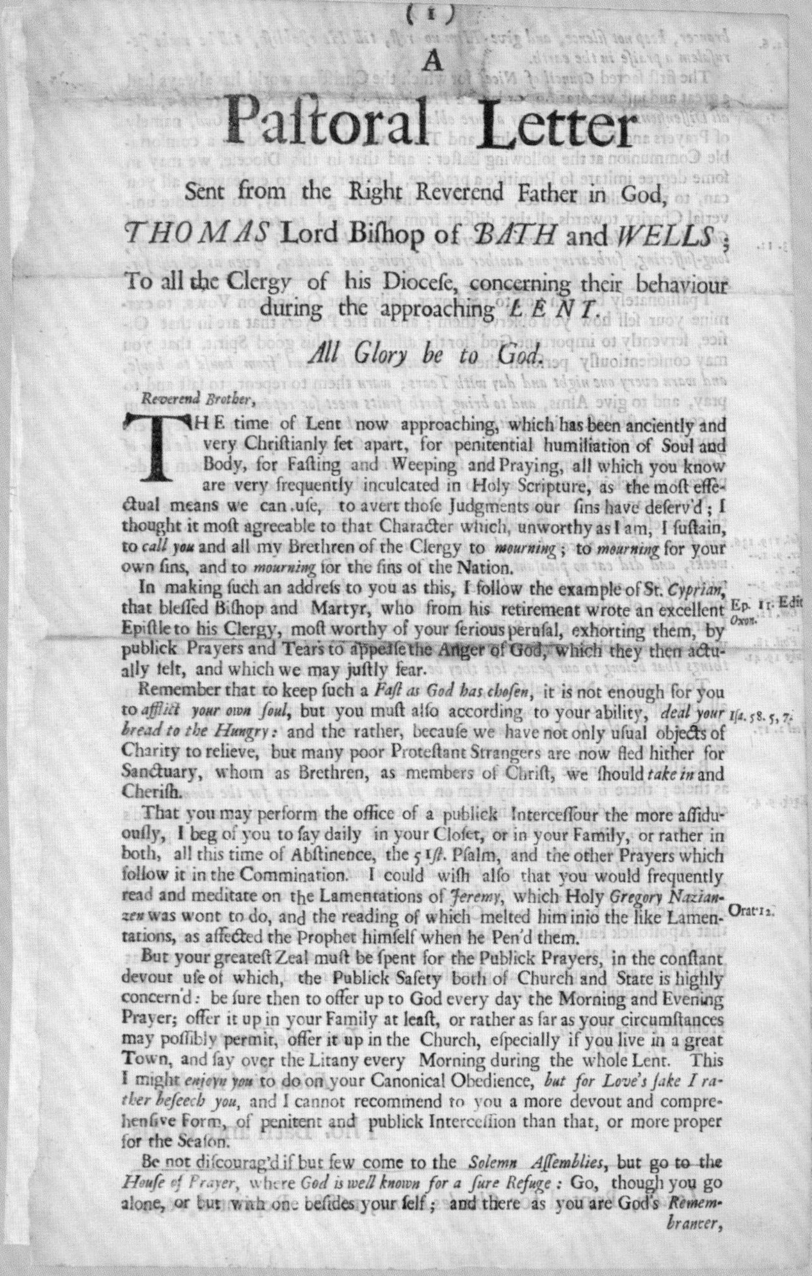

A
Paſtoral Letter

Sent from the Right Reverend Father in God,

THOMAS Lord Biſhop of *BATH* and *WELLS* ;

To all the Clergy of his Dioceſe, concerning their behaviour
during the approaching *LENT.*

All Glory be to God.

Reverend Brother,

THE time of Lent now approaching, which has been anciently and
very Chriſtianly ſet apart, for penitential humiliation of Soul and
Body, for Faſting and Weeping and Praying, all which you know
are very frequently inculcated in Holy Scripture, as the moſt effectual means we can uſe, to avert thoſe Judgments our ſins have deſerv'd; I
thought it moſt agreeable to that Character which, unworthy as I am, I ſuſtain,
to *call you* and all my Brethren of the Clergy to *mourning* ; to *mourning* for your
own ſins, and to *mourning* for the ſins of the Nation.

In making ſuch an addreſs to you as this, I follow the example of St. *Cyprian,*
that bleſſed Biſhop and Martyr, who from his retirement wrote an excellent
Epiſtle to his Clergy, moſt worthy of your ſerious peruſal, exhorting them, by
publick Prayers and Tears to appeaſe the Anger of God, which they then actually felt, and which we may juſtly fear.

Ep. 1; Edit
Oxon.

Remember that to keep ſuch a *Faſt as God has choſen,* it is not enough for you
to *afflict your own ſoul,* but you muſt alſo according to your ability, *deal your
bread to the Hungry:* and the rather, becauſe we have not only uſual objects of
Charity to relieve, but many poor Proteſtant Strangers are now fled hither for
Sanctuary, whom as Brethren, as members of Chriſt, we ſhould *take in* and
Cheriſh.

Iſa. 58. 5, 7.

That you may perform the office of a publick Interceſſour the more aſſidu-
ouſly, I beg of you to ſay daily in your Cloſet, or in your Family, or rather in
both, all this time of Abſtinence, the 51ſt. Pſalm, and the other Prayers which
follow it in the Commination. I could wiſh alſo that you would frequently
read and meditate on the Lamentations of *Jeremy,* which Holy *Gregory Nazian-
zen* was wont to do, and the reading of which melted him into the like Lamentations, as affected the Prophet himſelf when he Pen'd them.

Orat. 12.

But your greateſt Zeal muſt be ſpent for the Publick Prayers, in the conſtant
devout uſe of which, the Publick Safety both of Church and State is highly
concern'd: be ſure then to offer up to God every day the Morning and Evening
Prayer; offer it up in your Family at leaſt, or rather as far as your circumſtances
may poſſibly permit, offer it up in the Church, eſpecially if you live in a great
Town, and ſay over the Litany every Morning during the whole Lent. This
I might *enjoyn you* to do on your Canonical Obedience, *but for Love's ſake I rather beſeech you,* and I cannot recommend to you a more devout and compre-
henſive Form, of penitent and publick Interceſſion than that, or more proper
for the Seaſon.

Be not diſcourag'd if but few come to the *Solemn Aſſemblies,* but go to the
Houſe of Prayer, where God is well known for a ſure Refuge : Go, though you go
alone, or but with one beſides your ſelf ; and there as you are God's *Remem-*
brancer,

FIG. 76 *Thomas Ken's Pastoral Letter to the clergy of his diocese was
published towards Lent 1688. It suggests fasting, weeping and praying as the
most effectual means to 'avert those judgements our sins have deserv'd' – taken
to mean the policies pursued by the king. Later that year Ken was tried for
seditious libel as one of the seven bishops. He refused to take the oaths to the
new regime after the revolution and was deprived of his see.*

Between 1660 and 1715 eight bishops were removed from the House in this way. Seven of them were deprived of office in 1690 because of their failure to take the oaths to William and Mary. Their removal was bitterly contested. Spiritual authority, it was argued, could only be removed by a spiritual assembly – by Convocation, the Church's own Parliament. The non-juring bishop Thomas Ken, on the eve of his removal from his diocese, made a protest from his episcopal chair in Wells Cathedral asserting his 'canonical right' in the diocese.[18] The eighth bishop to be removed was Thomas Watson, James II's nominee to St David's. Although Watson took the oaths after the Revolution, he was nevertheless suspected of Jacobitism. He had few friends and many enemies. Convicted of simony and other clerical offences, he was deprived of his see in August 1699 – although he continued to sit in the House of Lords until the following February.

The strength of the House

Creations, inheritance, death, deprivation, exclusion by minority or through a refusal to take the oaths, all meant that the number of peers sitting in the House of Lords fluctuated constantly. At the end of the sixteenth century there were around fifty peers. By 1628, swollen by James I's creations, there were about 130. Despite Civil War creations, the House of Lords by the end of 1660 was little different in size: it stood at 131 peers, excluding minors and Thomas Howard, 5th duke of Norfolk, who was mentally incapacitated. It grew quickly to 162 in 1670, then more slowly to 172 in 1700. By 1710 it had risen to 190 – an increase almost entirely the result of the addition of the 16 Scottish representative peers. Over the next five years there was a more rapid growth. By the end of 1715 some 213 individuals were entitled to attend the House. A further 28 individuals were unable to sit because they were either under age or Catholic. The expansion was largely due to the influence on the queen of Robert Harley, earl of Oxford, who was responsible for the creation of 16 new peers (including himself) as well as summoning three others by writ of acceleration. By contrast George I was initially relatively parsimonious. Although a further expansion of the peerage was to come, between his accession and the end of 1715 he created only seven new peers. He concentrated instead on rewarding his supporters with promotions in the peerage.

The number of peers eligible to sit was not, however, an indicator of the real strength of the House. It was rare for the number of peers actually attending the House to reach three figures. The average daily attendance was at its highest during the 1670s when it reached 86. There were peaks on days when particularly contentious issues were debated – although some controversial matters could deter attendance if peers preferred to avoid committing themselves. The attempted impeachment of Clarendon in 1667, the votes on exclusion in 1680 and the regency in 1689, the occasional conformity bill in 1703 and the trial of Dr Sacheverell in 1710 attracted particularly high numbers. Attendance for the proceedings on Fenwick's attainder in 1696 was also high; the event that attracted the highest attendance was the declaration that William and Mary were joint monarchs on 7 February 1689. For much of the time, though, attendance was far lower. The House of Lords was actually run by a minority of the more energetic peers who regularly attended, men like William Nicolson, bishop of Carlisle, who could be found in the House on a Saturday afternoon in April 1709 five days before the end of the session, remaining there 'till after three, attending on private (and money) bills; in pure duty'.[19]

Among the others, and despite efforts to compel attendance (see below, pp. 270-2), there were many long-term absentees. Some were down to incapacity. The 2nd and 3rd earls of Newport both had severe learning difficulties and never tried to take their seats. Their younger brother, the 4th earl, regarded as 'nearly an idiot' sat only twice in 1675, the year he succeeded to the title. Thomas Howard, 5th duke of Norfolk, suffered severe brain damage as a young man and spent the rest of his life being cared for abroad. Some were too old and too frail to undertake the journey to Westminster, particularly the bishops, many of whom were already elderly when they were appointed. In January 1707, Bishop Hall of Bristol excused his attendance on the grounds that whenever he set foot in London he caught a cold that he could not shake off for a least a month. William Paget, 6th Baron Paget, was advised to stay away in 1673 until his 'present distempers' were alleviated: 'there is nothing worse for you both in regards of the piles and looseness than motion, and exposing yourself to take cold, which may soon cause a relapse into a more dangerous condition'.[20] An attempt to force peers to turn up in 1696 during the debates over the attainder of Sir John Fenwick, though remarkably successful, produced a string of plausible excuses from aged Members of the

Philip Bisse: a political bishop (1666–1721)

Philip Bisse was the son of a Gloucestershire clergyman. After New College, Oxford, he landed a domestic chaplaincy with Bridget Osborne, the widow of the earl of Plymouth. By 1704, he was married to her. The daughter of Thomas Osborne (earl of Danby and duke of Leeds), she brought him a formidable family connection: his new cousin by marriage, Robert Harley, later earl of Oxford, would prove his most influential patron. Bisse is generally seen as an urbane socialite, talented in aristocratic matchmaking and something of a Lothario (it was said that he kissed the duchess dowager of Northumberland by mistake, believing her to be a lady-in-waiting); but he was also an effective promoter of high Anglican ideals, and an adept promoter of himself. Preaching before the Commons in March 1710 – during the month of the Sacheverell trial – his rousing condemnation of the 'tedious and wasting war' accurately caught the Tory mood.[1] In another sermon, before the Lords on the commemoration of the Restoration, 29 May 1711, he looked back with considerable venom on the Interregnum regime that had been 'torn to pieces by the republican spirit' and infiltrated by 'the very dregs of the people'.[2]

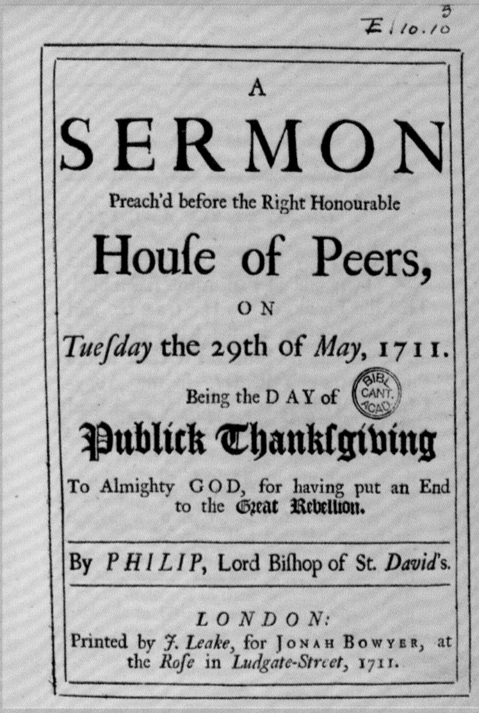

Bisse was ideally placed to land some promotion in the Church when Oxford formed a ministry after the Tory election landslide of 1710. He was appointed bishop of St David's in what was seen as a coup for moderate Tories associated with the lord treasurer. St David's was perhaps not the ideal see: he had no interest in Welsh culture, refused to subscribe to books in Welsh because it would 'obstruct the English tongue', and, unlike both his predecessor George Bull and successor Adam Ottley, insisted that only English was spoken in the charity schools he established.[3] His principal interests lay at Westminster, where he became a diligent member of the House of Lords. He was also closely involved in the management of Convocation, whose lower House was turning, under the guidance of Francis Atterbury (later bishop of Rochester) into a channel for the energies of high-flying Tory clergymen. Bisse was a regular attender at the meetings of Tory secular and ecc-

A

SERMON

Preach'd before the Right Honourable

House of Peers,

ON

Tuesday the 29th of *May,* 1711.

Being the D AY of

Publick Thanksgiving

To Almighty GOD, for having put an End to the Great Rebellion.

By *PHILIP*, Lord Bishop of St. *David's*.

LONDON:

Printed by *J. Leake,* for JONAH BOWYER, at the *Rose* in *Ludgate-Street,* 1711.

FIG. 77 *The House of Lords regularly commissioned sermons from its bishops to commemorate important historical dates: they were often used as opportunities to deliver strong political statements. This one by Bisse, delivered in 1711, celebrates the day in 1660 on which Charles II rode into the City of London and took possession of his kingdom. Sermons sold well and a sermon preached to the peers had a certain cachet.*

lesiastical politicians at the house of the then bishop of Rochester, Thomas Sprat, in which they tried to direct them.

In 1713 Bisse was translated to Hereford, a city firmly in the grip of the Tories. Entrenched as a member of the Harley-Foley political alliance in Herefordshire, Bisse came into conflict with the high steward of Hereford who later described him as 'the worst of bishops'.[4] It was assumed at court that Bisse belonged to the Tory faction that supported the Hanoverian succession, although he was not above attending a social gathering in 1713 with the incendiary Henry Sacheverell where the assembled company drank 'a great many loyal healths' to the Stuarts and musicians played a popular Jacobite song to 'universal acclamations'.[5] In 1714, while the coronation of George I sparked rioting in Hereford, Bisse infuriated some of Hereford's Tories by appearing before the clergy 'with a joyful and entirely pleased counte-

FIG. 78 *Philip Bisse,
engraved by George Vertue,
after Thomas Hill.*

*Reverendus admodum
in Christo Pater* PHILIPPUS BISSE *Episcopus* HEREFORDENSIS.

nance'.[6] Although Bisse's brother, whom he appointed to a prebend at the cathedral, settled happily down to promoting a collaboration between the cathedral choirs of Hereford, Gloucester and Worcester which became the Three Choirs Festival in 1724, Bisse himself made no bones about his hopes to shake the dust of Hereford from his feet and move to a more prestigious bishopric. It did not help his relationship with the town.

His expectations of succeeding to York after Archbishop Sharp's death were disappointed. Bisse's brand of churchmanship was no longer in favour after Anne's death; and, with Oxford ejected from government and persecuted by the Whigs, nor was his brand

of politics. He supported Oxford through impeachment; he may even, eventually, have flirted with the Jacobite cause. Bisse died in 1721, aged only fifty-four, and still in Hereford.

House. Among them were Thomas Howard, 3rd earl of Berkshire (nearly 80 and unable to walk), Bishop Beaw of Llandaff (also nearly 80 and having lost the use of a leg) and William Maynard, 2nd Baron Maynard (over 73 and with little prospect of recovery from illness).

Some Members were absent abroad on royal business, such as James Butler, duke of Ormond, who for much of his career after the Restoration was lord lieutenant of Ireland, or Denzil Holles, Baron Holles, who was ambassador to France from 1662 to 1666. Numerous other Members found regular attendance inconvenient for political or personal reasons: they disliked London, were out of favour with the court, or simply had more interesting things to do. The Catholic peer Marmaduke Langdale, 2nd Baron Langdale, claimed to be too poor to travel to London. At the Restoration the veteran presbyterian Algernon Percy, 4th earl of Northumberland, found the new regime unsympathetic and confided that although he would be in London 'I believe I shall not be very diligent in attending either the Parliament House, or the council table, finding myself grown too old for the gallantries of a young court'.[21] Charles Stanley, 8th earl of Derby, in high dudgeon over the government's attitude to his efforts to recover estates lost during the Interregnum (see below, p. 250), did not attend the House from 1663 to 1671. William Cavendish, duke of Newcastle, did not attend between August 1660 and his death in 1676, probably because his personal priorities lay in repairing his estates and local influence rather than in making a figure on the national political stage. He did visit London in 1665 and 1667 in company with his eccentric duchess in magnificent style, but he arrived after Parliament had been prorogued. His son Henry Cavendish, 2nd duke of Newcastle, pleaded illness to avoid attendance, but the real reason seems to have been a simple reluctance to get involved. 'When you consider the times and businesses are now on foot in Parliament time' explained his duchess to their daughter in the midst of anxieties about the Popish Plot, ''tis better to be from amongst them then with them.'[22] Edward Montagu, 2nd earl of Sandwich, lived abroad in the south of France from 1673 for his health until his death thirteen years later. The duke of Shrewsbury was absent from the House for almost ten years between 1696 and 1706, six of which he spent abroad, mainly in Montpellier and Rome.

Some peers were only galvanised into attendance when their personal interests were at stake. Nicholas Tufton, 3rd earl of Thanet, for example, turned out regularly for proceedings on a private bill to settle arrangements for the maintenance of his younger brothers in 1665, but then, 'much hypochondriac', dropped out of significant parliamentary business for over a decade.[23] What might often occasion a visit to the House was a claim of privilege, for the assertion and protection of the special rights which helped them to maintain their expensive lifestyle and their social and political pre-eminence were among the principal preoccupations of the peerage within parliament.

Revolution, 1688–1689

The request that William of Orange intervene in England fell on fertile ground. William, James's nephew as well as the husband of his daughter Mary, was already deeply concerned about James's alignment with Louis XIV and Louis's plans to renew hostilities with the Netherlands. In the spring of 1688, even before the invitation was received, and while France was distracted by campaigns in Germany and Italy, William had begun to assemble a fleet to invade England.

The invitation had asked him to assist in settling the country and to ensure the calling of a free Parliament. Of its seven signatories, five were members of the House of Lords: the now veteran politician Thomas Osborne, earl of Danby; Charles Talbot, 12th earl (later duke) of Shrewsbury; William Cavendish, 4th earl of Devonshire; Richard Lumley, Baron Lumley (later earl of Scarborough) and Henry Compton, bishop of London. One of the two commoners, Edward Russell (later earl of Orford), had had a promising naval career until the execution of his cousin and brother-in-law William, Lord Russell; the career of the second, Henry Sydney (later earl of Romney) had been similarly blighted by the execution of his brother Algernon. Two of the 'immortal seven' (Danby and Compton) were Tories, the rest either Whigs or Whiggish. Compton was close to James's younger daughter, Anne, and Lumley was a member of her household. Lumley and Shrewsbury were Protestant converts who had lost military commands for refusing to return to Catholicism.

The existence of neither the invitation nor William's invasion fleet was a secret. James's reaction was confused and uncertain: he prevaricated over whether to summon the Parliament for which he had been preparing. Meanwhile, the seven and their allies tried to muster their own support. Danby failed in September to recruit Philip Stanhope, 2nd earl of Chesterfield, who explained that 'I have ever had a natural aversion to the taking arms against my king' and urged Danby to reconsider for the sake of his own conscience.[1] Compton also failed to persuade Christopher Hatton, Viscount Hatton, to come off the fence. Others were more easily won over. Hatton's

FIG. 79 *Ignatius White (c.1626–1694), the imperial marquis d'Albeville and envoy extraordinary from James II to the Hague from 1687 celebrated the birth of James II's son in June 1688 with a series of splendid entertainments, and by commissioning this commemorative medal. Mary of Modena is shown in a bed proudly holding her baby. The canopy of the bed is embellished with the Stuart rose and Prince of Wales feathers.*

ward, Henry Yelverton, 15th Baron Grey of Ruthin (later Viscount Longueville), concealed his intention to join the rebels from his guardian. While William Stanley, 9th earl of Derby, was in London to see the king about resuming the lord lieutenancies of Lancashire and Cheshire, Bishop Compton discussed with him how to use the local militia in support of William's invasion – although in the end Derby failed to act decisively. The Cheshire Whig Henry Booth, 2nd Baron Delamer (later earl of Warrington), was already planning to support the Prince of Orange.

William landed at Torbay on 5 November. Most county militias provided little resistance; some joined the rebellion under the command of their former leaders. A formerly staunch Tory, John Granville, earl of Bath, handed over to William the west country militia together with Plymouth Castle and harbour (see

Jhro Königl. Hohejt Prjntz von Oranjen, Angelanget Jn Engeland Año. 1688.

below, p.160). The sacked lord lieutenant of Oxford-shire, James Bertie, earl of Abingdon, led a company to join William's invading army, while his replace-ment, Edward Henry Lee, earl of Lichfield, struggled to raise any forces for the king (see above, p.58). Princess Anne, her husband Prince George, Charles II's illegitimate son, Henry Fitzroy, duke of Grafton, and a large proportion of the senior officers of James's army, including John Churchill, Baron Churchill (later duke of Marlborough), all defected to William. James's army melted away. He fell back to London and called about forty peers to a 'great council' on 27 November. When it met, he was lectured by his former brother-in-law, Henry Hyde, 2nd earl of Clarendon, and when he appealed to William Russell, 5th earl of Bedford, he was rebuffed. 'Ah sir, I am old and feeble; I can do you but little service', Bedford responded, adding a bitter reference to the execution of his son, William, Lord Russell, pursued so vindic-tively by James in 1683: 'I once had a son that could have assisted you; but he is no more.' The king was left speechless.[2] He gave way to the demand to summon a new Parliament, but two weeks later, as William's forces approached London and rioting broke out, he hurried away to the Kent coast.

Much of the rioting was aimed at Catholics and James's closest allies. With government at a standstill, the peers took action to re-establish order. On 11 December 1688, 27 peers and bishops gathered at the Guildhall in London, where Laurence Hyde, earl of

FIG. 80 *The Prince of Orange landing at Torbay, 5 November 1688.*

Rochester, announced to the lord mayor and alder-men their intention of meeting 'that they might with better security consult and take the best means for the public weal'.[3] Then this select band of peers and bishops turned themselves into a provisional govern-ment, attending to the chaos in London and beyond. They moved to Whitehall, where they continued to meet until 15 December. On the king's unexpected return to the capital after his capture at Faversham they suspended their proceedings. Within a week, the king had left London for a second time, encouraged by the Prince of Orange: shortly afterwards he aban-doned the country for France. The lords reassem-bled, at first in the queen's presence chamber at St James's Palace on 21 December, and then in the House of Lords itself.

On Christmas Eve, an all-day debate in this assembly showed that momentum had passed to those determined to see the king either limited in his power or removed entirely. It decided that the govern-ment of the kingdom was 'extinct' and asked for William's agreement and assistance to summon a new 'Convention' Parliament. On Boxing Day, an assem-bly of some of the remaining Members of Charles II's last three Parliaments concurred. Elections held in the still-febrile atmosphere of early January 1689 pro-duced a House of Commons that was dominated,

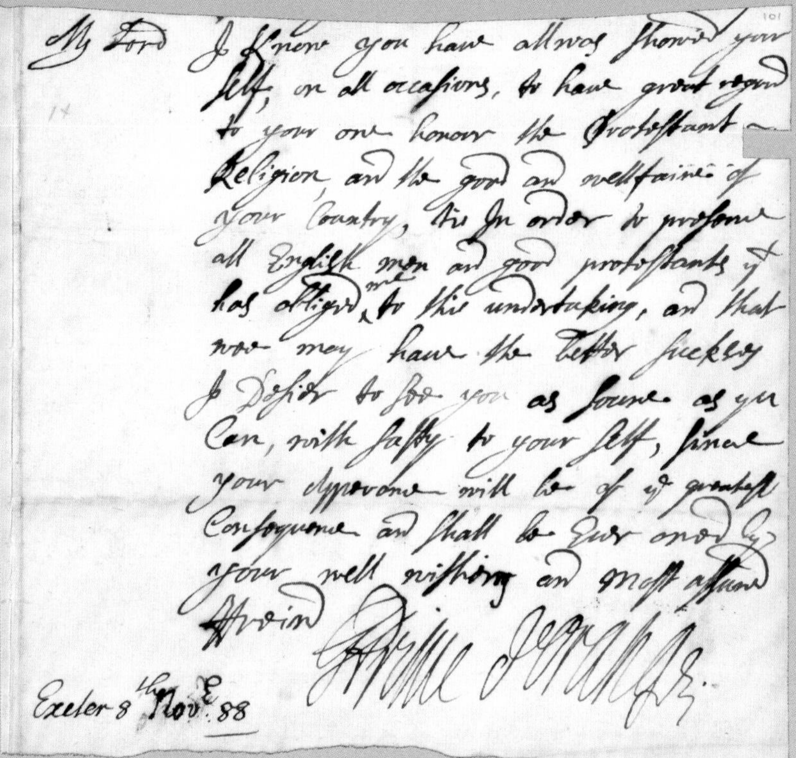

FIG. 81 *The Prince of Orange writes to John Granville, earl of Bath, on 8 and 20 November 1688, shortly after his landing in Devon. Bath had been placed in charge of the military stronghold of Plymouth by James II. The letter of 20 November (below) is William's response to Bath's offer to surrender the citadel to him.*

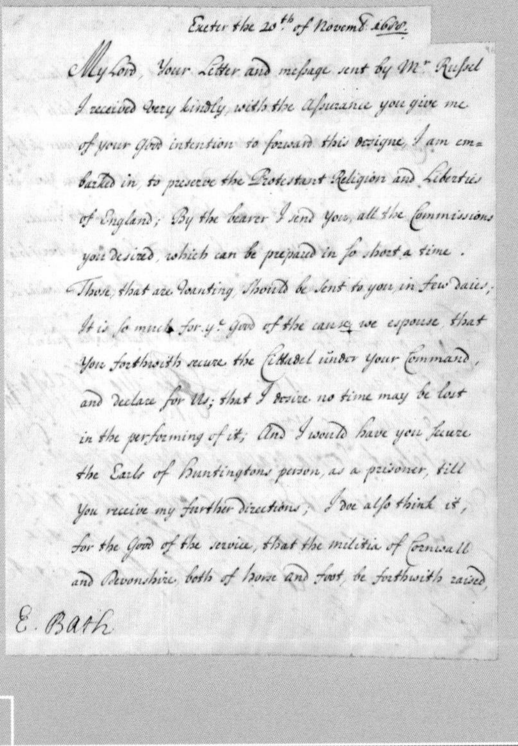

My Lord, I know you have allwas showed your self, on all occasions, to have great regard to your own honour the Protestant Religion and the good and wellfaire of your Country, tis In order to preserve all English men and good protestants yt has obliged me to this undertaking, and that wee may have the better successy I desire to see you as soone as yu Can, with safty to your self, since your apperance will be of yg greatest Consequence and shall be Ever owned by your well wishing and most assured friend

Exeter 8th Novr 88

Exeter the 20th of Novemb 1688

My Lord, Your Letter and message sent by Mr. Russel I received very kindly, with the Assurance you give me of your good intention to forward this designe, I am embarked in to preserve the Protestant Religion and Libertis of England; By the bearer I send You, all the Commissions you desired which can be prepared in so short a time. Those that are wanting, should be sent to you in few daies; It is so much for yr good of the cause, we espouse that you forthwith secure the Citadel under your Command, and declare for Us; that I desire no time may be lost in the performing of it; And I would have you secure the Earle of Huntingtons person, as a prisoner, till You receive my farther directions; I doe also think it, for the Good of the service, that the militia of Cornwall and Devonshire both of horse and foot, be forthwith raised,

E. Bath

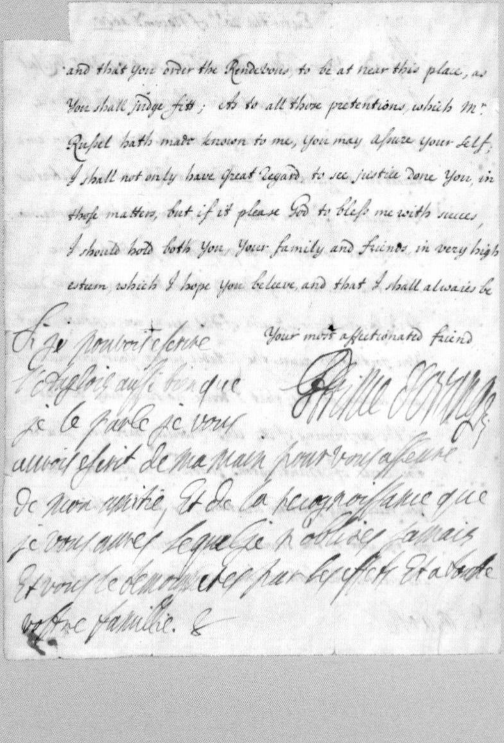

and that you order the Rendezvous to be at near this place, as You shall Judge fitt; As to all those pretentions, which Mr. Russel hath made known to me, you may assure your self, I shall not only have great Regard, to see justice done You, in those matters, but if it please God to bless me with succes, I should hold both You, Your family and friends, in very high esteem which I hope you believe, and that I shall alwaies be

Your most affectionated friend

Je ne pouvois escrire
L'Anglois aussi bien que
je le parle je vous
avois escrit de ma main pour vous asseure
de non mutte, Et de la recognoissance que
je vous avez lequelle n'oublie jamais
Et vous le benem...er par les efett Et a toute
votre famille. &

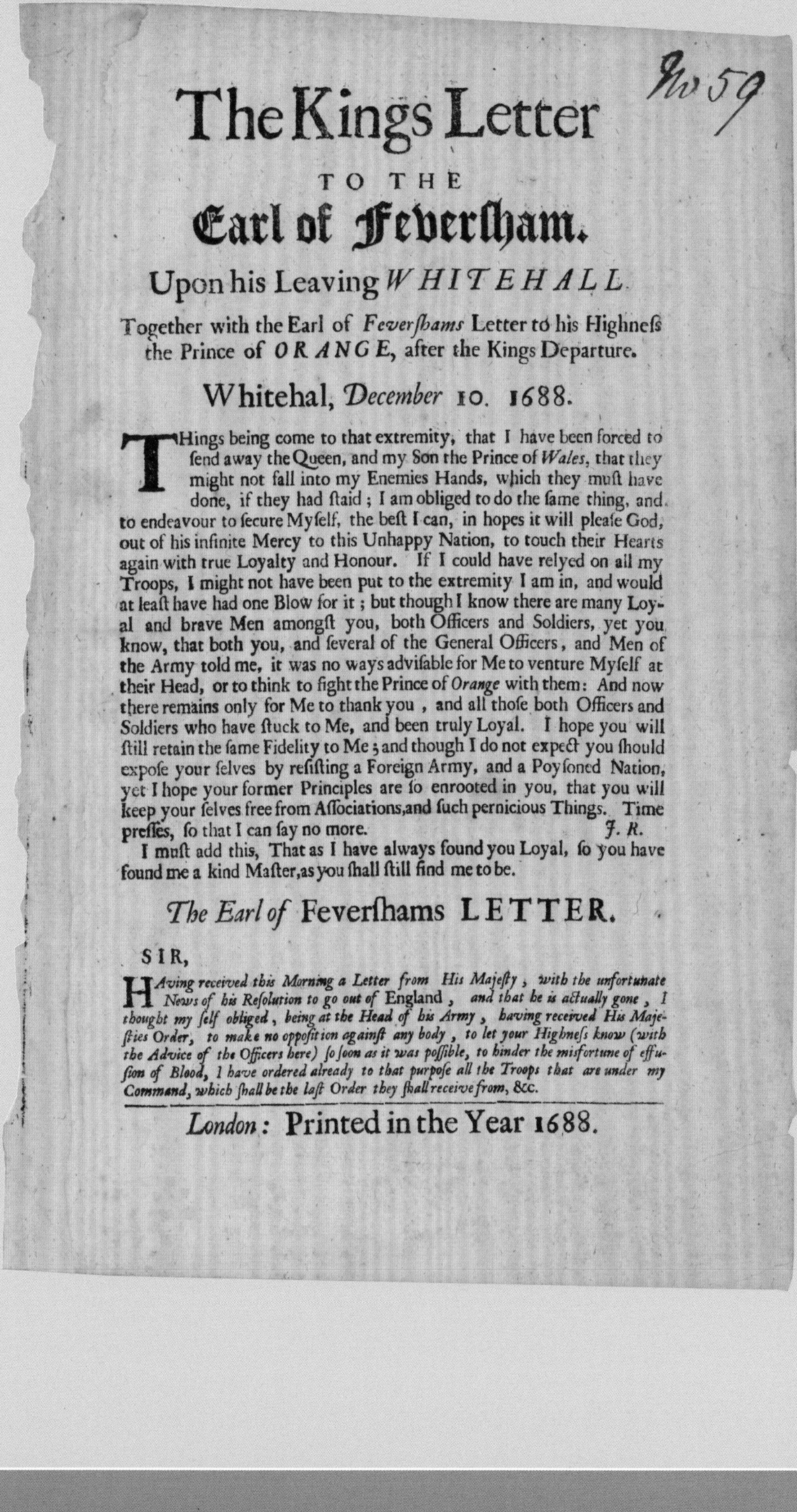

The Kings Letter

TO THE

Earl of Feversham.

Upon his Leaving WHITEHALL.

Together with the Earl of *Fevershams* Letter to his Highneſs the Prince of *ORANGE*, after the Kings Departure.

Whitehal, *December* 10. 1688.

THings being come to that extremity, that I have been forced to send away the Queen, and my Son the Prince of *Wales*, that they might not fall into my Enemies Hands, which they muſt have done, if they had ſtaid ; I am obliged to do the ſame thing, and to endeavour to ſecure Myſelf, the beſt I can, in hopes it will pleaſe God, out of his infinite Mercy to this Unhappy Nation, to touch their Hearts again with true Loyalty and Honour. If I could have relyed on all my Troops, I might not have been put to the extremity I am in, and would at leaſt have had one Blow for it ; but though I know there are many Loyal and brave Men amongſt you, both Officers and Soldiers, yet you know, that both you, and ſeveral of the General Officers, and Men of the Army told me, it was no ways adviſable for Me to venture Myſelf at their Head, or to think to fight the Prince of *Orange* with them: And now there remains only for Me to thank you , and all thoſe both Officers and Soldiers who have ſtuck to Me, and been truly Loyal. I hope you will ſtill retain the ſame Fidelity to Me ; and though I do not expect you ſhould expoſe your ſelves by reſiſting a Foreign Army, and a Poyſoned Nation, yet I hope your former Principles are ſo enrooted in you, that you will keep your ſelves free from Aſſociations, and ſuch pernicious Things. Time preſſes, ſo that I can ſay no more.   *J. R.*

I muſt add this, That as I have always found you Loyal, ſo you have found me a kind Maſter, as you ſhall ſtill find me to be.

The Earl of Fevershams LETTER.

SIR,

HAving received this Morning a Letter from His Majeſty, with the unfortunate News of his Reſolution to go out of England, and that he is actually gone, I thought my ſelf obliged, being at the Head of his Army, having received His Majeſties Order, to make no oppoſition againſt any body, to let your Highneſs know (with the Advice of the Officers here) ſo ſoon as it was poſſible, to hinder the misfortune of effuſion of Blood, I have ordered already to that purpoſe all the Troops that are under my Command, which ſhall be the laſt Order they ſhall receive from, &c.

London : Printed in the Year 1688.

FIG. 82 *As his army crumbled in front of Prince William's advance on London James II decided to leave the country. He left behind with Louis Duras, 2nd earl of Feversham, his most trusted military commander, this explanation dated 10 December of his decision to leave and his effective repudiation of any attempt to resist William of Orange by force. After writing the letter he made his way with a small party of loyal aides to Faversham in Kent, where he was ignominiously arrested by a Protestant mob, and brought back to London.*

6

will Doe desire you the Ld Marquis of Hallifax, the Earle of Shrewsbury, and the Ld Delamer to tell the King that it is thought convenient for the greater quiet of the City and for the greater safety of his person that he doe remove to Ham where he shall be attended by guards who will be ready to preserve him from any disturbance. given at Windsor the 17 day of December 1688

Prince D Orange

A similar Commission is at Althorpe

though not overwhelmed, by Whigs. On 28 January, six days after the Convention first assembled, the House of Commons voted that the king had 'abdicated the government' by 'breaking the original contract between king and people' and by having 'withdrawn himself out of the government' he had left the throne vacant. The vote caused consternation among Tories in the Lords, already aware of Whig plans to depose James formally and to confer the crown on William and his wife, Princess Mary. Only a handful of them – including Clarendon and Francis Turner, bishop of Ely – believed that James should be allowed to resume power; but all of them, firmly wedded to the principle of an indefeasible hereditary right, were horrified by the implication that the succession could be determined by Parliament.

Two days of open party warfare in the Lords, carried on 'with the greatest passion and violence' called up all the partisan hatreds of the last sixty years.[4] Tories tried to replace the word 'abdicated' with 'deserted' and rejected the idea that the throne was vacant. They proposed a regency instead – with William as regent during James' lifetime. Then William himself weighed in. So far he had scrupulously avoided advancing a claim to the throne but now, in command of the only viable military force in

His Majesties
REASONS
FOR
With-drawing Himself from *Rochester*. Writ with His own Hand, and Ordered to be Published.

The World cannot wonder at my with-drawing my Self now this Second time. I might have expected somewhat better Usage after what I writ to the P. of *Orange* by my Lord *Feversham*, and the Instructions I gave him; but instead of an Answer, such as I might have hoped for, What was I to expect after the Usage I received by the making the said Earl a *Prisoner*, against the Practice and Law of Nations; *The sending his own Guards at Eleven at Night to take Possession of the Posts at Whitehall*, without advertizing me in the least manner of it; *The sending to me at One a Clock, after Midnight, when I was in Bed, a kind of an Order by three Lords, to be gone out of mine own Palace, before Twelve that same Morning?* After all this, How could I hope to be safe, so long as I was in the Power of one, who had not only done this to me, and Invaded my Kingdoms without any just occasion given him for it, but that did by his first Declaration lay the greatest Aspersion upon me that Malice could invent, in that Clause of it which concerns my *Son*. I appeal to all that know me, nay, even to himself, that in their Consciences, neither he nor they can believe me *in the least capable of so unnatural a Villany*, nor of so little common sense, to be imposed on in a thing of such a nature as that. What had I then to expect from one who by all Arts hath taken such pains to make me appear as black as Hell to my own People, as well as to all the World besides? What effect that hath had at Home all mankind have seen, by so *general a defection* in my Army, as well as in the Nation amongst all sorts of People.

I was born *Free*, and desire to continue so; and tho I have *ventured my Life* very frankly, on several Occasions, for the Good and Honour of my Country, and am as free to do it again, (*and which I hope I shall yet do, as old as I am, to redeem it from the Slavery it is like to fall under*) yet I think it not convenient to expose my self to be Secured, as not to be at Liberty to Effect it; and for that reason do with-draw, but so as to be within call whensoever the Nations Eyes shall be opened, so as to see how they have been abused and imposed upon by the *specious Pretences of Religion and Property*. I hope it will please God to *touch* their Hearts, out of his infinite Mercy, and to make them sensible of the ill Condition they are in, and bring them to such a temper, that a *Legal Parliament* may be called; and that amongst other things which may be necessary to be done, they will agree to *Liberty of Conscience* for all Protestant Dissenters; and that those of my own Perswasion may be so far considered, and have such a share of it, as *they may live peaceably and quietly*, as Englishmen and Christians ought to do, and not to be obliged to *Transplant* themselves, which would be very grievous, especially to such as love their own Country; and I appeal to all men, who are considering men, and have had experience, whether any thing can make this Nation so great and flourishing as *Liberty of Conscience*. Some of our Neighbours dread it.

I could add much more to confirm all I have said, but now is not the proper time.

Rochester, Decemb. 22.
1688.

FIG. 84 *Instead of going to Ham, James asked to go to Rochester, and William agreed. A few days later he made a second, this time successful, attempt to leave, unimpeded by William. This is his second explanation of his departure.*

Resolved &c Luna 28° Jan.Ey 1688

That King James the Second haveing
endeavoured to subvert the Constitution of
the Kingdome by breaking the Originall Contract
betweene King and People, and by the Advice
of Jesuites and other wicked persons haveing
violated the fundamentall Lawes And
haveing withdrawne himselfe out of this
8 ... Kingdome has abdicated the Government
9 ... and that the Throne is thereby vacant.

HOUSE OF LORDS

FIG. 85 *The House of Commons' resolution that the king had
abdicated the government and that the throne was thereby vacant,
passed on 28 January, was bitterly debated in the Lords over two days.
They amended the word 'abdicated' to 'deserted', as is shown here, and
rejected the idea that there was a vacancy, because of resistance to the
notion that a hereditary monarchy could effectively become an elective
one. Eventually they were forced to cave in.*

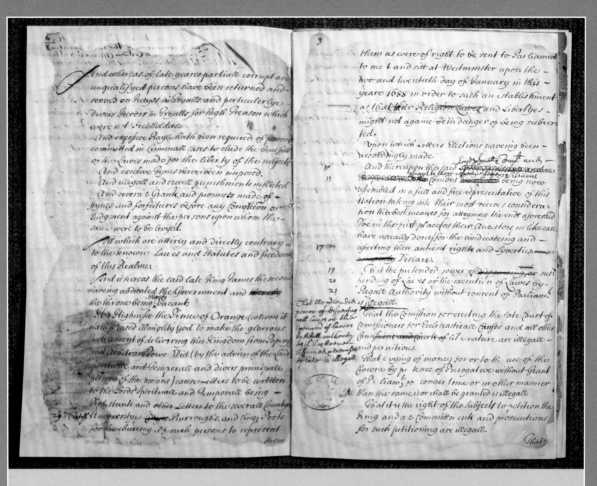

the country and firmly in control of London, he demanded the throne in his own right and in that of his wife. On 6 February the Whigs successfully marshalled their support in the Lords to support him. In his diary Clarendon described how 'all imaginable pains were taken to bring other lords to the House, who never used to come: as the earl of Lincoln, who, to confirm the opinion several had of his being half-mad, declared he came to do whatever my Lord Shrewsbury and Lord Mordaunt would have him'.[5] Edward Howard, the gouty 2nd earl of Carlisle 'was brought upon his crutches'. Even formerly staunch Tories like Nathaniel Crew, bishop of Durham, were persuaded to vote in William's favour. After the division Clarendon asked Thomas Tufton, 6th earl of Thanet, who had previously refused to acknowledge that the throne was vacant, why he 'came to leave us in this last vote'. Thanet responded that 'he was of our mind, and thought we had done ill in admitting the monarchy to be elective; for so this vote had made it: but he thought there was an absolute necessity of having a government; and he did not see it likely to be any other way than this'.[6] The Tory Daniel Finch,

FIG. 86 *The draft of the Declaration of Rights, which later became the Bill of Rights, which was brought from the House of Commons to the Lords on 8 February 1689. The Lords amendments are written on the document.*

2nd earl of Nottingham, who was prepared to recognise William as king *de facto* but not *de jure*, proposed new oaths that would allow others to assuage their consciences in the same way. These, after an initial struggle with the Commons, eventually passed into law.

On 13 February, both Houses went together 'in a body' to the Banqueting House in Whitehall, where they offered William and Mary the crown, together with a Declaration of Rights. The latter, which in statutory form would become known as the Bill of Rights, laid out the misgovernment of Charles II and James II and set out the principles which Parliament believed to be fundamental to the law and the constitution of England. It implied that the Revolution had restored an old order: but the feeling that an old order had been profoundly changed was hard to dispel, and few would guess quite how much – driven by the demands of war as much as by the formality of a new constitutional document – the government of England would change in the following quarter century.

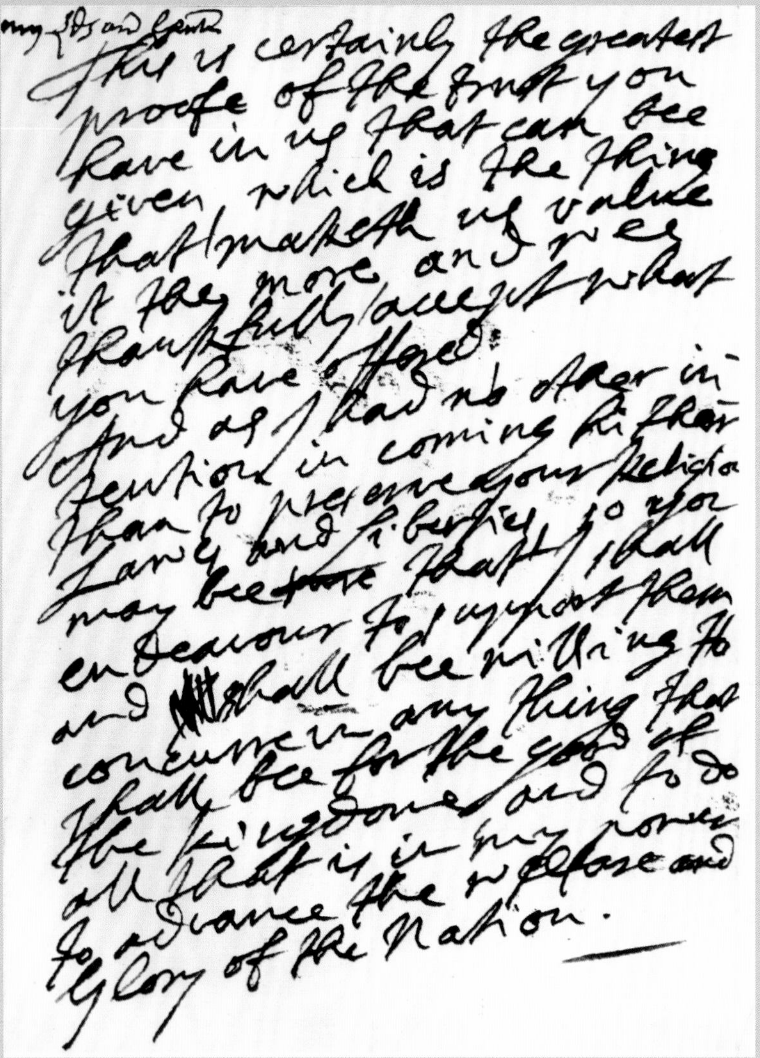

FIG. 87 *William of Orange's speech on accepting the throne, on 13 February 1689. This copy was requested by the House of Commons and printed and published by order of the House of Lords. It reads:*

My L[or]ds and Gent[leme]n
This is certainly the greatest proofe of the trust you have in us that can bee given, which is the thing that maketh us value it the more, and wee thankfully accept what you have offered.

And as I had no other intention in coming hither than to preserve your Religion Lawes and Liberties, so you may bee sure that I shall endeavour to support them and shall bee willing to concurre in any thing that shall bee for the good of the kingdome and to do all that is in my power to advance the welfare and Glory of the Nation.

Chapter 5

Honour, power and privilege

Precedence and distinction

Members of the House of Lords occupied a position conspicuously set apart from the great mass of the population. They were addressed with particular deference (usually 'my lord' or 'your grace', although these forms were not as generally used as they would become). Their possessions – silver and gold plate, architectural features, coaches, even funeral monuments – were identified with coats of arms distinguished from those of lesser distinction by supporters and a coronet (with decoration ranging from six pearls for a baron to eight strawberry leaves for a duke). Such emblems were supposed to command respect, although one story, perhaps apocryphal, described how the 'proud duke of Somerset' (Charles Seymour, the 6th duke) was tricked into giving precedence to a mere commoner. Sir James Delaval placed the arms of the duke of Norfolk on a coach and surrounded it with servants in the Norfolk livery. When Somerset appeared on the same road, Delaval's hirelings called out 'the duke of Norfolk' and, the dukedom of Norfolk being senior to that of Somerset, Somerset promptly ordered his own coach to pull over to allow Norfolk's coach to pass unhindered.

It was the job of the heralds of the college of arms to supervise and enforce the rules relating to the display of such marks of distinction. In January 1668, for example, Sir Edward Walker, garter king of arms, imprisoned a painter-stainer called Parker for marshalling the funeral of Charles Gerard, 4th Baron Gerard, without proper authorisation: Parker's offence was aggravated by the display of false arms including a coronet with eight pearls instead of six. Such matters were not the concern of the House of Lords itself. It did, though, routinely assert its right to the respect it thought was due to it as an institution, a respect that was deeply

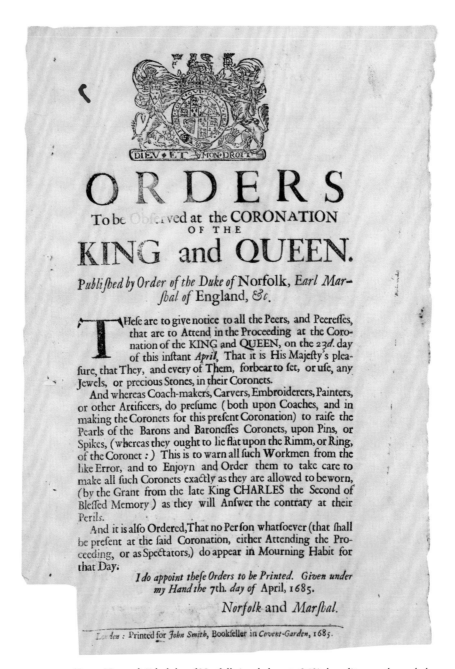

ORDERS

To be Observed at the CORONATION
OF THE

KING and QUEEN.

Published by Order of the Duke of Norfolk, *Earl Marshal of* England, *&c.*

These are to give notice to all the Peers, and Peeresses,
that are to Attend in the Proceeding at the Coronation of the KING and QUEEN, on the 23*d.* day
of this instant *April,* That it is His Majesty's pleasure, that They, and every of Them, forbear to set, or use, any
Jewels, or precious Stones, in their Coronets.

And whereas Coach-makers, Carvers, Embroiderers, Painters,
or other Artificers, do presume (both upon Coaches, and in
making the Coronets for this present Coronation) to raise the
Pearls of the Barons and Baronesses Coronets, upon Pins, or
Spikes, (whereas they ought to lie flat upon the Rimm, or Ring,
of the Coronet :) This is to warn all such Workmen from the
like Error, and to Enjoyn and Order them to take care to
make all such Coronets exactly as they are allowed to be worn,
(by the Grant from the late King CHARLES the Second of
Blessed Memory) as they will Answer the contrary at their
Perils.

And it is also Ordered, That no Person whatsoever (that shall
be present at the said Coronation, either Attending the Proceeding, or as Spectators,) do appear in Mourning Habit for
that Day.

*I do appoint these Orders to be Printed. Given under
my Hand the* 7th. *day of* April, 1685.

Norfolk and *Marshal.*

London : Printed for *John Smith,* Bookseller in *Covent-Garden,* 1685.

FIG. 88 *Henry Howard, 7th duke of Norfolk (see below, p. 260), hereditary earl marshal
of England, was responsible for the ceremonial of the coronation of James II and his
consort, Mary of Modena. His instructions suggest that the peers would have been
commissioning robes and coronets for the occasion. The sudden demand for appropriate
textiles led to inflated prices and profiteering.*

A PROSPECT OF THE INSIDE OF WESTMINSTER HALL,
Shewing how the KING and QUEEN, with the NOBILITY and Others, did Sit at DINNER on the day of the CORONATION, 23 Apr. 1685.
With the manner of Serving up the First Course of Hot Meat to their Majesties Table.

entangled with the deference which individual peers expected, and almost impossible to unravel from it. Some of the actions taken by the House were more or less practical. It regularly instructed the Westminster authorities to prevent traffic jams (or as they would put it 'stoppages in the streets') and to implement special parking restrictions in order to enable the peers to travel freely and speedily to the House. On at least one occasion the House reprimanded the deputy steward of Westminster for his failure to protect them from the effect of 'stoppages'. Frequently, the House was simply asserting its own superiority and the superiority of its members over others involved in Parliament. It insisted, for example, that those who were not peers (for example, the judges in attendance on the House) should remove their hats in the House. At the ceremonies when Parliament was prorogued or adjourned and at committees and conferences the distinction between peers and commoners was reinforced by making members of the Commons stand, hatless, whilst the peers

FIG. 89 *'The nobility and others' at the banquet for the coronation of James II in Westminster Hall on 23 April 1685.*

Edward Stillingfleet
(1635–99) and
comprehension

dward Stillingfleet was one of the intellectual stars of the Restoration Church.
A fellow of St John's College, Cambridge,
in the 1650s, his 1661 tract *Irenicum*
was a key text in the debate about how far the
Church of England should attempt to accommodate
Presbyterians, arguing that 'sober' dissenters be
accommodated within a broader Church of England.
Stillingfleet made lasting enemies for recommending
'latitude' in the relationship of the Church with its
enemies and was branded 'an old knave' for daring
to suggest that Parliament could tamper with the constitution of the Church.[1]

Stillingfleet was also a natural and very popular
preacher. Thomas Wriothesley, 4th earl of Southampton, presented him to the prestigious and wealthy
inner city parish of St Andrew's, Holborn in 1665,
and by 1669 there was standing room only when he
preached there. He preached the fast sermon before
the Commons after the Great Fire in 1666, was read
constantly by the devout Mary Rich, countess of
Warwick, and became required reading for the likes
of Andrew Marvell the poet and presbyterian, and
Philip Wharton, 4th Baron Wharton, a friend of the
dissenters.

The most politically sophisticated of churchmen,
Stillingfleet was just as much in demand as a strategist
and negotiator. In 1674 he helped to draft a comprehension bill, even though by then his views about just
how far the Church should lean to comprehend moderate dissenters had become relatively conservative.
Promoted to the pivotal London position of dean of
St Paul's in 1678, he formed a close and important
alliance with the bishop of London, Henry Compton,
and with the lord chancellor, Heneage Finch, earl of
Nottingham. The connection with Nottingham and
with his son, Daniel Finch, the 2nd earl, would last
for the remainder of Stillingfleet's life.

During the Popish Plot crisis, Stillingfleet's persistent attacks on Catholics led to rumours that he
might be assassinated and his parishioners set up a
bodyguard to protect him. Despite his outspokenness,
Stillingfleet's slide towards conservative politics continued. At the time of the impeachment of Thomas

Osborne, earl of Danby, he used his considerable
knowledge of Church history to try to assist the minister, refuting the argument put by Denzil Holles,
Baron Holles, that bishops should not be allowed to
vote in such trials. By now his commitment to comprehension had shrivelled to a demand that nonconformists should set aside their differences with the
Church in order to strengthen it against the Catholic
threat. In 1680 he opposed the comprehension bill.

During the reign of James II, Stillingfleet worked
closely, if warily, with Compton and the 2nd earl
of Nottingham against the king's promotion of
Catholicism and was closely in touch with Gilbert
Burnet at the court of William, Prince of Orange.
Immediately after the Revolution, he worked hand in
glove with Nottingham on a new comprehension
scheme, designed to consolidate the united Protestant
front which had mobilized against James II.
Nottingham introduced the bill for uniting Protestants into the Lords in March 1689. It was lost
because of the adamant opposition of most Tories;
dissenters themselves were not very interested in the
small compromises on offer anyway. Only the
Toleration Act, which had been designed as a comple-
mentary measure, was passed.

Despite his central role in the religious politics
of the previous three decades, it was not until October
1689 that Stillingfleet was finally promoted to a bish-
opric, that of Worcester. He launched a moral crusade
in his diocese, cajoling his flock 'to discard the pro-
fane, sumptuous expenses of luxury, of debauchery,
of gaiety of clothes' and to give their money to charity.[2] His contributions to the House of Lords, however, were unimpressive: he was a martyr to gout –
for the relief of which he drank a pint of cow's urine
each morning – and reluctant to make the journey to
London. He became increasingly cantankerous (one
scholarly exchange was described as 'the fighting of
two cocks on a dung-hill'),[3] increasingly conservative,
and increasingly selfish (he annoyed his colleagues
with his determination to promote his son in the
Church, making himself 'so unpleasant on the subject'
that he almost wrecked a commission on church
preferments).[4]

Edwardus Stillingfleet S.T.P. Epis. Wigorn. Eccles. S.ti Paul. Decanus
Nat. 17 April. A.D. 1635 Denatus 27 Mar. A.D. 1699

As a result he was passed over when the archbishopric of Canterbury became vacant in 1694, and it went instead to his friend Thomas Tenison. Stillingfleet died in 1699, leaving a massive library, the cream of which was snapped up by the bibliophile Robert Harley, later earl of Oxford.

FIG. 90 *Edward Stillingfleet, by Mary Beale.*

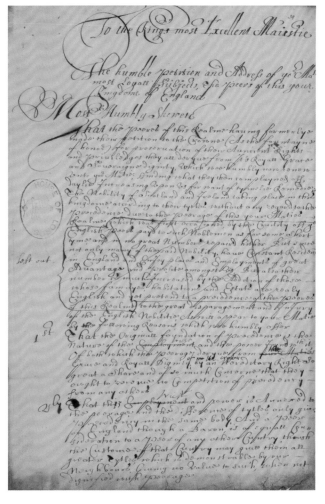

FIG.91 *Draft of a petition to the crown regarding the precedence of foreign (i.e. Scots and Irish) nobility, March 1668.*

remained seated and 'covered'. Even when the House was not in session 'so much respect is to be paid to that room as none but members of the House ought to be covered there'.[1] Questions about the wearing of hats took up a large amount of time in settling procedure for the proposed impeachment of John Mordaunt, Viscount Mordaunt and for the Norfolk divorce case (see p. 260). Even in April 1689, in the midst of the constitutional ferment of the revolution, the committee for privileges spent much time and energy considering the circumstances under which peers could wear hats in the presence of the monarch. An inadvertent concession might jeopardise the position of the peerage as a whole: Thomas Thynne, created Viscount Weymouth in 1682 (see below, p. 312), expected to be named to the commission that would try the Monmouth rebels in 1685. Should he or should he not give place to the judges? It was not (or so he said) his own honour that concerned him for 'I am little concerned for my self, yet I would not incur the censure of the House for losing what belongs to the peers'.[2]

The claims of those termed 'foreign' nobility – those in possession of Scottish, or more particularly Irish, peerages – were a particularly thorny problem. Granting Irish peerages had long provided the crown with a way to grant honours without diluting the exclusivity of the English peerage. Many of those who possessed them had little or no connection to Ireland. Complaints about Irish peers claiming parity with equivalent ranks in the English peerage had been made in 1629 and 1641. Further complaints were investigated by the House in 1662, 1666 and 1667–8. The 1662 complaint resulted in an abortive bill, that of 1666 resulted first in a request for a statute and then a petition to the king emphasising the importance of preserving

> the peerage in their full lustre, and fruition of all their privileges, they being the best, safest, and most natural fence of monarchy against the popular distempers of this last age; we shall with great assurance humbly beseech your majesty, that you will be graciously pleased to establish some rule for regulating this matter in the future; that the inconveniencies to your nobility and government, which may happen hereby, may be seasonably thereby prevented and avoided.[3]

In 1671 when the House anticipated problems with the Irish peers at the funeral of the duchess of York, it took pre-emptive action and ordered that 'the peers of this realm shall meet in this House, and go in a body by themselves, according to their places in this House; and that garter king at arms have notice hereof, to the end he may take care that no foreign nobility shall interpose'.[4] In 1668 the peers complained that peers of 'other kingdoms' had coronets with six pearls emblazoned on their coaches 'which none ought to do but English barons'.[5] In 1677 they again demanded an investigation into the right of Scots and Irish peers to display coronets on their coaches. That year, however, they seemed to recognize the rights of the Scottish and Irish peers, when they contemplated making it illegal for men who had not been 'admitted peers by sitting in the Parliaments of the three nations according as their honours are ... [to] place coronets on their coaches and be called lords'.[6] On this occasion, the particular objects of their anger were Robert Villiers, *soi-disant*

Viscount Purbeck, and Charles Knollys, *soi-disant* earl of Banbury (see above, pp. 125, 127-9, 146). Knollys was again aimed at in 1685 when it was rumoured that the earl marshal, the head of the college of arms, would force him to remove a coronet from his coach.

Formal rights and immunities

Such marks of precedence and distinction were only the most conspicuous of the privileges enjoyed by the members of the House of Lords. A series of formal rights and immunities were the most valuable. These came to them both because of their titles (privilege of peerage) and because of their membership of the House of Lords (privilege of Parliament). The situation of the bishops – who were not peers – was different. Shortly after the bishops were readmitted to the House in 1661, the old Presbyterian Algernon Percy, 4th earl of Northumberland, complained that 'The bishops are not contented to be restored unto all they formerly enjoyed, but now they pretend to be peers likewise, and that point is at present under consideration before the committee for privileges.'[7] The committee decided that they were entitled to privilege of Parliament but not to privilege of peerage. When, after 1678 the right to sit in the House was withdrawn from Catholic peers, their right to privilege of Parliament (but not privilege of peerage) should have lapsed as well, although this was not confirmed until 1692 and was still disputed a century later.

Entitlement to the two types of privilege was ill defined and often illogical. Guardians of underage peers managed to claim privilege of Parliament (as Lord Mohun's guardians did in 1667) even though their wards were unable to sit in the House. In 1685 however, the committee for privileges decided that 'Privilege of Parliament ought not to be allowed to peers in cases wherein they are only trustees'.[8] An attempt to prosecute Henry Howard, earl of Norwich (later 6th duke of Norfolk), and his two sons led to a declaration in 1674 that the children of peers could claim privilege of Parliament in certain cases if unmarried, under age and still living with their fathers and they could continue to enjoy it in a more limited range of cases after they came of age, provided that they were unmarried and living with their fathers.

Before 1680 a number of peers' widows also benefited from privilege of Parliament. When the dowager Baroness De la Warr, widow of Henry West, 4th Baron De la Warr, was sued by her tailor in 1671, she claimed privilege against him and his bailiffs: the bailiffs, she alleged, had broken into her house, taken an inventory of her goods and 'threatened to take the said Lady De la Warr alive or dead; and uttered other vilifying language, contrary to the honour due to the peerage of this kingdom, and privilege of Parliament, although they were forewarned that she was a peeress, and had privilege of Parliament'. The House seems, initially at least, to have accepted her claim that she was entitled to both privilege of peerage and privilege of Parliament, despite the fact that she was not entitled to sit in Parliament, was not a peeress in her own right and her husband had been dead for more than forty years.[9] In 1661 the House resolved that the widow of Richard Lennard, 13th Baron Dacre, had forfeited her right to privilege (recorded in the reference to the committee for privileges as privilege of Parliament but in the response of the judges as privilege of peerage) because she had married a commoner, David Walter. In 1675, the House suspended the right of noblewomen and the wives and widows of peers to claim privilege of Parliament; two years later it decided to reinstate it. As a result in 1678 – at the height of the Popish Plot, with the Catholic peers in the Tower on charges of treason and in the midst of debates over the Test Act – the Catholic dowager marchioness of Worcester was able to obtain a declaration 'That all peers, peers' widows (who have not since married to commoners), and the wives of peers, ought to enjoy the privilege of Parliament, and not be comprehended within the penalties enjoined by the proclamation for banishing papists from London and Westminster'. The House changed its mind again in 1680 when it considered another claim from Elizabeth Walter, the former Lady Dacre, who had now received a peerage, as countess of Sheppey, in her own right for life. In dismissing her request the House ruled 'That privilege of Parliament shall not be allowed to noblewomen or widows of peers; saving the right of peerage'.[10] In 1693 the House confirmed that ruling when it resolved that privilege of Parliament did not apply to underage peers, the wives of peers or the widows of peers who had subsequently married commoners.[11]

Privilege of Parliament

Privilege of Parliament was of incalculable value to peers with complex legal and financial affairs and frequently ensnared in debt. It was defined only by the decisions of the House. Although it was shared by Members of the House of Commons, each House made its own rulings and there was no mechanism for standardising them. Variations in interpretation were not unusual. Privilege of Parliament included the right to freedom of speech in Parliament (see above, p. 137, below, p. 215); but its chief practical value to Members of both Houses lay in the fact that, under the guise of preventing interference with their parliamentary duties, it could be used to avoid arrest for debt (although peers were also protected in this by privilege of peerage) and to delay legal action against them. The House, for example, ordered a stay in the proceedings for debt initiated by Edward Higgins against Thomas Savage, 3rd Earl Rivers, in 1661, after Higgins had seized his coach and six horses. Richard Boyle, Baron Clifford of Lanesborough, used it against two individuals who had 'shut up the way, and barred the passage for coaches' to his house.[12] Richard Vaughan, 2nd earl of Carbery in the Irish peerage, who sat in the Lords as Baron Vaughan, called on privilege during a violent local feud in order to secure the return of corn illicitly removed from his barn.[13]

Privilege of Parliament enabled members of the Lords to protect not only themselves, but their servants, their lands and other property rights. The most common use, indeed, was to protect the servants of peers and bishops from arrest for debt (which could sometimes be an attempt to harass their master during a dispute). The arrest of Edward Cherry, domestic chaplain to Earl Rivers, in 1663, for example, may well have been connected to Rivers' own money troubles; in 1671 a servant of Thomas Windsor, 7th Baron Windsor, was arrested at the behest of one of Windsor's creditors. The application of privilege in such cases was governed by a 'remembrance' of the Lords of 28 May 1624 which emphasised the need to take care that only immediate servants should benefit and instructed its members to 'remember the ground of this privilege, which was only in respect they should not be distracted, by the trouble of their servants, from attending the serious affairs of the kingdom; and that, therefore, they will not pervert that privilege to the public injustice of the kingdom'.[14]

In practice these instructions were simply ignored; protections were issued to tradesmen, lawyers and tenants. Worse still, forged protections were offered for cash. Late in 1661 the House declared that protections issued to 'those who were not their lordships' menial servants, or persons necessarily employed about their estates, are void, and of none effect' and warned against forgeries.[15] Within a month of repeating these instructions in 1663 the House was investigating the case of Thomas Sheircliffe or Shawcliffe, who had paid £2 to one of the lord chamberlain's servants for a protection signed by John Carey, Baron Hunsdon. Shawcliffe wanted to use it in a dispute with his landlord and was so grateful that he went personally to thank Hunsdon – who promptly identified the protection as a forgery and reported it to the House. Shawcliffe's protection was perhaps suspiciously cheap: in 1664 it was said they could be had for £20.

Protections issued by members of both Houses of Parliament were widely resented. For tradespeople, denied redress for non-payment by men who relied on their membership of Parliament to ratchet up huge debts, they were potentially ruinous. A pamphlet published in 1662 referred to them as one of the new burdens imposed on the City of London since 1660.[16] In his speech closing the parliamentary session in May that year, the king referred to the 'great clamour against the multitude of protections'.[17] In the midst of the furore over privilege created by the confrontation over *Thomas Skinner v. The East India Company* in 1668 (see above, p. 24), Sir Roger Twysden wrote to Sir Heneage Finch (the future lord chancellor and earl of Nottingham) arguing that protections could no longer be justified:

> It is true in former times, when 14 days or three weeks concluded a session, it might be tolerated, but now they last most part of the year and protect from the hand of justice not less than 10,000 men, I shall leave it to you the consideration whether, if there be such a right, it be not fit to be removed.[18]

The figure of 10,000 was probably an exaggeration; but there may have been thousands of people under the protection of members of both Houses. Nevertheless almost the only restriction imposed by the House of Lords on protections issued by its Members before 1689 was a decision in 1680 that a letter of protection could not exempt the holder from parochial office.

A serious intent to address abuses in protections only emerged after the Revolution. Although the annual sessions of Parliament after 1689 made privilege much more burdensome, the first sign that the problem would be tackled predated the realization that Parliaments would be called annually. In June 1689 a complaint was made against a protection issued by George Howard, 4th earl of Suffolk.[19] Two months later the

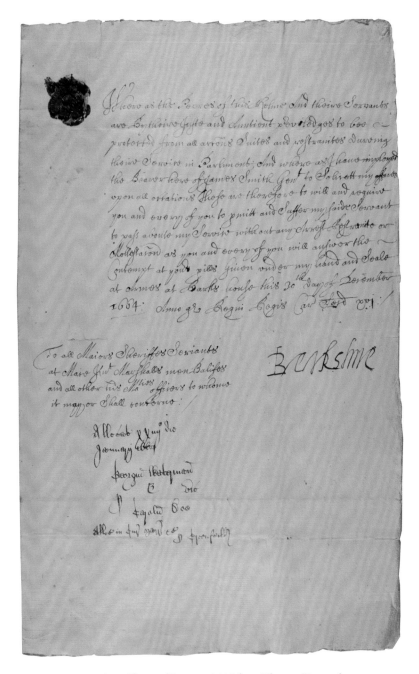

FIG. 92 *A certificate of January 1665 from Thomas Howard,*
earl of Berkshire, indicating that James Smith, gentleman, was
protected by his privilege of peerage, and could 'pass about my
service without any arrest restraint or molestation'.

House learned that one John Trewolla claimed a 'pretended protection' from Philip Wharton, 4th Baron Wharton.[20] Similar complaints were made in the Commons over the winter of 1689–90. The Commons demanded a list of protections and issued a set of rules to regulate their use. The House of Lords followed suit, ordering that:

> for the future there shall no protection or protections be allowed to be
> good, valid, or of any effect, unless they be first entered in the
> Parliament office at Westminster; and the protection, so by such peer or
> Member certified, shall be entered by the clerk of the Parliaments, or
> his deputy; and that in every such protection, that shall be so allowed
> by the clerk or his deputy to be entered, there shall be mentioned in it,
> the nature or quality of such person so protected, and what office or
> place he is in under such peer or member of this House. [21]

Several of the protections produced to the House as a result were found to be forged and two of the forgers were identified and arrested. Abuses continued regardless. When in December 1690 protections issued by four peers were challenged, two of them (George Fitzroy, duke of Northumberland and Thomas Parker, 15th Baron Morley) claimed to be ignorant of the rules. The other two, Suffolk, and Edward Clinton, 5th earl of Lincoln, failed to attend and had all their protections vacated by the House. One of Lincoln's protections had been used to prevent a victim from seeking legal redress against a gang who had imprisoned him in a turret 'under strict guard, without being allowed candle, pen, ink, paper, meat or drink'. Investigations into Morley's activities in 1690 showed that he had registered 90 protections in London and a further 60 in Lancashire, Yorkshire and Westmorland. Hornby, the nearest town to his home at Hornby Castle, had been turned into what was effectively his own personal debtors' sanctuary. It was said that 'no sheriff's officer dare attempt to arrest any inhabitant without his lordship's licence first had, several bailiffs, who have attempted to do so, having been whipped and put in the stocks by his lordship's order.'[22] Continuing efforts to control abuses resulted in Morley's committal to the Tower in January 1692.

If Morley's imprisonment were meant as a salutary lesson to others, it was only partially successful. Northumberland and Lincoln were hauled before the House for a second time in 1692. In 1694 Hugh Cholmondley, Baron Cholmondeley, refused to take a man in financial difficulties into his service – the man was no doubt seeking to shelter under his protection – because he had already appointed one such failed gentleman and feared

Die Mercurij 27° Januarij, 1696.

HE House this Day Reading the Names of the Persons Entred in the Book of Protections, It is Ordered by the Lords Spiritual and Temporal in Parliament Assembled, That all Written Protections given by any Lord of this House, shall be, and are hereby Vacated and made Void, and that for the future no Lord of this House shall give any Written Protection to any Person whatsoever, and this Order to be fixed on the Doors of this House, and *Westminster* Hall.

Matth. Johnson,
Cler' Parliamentor'

Die Lunæ 4° Julij, 1698.

IT is this Day Ordered by the Lords Spiritual and Temporal in Parliament Assembled, That the Order made the last Session of Parliament, on the Twenty seventh of *January*, One thousand six hundred ninety six, for Vacating all Written Protections, shall be forthwith Printed and Published, and be put upon the Doors of this House, the Doors of *Westminster* Hall, the *Royal Exchange* in *London*, the Sheriffs Office, and other Publick Places; to the End all Persons who think themselves therein Concerned may have Notice thereof.

Matth. Johnson,
Cler' Parliamentor'

London, Printed by *Charles Bill*, and the Executrix of *Thomas Newcomb*, deceas'd; Printers to the King's most Excellent Majesty. 1698.

becoming 'notorious for it'.[23] The Fenwick affair in 1696 revealed another scandal. Daniel Ryan, an Irish tailor, desperately wanted a post in the service of Charles Mordaunt, earl of Monmouth. Ryan stated that 'If he could be protected as my lord's servant (which was all he designed in it), he did not care if he made my lord's liveries for nothing' and offered a substantial bribe to get the job 'only to come once a month, to appear as a servant, to cover the protection'.[24] In January 1697, the House banned written protections (though this was only made into a formal standing order in 1712). The ban had little effect on Morley, who was again in trouble the very same year. A more serious effort to limit the abuse of parliamentary privilege was launched that year, with a bill designed to restrict its potential to delay private litigation. Another such bill was initiated in the Lords

Getting away with murder?
Charles Mohun, 4th Baron
Mohun (1677–1712)

harles Mohun was barely five months old when he succeeded in 1677 as 4th Baron Mohun. Both of his parents had hot tempers: his father was 'run through the guts' in a fight behind Southampton House in Bloomsbury; his mother Philippa, described as an 'impudent baggage' by her own father, Arthur Annesley, earl of Anglesey, was involved in a brawl shortly after her husband's death. Mohun inherited little apart from his title and his parents' unruliness. In December 1692, still only fifteen, he joined his friend Richard Hill in a bizarre attempt to kidnap the actor Anne Bracegirdle. When their haphazard plans fell apart, they turned instead on a passer-by, the actor William Mountfort whom they believed to be Anne Bracegirdle's lover. While Mohun distracted Mountfort, Hill stabbed him. Mountfort, with a wound in his chest 20 inches deep, died the next day.

Mohun's trial for murder began in the House of Lords on 31 January 1693. The trial was a sensation, attracting 'a glorious appearance of ladies' as well as the king himself.[1] It was not claimed that Mohun was the killer but, as the solicitor general argued, 'if he was privy, and knew of Hill's design, and stayed there for that purpose, to give him assistance in it ... he will be as much guilty of the murther, as Hill that actually killed him.' The prosecution brought evidence that after the failure of their kidnapping attempt, Hill and Mohun had fuelled their aggression with drink while waiting for Mountfort outside the Bracegirdle house with drawn swords. Mohun's witnesses testified that they were intending to find an opportunity to apologise for their actions, that Mountfort had drawn his sword and had been killed in a fair fight. The evidence of at least one of these witnesses differed in several important details from his earlier statements; that of another was tainted by allegations that she had deliberately disappeared to avoid testifying to the coroner.

The peers spent several days discussing their verdict, eventually seeking the advice of the judges to clarify the crucial issue: whether Mohun's involvement amounted to murder. When the vote was taken, 14 peers declared him guilty but 69, including

Thomas Osborne, marquess of Carmarthen, the presiding officer, voted to acquit. 'The evidence ... would have endanger'd a commoner', remarked one observer.[2] Social status certainly influenced the outcome of the case – one 'great lord' declared that Mountfort 'was but a player, and they and fiddlers are rogues'[3] – although Mohun's youth did as well.

Towards the end of 1694 Mohun was involved in another brawl, this time with a Cornish Member of the Commons, Francis Scobell. There were further incidents. In the autumn of 1697, still several months short of his 21st birthday, he again found himself accused of murder. Arrogant as ever, he was placed under close confinement in the Tower of London because, as its governor explained 'his lordship was so exceeding rude that he could not tell how to deal with him'.[4] It was estimated that the trial would cost £3,000, but Mohun's contemporaries predicted that he would again walk free. At worst they anticipated a verdict of manslaughter which would effectively be nullified by his entitlement to privilege of peerage. Although the House of Lords ordered preparations to be made, no trial was held. In April 1698 Mohun was released on bail.

Just six months later Mohun was again involved in a fatal fight. Together with his equally vicious friend, Edward Rich, 6th earl of Warwick, he had been drinking with four companions when a quarrel arose between two of them, Richard Coote and Richard French. Well after midnight, the entire party went to fight in nearby Leicester Square, and, in the dark, Coote was killed. Afterwards Warwick and Mohun both fled the country, although they returned in the spring of the following year to face trial by their peers. Warwick explained that they had left the country merely to avoid the inconvenience of a long spell in gaol awaiting the sitting of Parliament. The witnesses, a mixture of lowly paid sedan chairmen and tavern staff, told a consistent (or possibly well-rehearsed) story in which Warwick and Mohun were cast, improbably, as peacemakers. Although an investigation suggested that the fatal wound was probably inflicted by Warwick's sword, the verdicts were unan-

FIG. 95 *Charles Mohun, 4th Baron Mohun, by Sir Godfrey Kneller.*

imous: Warwick was found guilty of manslaughter, Mohun was acquitted. When Mohun fell ill later that year at least one contemporary remarked that 'his death will be no loss to the nation'.[5]

Mohun was suspected of yet another killing in 1701. In the same year he inherited much of the Macclesfield estate and became embroiled in litigation with a rival claimant, his wife's brother-in-law, the Scottish peer James Hamilton, 4th duke of Hamilton (see above, p. 88). In 1712, with the legal actions still ongoing, Hamilton accused one of Mohun's witnesses of perjury. Mohun challenged Hamilton to a duel. The two men fought in Hyde Park where 'Duke Hamilton was run through the right arm at the first thrust and at the same time he ran Lord Mohun through the breast sideways, this made 'em close and so they fell to stabbing till both fell'.[6] Both Mohun and Hamilton died of their wounds.

FIG. 96 *It is unknown whether this anonymous drawing of the duel between Mohun and Hamilton bears any relation to reality.*

in 1701, but was dropped in favour of a bill from the Commons, which finally passed, although it only addressed part of the broader issues associated with privilege.

Privilege of peerage

Privilege of peerage encompassed a collection of rights and immunities founded partly on custom, partly on statute and partly on the whim of the House of Lords. It included, most fundamentally, the right to sit and vote in the House (although this, as has been seen, was far from straightforward). A few of them were valuable, but not especially contentious: the mid-sixteenth century statute of pluralities, for example, enabled the chaplains of peers and bishops to supplement their income by holding several livings at once, despite the general prohibition on pluralities. Members were entitled to nominate chaplains on a sliding scale based on rank: eight for an archbishop; six for a bishop; five for earls and marquesses; four for viscounts; three for barons; two for widows of peers. Peers' right of access to the sovereign, acknowledged as a privilege of peerage after 1715, may have existed before then, although Godolphin complained bitterly to Marlborough about Queen Anne's decision to see the opposition peer John Thompson, Baron Haversham: 'it was not hard to make a judgment of what was like to happen next winter, when people of his behaviour could meet with encouragement to come to court.'[25] Peers could not be summoned to answer actions in chancery but had to be invited by letter, and in a court of law they testified on honour rather than oath.

The most conspicuous privilege of peerage, apart from the right to be summoned to the House, was the right to trial by fellow peers in cases of treason or felony. The procedures were set out in a statute of 1547. Proceedings began in the ordinary criminal courts, but were transferred either to the House of Lords itself, formally reconstituted as the court of the lord high steward, or (if Parliament were not sitting) to a specially convened court of the lord high steward to which 20-35 peers were summoned as triers. After 1689 Parliament sat so regularly that there was no need for the separate court, and the 1696 Treason Act required all peers with the right to sit and vote to be summoned, removing any real distinction between the court and the House and preventing the crown from trying to determine the outcome by selecting the triers. The verdict was by majority vote given in reverse order of precedence, the most junior peer being the first to declare his decision. The trials took place in Westminster Hall where they became popular events and society occasions. At the trial of Lord Morley in 1666 two private rooms were erected in the Hall, one for the king and queen who attended incognito with their attendants and one for other members of the royal family. Accommodation was also provided for the Spanish and Swedish ambassadors, 'divers ladies and persons of honour' and those peers who had not been summoned as triers.[26]

Other than impeachments of peers (which, despite the similarity of subject matter, followed different procedural rules making privilege of peerage irrelevant), between 1660 and 1715 only two trials of peers did not take place in the court of lord high steward. In 1687 William Cavendish, 4th earl (later duke) of Devonshire, and prominent opposition spokesman, was accused of assault. Since assault was a misdemeanour, rather than a felony, his plea of privilege was over-ruled and he was tried in the court of king's bench where he was punished for his politics rather than his offence and fined £30,000. The second case was that of Arthur Herbert, earl of Torrington, who was court martialled for his part in the naval defeat off Beachy Head under articles of war by a board made up mainly of commoner officers in 1690. The House reluctantly agreed that under such circumstances privilege did not apply, although in 1703 it secured provision in the Mutiny Act to ensure that peers in military service abroad who were charged with felony or treason and who were not then tried by court martial could be tried by their peers when they returned to England.[27]

In any case, very few peers were tried for felonies. Frequently they were pardoned before the case reached the formality of an indictment. One of the most notorious cases of a pardon was the fatal wounding of Francis Talbot, 11th earl of Shrewsbury, in January 1668 by George Villiers, 2nd duke of Buckingham, in a duel over Buckingham's notoriously indiscreet affair with Shrewsbury's countess. It was a surprise that the duel had taken place at all, since Shrewsbury had been remarkably tolerant over his wife's indiscretions for several years; moreover, Buckingham had been regarded as a coward since two years before, when he had avoided a duel with Thomas Belasyse, 2nd Viscount Fauconberg (all the participants had drawn their swords to fight, 'but the duke ... had more mind to parley than to fight, and kept his in his scabbard, till taking some verbal and superficial satisfaction of my Lord Falconbrige [Fauconberg], the dispute went no further').[28] This time, Shrewsbury

'Not guilty upon honour':
Thomas Brown on peerage trials

 ur Peers have often for themselves rebell'd
When did they for the People take
the Field?
Led not by Love, but Interest and Pride,
They would not let the Prince their Vassals ride.
That Pow'r they to themselves reserv'd alone,
And so thro' thick and thin they spur'd old Roan.
  To Fact and long Experience I appeal,
How fairly to themselves they Justice deal;
For if my Lord, o'er-power'd by Wine and Whore,
The next he meets, does thro' the Entrails scow'r,
Tis pity, his relenting Brethren cry,
That for his first Offence the Youth shou'd die;
Come, he'll grow grave, Virtue and he'll be Friends,

And by his Voting make the Crown amends.
Tis true a most magnificent Parade
Of Law, to please the gaping Mob, is made.
Scaffolds are rais'd in the Litigious Hall,
The Maces glitter, and the Serjeants bawl.
So long they wrangle, and so oft they stop,
The wearied Ladies do their Moisture drop.
This is the Court (they say) keeps all in awe,
Gives Life to Justice, Vigour to the Law.
True, they quote *Law*, and they do prattle on her,
What's the Result? *Not guilty upon Honour.*

Works of Mr Thomas Brown, Serious and Comical,
5th edition, 1720, p. 147

---

threatened to pistol whip Buckingham every time they met if the challenge were refused. They met, each accompanied by two seconds, at Barn Elms, near Putney, and all six men began to fight. By the end, one of Buckingham's seconds was dead and Shrewsbury was badly wounded. Charles II was said to be enraged and Buckingham went to ground for a while, giving his enemies hope that 'the great minister of state ... will lose his master's ear, and be obstructed in his influencing either Houses'.[29] In less than two weeks, though, the king had convinced himself that the real fault was Shrewsbury's and ordered pardons for all the participants. Shrewsbury died two months after the duel. The doctors declared that he had died of natural causes but few believed them, preferring the more obvious explanation that this was an official cover-up aimed at protecting Buckingham (and the king who had pardoned him) from blame.

Buckingham's escape from trial for murder was not unusual. Duelling was to some extent a special case, as even when prosecuted in the ordinary courts, men who killed their opponents in a duel were frequently acquitted, as long as the rules of honour had been followed. But when, three years later, a group of young courtiers, including the king's illegitimate son James Scott, duke of Monmouth, and Christopher Monck,

Scandalum magnatum: libel and politics

ne of the first peers after the Restoration to sue on a charge of *scandalum magnatum* was Henry Pierrepont, marquess of Dorchester, who brought a case against one Powle in the court of common pleas in February 1664 for saying that Dorchester was 'no more to be regarded than that dog'. Dorchester was awarded 1,000 marks in compensation.[1] Sometime in the early 1670s Edward Montagu, 2nd Baron Montagu of Boughton, brought an action against a kinsman, Francis Lane, who had been a thorn in his side for several years. One deponent gave testimony that Lane had slandered Montagu in 1666 at 'several times in several places' claiming that he 'was an enemy to the king.'[2] Three years later, Lane told Basil Feilding, 2nd earl of Denbigh, that he had informed one of the secretaries of state of Montagu's 'disloyalty and disaffection',[3] and at about the same time made free to another acquaintance, 'saying the Lord Montagu was a base unworthy person'.[4] Lane continued his campaign before several witnesses, describing Montagu as 'a mongrel and not a Montagu and that his true name was Ladds and that his ancestors changed their name and arrogated to themselves the name of Montagu'. His rant encompassed the whole Montagu family, including Edward Montagu, first earl of Sandwich, then ambassador to Madrid:

> he hoped he should see in a short time never a Montagu in England have their heads upon their shoulders, and that the Lord Sandwich was a coward and he looked upon him as a condemned person already and that it was well he was gone into Spain or else his head had been cut off before this time.[5]

By the mid-1670s *scandalum magnatum* was being used freely by peers responding to attacks during elections. In April 1676 Anthony Ashley Cooper, earl of Shaftesbury, brought a case against John Digby, styled Lord Digby (heir to the earldom of Bristol), for accusing Shaftesbury of being 'a fanatic and a traitor and by God I will have your head the next sessions of Parliament'.[6] Shaftesbury won his case, but it was speculated that he would gain no very considerable damages as 'the foreman of the jury is my Lord Digby's friend'. Henry Hyde, 2nd earl of Clarendon, fared little better against Thomas Hooper, who had accused the earl of being a papist during the election at Christchurch in Hampshire in 1681. Although Clarendon sought £5,000 damages, he was awarded only 100 marks and 40 shillings costs by the jury. Hooper had claimed that Clarendon had insulted him first and threatened to 'fillip' him on the nose. At the election of a new town clerk in Oxford in 1681, the Tory James Bertie, earl of Abingdon, had a furious row with the city's former Member of the Commons, the venerable Whig, Brome Whorwood. Abingdon called Whorwood an 'old fool'; Whorwood called Abingdon a young one. Abingdon sued for *scandalum magnatum*; Whorwood brought a charge of battery against the earl. In the end, John Fell, bishop of Oxford, managed to smooth things over. The previous year George Villiers, 2nd duke of Buckingham, had left nothing to chance. Having 'two or three' trials pending at the Buckingham assizes he sent the judges a side of venison and was awarded £1,000 following his successful prosecution of one Howard, a local barber.[7]

It was James, duke of York, who used *scandalum magnatum* most effectively, developing it into a crippling weapon against his Whig antagonists after his return to England from exile in Scotland in 1682. He won damages of £100,000 from Thomas Pilkington, a former Whig Member of the Commons and sheriff of London, who was alleged to have accused York of having a hand in the Great Fire of London and of planning to 'cut the citizens' throats'.[8] He sued Titus Oates, and a raft of former Whig Members of the Commons – John Upton, Sir Francis Drake, Sir George Speke and John Dutton Colt – as well as the Speaker, William Williams. Damages were awarded against Colt of £100,000. Associates of York used the same device: Henry Mordaunt, 2nd earl of Peterborough, James Butler, duke of Ormond, Henry Somerset, duke of Beaufort, Clarendon, George Jeffreys, Baron Jeffreys and Charles North, 5th Baron

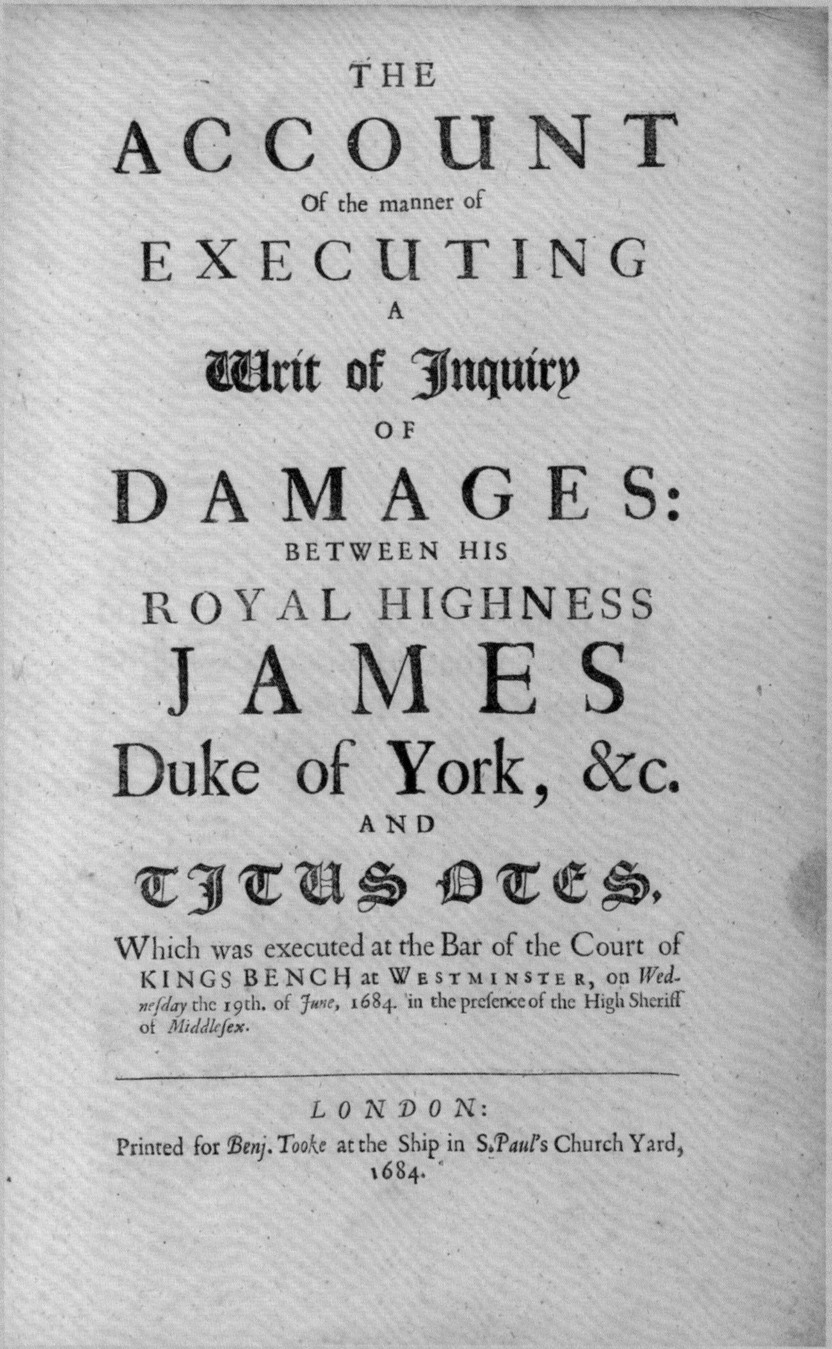

THE
ACCOUNT
Of the manner of
EXECUTING
A
𝔚rit of 𝔍nquiry
OF
DAMAGES:
BETWEEN HIS
ROYAL HIGHNESS
JAMES
Duke of York, &c.
AND
𝔗𝔦𝔱𝔲𝔰 𝔒𝔱𝔢𝔰,

Which was executed at the Bar of the Court of
KINGS BENCH at WESTMINSTER, on *Wed-nesday* the 19th. of *June,* 1684. in the presence of the High Sheriff
of *Middlesex.*

LONDON:
Printed for *Benj. Tooke* at the Ship in S. *Paul's* Church Yard,
1684.

FIG. 97 *In 1684 James duke of York sued Titus Oates, the originator of the Popish Plot and the initial allegations about the involvement of the duke and his circle. York was awarded £100,000 in damages. Oates was put in the Compter prison when he defaulted on payment. He was later prosecuted for perjury.*

North. Lord North in 1683, however, accepted the apology of the man he had sued in lieu of damages, 'and so it ended to his lordship's great commendation'.[9] These cases partly lay behind the 1689 Bill of Rights' condemnation of excessive fines and 'cruel and unusual punishments'. After the overthrow of James II in 1688, the use of actions of *scandalum magnatum* to cow political opponents ceased and the use of the device declined, although it was not abolished until 1887.

2nd duke of Albemarle, killed a beadle during a disturbance at a brothel, they, too, were pardoned before a trial could be held. Richard Savage, the future 4th Earl Rivers, was similarly pardoned when he was indicted for his part in an affray in which he together with his brother and three equally drunken friends attacked and killed one William Cole.

Those whose cases did get to trial found, as the satirist Thomas Brown complained, that their fellow peers were just as generous as the king. Philip Herbert, 7th earl of Pembroke, was tried for murder by the House in 1678 after killing a man in a confused brawl – he had taken offence when someone had claimed to be 'as good, or better a gentleman' than Pembroke. Even before the trial it was reported that Pembroke would be pardoned if convicted. In the event he was found guilty of manslaughter, which implied that Pembroke's vicious attack was a justifiable reaction to intolerable provocation; he was allowed to claim benefit of clergy, which meant that he could go free. In the mid-eighteenth century the trial and conviction for murder of Laurence Shirley, 4th Earl Ferrers, was paraded as proof that all were equal under the law: in the later seventeenth century the peers' unique rights and privileges, their special relationship with the crown and deference to their exalted status meant that the criminal law barely reached them.

Peers possessed another and, as used in the politically tense final years of Charles II's reign, particularly pernicious, privilege through the medieval statutes of *scandalum magnatum* (see above, p. 188). These created an aggravated offence of libel against great officers of state, a term which encompassed members of the House of Lords, and opened up the possibility of virtually unlimited fines and damages. Such actions had been curtailed by the abolition of the court of star chamber in 1641, but they were revived following the Restoration and later proved to be a useful political weapon, employed to particular effect by peers on both sides of the question during the Exclusion Crisis. They were used ruthlessly by the governments of Charles II and James II against their opponents. In 1686 Speaker Sir William Williams rapidly changed his political allegiances when faced with a £10,000 fine for authorising the publication of Dangerfield's Whiggish *Narrative* of the Popish Plot, and hence (it was claimed) libelling James, duke of York. He was sued for a similar sum for libelling York's close friend and supporter Henry Mordaunt, 2nd earl of Peterborough, in the same publication. Peterborough also prosecuted the printer of the *Narrative* and several of the booksellers who had sold it.

He drove at least one of the booksellers to insolvency. The printer embraced the Roman Catholic Church as a way of securing the king's favour and evading payment.

Peers routinely attempted to assert their right to special treatment in new statutes. They insisted in 1660 that their taxes should not be assessed by mere commoners, although on a number of subsequent occasions the government pressurised them to give way, rather than risk the loss of essential financial legislation. Peers insisted on special provisions in the 1662 militia bill, and although compromises were eventually reached, debates over the conventicle bill in 1664 and again in 1670 stumbled over their insistence that their houses should be exempt from search except under the king's warrant. At the height of the London plague of 1665, legislation to control the movement of the sick was defeated by the obstinacy of peers who refused to permit their houses to be shut up even if infected. Keeping track of how to deal with peers was a major headache for local officials; a series of notes compiled by Sir Willoughby Aston about the duties of deputy lieutenants – the leaders of the county militia – included headings like 'noblemen's houses how searched', 'how peers are to be taxed' and guidelines about the requirements for oath taking as they applied to peers.[30]

Privilege was fundamental to the power and status of the peerage. The earl of Northampton suggested in 1679 that 'the thickest head of hair may be pulled out hair by hair: if you part with one privilege and another you may at last lose all', and his sentiment – that the loss of any privilege could easily lead to the end of the special status of the peerage within society – was widely shared.[31] From the Restoration to the Revolution, the Lords had been particularly assertive about their privileges, determined to claim them and tenacious to defend them. Parliament was an essential part of their system of power and privilege: Parliament was coming to be the arbiter of who could be regarded as a peer; some of their privileges derived from Parliament, and it was only because they participated directly in Parliament that peers and bishops were able to defend their privileges so effectively. Besides privilege, Parliament provided the peers and the bishops with many other ways of pursuing their collective and individual interests, and carrying on their personal disputes. Most of all, of course, it enabled them to exercise their personal influence within national politics. How the peers used Parliament, and how the House of Lords worked, is the concern of the next two chapters.

Allegiance, conspiracy and confusion: the legacy of revolution, 1689–97

In three months a Revolution had transformed the politics and constitution of England. Over the next twenty-five years, against the backdrop of a series of intense wars with France, her politicians would struggle to get to grips with what it meant. Was the Revolution permanent? Few were sure, and many hedged their bets by maintaining contacts with James II, now established at St Germain-en-Laye to the west of Paris. Uncertainty about which of them were engaged in a probably treasonous correspondence with James's court fuelled a paranoid and poisonous political atmosphere.

Was the Revolution justified? The most radical Whigs accepted with alacrity the deposition by the people and Parliament of the rightful monarch and the exclusion of his proper heir from succession to the throne. The most ideologically consistent of Tories regarded it as a crime and viewed their more pragmatic colleagues who went along with it as time-servers and hypocrites. A handful of major politicians – among them Henry Hyde, 2nd earl of Clarendon – refused to take the oaths of allegiance to the new monarchs and, as non-jurors, had to forego all public office. A small number of Tories became Jacobites, pledging their assistance to the exiled monarch's bid to regain the throne. The great majority of politicians and churchmen – Whigs and Tories alike – uncomfortably came to terms with the Revolution, seeking ways to justify it that avoided jeopardising the accepted order of things.

What sort of politics would emerge from the Revolution? The sense of common purpose against James II's Catholic project of 1687 and 1688 was eroded by the arguments of early 1689. They had reminded Tories of the links between Whig ideas and the bloody deposition of Charles I; they had convinced Whigs that the divine right of kings – never mind how pernicious the kings themselves might be – was the bedrock of Toryism. The clearest dividing line remained the Church. A belief that the Revolution might result in a reconciliation between the Church and the dissenters was strangled in 1689. The Tories were willing now to let dissenters worship in their own meeting houses – Daniel Finch, 2nd earl of Nottingham's Toleration Act was passed – but they vigorously rejected the idea that they might take part in, and dilute the purity of, the established Church and its liturgy. The leader of the most uncompromising Tories, the 2nd earl of Clarendon, after walking with one of the proposers of a 'comprehension' bill, the prominent Whig clergyman, Thomas Tenison, in the Apothecaries' Garden in April 1689, was mystified as to how 'so good a man' should be involved in such a scheme.[1] Dissenters were in any case by now

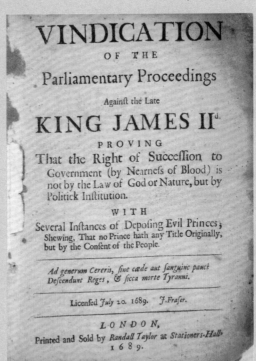

FIG. 98 *One of the many contributions to the hot public debate on the nature and meaning of the Revolution. Tories were deeply uncomfortable with the idea that the hereditary principle had been overturned, and the suggestion advanced in this pamphlet that the right of succession to the crown could be simply altered by Parliament was anathema.*

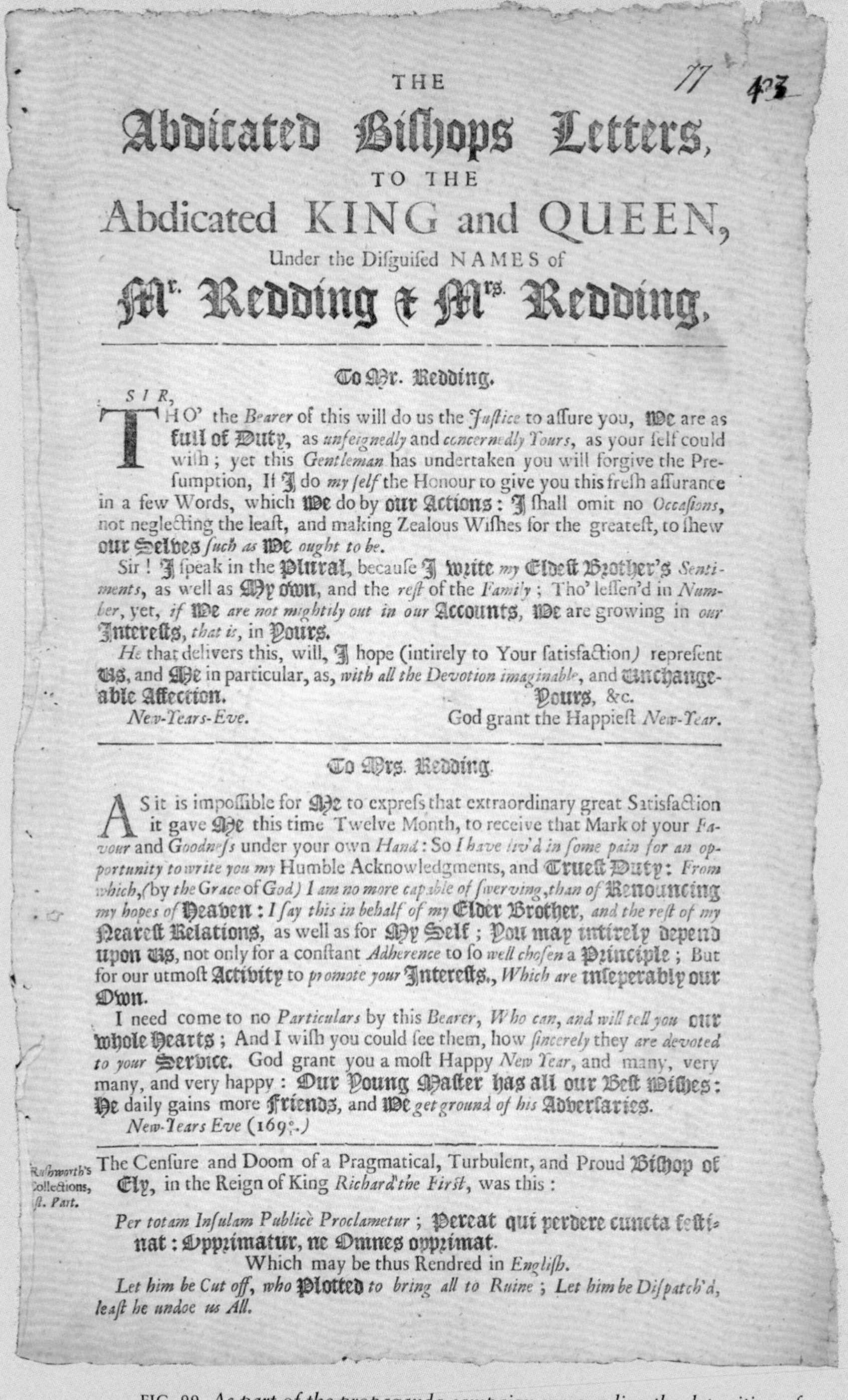

THE
Abdicated Bishops Letters,
TO THE
Abdicated KING and QUEEN,
Under the Disguised NAMES of
Mr. Redding & Mrs. Redding.

To Mr. Redding.

SIR,

THO' the *Bearer* of this will do us the *Justice* to assure you, We are as full of Duty, as *unfeignedly* and *concernedly Yours*, as your self could wish; yet this *Gentleman* has undertaken you will forgive the Presumption, If I do *my self* the Honour to give you this fresh assurance in a few Words, which We do by our Actions: I shall omit no *Occasions*, not neglecting the least, and making Zealous Wishes for the greatest, to shew our Selves *such as* We *ought to be*.

Sir! I speak in the Plural, because I write *my* Eldest Brother's *Sentiments*, as well as My own, and the *rest* of the *Family*; Tho' lessen'd in *Number*, yet, if We *are not mightily out in our* Accounts, We are growing in *our* Interests, *that is*, in Yours.

He that delivers this, will, I hope (intirely to Your *satisfaction*) represent Us, and Me in particular, as, *with all the Devotion imaginable*, and Unchangeable Affection.

     Yours, &c.

New-Years-Eve.   God grant the Happiest *New-Year*.

To Mrs. Redding.

AS it is impossible for Me to express that extraordinary great Satisfaction it gave Me this time Twelve Month, to receive that Mark of your *Favour* and *Goodness* under your own *Hand*: So *I have liv'd in some pain for an opportunity to write you my* Humble Acknowledgments, and Truest Duty: *From which, (by the* Grace *of God) I am no more capable of swerving, than of* Renouncing *my hopes of* Heaven: *I say this in behalf of my* Elder Brother, *and the rest of my* Nearest Relations, as well as for My Self; You may intirely depend upon Us, not only for a constant *Adherence* to so *well chosen* a Principle; But for our utmost Activity to *promote your* Interests., Which are inseperably our Own.

I need come to no *Particulars* by this *Bearer, Who can, and will tell you* our whole Hearts; And I wish you could see them, how *sincerely they are devoted to your* Service. God grant you a most Happy *New Year*, and many, very many, and very happy: Our Young Master has all our Best Wishes: He daily gains more Friends, and We *get ground of his Adversaries*.

     New-Years Eve (169?.)

Rushworth's Collections, 3. Part. The Censure and Doom of a Pragmatical, Turbulent, and Proud Bishop of Ely, in the Reign of King *Richard the First*, was this:

Per totam Insulam Publice Proclametur; Pereat qui perdere cuncta festinat: Opprimatur, ne Omnes opprimat.

     Which may be thus Rendred in *English*.

Let him be Cut off, who Plotted *to bring all to* Ruine; *Let him be Dispatch'd, least he undoe us All*.

FIG. 99 *As part of the propaganda campaign surrounding the deposition of James II, there were strenuous efforts to identify the deprived bishops as Jacobite sympathisers. Here the non-juring bishops are made to express their support for James II's son, the Prince of Wales ('our young master') as the legitimate heir to his father's throne.*

FIG. 100 *This medal was struck to mark the defeat in Ireland of James II. William and Mary are depicted as a lion and lioness with the Jacobites as Hydra, the many headed serpent. The lion tramples Hydra whilst a spaniel (regarded as a quintessentially English dog and celebrated for its loyalty) demonstrates its devotion to the lioness. The inscription, PARCERE SVBIECTIS ET DEBELLARE SVPERBOS, is a quotation from Virgil's Aeneid: 'spare the conquered and overcome the proud'.*

less interested in a reconciliation with the Church of England, and were more interested in obtaining the abolition of the sacramental test which limited their access to office. Although they secured the support of the king, Tories bitterly resisted that, too, regarding it, in Nottingham's words, as 'dangerous to admit any kind of Dissenters into any share of the Government'.[2] Whigs ensured that the new oath of allegiance to William and Mary – though carefully worded to fudge the issue of whether they were, or were not, the rightful rulers – was imposed on the clergy. It was more than some Tory consciences could accept. Around four hundred clergymen and nearly a third of the episcopate – Archbishop Sancroft of Canterbury, Bishops Ken of Bath and Wells, Lake of Chichester, Turner of Ely, White of Peterborough, Thomas of Worcester, Frampton of Gloucester and Lloyd of Norwich – refused to swear. Six of them were subsequently deprived of office: Lake died in August 1689 before the deprivation came into effect, and another bishop, Cartwright of Chester, who had gone to join James II in Ireland, died in April 1689.

All this showed that the party divisions of the early 1680s were still very much present. But there was plenty to confuse them. The Revolution had resulted in England's immediate engagement in a gruelling war with France, which required heavy and continuous taxation and the expansion of the military and state bureaucracy. It spurred the development of a new and complex system of deficit finance dependent on the growing London money market. Many of the aristocracy and the country gentlemen who sat in Parliament, of both parties, were convinced that it was forging a new and corrupt political elite. William himself was widely regarded as intent on bleeding English resources – men, arms and money – to pursue a war that was designed primarily to protect the interests of his homeland and England's commercial rival, the Dutch republic. Discontented Whigs and Tories alike adopted some of the anti-government attitudes and language of the 'country' politicians of the 1670s.

Who would benefit from the Revolution? Whigs regarded themselves as the natural party of Revolution government. They resented William's willingness to turn for advice and support to some of the discredited politicians of the previous regime. Thomas Osborne, now marquess of Carmarthen, Robert Spencer, 2nd earl of Sunderland, and George Savile, marquess of Halifax, all of whom quickly became indispensable advisers to the new King, were regarded with especial venom for their roles in the governments of Charles II and of James II. William turned often, too often for his new English subjects, to the advice of tried and tested supporters amongst his fellow countrymen: William Henry van Nassau van Zuylestein, created earl of Rochford; Hans Willem Bentinck, created earl of Portland; and Arnold Joost van Keppel, created earl of Albemarle in 1697.

How would the Revolution affect the role of the Lords? The immense burden of the war with France into which England was plunged by the Revolution, made taxation – and hence control of the House of Commons – even more central to government concerns. The king's ministers needed to construct coalitions in the Commons to secure key votes for supply, basing them around party allies, the employees of the crown, their personal connections and their powers of persuasion. Peers were nevertheless at the heart of Revolution politics: both individually, as the key min-

FIG. 101 *The new and fragile regime was constantly wary of possible Jacobite plots. Revelations in the spring of 1692 of a possible invasion led to this proclamation for the arrest of several Jacobite sympathisers, including Edward Lee, earl of Lichfield and Sir John Fenwick (see above, p. 58 and below, p. 216). John Churchill, earl (later duke) of Marlborough, had been arrested five days earlier, creating a deep rift between the queen and her sister, Princess Anne.*

isters and politicians, deeply involved in the management of the Commons; and collectively, as a body which, with careful planning and organisation, was able to frustrate the designs of whatever majorities had been built in the lower House. The political dynamics of the House of Lords were difficult to pin down. The Lords had its party zealots, men like the Whigs Charles Powlett, promoted from marquess of Winchester to duke of Bolton, and Charles Gerard, earl of Macclesfield, who in November 1689 set in motion a set of inquiries into abuses of the past fifteen years. Yet party was far from the only factor in the complex politics of the Lords. William created fourteen new peerages in April and May 1689, but they showed no clear party bias. Naturally, the influence of the crown was much more closely felt in the Lords than it was in the Commons, and if the ideological politics of Whig and Tory, country and court, were significant, the politics of the Lords was confused by intense personal and family ambitions, rivalries, friendships and loyalties, many of which had long histories, and in which even newly ennobled peers, linked to the same families by blood and marriage, were equally involved.

Their Excellencies
THE LORDS JUSTICES OF ENGLAND,
For the Administration of the Government during the Absence of the KING.

A mixed ministry

William struggled to hold together ministries incorporating ministers from both parties, as they fought out their personal and party rivalries in Parliament. When he dissolved the Convention and summoned a new Parliament in 1690, the elections strengthened the Tories in the Commons. Whigs tested and provoked them in the Lords. Setbacks in the war produced recriminations between the ministers, and suspicions about the allegiance of senior ministers and military officers were never far from the surface. Well founded doubts about the loyalty of the prominent general John Churchill, earl, later duke of Marlborough led to his dismissal in 1692, and a rupture between the king and queen on the one hand, and the heir apparent, the queen's sister Princess Anne, to whom Marlborough and his wife were especially close, on the other.

By 1693, coaxed by a Sunderland now returned from exile and attempting a political rehabilitation (see above, p. 134), William had begun to move towards the Whigs as he searched for a more stable basis for his government. Always ambiguous in his political actions and affiliations, Sunderland was said to have countered the king's objections by pointing out 'that it was very true that the Tories were better friends to monarchy than the Whigs were, but then

his majesty was to consider that he was not their monarch'.[3] He projected a new court party, distributing offers of money, office and promotions among the peerage. He assembled the Whig leaders at his house at Althorp, even though many of them regarded the former *éminence grise* of James II with outright hostility – a former friend and colleague, Sidney Godolphin, Baron (later earl of) Godolphin declared that Sunderland 'deserved rather to be impeached than to be preferred'.[4] In the autumn of 1693, with both Houses demanding enquiries into the mismanagement of the war, William dismissed the Tory secretary of state Nottingham, and over the winter of 1693/4 he employed Mrs Lundy, the mistress of Charles Talbot, 12th earl of Shrewsbury, and his own mistress, Mrs Villiers (later countess of Orkney), to entice Shrewsbury into office as the linchpin of a mainly Whig ministry. Shrewsbury's price was the king's agreement to one of the Whigs' favourite projects, limiting Parliament to three year terms (the Triennial Act). A flurry of appointments, honours (including dukedoms for four key Whig politicians – Shrewsbury, William Cavendish, 4th earl of Devonshire, William Russell, 5th earl of Bedford and John Holles, 4th earl of Clare) and purges in early 1694 tightened the new ministers', and Sunderland's, grip on power. 'Let [the king] be steady and go on in making the changes intended' wrote Sunderland to Portland 'and he may be sure his business will mend every day'.[5]

The Junto

At the end of December 1694 the unexpected death of the queen seemed to threaten the fragile legitimacy of William's government. In the event, by underlining its vulnerability, it bolstered loyalty to William and brought about a reconciliation with Princess Anne. Over the following two years, Whig grandees gradually consolidated themselves in power and distanced themselves from Sunderland. A series of explosive allegations of bribery resulted in the removal from office of the compliant but Tory Speaker of the Commons, Sir John Trevor, along with Sunderland's

The Right Hono^ble Admiral RUSSELL

Prined & Sold by Tho: Bakewell Next & Horn Tavern in Fleet Street.

FIG. 103
The admiral, Junto leader and one of the seven signatories to the invitation to William of Orange, Edward Russell (1653–1727), later ennobled as earl of Orford. Mezzotint by William Faithorne the younger.

Commons ally, Henry Guy, the secretary to the Treasury. They blackened the reputation of John Sheffield, marquess of Normanby, Sunderland's associate in the Lords, (who escaped formal censure by a mere four votes). Shortly afterwards it was revealed that the East India Company, desperately fighting off challenges to its monopoly, had bought 'special services' from members of both Houses. They included Thomas Osborne, who had recently been promoted duke of Leeds. Despite his status as one of the 'immortal seven', Leeds had never overcome Whig

hostility and now found himself impeached by the Commons for the second time in his career. He claimed that the allegations had been fabricated by the Whigs for political purposes; but his case was not improved by the disappearance of a key witness and his attempts to 'debauch' poor peers by entertaining them at Hell tavern in Westminster.[6]

The Whigs had made a significant advance towards dominating the ministry. Shrewsbury, despite frequent bouts of ill health, remained the cornerstone of the administration; but much of the responsibility

FIG. 104
The story of the Assassination Plot of 1696 is told in this broadside. It begins with James II receiving the pope's blessing, via the papal nuncio, and ends with the execution of the conspirators, after the 'eye of providence' saved William III from the assassins. The print was presumably produced before the attainder of Fenwick.

for parliamentary management was effectively handed to a group of ambitious and able Commons politicians collectively known as the Junto: the brilliant lawyer, Sir John Somers; Edward Russell, one of the 'immortal seven', now an admiral; Charles Montagu, the chancellor of the exchequer and financial expert, and Thomas Wharton, the son of the 4th Baron Wharton. Montagu and Thomas Wharton had been responsible for the disgrace of Trevor and the impeachment of Leeds. William disliked them all, especially Montagu and Wharton, but they offered the welcome prospect of a united and effective leadership over the Commons.

The discovery of a Jacobite plot in 1696 – an attempt to assassinate William III co-ordinated with a Jacobite rising in alliance with the French – produced a tide of Williamite fervour of which the Whigs took full advantage. Both Houses voted for the formation of an 'Association for the safety of the king's person and defence of his government'. In the Lords, each Member was asked to make an explicit repudiation of James II and his son, and to commit themselves 'in case His Majesty come to any violent or untimely death ... to unite, associate, and stand by each other, in revenging the same upon his enemies and their adherents'. [7] The 2nd earl of Nottingham and eighteen other peers refused to subscribe and the bishops balked at signing up to a bloodthirsty act of revenge.[8] The Association was not compulsory. Yet it was so clear a test of loyalty that those who refused it effectively labelled themselves as crypto-Jacobites. Three privy councillors who refused to sign (Nottingham and Normanby in the Lords and Seymour in the Commons) were removed from the council by the king himself in March. In April 1696, a new act made signing the Association compulsory for members of the Commons (but not for the Lords) and for office holders. Philip Stanhope, 2nd earl of Chesterfield, who had successfully argued in the House against a requirement that all those who refused to sign should forfeit their hereditary offices (such as his own as warden of the Chase of Thorny Woods), personally presented the king with a memorandum against the Association: 'I have already taken the oath of allegiance and if that cannot bind me I am sure that no other oath will, but besides I have a greater aversion against the taking of solemn oaths, than many other men have'.[9]

One of the Jacobite conspirators was captured in June. Sir John Fenwick, married to the aunt of Charles Howard, 3rd earl of Carlisle, was a Northumberland gentleman with heavy debts and poor judgement who had contracted a strong dislike of William III while serving in the English and Dutch armies before the Revolution. Presented with legal problems in prosecuting him through the courts, Ministers decided on a show trial in Parliament, by means of a bill of attainder. The spectacle helped to distract attention from a liquidity crisis that had disrupted the king's military campaign abroad and caused economic hardship at home, but it generated immense legal and political controversy. Some Whigs were troubled by the legal issues involved, and Tories flocked to protect Fenwick – a man caught out in the confused political world created by the Revolution. The attainder threatened to backfire against the

Whigs themselves when in the Lords the dissident Whig, Charles Mordaunt, earl of Monmouth (later 3rd earl of Peterborough) tried to hijack the proceedings in pursuit of his own vendetta against Shrewsbury and the Junto. Fenwick's allegations about ministers' contacts with the Jacobite court turned Shrewsbury, who had retired to Gloucestershire as an invalid, into a nervous wreck, requiring constant soothing messages from his friends and allies to coax him back to London. The bill finally received royal assent in January 1697. Fenwick was executed soon afterwards (see below, p. 216).

It was the high point in the career of the Whig Junto, and was followed by the translation of Somers and Russell to the House of Lords (as Baron Somers and earl of Orford respectively). Thomas Wharton had become 5th Baron Wharton a year earlier (the other Junto member, Charles Montagu, was created Baron Halifax in 1700 and earl of Halifax in 1714). Their arrival brought to the House a group of men who had developed exceptional political skills in managing the Commons. Their promotion to the peerage contributed to the Junto's loss of grip in the lower House; but in the upper, the Whigs began to play their hand with remarkable skill and assurance.

Chapter 6

The House of Lords at work

The Chamber

Except for the two occasions in the period when Parliament met in Oxford, the House of Lords sat in the queen's chamber of the old Palace of Westminster, which had ceased to be a royal residence after a fire in 1512. The Lords chamber was narrow, about 70 feet long by 27 feet wide (the present chamber of the House of Lords is 80 feet long by 45 feet wide). A bar at its northern end marked the formal limit of the House, the area beyond it usually occupied by the peers' 'necessary attendants'. (Peers were supposed, under an order of March 1670, to go beyond the bar to have private conversations, rather than disturb the debate in the chamber.) The part of the chamber in which the Lords sat was only 54 feet long. In 1679, George Villiers, 2nd duke of Buckingham described the chamber as 'strait and scant' and mischievously suggested that more temporal peers could be accommodated by removing the bishops.[1] A 1673 proposal by Christopher Wren to enlarge the chamber was not proceeded with. It had been refurbished during 1623–24 by Inigo Jones, involving, amongst other things, the installation of a new ceiling, with a plaster barrel vault painted *tromp-l'oeil* with imitation coffering. Around the walls hung tapestries depicting the defeat of the Spanish Armada in 1588, created to designs by Cornelius Vroom for Lord High Admiral Charles Howard, Baron Howard of Effingham (created earl of Nottingham in 1597). Nottingham sold the tapestries to James I and they were moved to the House later where they remained until they perished in the fire of 1834. The House was poorly lit by a window at the north end and by dormers in the ceiling. It was often dark inside. A fireplace on the eastern side supplied the only heating. A gallery was erected with four rows of benches in 1704 at the north end of the chamber to accommodate some

FIG. 105 *Queen Anne in the House of Lords, c. 1710, by Peter Tillemans.*

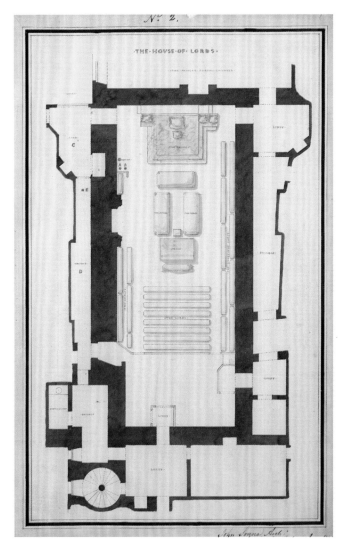

FIG. 106 *Plan of the layout of the House of Lords in 1794, by Sir John Soane. The chamber had hardly changed since 1715.*

of those – probably the queen's ladies in waiting – who might attend on formal occasions when the queen came to the House. It was disliked by the Lords as it encroached on the entrance to the chamber, and it was removed in 1711.

Commoners who had business with the House, as witnesses, defendants, counsel or petitioners, were not permitted to enter the chamber but had to stand at the bar in order to present their cases or be interrogated. Members of the House of Commons stood at the bar to listen to the monarch's speech. Commoners occasionally also stood at the bar in order

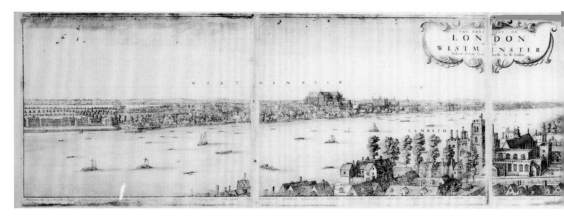

FIG. 108 (BELOW) *View of Westminster Hall and Abbey with the River Thames, engraved by Wenceslaus Hollar. No. 1 is Westminster Abbey; 2 is the Henry VII Chapel, 3 St Margaret's Church. No. 4 is St Stephen's Chapel, the old House of Commons. The House of Lords is contained within the buildings to the left of the House of Commons, behind the trees.*

to observe the Lords at work, although they had no right to do so and were more likely to be driven to surreptitious eavesdropping at the doors. The Member for Berwickshire, George Baillie of Jerviswood, stood for about eight hours with 'a multitude of people at my back the whole day' listening to the debate on Sacheverell's trial in March 1710.[2] In 1664 the diarist Samuel Pepys (though not even a Member of the Commons) crowded in at the back to hear the king's speech. Pepys spent another morning at the door of the House of Lords on 28 January 1667 with 'many hundreds of people' listening to what he described as a conference between the Houses on the procedural issues associated with the proposed impeachment of John Mordaunt, Viscount Mordaunt.[3] About twenty

FIG. 107 *Wenceslaus Hollar,* The prospect of London and Westminster taken from Lambeth.

FIG. 109 (BELOW) *Wenceslaus Hollar's print of 1647, showing the House of Commons (Parliament House), Westminster Hall, and Westminster Abbey. The House of Lords is out of sight, to the left of the area shown.*

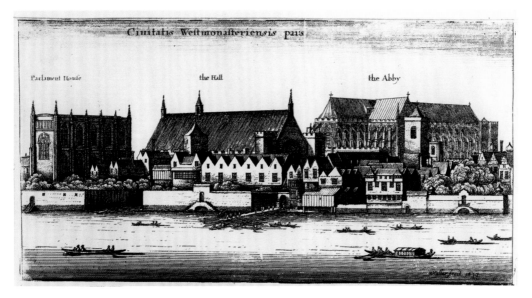

years later another diarist, John Evelyn, similarly overheard a Lords debate by positioning himself 'by the princes lodgings at the door of the lobby to the House'.[4] The possibility of 'strangers' eavesdropping (as well as obstructing free passage) lay behind orders like the one the House made in 1678 that the Painted Chamber and the various lobbies 'be kept clear from all footmen, and all other persons not having business with the Lords (except such gentlemen and pages as attend the lords and their assistants)'.[5]

At the opposite end of the chamber to the bar stood the throne. Chairs stood either side of it for the accommodation of royal princes. The chair to the right was reserved for a Prince of Wales, but during the reign

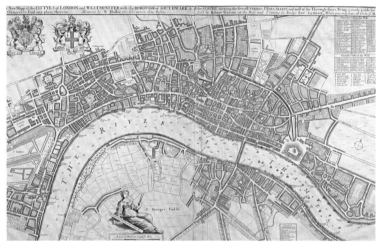

FIG. 111 *Map of the Cities of London and Westminster, Southwark and the suburbs, engraved by Wenceslaus Hollar, c. 1680.*

FIG. 110 *The west central area of London, engraved by Wenceslaus Hollar in the 1660s, the only executed plate of his uncompleted project to create a plan of the whole of the City. The plan shows a number of the large houses occupied by the nobility, especially on the Strand, including Worcester House, belonging to the marquess of Worcester, but let out during the early 1660s to the earl of Clarendon; Exeter House, belonging to the earls of Exeter, but altered to retail property in 1676; Bedford House; Salisbury House and Arundel House.*

FIG. 112 (OPPOSITE)
*A plan of the Palace
of Westminster and
Westminster Abbey
showing the
arrangements for
the coronation
procession in 1685
from Francis
Sandford's* The
history of the
coronation of the
most high monarch
James II *(1687).
The House of Lords
is shown in the top
left hand corner.*

of Charles II it was used by James, duke of York as heir apparent. The spaces behind the throne or the steps of the throne itself were used by Members of the Commons and elder sons of peers attending the Lords to listen to the proceedings. The elder sons of peers may have trespassed further than this, for an order made in January 1695 emphasised that they were not permitted 'at any time when the House is sitting, [to] presume to come into the House, farther than the upper end of the archbishops bench'.[6] Sometimes permission was granted to close political associates of peers who were not Members to stand there. The king's presence in the House seems to have upset matters considerably: in 1673 the Lords complained about 'the coming in and sitting of divers persons (not being peers of this realm) upon the earls, bishops and barons benches in the House of Peers, at such times as His Majesty shall be present there'.[7] Ladies who wished to attend proceedings (in the absence of a gallery) 'placed themselves behind the curtains on each side of the throne'. Anthony Ashley Cooper, earl of Shaftesbury was said to have complained in 1675 of 'those droves of ladies that attended all causes', and claimed 'that men hired or borrowed of their friends handsome sisters, or daughters, to deliver their petitions'.[8] In front of the throne, three woolsacks provided seating for the Speaker of the House and for the judges and other legal assistants. In front of the woolsacks, the clerks were provided with a table and chairs.

The Members of the House sat on benches covered in red cloth. In theory the bishops, the lords spiritual, sat on the eastern side of the chamber and the lords temporal sat facing them on the western side, with the earls and the great officers of state on the front bench and barons behind and any overflow on the cross benches. A statute passed during the reign of Henry VIII determined the order in which the peers were supposed to sit. For the lords temporal highest precedence went to royal dukes (the sons, brothers, uncles and nephews of the king). Next came the great officers of state (the lord chancellor, lord treasurer, lord president of the council and lord privy seal) irrespective of their actual rank in the peerage. They were followed by the rest of the peerage, sitting first in order of rank, then by date of creation. For the lords spiritual, the highest ranking went to the archbishops of Canterbury and York, then to the bishops of London, Durham and Winchester and then the remaining bishops in order of the date of their first consecration. Frequently repeated injunctions for members to sit in, and to speak from, their places suggests that in practice

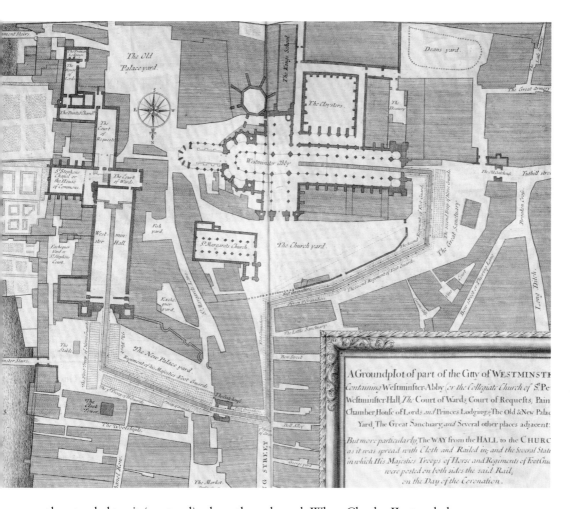

A Groundplot of part of the City of WESTMINSTE
Containing Westminster-Abby (or the Collegiate Church of St. Pet
Westminster-Hall, Th: Court of Wards, Court of Requests, Paint
Chamber, House of Lords and Princes Lodgings, The Old & New Palac
Yard, The Great Sanctuary, and Several other places adjacent:

But more particularly, The WAY from the HALL to the CHURC
as it was spread with Cloth and Railed in; and the several Stati
in which His Majesties Troops of Horse and Regiments of Foot Gua
were posted on both sides the said Rail,
on the Day of the Coronation.

they tended to sit (or stand) where they pleased. When Charles II attended the House informally it was only natural that members should join him sitting near the fireplace. Indeed in a large and chilly room the fireplace would always attract Members and the order of 1695 for preserving regularity in proceedings stated that members of the House should 'not stand before the fire, or sit on the woolsack (except such lords as have particular leave to do so); nor any temporal lords sit on the bishops benches.' It is also likely that some members preferred to speak from a position close to the clerks' table rather than from the benches, especially as there were occasions, such as the debates on the attainder of Sir John Fenwick in 1696, when the number of peers present outstripped the actual seating capacity.

Provision for refreshment was probably limited, although there is little evidence on the subject. Refreshments were apparently sometimes provided in adjacent rooms. An entry in the diary of Charles Bennet, 2nd Baron Ossulston mentions dining in Black Rod's chamber in February 1704; there is a reference elsewhere to refreshments being provided on one occasion in the rooms near the Prince's Lodgings. When the House adjourned for refreshments during debates on the imprisonment of Danby and the Catholic peers in May 1685 it did so for only fifteen minutes to 'the adjacent rooms'.[9] A similar adjournment during the second reading of the Fenwick attainder bill lasted for half an hour. There had once been an alehouse underneath the Prince's Lodgings but it had been suppressed in 1644. There were numerous other taverns and coffee houses in the vicinity. There was a tavern in Palace Yard in 1667; in 1697 John West, 6th Baron De la Warr and George Neville, 13th Baron Abergavenny, left the chamber at 11 a.m. to dine at a cook's shop. A newspaper advertisement reveals the existence of Waghorn's coffee house 'next the House of Lords'.[10] A 'bog house' was situated off a passage on the eastern side of the House. In addition, eighteen chamber pots, renewed annually by the lord chamberlain's department, were provided in the 'Lords smoking room' (it is not known where this was). The great officers of state may have been able to take advantage of the lord privy seal's 'inner room' which accommodated a close stool with two pans as well as 'Turkey work' chairs.

As is evident, the chamber was surrounded by a warren of smaller rooms that functioned as government offices, committee and conference rooms and lobbies or waiting rooms. The largest of them was the Painted Chamber which usually served as a committee and conference room but which was turned into a robing room for the monarch on formal state occasions. Occasionally it was used for the lying-in-state of important personages such as the duchess of York in 1671 and Prince George of Denmark in 1708. After his death, the body of the 2nd duke of Buckingham lay in state in the smaller Prince's Chamber. The splendour of his funeral was described by Roger Morrice:

> The nobility of England that were in town had notice and were desired to meet in the Lords House to pay the last testimony of respect to him, and to accompany his body to the grave and there they very generally did meet, and about eleven a clock at night his corpse were brought out of the Prince's lodgings, and with great pomp and ceremony, and with a great appearance of the nobility, especially seven ladies, and of people

of all other conditions, so that the concourse was very great through the Palace Yard and through the Abbey, and was laid in the stately vault by [adjacent to] the duke his father.[11]

The House of Lords in session

The ceremonial opening or closure of the Parliament and its sessions was a major political and social event. In 1685 it was said that James II intended to walk to Parliament in his robes, followed by the peers in robes and coronets 'purposely to gratify his people that they may see a splendid show'.[12] Some of the orders for preventing the access of outsiders to the lobbies and other approaches to the chamber were prompted by the peers' annoyance at crowds of commoners anxious to catch a glimpse of their monarch.

On such occasions the monarch used the nearby Painted Chamber to change into his or her 'regal robes' and to don the crown before delivering a speech from the throne to the assembled members of both Houses or giving the royal assent. On normal business days members of the Lords attended in their everyday clothes, but since at least 1614, the peers had marked state occasions by wearing parliamentary robes, made of fine scarlet cloth trimmed with miniver bars (four rows for a duke, three and a half for a marquess, three for an earl, two and a half for a viscount and two for a baron). Special orders were issued in April 1696 to ensure that the peers wore their robes when the king came to give the royal assent to various bills and that ladies were excluded so that the ceremony could be better observed by the Venetian ambassador. Parliamentary robes were also worn when a peer was tried in the House. The robes were expensive, and some peers borrowed them, as Charles Bruce, styled Lord Bruce (and later 3rd earl of Ailesbury), was advised to do when he was summoned to the House by a writ of acceleration in 1711. A set of robes stolen from Lord Stourton in the early seventeenth century was valued at £74, although these may have been the more elaborate robes worn at a coronation: the sudden demand for velvet and ermine at the accession of James II in 1685 made these even more expensive than they would otherwise have been.

It might take some time for the Lords to get down to serious business. Often a ministry's principal focus early in a session was on the House of Commons and securing a supply bill. Members of the Lords often thought it possible to delay their arrival because the first week or two

'So much pain and so little pleasure': Charles Talbot, duke of Shrewsbury (1660–1718)

ne of the 'immortal seven' who signed the invitation to William III and a prominent convert from Catholicism, Charles Talbot, 12th earl, later duke, of Shrewsbury, enjoyed both 'the respect of all parties and the good-will of the king'.[1] The greatest bar to his acquiring an almost unrivalled level of authority was his atrocious health. In early manhood he lost one eye and narrowly avoided losing the other; he also suffered from crippling bouts of sickness during which he would spit blood. His attention to business was regularly interrupted by long periods of convalescence in the country, a sickly languor that infuriated friends and enemies alike. William III found his condition especially frustrating as he relied on Shrewsbury as a bridge between the Whigs and his other indispensable servant, the earl of Sunderland. On one occasion, prostrated with pain from an attack of gout, Shrewsbury disconsolately asked 'what one does in a world where there is so much pain and so little pleasure?'

Raised by his Catholic Brudenell relations following his father's death from wounds sustained in a notorious duel with his mother's lover, George Villiers, 2nd duke of Buckingham (see above, p. 186), Shrewsbury was educated abroad, but by the time of the Popish Plot he had fallen under the sway of the charismatic clergyman, John Tillotson, who converted him to the Church of England. The accession of the Catholic James II failed to undermine Shrewsbury's newfound Anglicanism. He accompanied the Prince of Orange in the invasion fleet in November 1688, and was rapidly promoted by the new king. He was raised to a dukedom, appointed to the lord lieutenancies of Hertfordshire and Worcestershire and, most importantly, to national office as one of the secretaries of state.

Although a Whig and a close friend of Thomas Wharton (later marquess of Wharton), one of the Junto's leaders, Shrewsbury was at heart a moderate, and he enjoyed cordial relations with Whigs, Tories and Jacobites alike. His association with the latter led to his being named by Sir John Fenwick in 1696 as being involved in Jacobite plotting, but his friends among the Whigs ensured that his name was cleared and saw to it that Fenwick was executed before he could do any more damage to Shrewsbury's reputation (see below, p.216). Despite this support and his own undoubted ambition, Shrewsbury appears to have been singularly poorly equipped to deal with the cut and thrust of late seventeenth century political life. Fenwick's accusations unnerved him, as did a number of other more or less minor complaints brought against him by a variety of disappointed people with axes to grind. The whole experience of government shattered his nerves and at regular intervals throughout the 1690s he pleaded with the king to accept his resignation. The result was that from 1689 until his death, Shrewsbury held a succession of offices, punctuated by periods of self-imposed purdah.

By 1700 Shrewsbury had taken as much as he was able to stand of English political life. He dreaded Parliaments, complaining later in life that 'so many things unexpected fall out in a sessions, that I have often found those most difficult, who at first had the greatest appearance of easiness'.[2] In November he left for the warmer climes of Southern France and Italy. He lived in Rome for almost four years, immune to the Pope's efforts to reconvert him: he even succeeded in converting his kinsman, George Brudenell, 3rd earl of Cardigan, to Protestantism under the Vatican's nose.

He returned to England in January 1706. His long sojourn abroad and the widespread belief that before leaving for his self-imposed exile he had counselled the then king against retaining the Whigs in office meant that he was now viewed with suspicion by his former friends in the Junto. The Junto's hostility and his waning friendship with John Churchill, duke of Marlborough, manoeuvred him into the orbit of Robert Harley (later earl of Oxford), and from 1708 until the death of Anne, Shrewsbury and Harley co-operated to construct a court party, largely Tory in character, but also comprising moderate Whigs. Shrewsbury's close relationship with the queen and dislike of the costliness of war further served to distance him from the Whig party, which was so closely identified with the ongoing conflict.

FIG. 113 *Charles Talbot, duke of Shrewsbury, by Sir Godfrey Kneller.*

Shrewsbury's change of sides had lost him his reputation as an honest broker and the sympathy of many of his old friends. He also appears to have lost some of his former charm. On being appointed lord chamberlain in 1710 in place of Henry Grey, 12th earl of Kent, nicknamed 'the bug', Shrewsbury was reminded that he had once asserted that he would never turn anyone out of their place, only to respond that he had not broken his word since the bug was nobody.[3] The duchess of Marlborough's confidant, Arthur Maynwaring, reflected the Whigs' increasing dislike of their former darling, commenting that Shrewsbury 'will trim and shuffle between [the two parties] as well and as long as he can, professing and lying to both sides, and making his court all the while

to the queen by doing so'.[4] Despite this loss of trust, on the death of Anne Shrewsbury was nominated lord high treasurer as a compromise to forestall the ambitions of Henry St John, Viscount Bolingbroke. Shrewsbury resigned the place within months of the Hanoverian accession, but remained an influential political figure for the few remaining years of his life.

would be occupied with less important matters (although they were not always right). How the House organised its business – how it established the orders of the day – remains obscure. If it followed later practice then it was up to individual members themselves to set down the business for which they were responsible for specific days. The business would then be taken in the order in which it had been set down, rather than in order of importance. The order of business for a particular day might be set aside when the House could be persuaded that other matters were of greater significance. On 5 June 1713, for example, the Scots representative peer John Elphinstone, 4th Lord Balmerinoch, moved 'to put off the order of the day [for the second reading of the malt tax bill] and to appoint Monday next for taking into consideration the state of the nation with regard to the 14 or other articles of the Union which had relation to the malt tax'. It is possible that some influence over the day's business was exercised by the clerk of the Parliaments and the chancellor in consultation together before being put to the House.

The procedures of the House of Lords were broadly similar to those of the lower House. It normally sat for six days a week (very occasionally it might meet on a Sunday). It would assemble in the morning, convening again in the afternoon if business required, especially in the rush to complete business at the end of a session. The Speaker presided from the woolsack, although unlike the practice in the Commons, Members of the Lords did not address their remarks to their Speaker but to their fellow Members. A standing order made in 1626 required them to avoid 'personal sharpness, or taxing speeches' so that 'as nothing offensive is to be spoken, so nothing is to be ill taken, if the party that spoke shall presently make a fair exposition or clear denial of the words that might bear any ill construction'.[13] In a body of men so devoted to their honour and dignity, heat was common and offence taken frequently, and given the proclivity of the peers for duelling, such a regulation was much needed, especially as peers wore their swords in the chamber.

The House was often required to intervene to head off confrontations between Members. The king himself reprimanded peers in 1671 for 'very great disorders... both at the hearing of causes, and in debates among themselves'.[14] Several peers were notorious for their quick tempers. Two of them, Henry Pierrepont, marquess of Dorchester, and Buckingham, clashed at a conference on the Canary Company held in the Painted Chamber on 19 December 1666. Edward Hyde, earl of Clarendon commented that already 'there was no good correspondence' between these two peers and 'their mutual undervaluing each other always disposed them to affect any opportunity to manifest it'. Finding themselves neighbours, a jostling for space soon led to an exchange of insults and then proceeded to an unseemly fistfight,

> in which the marquis, who was the lower of the two in stature, and was less active in his limbs, lost his periwig, and received some rudeness, which nobody imputed to his want of courage, which was ever less questioned than that of the other . . . The marquis had much of the duke's hair in his hands to recompense for his pulling of his periwig, which he could not reach high enough to do to the other.[15]

The House, astonished at this 'misdemeanour, greater than had ever happened, in that place and upon such an occasion', committed both peers to the Tower, and it was only after both of them submitted humble apologies to the House (Buckingham doing so rather more reluctantly) that they were readmitted to their seats some days later. The same year, during debates over the Irish cattle bill, Thomas Butler, earl of Ossory in the Irish peerage, who sat in the House of Lords by virtue of his English peerage as Lord Butler, upset Baron Ashley (later earl of Shaftesbury) by referring to him, accurately enough, as one of Cromwell's counsellors. Ossory had to leave the chamber while the incident was discussed and was then called back in, reprimanded and told to apologise to the House and then to Ashley. The process was then repeated all over again in response to another complaint on behalf of the duke of Buckingham.[16]

It was not just personal aspersions that got peers into trouble, but also anything that was, or could be twisted into, disrespect to the king or the House. There was an enormous row when in 1677 Buckingham questioned whether Parliament had been dissolved by the long prorogation, and John Frescheville, Baron Frescheville, a close associate of his opponent the earl of Danby, claimed that Buckingham's words constituted a disrespect to the House itself. He proposed that Buckingham should be called to the bar and 'proceeded with as should be thought fit'; Buckingham's ally, Shaftesbury, weighed in to protest that 'the motion of calling to the Bar took away all liberty and freedom of speech in Parliament'.[17] Shaftesbury, Buckingham and others were, indeed, subsequently committed to the Tower for contempt of the House. Shaftesbury's imprisonment was described by his counsel as a punishment 'for using his just freedom of speech in parliament'.[18]

The Fenwick attainder, 1696

FIG. 114 *Sir John Fenwick (c. 1645–1697), by Robert White.*

Hot-tempered, inept and violently antagonistic to the new regime of William III and Mary, Sir John Fenwick was attainted by Parliament and executed for treason in January 1697. Arrested the previous June after the discovery of an attempt to assassinate William III, he was undoubtedly deeply involved in Jacobite conspiracies; whether he posed a real threat to William III's regime was another matter. The prosecution case against him was weak. To prove an act of treason, statute law required the testimony of two credible witnesses. In Fenwick's case the two witnesses were George Porter and Cardell Goodman, whose not completely credible testimony had already sent some of those accused of complicity in the assassination plot to the gallows.

The ministry hoped that Fenwick might save his life by exposing his fellow conspirators. All he did was to make a string of unsupported allegations against key ministerial and military figures including Charles Talbot, duke of Shrewsbury, Sidney Godolphin, Baron Godolphin, John Churchill, earl of Marlborough and Admiral Russell. Meanwhile, Goodman vanished. Without him, the prosecution no longer had its two witnesses. To overcome the problem, the ministry decided to proceed by a bill of attainder, for which normal legal procedures could be ignored. Profound unease about proceedings that aped a trial but lacked any legal or evidential safeguards was reflected in the division lobbies in the Commons: a majority of 92 for the first reading of the bill dwindled to 33 by the third. Even stalwart Whigs like Thomas Wharton, 5th Baron Wharton, interpreted what happened in the Commons as no more than a pretence at 'fair dealing'.[1]

The bill arrived in the House of Lords with the Christmas recess looming. Whig anxiety about it was evident. In December the second reading was moved by three court dependants (Thomas Grey, 2nd earl of Stamford, Charles Powlett, duke of Bolton and Aubrey de Vere, 20th earl of Oxford). Bolton argued 'that nobody could be for the government and against the bill'.[2] The House enforced attendance by threatening absentees with imprisonment and as a result

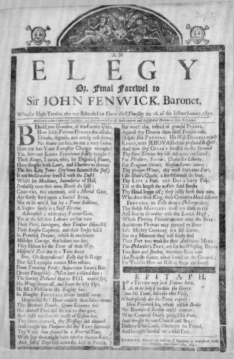

FIG. 115

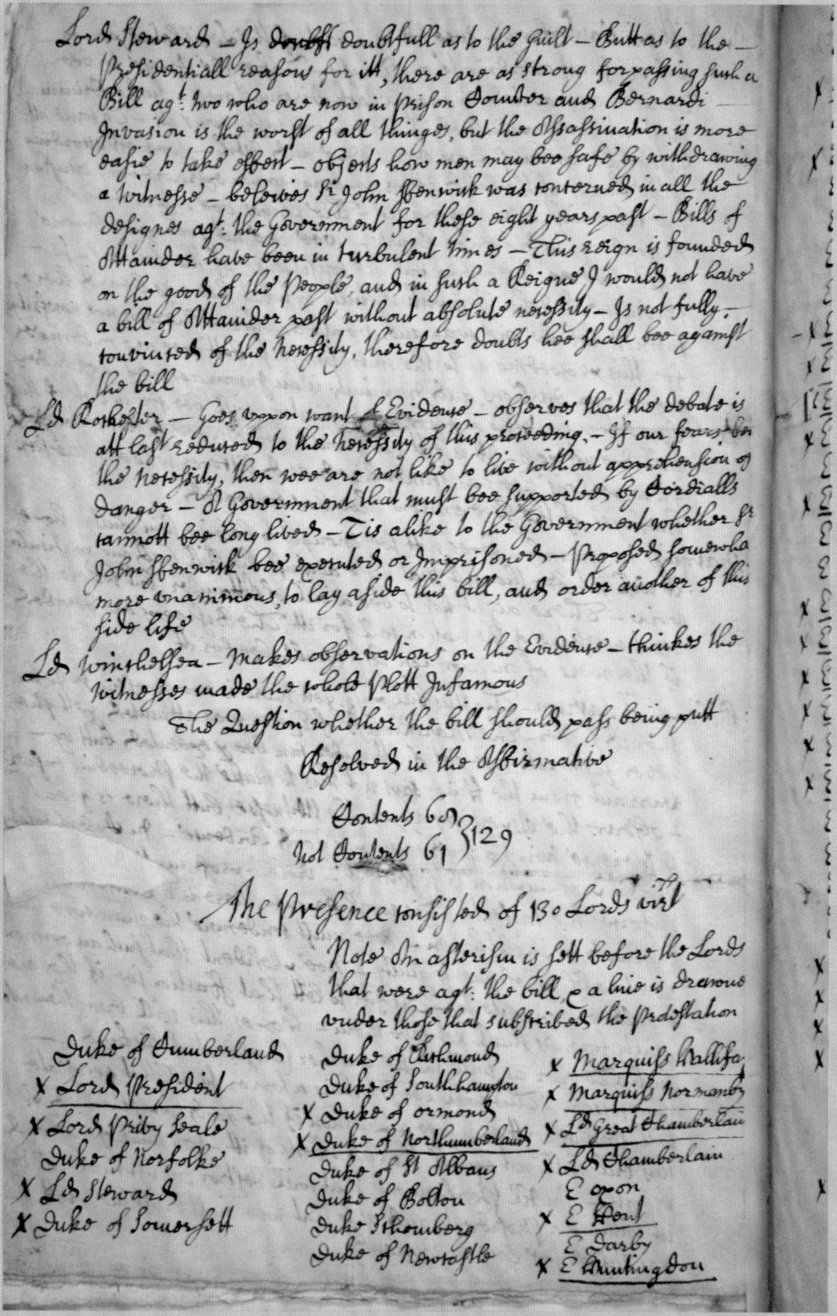

Lord Steward – Is doubtfull as to the guilt – But as to the
Prudentiall reason for it, there are as strong for passing such a
Bill agt. two who are now in prison Cowper and Bernardi –
Invasion is the worst of all thinges, but the Assassination is more
easie to take effect – observs how men may bee safe by withdrawing
a witnesse – besides Si John ffenwick was concerned in all the
designes agt. the Government for these eight years past – Bills of
Attainder have been in turbulent times – This reign is founded
on the good of the people, and in such a Reigne I would not have
a bill of Attainder past without absolute necessity – Is not fully
convinced of the necessity, therefore doubts hee shall bee agaynst
the bill

Ld Rochester – Goes upon want of Evidence – observes that the debate is
att last reduced to the necessity of this proceeding – If our fears bee
the necessity, then wee are not like to live without apprehension of
danger – A Government that must bee supported by Cordialls
cannott bee long lived – Tis alike to the Government whether Si
John ffenwick bee executed or imprisoned – Proposed somewhat
more unanimous to lay aside this bill, and order another of this
side life

Ld Winchelsea – Makes observations on the Evidence – thinkes the
witnesses made the whole Plott Infamous

The Question whether the bill should pass being putt

Resolved in the Affirmative

Contents 68
Not Contents 61 ⎱ 129

The Presence consisted of 130 Lords

Note An asterism is sett before the Lords
that were agt. the bill & a line is drawne
under those that subscribed the Protestation

Duke of Cumberland   Duke of Richmond   x Marquiss Hallifax
x Lord President   Duke of Southhampton   x Marquiss Normanby
x Lord Privy Seale   x Duke of Ormond   x Ld Great Chamberlain
  Duke of Norfolke   x Duke of Northumberland x Ld Chamberlain
x Ld Steward   Duke of St Albans   E Oxon
x Duke of Somersett   Duke of Bolton   x E Kent
                           Duke of Schomberg   E Darby
                           Duke of Newcastle   x E Huntingdon

FIG. 116 Although the House did not allow reporting of its proceedings in this
period, occasionally peers took notes of the debates. There are surviving manuscript
notes of the debates on the Fenwick attainder together with a copy of the division list,
which is annotated to show which opponents of the bill then went on to enter a
formal protest against its passage. The protest itself emphasises that 'bills of attainder
against persons in prison … are of a dangerous consequence to the lives of the
subjects, and as we conceive may tend to the subversion of the laws of this kingdom'.

217

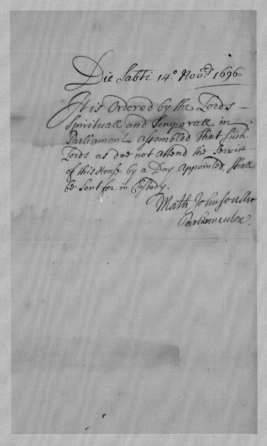

FIG. 117 *The controversy surrounding the Fenwick attainder led the House to order Members to attend. In a polite covering letter, the lord keeper, John Somers, informs Christopher Hatton, Viscount Hatton that he is required to attend. The order itself is more blunt: it states that defaulters will be 'sent for in custody'.*

between 133 and 151 peers were present over the three days of debate – the highest attendances recorded at any time between 1660 and 1714 apart from the declaration that William and Mary were joint monarchs in February 1689. Many peers had attended the debates in the Commons so were already familiar with the issues. Laurence Hyde, earl of Rochester, Henry Compton, bishop of London, Daniel Finch, 2nd earl of Nottingham and Thomas Osborne, duke of Leeds recited the by now well-worn objections to accepting a lower standard of proof than in a court of law, and appealed to the privileges of the House: allowing such a bill to start in the Commons, they claimed, undermined the Lords' claim to judicature. It signalled that the government was in 'a very tottering condition, when for its preservation, it's forced to leap over all our laws and fly to so extraordinary a method to take away the life of one poor man.'[3] Even some ministers were unnerved by the arguments. The lord privy seal, Thomas Herbert, 8th earl of Pembroke, announced that he would vote for the second reading in hopes of inducing further revelations from Fenwick but was unde-

cided about the third. Tory peers held out a lifeline to such waverers, suggesting that Fenwick should be imprisoned for life.

The attainder passed its second reading by a mere 18 votes, and ministers were faced with a real fight to prevent support for the bill ebbing away completely. Thomas Tenison, archbishop of Canterbury, despite the convention established some twenty years earlier that bishops should not vote in blood cases, 'spoke for it with the eloquence and courage of St Paul'.[4] The bill obtained a third reading by just seven. It received the royal assent on 11 January. In what by the standards of the day was interpreted as a magnanimous gesture the king allowed Fenwick to be beheaded rather than suffer the ignominy of being hanged.

The presence of the king was a natural dampener on the freedom of debate. Charles II first began to attend during debates on the conventicle bill in March 1670, when he told the House that he had come 'to renew a custom of his predecessors, long discontinued, to be present at debates, but not to interrupt the freedom thereof'.[19] His assurances sit awkwardly against the report that he 'heard the debate about the conventicle bill, and promoted it with all his vigour, so that there is no doubt of its passing'[20] and his known interest in the fate of the Roos divorce bill, the debates on which he also attended. The House offered him its thanks for the honour he did them by his attendance but Gilbert Holles, 3rd earl of Clare, was bold enough openly to accuse the king of preventing 'freedom of debate' when he attended the House for the second reading of the subsidy bill in February 1671.[21] At that debate John Lucas, Baron Lucas, made 'a fervent bold speech' against the government, copies of which were widely circulated.[22] The king continued nevertheless to attend on a daily basis, staying 'at least three or four hours to hear the debates held on every subject which is raised there'.[23] James II also attended regularly; William III and Anne only occasionally.

The House normally came to its decisions without a formal vote, by gauging whether the shouts of the 'contents' or the 'not contents' were loudest. A formal division, required when the decision was challenged, involved the contents standing and the not contents remaining seated. In April 1675, in a division on the test bill, 'it being candlelight and therefore difficult to tell the House' it was decided that the contents should withdraw below the bar of the House, so that they could be counted by a teller as they passed back through it. The 'not contents' were to remain in the chamber to be counted.[24] In November 1691 this method was officially adopted and added to the standing orders. A different, and probably far older, method of voting was sometimes used for formal proceedings, including trials. The Members of the House would vote one by one, in reverse order of precedence, by standing and declaring 'content' or 'not content' or, in the case of trials, guilty or not guilty 'upon my honour'. No formal means of registering abstention was available: those who wished to abstain had to leave the chamber altogether. It is not clear when the practice of withdrawing to the woolsacks or the steps of the throne developed as a method of abstention, although it may well have been in use long before it was first recorded in 1733. Some regarded it as improper to vote without having heard the evidence, at least in judicial business,

FIG. 118 *Sir Orlando Bridgeman (1609–74), by William Faithorne, 1671.*
Bridgeman, an eminent lawyer, regularly presided over the House of Lords
during the illnesses of the lord chancellor, Edward Hyde, earl of Clarendon.
When Clarendon was dismissed in August 1667, Bridgeman was appointed
lord keeper. He was himself dismissed in 1672 following his refusal to put
the seal onto the Declaration of Indulgence that year.

FIG. 119 *Heneage Finch, earl of Nottingham (1621–82), after Sir Godfrey Kneller. A distinguished lawyer with an impeccable record of service to the crown Finch was appointed lord keeper in succession to Anthony Ashley Cooper, earl of Shaftesbury in 1673. He became lord chancellor in 1675. He received a peerage as Baron Finch in 1674 and was promoted to an earldom in 1681.*

although this was not a formal requirement. When, two days before Christmas 1696 the House prepared to divide on the attainder of Sir John Fenwick, Archbishop Tenison stopped the newly consecrated bishop of Chichester, John Williams, who was rushing to robe himself in time for the vote, and advised him to be cautious since Williams had not been at the debates to judge the merits of the case for himself.

A distinctive aspect of procedure in the Lords was the right to enter a protest or dissent when an individual or group of peers disagreed with the result of a division. The distinction between a dissent and a protest

FIG. 120 (OPPOSITE)
George Jeffreys, Baron Jeffreys (1648–89), after John Riley. George Jeffreys developed a large and lucrative legal practice through his mastery of courtroom advocacy. He became closely associated with James, duke of York whom he served as solicitor general from 1679. Jeffreys received his peerage in 1685 and later that year presided over the notorious 'bloody assizes' at which some 200 supporters of Monmouth's rebellion were convicted and executed, with many more transported to the West Indies. He became lord chancellor in September 1685.

was not clear, although dissent usually implied a simple statement of disagreement whilst a protest was a more discursive document which explained the reasons for the disagreement. Protests were recorded in the Lords Journal, from which they could be extracted, printed and circulated. They were thus an ideal vehicle for publicising opposition policies. Shaftesbury was an early master of the use of protests as part of a propaganda offensive to influence extra-parliamentary opinion and to stimulate support in the Commons.

When peers wanted a more informal discussion (so that, for example, they might speak more than once in a particular debate) the House resolved itself into a committee of the whole House. Detailed scrutiny of legislation or particular matters was remitted to committees which could be authorised to meet nearby, usually in the Prince's Lodgings, but sometimes in the chairman's own house. Much still remains to be discovered about the workings of such committees. Theoretically they were 'select' – that is, they consisted of a few chosen members – but from the early 1660s when particularly contentious matters were referred to committees it became usual to appoint all the members present in the chamber. After the Revolution this practice seems to have been extended to all committees.

The office of chairman of committees emerged after 1714 when the first identifiable occupant of the (as yet officially unrecognized) post was Edward Hyde, 3rd earl of Clarendon (see p. 228). Before 1714 the work of chairing committees was shared between a small group of individuals. John Egerton, 2nd earl of Bridgwater, for example, chaired the committees dealing with the religious settlement in the 1660s; Richard Sackville, 5th earl of Dorset, was active in chairing committees at the same time; and Bridgwater's son and namesake the 3rd earl was also an active committee chairman during the 1690s. It is not yet understood why these men became so prominent in committee work, and how involved they were in the management of business. Those named to a committee did not necessarily participate in its work, and in practice it could be difficult to secure a sufficient number of peers to take part. Bishop Nicolson's diary records his attendance along with four other bishops and two lords temporal on Christmas Eve 1702 at a committee which dealt with three private bills. The committee had thus barely met its quorum (five) although seventy-four members of the House – all of those present in the House when it was committed – had been named to it.

FIG. 121 *William Cowper, Baron (later Earl) Cowper (1665–1723), by Jonathan Richardson.*
William Cowper's private life enabled his Tory opponents to accuse him of bigamy or polygamy.
His political career was given an initial boost by his friendship with the Junto whig John Somers,
later Baron Somers, but he was also on good terms with Sarah Churchill, duchess of Marlborough
and it was through the influence of the duumvirs, John Churchill, duke of Marlborough, and Sidney
Godolphin, Baron Godolphin, that he became lord keeper in 1705 (one of the youngest ever to be
appointed). In 1707 he became the first lord chancellor of Great Britain. He lost office under the
ministry of Robert Harley, earl of Oxford, but was reinstated at the accession of George I.

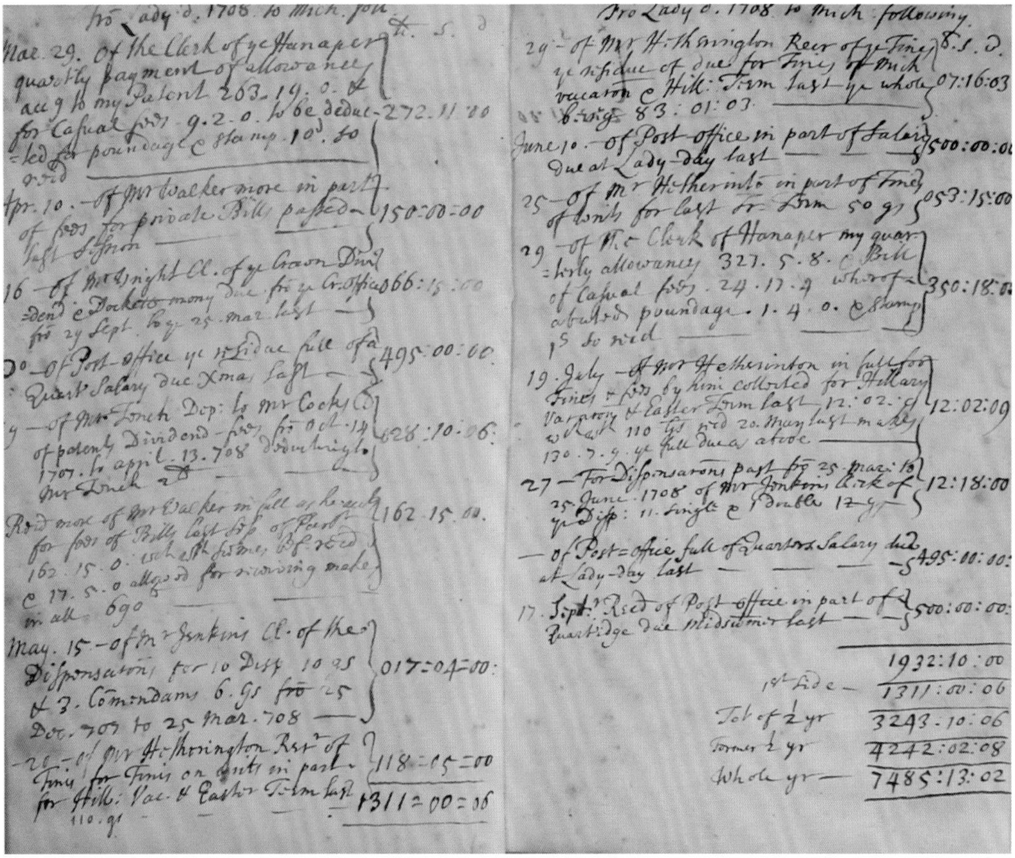

	1932:10:00
1st side	1311:00:06
Tot of ½ yr	3243:10:06
Former ½ yr	4242:02:08
Whole yr	7485:13:02

FIG. 122 *These pages from the diary of William Cowper, Baron Cowper, during his time as lord chancellor, show that he received more than £300 in fees on bills over a six month period in 1708.*

The officers of the House

The presiding officer or Speaker of the House of Lords was normally the keeper of the great seal, either the lord chancellor or the lord keeper, appointed by the crown. The post was almost always filled by a lawyer, often a man who had filled other senior legal offices, frequently a senior political figure. Four of the men who filled the office between the fall of Clarendon in 1667 and the accession of George I in 1714 (Heneage Finch, later Baron Finch and earl of Nottingham; Francis North, later Baron Guilford; John Somers, later Baron Somers; Simon Harcourt, Viscount Harcourt) had served as solicitor general and attorney general; Sir Orlando Bridgeman and Guilford had also been chief justices of the court of common pleas. All but one were lawyers, though Nathan Wright, appointed lord keeper in 1700, was a relatively undistinguished one. The

FIG. 123 (OPPOSITE)
Officers of the House derived much of their income from fees charged for various services. The documents reproduced here are bills for fees incurred on the admission of the earl of Dorset to the House (£5 10s apiece to black rod and the clerk); and in the promotion of a bill in the House (£25, including £10 to the lord chancellor).

exception was the earl of Shaftesbury, who when appointed in 1673 had been chancellor of the exchequer since 1661 but had never been trained in the law. Commoners appointed to the office were normally created peers, although rarely before they had served for several years. The office was a lucrative one: William Cowper's accounts show that he received more than £1,000 in fees as Speaker of the House of Lords in a single year as well as his salary of £4,000 as lord keeper (see fig. 120).

Others might preside if the chancellor or keeper was sick or unavailable. Edward Montagu, 2nd earl of Manchester, chaired the House in the first days of the Convention in 1660, and George Savile, marquess of Halifax, performed a similar service in the Convention of 1689. The House had the right, in the absence of its Speaker, to elect a candidate of its own, but this was not normally necessary as the deficiency was supplied by the appointment of substitutes by a commission under the great seal. In the early 1660s the substitute was often the lord privy seal, but it later became customary to nominate one of the judges.

Proceedings in the House of Lords were governed collectively by its Members rather than by any single individual, and therefore the Speaker had less formal power than his counterpart in the Commons. Despite this, he played a highly influential role in organising the business and proceedings of the House. He normally used his influence to promote the interests of the crown. In some respects, the lord chancellor or lord keeper represented the king: until the 1679 Parliament he routinely made the speech to both Houses at the beginning of each session outlining the reasons for which Parliament had been summoned. Outside Parliament lord chancellors and lord keepers held in their hands considerable powers over appointments in church and state. They were able to nominate and remove justices of the peace, and sway the appointment of judges and grants of livings. Their office issued the writs for elections: there was a storm against the earl of Shaftesbury in 1673 when it was alleged that he had manipulated the timing of writs for by-elections in order to influence the results.

The principal executive officer of the House, responsible for preparing the minutes of the House, was the clerk of the Parliaments, appointed by the crown by letters patent. From 1660 to 1715 there were only two clerks: John Browne and Matthew Johnson. John Browne obtained the office in 1638, lost it when the House of Lords was abolished in 1649, but was reinstated (despite his record of support for the parliamentarian

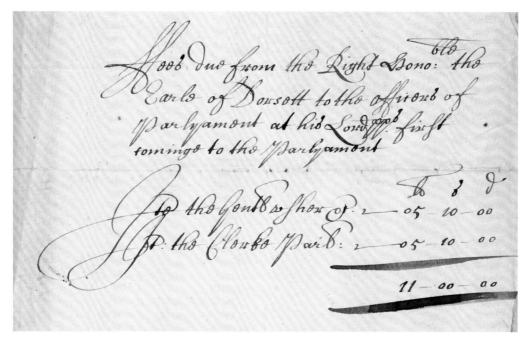

ffees due from the Right Hono: the
Earle of Dorsett to the officers of
Parlyament at his Lordshipps first
cominge to the Parlyament

                                                li s d

To the Gentl usher of: — 05 — 10 — 00
To the Clerke Parll: — 05 — 10 — 00

                                       11 — 00 — 00

ffees due from the Right hono: the
Earle of Dorsett for his bill in the house
of Peeres.

Imp: to the Lord Chamberlan his fee 10 — 00 — 0
Item the Clerke of the Parll office — 07 — 00 — 0
It the Gentusher fee — 05 — 00 — 0
It the yoman and messeng. — 02 — 00 — 0
It the yoman vssher fee — 01 — 00 — 0

                                25 — 00 — 0

It the engrossing of the three the
first p[er] 17s 4d the rest 10s

A committee chairman: Edward Hyde, 3rd earl of Clarendon (1661–1723)

The nineteenth century historian Thomas Macaulay reckoned the third earl of Clarendon a man of 'slender abilities, loose principles, and violent temper'.[1] Clarendon's father appears to have agreed at least in the latter judgement, pleading in the wake of one of his son's outbursts 'God send he does not at one time or other run himself into some great inconvenience by his passion'.[2] Lord Cornbury (as he was styled before he succeeded to the earldom) had been one of the first to defect to William of Orange in 1688. Despite this he was tarnished by his father's adherence to the cause of James II and by his own refusal to accompany Prince George of Denmark, in whose household he served as master of the horse, to the campaign in Ireland. It was not until the accession of his cousin, Queen Anne, that Cornbury was able to secure any particularly notable marks of favour with his appointment to the governorship of New York, where he was a spectacular failure (see above, p. 106).

Despite this inauspicious beginning, on his accession to the earldom in 1709 and his return to England, Clarendon became one of the most assiduous members of the House. It was perhaps for this reason that he became one of the most frequently named committee chairmen. During the session of 1710–11 he chaired nine committees of the whole House and eight select committees, but by 1720 he had effectively monopolized the position, chairing all of the 42 committees of the whole and 46 of the 62 select committees in the 1720–21 session.

It was probably Clarendon's lack of other commitments and his financial insecurity – he depended on the queen and the ministry for regular handouts and for lodgings in Somerset House – that ensured his regular attendance in the House and thus his suitability for the drudgery of the task of overseeing the House's committee-work. Certainly, in no other regard did he manage to distinguish himself. Having suffered the loss of his only son and heir in 1713 through excessive alcohol consumption, which he accounted a 'very great misfortune, a load of grief too heavy for man to bear without the assistance of the mercy of God',[3] Clarendon was appointed envoy to Hanover in 1714. The appointment was regarded as a triumph for Henry St John, Viscount Bolingbroke, whose candidate for the mission Clarendon was believed to be, in preference to Henry Paget, 8th Baron Paget, nominated by Robert Harley, earl of Oxford. The Hanoverian envoy, von Bothmer, was less happy, calling him 'a selfish and presumptuous fool', and dragging up an old story about him dressing up as a woman in America in order to represent the queen. His posting was cut short by the sudden death of the queen in August, leaving Clarendon 'struck dumb' with grief for 'the loss of the best queen, the best mistress, and the best friend, but the only friend I had in the world'.[4] Although George I assured Clarendon of his friendship, he benefited little from the new regime, and was left with no alternatives but to carve out a niche for himself as a parliamentary workhorse. Consequently, following his return to England, he once again took up committee work. Nine years later he died 'in obscurity and deeply in debt' at his lodgings in Chelsea. In the absence of a son, the earldom passed to his nephew, Henry Hyde, 2nd earl of Rochester.

cause) in 1660 and continued until his death in 1691. He had been admitted to the Middle Temple in 1628, but was never called to the bar. Browne was prosperous, having inherited a substantial estate from his uncle and adoptive parent, a City merchant, and was well connected. His first wife was the sister of John Crew, the future Baron Crew, and he remained on close terms with the Crew family long after her death; his second was the daughter of John Packer, clerk of the privy seal and secretary to the 2nd duke of Buckingham. Given the intermittent nature of parliamentary sessions before 1689, Browne's duties cannot have been onerous. He had both the time and the means to pursue other interests including amassing an important collection of musical manuscripts. Browne's successor, Matthew Johnson, served from 1691 to 1716. He had been assistant or secretary to the future lord chancellor, John Somers, later Baron Somers.

The clerk made money from fees charged to peers and the promoters of bills for for many of his services – for example £4 10s for the introduction of a new marquess or earl, and £7 when a private bill was passed. He was assisted by under clerks, although how many is uncertain because several were employed privately by the official clerks. They included a clerk assistant, who was also entitled to fees (he, for example, received £1 at the entrance of a new marquess or earl). The existence of a reading clerk who sat at the table of the House alongside the clerk of the Parliaments can be traced to at least 1662, when the Lords ordered that the sum of 40s which had been paid for the 'entertainment' of a committee sitting on a private bill should be paid instead to the reading clerk (John Walker). The next reading clerk, in around 1664, was John Relfe, whose collection of notes on procedure survives in the Parliamentary Archives. He was succeeded by Matthew Johnson.

The gentleman usher of the black rod was responsible for the security of the House and for its domestic arrangements. He derived his title from his staff of office, made of ebony and topped with a gold lion, and was customarily a senior officer of the royal household – the gentleman usher daily waiter – responsible to the lord chamberlain, who had authority over all the under officers above stairs. His duties as black rod included constant attendance on the House, clearing the areas outside the chamber of strangers and arresting those guilty of breach of privilege or of otherwise disturbing the proceedings of the House. Arrest by black rod was not necessarily an unpleasant experience. Pepys's friend William Joyce was arrested in 1664 by order of the House. Black rod 'did direct one of his messengers to take him in custody, and so he was peaceably conducted to the Swan-with-Two-Necks in Tuttle Street, to a handsome dining room, and there was most civilly used – my uncle Fenner and his brother Anthony and some other friends being with him'.[25] Black rod carried the king's commands to the Commons to attend him in the House of Lords. He was responsible for the domestic establishment of the House (the yeoman usher, doorkeepers, messengers and other staff), and made all the necessary arrangements for the accommodation of the House. The holders of the office included a distinguished naval officer, Admiral Sir David Mitchell (1698–1710) who appointed a deputy to act for him when absent on naval duty, but they also included the poet and literary critic Sir Fleetwood Sheppard, who was described by one of his contemporaries as Charles II's pimp. The post was probably much sought after. As gentlemen usher daily waiter, black rod was able to dispense, or at the very least influence the distribution of, the patronage of the lord chamberlain. Sheppard, who was close to the lord chamberlain (Charles Sackville, 6th earl of Dorset), was accused by his contemporaries of selling offices in Dorset's gift. Like his predecessor, Sir Edward Carteret, he was keeper of the Little Park at Windsor. Another of his predecessors, Sir Thomas Duppa, was sub-collector of the tenths of the clergy in the diocese of Exeter. Like the clerks, black rod was entitled to substantial fees derived from the business of the House: he claimed £20, for example, for arresting a peer and conveying him to the Tower and, like the clerk, £4 10s at the introduction of an earl or marquess.

Reporting the House

Although it is sometimes possible to piece together accounts of proceedings in the House of Lords, much of what went on each day remains obscure. Unlike the Commons after 1680 the Lords did not even print a bare minute of their proceedings, the 'Votes'. The House's Journal was only printed retrospectively in the second half of the eighteenth century. Members of the House were entitled to obtain copies of the Journal, and the supply of copies either in bound sets or as loose pages relating to a particular day's business provided a useful source of extra income for the clerks. The surviving papers of Theophilus Hastings, 7th earl of Huntingdon, include copies of the minutes of the House and a promise to write weekly, all in the hand of John Relfe, the reading clerk. The circulation of such items was nevertheless limited, probably to Members of the House. The Journal anyway recorded only the House's formal decisions, and gave no details of speeches, voting figures and the names of those responsible for formulating and moving business.

The peers were sometimes prepared to countenance the publication of authorised accounts of certain proceedings: the monarch's and lord chancellor's speeches, their own addresses to the crown, sermons preached to the House on special occasions, specific orders such as the various declarations against protections, and authorised accounts of criminal trials held before them, such as that of William Howard, Viscount Stafford, in 1680 (see below, p. 266). They were however extremely resistant to unauthorised attempts to publish accounts of their activities. In 1660 one of the earliest actions of the House of Lords in the Convention Parliament was to pass an order that no account of their activities was to be printed without permission.[26]

In practice, however, information about the Lords' proceedings leaked out of the House through the conversations and correspondence of its members and officers and through the well-documented practice of 'strangers', such as Pepys and Evelyn, eavesdropping at the door or in the lobbies (see above p. 204). One eavesdropper, a Mr Blaney, seems to have been the originator of all the surviving accounts of the conference of 6 February 1689 on the question of James II's supposed abdication. The peers themselves, sometimes for reasons of political advantage and sometimes out of pure vanity, also occasionally conspired to ensure their words reached a wider audience. Shaftesbury's political propaganda machine during the 1670s was serviced by the booksellers Thomas Collins and John Starkey who provided copies of parliamentary speeches, addresses and votes 'perfect true, or artificially corrupted'.[27] A speech by the earl himself, delivered on 23 December 1680, was taken down by Philip Wharton, 4th Baron Wharton, who then passed his notes on to William Russell, 5th earl of Bedford, who in turn passed them on to his son, Lord Russell, who conveyed them to the printer, Francis Smith: the whole chain purposely designed to protect each person from accusations of breaching the House's privilege.

Many accounts of parliamentary proceedings and parliamentary speeches were circulated in manuscript through coffee shops as well as to individual subscribers in the form of newsletters. Copies of one popular item, the notorious 1671 speech on the supply bill by John Lucas, Baron

'High feeding and smart drinking': clubs, dinners and party politics

n Aphra Behn's 1682 play *The City Heiress*, Tom Wilding tells the buffoonish Whig Sir Timothy Treat-All that 'High feeding and smart drinking gains more to the party than your smart preaching'.[1] Dining and drinking were indeed essential components of Westminster politics, opportunities to plot strategies and to foster party ties. Such gatherings first became noticeable and controversial in the feverish atmosphere of the Popish Plot and Exclusion Crisis. Meeting in the City of London, so close geographically to the court at Westminster but very far from it politically, were several centres of opposition to the current administration. The most prominent of them was the Green Ribbon Club, which met at the King's Head Tavern at the corner of Fleet Street and Chancery Lane. It consisted largely of commoners, although two radical Whig peers, Ford Grey, Baron Grey of Warke (see above, p. 238) and William Howard, 3rd Baron Howard of Escrick, were also accepted as members and helped to engineer some of its more infamous demonstrations of anti-Catholic activism, such as the pope-burning processions of 1679–81. Grey and Howard were also members of a group made up exclusively of peers, which first met at the Swan Tavern in Fish Street in the City in late November 1679 and 'resolved to continue a club there once a week'.[2] The group, which also included Theophilus Hastings, 7th earl of Huntingdon, Gilbert Holles, 3rd earl of Clare, and Thomas Grey, 2nd earl of Stamford, was responsible for the petition of sixteen peers presented to Charles II on 6 December calling for the immediate meeting of Parliament. As well as such private gatherings, politicians organised public dinners, designed to encourage their supporters. After March 1681, with no prospect of another Parliament, such feasts became larger and more politicized for, as Shaftesbury explained while planning the 500-strong 'Protestant Feast' of 22 April 1682, 'at present we have no way to let them see our power and formidability but appearing in public'.[3]

The reign of Anne saw an explosion of such political clubs as the party battle grew to its virulent height. Some were primarily for backbenchers in the

FIG. 124 *The first coffee houses in England appeared during the 1650s. During the 1670s there was a debate on the political, moral and physical threat they might pose (Figs 125, 126 opposite), which helped to provoke an unenforced proclamation requiring their suppression in 1675 (Fig. 127 below). By Queen Anne's death in 1714 there were some 500 in London alone, many catering to specialised clienteles: Lloyds of London, for example, famously had its origins in a coffee house where insurance brokers met, socialised and did business. Coffee houses became central to the political culture of the day, providing opportunities for partisan debate and discussion as well as cheap access to newspapers and pamphlets.*

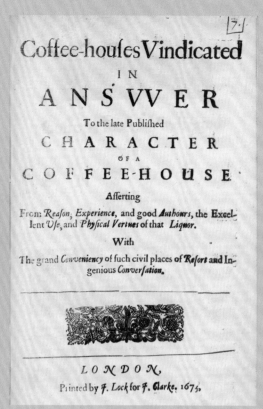

THE

CHARACTER

OF

A Coffee-House,

WITH THE

SYMPTOMES

OF A

TOWN-WIT.

With Allowance, April 11ᵗʰ *1673.*

LONDON,

Printed for *Jonathan Edwin*, at the three Roses in *Lud-Gate-Street*, 1673.

FIG. 125

Coffee-houses Vindicated

IN

ANSWER

To the late Published

CHARACTER

OF A

COFFEE-HOUSE

Asserting

From *Reason*, *Experience*, and good *Authours*, the Excellent *Use*, and *Physical Vertues* of that *Liquor*.

With

The grand *Conveniency* of such civil places of *Resort* and Ingenious *Conversation*.

LONDON,

Printed by *J. Lock* for *J. Clarke*, 1675,

FIG. 126

Commons, such as the violently Tory 'October Club', but others aimed at a more exclusive and aristocratic membership. From the summer of 1711 Henry St John, later Viscount Bolingbroke, and his friend Jonathan Swift worked to recruit Tory peers for the Brothers' Club: by 1712 its membership consisted almost entirely of those who had been promoted to the British House of Lords by the Tory ministry which had come to power in 1710, including Charles Boyle, Baron Boyle (earl of Orrery in the Irish peerage), George Hay, Baron Hay (Viscount Dupplin in the Scottish peerage), Samuel Masham, Baron Masham, Allen Bathurst, Baron Bathurst and Simon Harcourt, Baron Harcourt. Much drinking and merry-making went on at its meetings, but St John assured Orrery of the society's true intent: 'A number of valuable people will be kept in the same mind and others will be made converts to their opinions'.[4] The Brothers' was not to be confused with the Society of the Board of Brothers, founded in 1709 by the Tory Henry Somerset, 2nd duke of Beaufort, which was less exclusive and which placed more emphasis on heavy drinking than on political management. The most famous and socially exclusive political club of this period was

the Kit Cat Club, founded about 1700 to gather together supporters of the Hanoverian succession. During Anne's reign it included the cream of the Whig aristocracy: the dukes of Newcastle, Somerset, Devonshire, Grafton and Richmond, the earls of Sunderland, Carlisle, Kingston, Dorset and Manchester and Lords Wharton, Halifax, Somers, Cowper and Mohun, as well as prominent members of the Commons such as Sir Robert Walpole.

The many coffee houses and taverns of London were also favoured venues for politics and news. Tories by and large frequented the Cocoa Tree in Pall Mall or Ozinda's Chocolate House in St James's Street, while the Whigs haunted the St James's Coffee House further down the same street. There were occasional dinner meetings organized by party leaders for their followers, in which strategy and tactics were invariably discussed. The diary of the second-rank Whig, Charles Bennet, 2nd Baron Ossulston, reveals that he frequently ended a day in the House of Lords with a dinner in a tavern with a group of friends and associates and that occasionally, when important divisions were coming up, he would be called to large-scale meetings at the London townhouse of one of the

By the King.

A PROCLAMATION
FOR THE
Suppression of Coffee-Houses.

CHARLES R.

Hereas it is most apparent, that the Multitude of Coffee-houses of late years set up and kept within this Kingdom, the Dominion of Wales, and the Town of Berwick upon Tweed, and the great resort of Idle and disaffected persons to them, have produced very evil and dangerous effects; as well for that many Tradesmen and others, do therein mis-spend much of their time, which might and probably would otherwise be imployed in and about their Lawful Callings and Affairs; but also, for that in such Houses, and by occasion of the meetings of such persons therein, divers False, Malitious and Scandalous Reports are devised and spread abroad, to the Defamation of His Majesties Government, and to the Disturbance of the Peace and Quiet of the Realm; His Majesty hath thought it fit and necessary, That the said Coffee-Houses be (for the future) Put down and Suppressed, and doth (with the Advice of His Privy Council) by this His Royal Proclamation, Strictly Charge and Command all manner of

persons, That they or any of them do not presume from and after the Tenth day of January next ensuing, to keep any Publick Coffee-house, or to Utter or sell by retail, in his, her or their house or houses (to be spent or consumed within the same) any Coffee, Chocolet, Sherbett or Tea, as they will answer the contrary at their utmost perils.

And for the better accomplishment of this his Majesties Royal Pleasure, his Majesty doth hereby will and require the Justices of Peace within their several Countries, and the Chief Magistrates in all Cities and Towns Corporate, that they do at their next respective General Sessions of the peace (to be holden within their several and respective Counties, Divisions and Precincts) recall and make void all Licenses at any time heretofore Granted, for the selling or Retailing of any Coffee, Chocolet, Sherbett or Tea. And that they or any of them do not (for the future) make or grant any such License or Licenses, to any person or persons whatsoever. And his Majesty doth further hereby declare, that if any person or persons shall take upon them, him or her, after his, her or their License or Licenses recalled, or otherwise without License, to sell by retail (as aforesaid) any of the Liquors aforesaid, that then the person or persons so Offending, shall not only be proceeded against, upon the Statute made in the Fifteenth year of His Majesties Reign (which gives the forfeiture of five pounds for every moneth wherein he, she or they shall offend therein) but shall (in case they persevere to Offend) receive the severest punishments that may by Law be inflicted.

Given at Our Court at *Whitehall*, this Nine and twentieth day of *December* 1675. in the Seven and twentieth year of Our Reign.

God save the King.

LONDON,
Printed by the Assigns of *John Bill*, and *Christopher Barker*,
Printers to the Kings most Excellent Majesty, 1675.

FIG. 127

Whig leaders. On 17 December 1703, for example, when the occasional conformity bill was before the House, Ossulston attended a grand supper at the St James's residence of Charles Spencer, 3rd earl of Sunderland, where he was joined by fourteen named peers, and 'some others I do not remember'. Ossulston also attended another meeting of eighteen peers at Sunderland's in February 1704 where 'tea drunk and our discourse was only about the Scotch Plot'.[5]

Lucas, survive in many manuscript collections. The emergence of a commercial publishing industry made the political, financial and narcissistic rewards for this kind of journalism even greater. During Anne's reign, John Thompson, Baron Haversham, a disgruntled Whig with decidedly dissenting sympathies who turned his coat to ally with high church Tories, made a habit of attending Parliament for the sole purpose of making one big set speech. Haversham cultivated the press: at one stage he was said to be patron of the political journalist John Tutchin. He ensured that his speeches were printed and sold in the streets to an avid and very appreciative reading public. In 1709 one enterprising street seller took advantage of the heightened demand created by the announcement of Haversham's latest speech to unload copies of old stock before the new one could be printed and distributed.

Haversham was not prosecuted for the publication of his speeches. From time to time, however, the House would take action. Lord Lucas's speech was burnt by the common hangman by order of the House, and the shame it brought on him was said to have contributed to his death shortly afterwards. In February 1689 the printing of a list of those who 'who deserted, (not protested)' against the vote on the use of the words 'abdicated' and 'the throne vacant' led to orders to arrest several printers, although it is not known whether they were put into effect.[28] Early in 1699 the House learned that the entrepreneurial printer, John Churchill, had produced a set of *Cases in Parliament resolved and adjudged, upon petitions and writs of error*. The House first reprimanded Churchill, then passed a new standing order to the effect that it was a breach of the privilege of the House for any person to publish or print anything relevant to their proceedings without the leave of the House.

Churchill's real offence may have been to have spotted a market opportunity that could otherwise have provided the House's officers with an additional income; it was the clerks who profited from the sale of printed copies of the monarch's speech and the address to the crown. The first concerted attempt to circumvent the ban came in 1711 when Abel Boyer began to publish the monthly periodical *The political state of Great Britain* which included accounts of debates in both Houses. Boyer was arrested, imprisoned and reprimanded by the House in March 1711 and thereafter paid lip service to the proscription by publishing only during the recess and identifying the speakers by transparent disguises (Lord H——x instead of Lord Halifax, for example). A further clampdown on reporting came after our period and it was not until the last quarter of the eighteenth century that Parliamentary reporting became properly established.

The Lords and the Commons

There were many and close links, both political and personal, between individual peers and individual Members of the House of Commons. Despite this, there were frequent disagreements between the two Houses. For the most part, these were about the details of legislation, and could be reasonably easily resolved though conferences, which were usually held in the Painted Chamber. They could be requested by either House, although it was the prerogative of the Lords to name the time and place of meeting. They could be structured or unstructured. An unstructured or 'free' conference allowed a wide ranging discussion enabling a real dialogue between the Houses rather than obliging them to stick to a predetermined stance. In a structured conference the agenda was decided in detail in advance. In such cases both Houses would prepare their arguments beforehand, and once these lines to take had been agreed to by the House 'no lord is to speak contrary to what was the general sense of this House'.[29] Structured conferences were used to present the Lords' case during the inter-house dispute over *Thomas Skinner v. The East India Company* which brought Parliament to a standstill in 1668 (see above, p. 24). The committee of privileges prepared almost every detail for the conference of 8 May 1668. They wrote and approved a draft introductory speech to be delivered by the duke of Buckingham and a supporting speech to be delivered by Arthur Capell, earl of Essex. They instructed Lord Holles to research ancient records and Arthur Annesley, earl of Anglesey, to research modern ones in order to be able to cite precedents. Charles Howard, Baron Howard of Charlton, was to speak to the East India Company petition that had sparked the interest of the Commons, and Lord Lucas was to answer the arguments advanced by the Commons managers.

In the conferences on the Skinner case, considerable effort was expended, for political reasons, on preventing an agreement. When the dispute was more straightforward, the arguments could be smoothed over, probably with the help of negotiations behind the scenes. In 1661 differences over the corporations bill threatened to bring parliament to a standstill. The Lords' insistence that the bill fail unless their amendments were accepted led to an ill tempered meeting at which Lord Falkland (who sat in the Commons as the Member for Oxfordshire but held a Scots peerage) proposed the production of a printed remonstrance justifying the Commons' actions. The differences were overcome only by the careful management of the solicitor general, Sir Heneage Finch (later earl of Nottingham). Acting on behalf of the court, Finch 'so calmed the tempers of their minds' that the Lords not only agreed to the necessity for a bill but decided that it should be the first priority in the next session 'for which composure [he] had ... the thanks of the king and duke'.[30]

Where clashes between the Commons and the Lords related to the respective privileges of either House they were much more difficult to resolve. Both Houses had established distinctive roles, which they jealously defended from interference by the other. On three occasions the claim to judicature aroused the indignation of the Commons when they were led to believe that it was being used to affect their right to settle their own affairs, or to interfere with its membership. During the House's hearings on the case of *Thomas Skinner v. the East India Company* in 1668, the East India Company got the Commons to challenge the jurisdiction of the House of Lords in a case of first instance rather than appeal, arguing that the absence of a jury amounted to 'the introducing of an arbitrary way of proceeding' and, because the case involved several members of the lower House, that it was contrary to the privileges of the Commons. The case ended in a stalemate and the king managed to suppress the whole affair in 1670 (see above, p. 24). In *Sherley v. Fagg*, which reached the Lords in 1675, Dr Thomas Sherley sought to overturn a chancery decree. His opponent was a Member of the Commons, and this was used to provoke the resistance of the lower House, largely in order to disrupt the session and halt controversial legislation. A third case (*Ashby v. White*) arose out of the general election of 1701 and related to the rights of individual electors: in the Commons it was claimed that for the Lords to presume to adjudicate on the details of an election dispute was an unwarranted interference with the independence of the lower House, and, they implied, was a political attempt to pervert justice and the constitution (see below, p. 284).

The House of Commons insisted on its own unique constitutional role in its exclusive right to initiate taxation. In itself, this was uncontroversial: the Lords accepted that it was appropriate for the lower House, as representatives of the people, to decide on taxation of commoners.

The radical Whig: Ford Grey, 3rd Baron Grey of Warke and earl of Tankerville (1655–1701)

ord Grey, 3rd Baron Grey of Warke was best known to contemporaries, as now, for his incestuous liaison in 1682 with his sister-in-law Henrietta, the daughter, like his legal wife Mary, of George Berkeley, earl of Berkeley, which appeared lightly fictionalized in Aphra Behn's *Love-Letters between a nobleman and his sister.* Grey of Warke was also one of the ablest and most committed Whigs, whose political skills, both within parliament and outside it, were a key asset for his party in the campaigns of 1679–83.

Grey's grandfather, the first baron, had been a prominent opponent of Charles I, and his great-uncle was Cromwell's right-hand man General Henry Ireton. It was little wonder that Grey would be an opponent of the Catholic duke of York and of the episcopal Church of England, although he had certainly left behind the puritan morality of his grandfather. Taking his seat in the House of Lords in February 1677, barely aged 21, Grey quickly became closely associated with the attacks of Anthony Ashley Cooper, earl of Shaftesbury, on James, duke of York and Thomas Osborne, earl of Danby. An apochryphal story about the passage of the Habeas Corpus Act in 1679 suggests that contemporaries recognized Grey's quick-wittedness and his unscrupulous support for his cause. A teller in favour of the bill in a procedural division, he 'as a jest at first' counted a particularly fat peer as ten votes on his side. When nobody noticed, he let the miscounted tally stand and his side won by two votes, rather than losing by eight. His youth, vigour, and common touch, similar qualities to those of his friend and hunting companion James Scott, duke of Monmouth, also made him popular outside Westminster, and in 1679–81 he was effective in getting exclusionist candidates elected in Northumberland, Essex, and Sussex, the counties where his principal estates lay. The bishop of Chichester, Guy Carleton, looked on in frustration as Grey managed the election of the old republican plotter John Braman for all three Exclusion Parliaments. He dubbed Grey 'the elector-general' of Chichester.[1] Grey was at the heart, too, of the large set pieces of political theatre staged in London during the ex-

THE
AMOURS
OF
PHILANDER
AND
SILVIA:
Being the Third and Laſt Part
OF THE
Love-Letters
Between a
NOBLE-MAN
AND HIS
SISTER.
by A. B.

LONDON,
Printed for *Joseph Hindmarſh*, at the *Golden-Ball*
in *Cornhill*; and *Jacob Tonson*, at the *Judge's-
Head* in *Chancery-lane*, 1693.

FIG. 128 *The third volume of Aphra Behn's* Love letters between a nobleman and his sister, *which fictionalises the affair between Grey of Warke and his sister-in-law, and his involvement in Monmouth's rebellion.*

clusion crisis: the pope-burning processions, lavish public dinners and the 'monster petition' campaign, demanding that Parliament be convened, presented to the king in January 1680.

By the time the parliamentary exclusion campaign was brought to an end in March 1681 by the

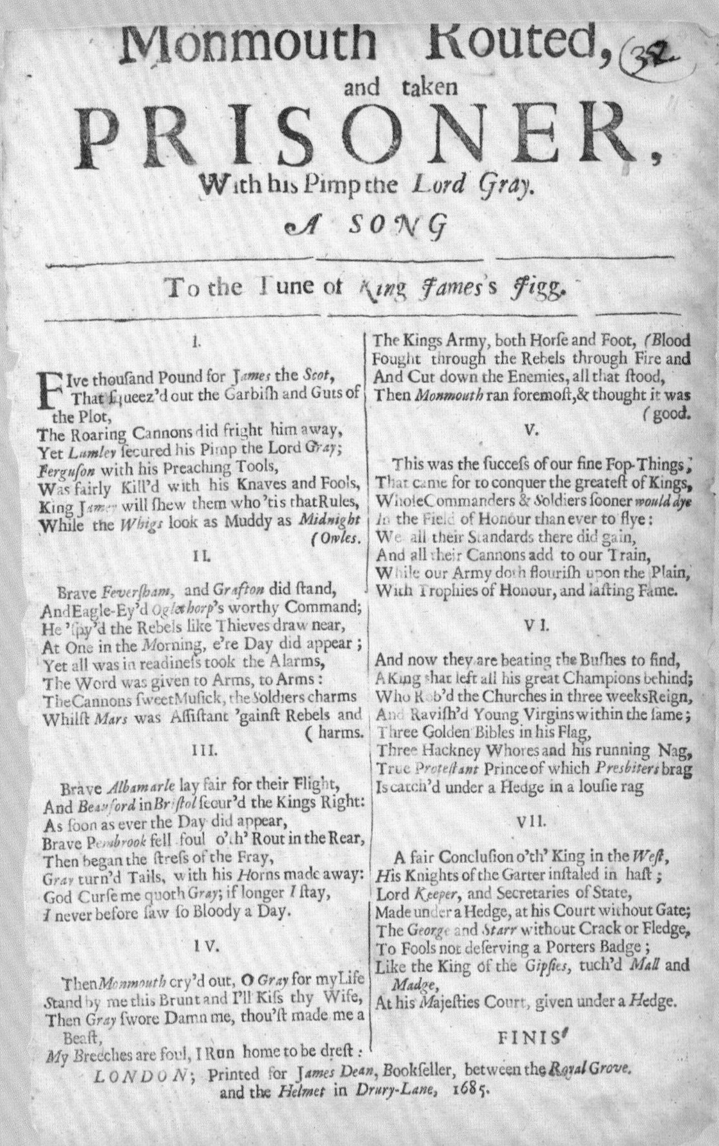

Monmouth Routed, (32

and taken

PRISONER,

With his Pimp the *Lord Gray.*

A SONG

To the Tune of *King James's Jigg.*

I.

Ive thousand Pound for *James* the *Scot*,
That squeez'd out the Garbish and Guts of
the Plot,
The Roaring Cannons did fright him away,
Yet *Lumley* secured his Pimp the Lord *Gray*;
Ferguson with his Preaching Tools,
Was fairly Kill'd with his Knaves and Fools,
King *James* will shew them who'tis that Rules,
While the *Whigs* look as Muddy as *Midnight*
(Owles.

II.

Brave *Feversham*, and *Grafton* did stand,
And Eagle-Ey'd *Oglethorp's* worthy Command;
He 'spy'd the Rebels like Thieves draw near,
At One in the Morning, e're Day did appear ;
Yet all was in readiness took the Alarms,
The Word was given to Arms, to Arms ;
The Cannons sweet Musick, the Soldiers charms
Whilst *Mars* was Assistant 'gainst Rebels and
(harms.

III.

Brave *Albamarle* lay fair for their Flight,
And *Beauford* in *Bristol* secur'd the Kings Right:
As soon as ever the Day did appear,
Brave *Pembrook* fell foul o'th' Rout in the Rear,
Then began the stress of the Fray,
Gray turn'd Tails, with his *Horns* made away:
God Curse me quoth *Gray*; if longer *I* stay,
I never before saw so Bloody a Day.

IV.

Then *Monmouth* cry'd out, O *Gray* for my Life
Stand by me this Brunt and I'll Kiss thy Wife,
Then *Gray* swore Damn me, thou'st made me a
Beast,
My Breeches are foul, I Run home to be drest :

The Kings Army, both Horse and Foot, (Blood
Fought through the Rebels through Fire and
And Cut down the Enemies, all that stood,
Then *Monmouth* ran foremost, & thought it was
(good.

V.

This was the success of our fine Fop-Things,
That came for to conquer the greatest of Kings,
Whole Commanders & Soldiers sooner *would dye*
In the Field of Honour than ever to flye :
We all their Standards there did gain,
And all their Cannons add to our Train,
While our Army doth flourish upon the Plain,
With Trophies of Honour, and lasting Fame.

VI.

And now they are beating the Bushes to find,
A King that left all his great Champions behind;
Who Rob'd the Churches in three weeks Reign,
And Ravish'd Young Virgins within the same ;
Three Golden Bibles in his Flag,
Three Hackney Whores and his running Nag,
True *Protestant* Prince of which *Presbiters* brag
Is catch'd under a Hedge in a lousie rag

VII.

A fair Conclusion o'th' King in the *West*,
His Knights of the Garter instaled in hast ;
Lord *Keeper*, and Secretaries of State,
Made under a Hedge, at his Court without Gate;
The *George* and *Starr* without Crack or Fledge,
To Fools not deserving a Porters Badge ;
Like the King of the *Gipses*, tuch'd *Mall* and
Madge,
At his Majesties Court, given under a Hedge.

FINIS

LONDON; Printed for *James Dean*, Bookseller, between the *Royal Grove*,
and the *Helmet* in *Drury-Lane*, 1685.

FIG. 129 *Broadside verses pour scorn on Monmouth ('James the Scot'), his 'Pimp the Lord Gray' and other associates while praising the efforts of the loyal nobility to suppress the rebellion.*

dissolution of the Oxford Parliament, Grey was involved in more dangerous activities. He helped to organize the violent and rigged election of the Whig sheriffs of London in 1682, and was at the centre of a number of plots for a popular uprising or the murder of the royal brothers. Arrested in June 1683 when he was implicated in the Rye House Plot, he managed to escape to Germany, where he was joined by his lover Henrietta Berkeley and later by Monmouth.

Grey was the only nobleman to join Monmouth in his fatal revolt against James II in 1685. Despite his complete lack of military experience, he was appointed commander of cavalry in Monmouth's makeshift army. They were routed at Sedgemoor owing, contemporaries gleefully insisted, to his incompetence and cowardice. Grey and Monmouth fled the battle together, but took different routes, and were captured separately. Unlike Monmouth, Grey was kept alive, but only so that the crown could make good use of him for its own ends. His substantial estates were confiscated, and the income diverted to the current favourite at court, Laurence Hyde, earl of Rochester. Grey, in exchange for his life, was forced to write out a confession of his long involvement in

FIG. 130 *Ford Grey, 3rd Baron Grey of Warke in a print made on the continent in 1689.*

conspiracies against the Stuart brothers. It was used by the government to charge other known enemies of the regime with treason and to vindicate its previous executions.

Having barely escaped with his life, Grey kept a low profile for the rest of James II's reign and during the beginning of William III's, although he did appear in the House in 1689 to vote in favour of William and Mary's right to the throne. He waited until early 1695, when he could be confident that William of Orange was one Protestant pretender who was securely seated on the English throne, before he made his return to politics with the resurgent Whigs. So effective a party spokesman in the House was he that

in June 1695 he was promoted in the peerage as earl of Tankerville (a town in Normandy where an ancestor had performed valiant military service for Henry V). From then on offices and honours came thick and fast: privy council, board of trade, first lord of the treasury, and finally, in November 1699, lord privy seal. Tankerville died in this office aged 45 on 24 June 1701, the same day on which the king assented to the Act of Settlement, which ensured by statute the Protestant succession to the English throne.

What they did not accept was the Commons' assumption that their privilege over taxation, or money bills, covered any bill that imposed fees, fines or forfeitures, nor that they could have no say in amending them. In 1661 the Commons rejected an otherwise innocuous bill from the Lords designed to improve the state of the streets in Westminster because it laid 'a charge upon the people' and 'bills of that nature ought to be first considered here'.[31] As Edward Hyde, earl of Clarendon, remarked, the lower House was 'the immediate representative of the people, it is presumed that they best know what they can bear and are willing to submit to, and what they propose to give is proportionable to what they can spare; and therefore the lords use not to put any stop in the passage of such bills'. Taxes, though, were 'as much the gift and present from the house of peers as they are from the House of Commons' and so required the approval of the upper House. Clarendon insisted that the Lords 'may alter any clause in them [money bills], that they do not think to the good of the people'.[32] A similar claim was made in 1671 in Lord Lucas's notorious speech on the supply bill. Lucas, appalled at the vast sums involved, condemned 'this over liberal humour of the Commons' and insisted that the Lords could and should amend money bills since otherwise all property was at the mercy of the Commons so that 'your Lordships have nothing that you can properly call your own'.[33]

In practice, the Lords usually accepted that they should not revise money bills. The greatest rows occurred when the Commons took advantage of this by 'tacking' to them controversial provisions which had nothing to do with finance. In February 1692, when the substance of a bill for taking public accounts which had already failed to pass through the Lords was added to the poll bill, the peers made a point of recording that:

> The Lords in Parliament, being extremely sensible of that
> imminent danger, to which not only this nation, but a great part
> of Christendom might be exposed, if either the necessary supply
> of money, or his majesty's voyage beyond sea in this extraordinary
> conjuncture should receive any delay, have agreed to the bill,
> entitled, an act for raising money by a poll, payable quarterly,
> for one year, for the carrying on a vigorous war against France,
> without any amendments; and, out of zeal to the public good,
> have purposely avoided to take notice of the irregularities relating
> to the clause for taking the accounts. But, to prevent any ill
> consequences from such a precedent for the future, they have
> thought fit to declare solemnly, and to enter upon their books

FIG. 131 Het hoog en lager-huys van Engelandt: *a Dutch print of 1689, by Romeyn de Hooghe, purports to show the House of Lords meeting with the king, William III, on the throne. The topographical detail is highly inaccurate.*

for a record to all posterity, that they will not hereafter admit, upon any occasion whatsoever, of a proceeding so contrary to the rules and methods of Parliament.[34]

'Tacking' was used again in 1699 and 1700. Anger over the 1700 bill was assiduously stoked by the Whigs and it passed the House by only a single vote, despite strong pressure from the king. To the peers it seemed that their giving way 'has had no other effect but to introduce greater impositions upon them' and they warned of their determination to 'transmit the government and their own rights and privileges to their posterity, in the same state and condition that they were derived down to them from their ancestors'.[35] In 1702 there was another threat of a tack, this time to secure the passage of the failed occasional conformity bill. To pre-empt it, the Lords passed a new standing order declaring 'That the annexing any

clause or clauses to a bill of aid or supply, the matter of which is foreign
to, and different from, the matter of the said bill of aid or supply, is unpar-
liamentary, and tends to the destruction of the constitution of this government'.[36] When in 1704 the Commons again resorted to a tack their
bill was decisively thrown out at its second reading.

These confrontations constituted some of the greatest dramas of
parliamentary life, excitedly reported across London and the rest of the
country and attracting intense political interest. Much of the business in
the Lords was more humdrum and less controversial. But all of it required
sustained attention and effort on the part of a large group of people –
peers and bishops, promoters, officials – to achieve the desired result,
often in a race to complete it during the short period in which the House
sat, or in which the attention and sympathy of its members was engaged.

War and peace, 1697–1702

aving drifted into stalemate, the war against France was brought to an end in September 1697 with the Treaty of Ryswick. Parliamentarians looked forward to the disbandment of the forces and relief from high taxes. William III did not. War, he calculated, would be renewed if the death of the ailing and childless King Charles II of Spain destroyed the balance of power in Europe by uniting the crowns of Spain and France. Proponents of a speedy demobilisation, both Whig and Tory, were drawn towards the 'country' attitudes espoused in the Commons by the Whigs Robert Harley and Paul Foley, whose attacks on waste and corruption in government had already drawn support from both parties. The 1698 elections saw a resurgence of support for country ideals and a vigorous hostility to taxes and placemen. When Parliament met, the Commons rejected William's request for sufficient funding to retain a permanent force of 10,000 men, including his crack Dutch troops.

William threatened to leave England for good. His frantic ministers considered the possibility of renewing the fight in the Lords but, as secretary of state James Vernon lamented, this would inevitably result in a conflict between the Houses: 'questions are already moved whether it be a money bill, so as to exclude the Lords from making alterations in it, and what would be the consequences of their rejecting it. But that looks like a remedy worse than the disease'.[1] The government had to back down, and William to accept the cuts required by the Commons. The Commons provoked both him and the Lords more still by tacking onto two money bills clauses about the distribution of the Irish estates confiscated from supporters of James II. At the end of the session on 4 May 1698, it was observed, with some understatement, that 'The Lords and Commons are not parted extraordinary friends'.[2]

For William, always a reluctant collaborator with the Junto, the 1698 session was further evidence that they were incapable of serving him effectively. There was, however, no real alternative. Although he had finally brought his preferred adviser, Robert Spencer, 2nd earl of Sunderland, formally into office as lord chamberlain in April 1697, Sunderland gave it up by the end of the year, recognising that it exposed him to even greater hostility – wanting to place himself 'out of gunshot', as he put it.[3] His chances of returning to power were ended when, in the summer of 1698, Charles Montagu secured a promise of £2,000,000 from a group of merchants who wanted to overturn the East India Company's monopoly of trade with the East Indies. In so doing he transformed the king's finances and (temporarily at least) his opinion of the Junto.

Trouble in Parliament continued. During the 1699–1700 session further inquiries into the disposition of forfeited Irish estates revealed just how extensive were the grants that William had made to his Dutch favourites. In what was now a regular tactic, the Commons, determined that these grants should be revoked, coupled a provision to do so to a money bill. This time William was determined to resist in the Lords, against the advice of Sunderland and the key figures in the Junto. He incited the peers – a number of whom were themselves beneficiaries of the estates – to reject the important provisions of the bill in early April 1700. The ensuing confrontation between the Houses was fuelled by indignation in the Commons at the peers' defence of the exorbitant favours showered on the king's foreign advisers. William was forced to back down. Persuading the Lords to do likewise was more easily said than done. Only after a furious row over the precise meaning of a tied division did the House surrender to the Commons. As part of his own humble pie the king had to accept a statutory commission to examine debts incurred by the various branches of the military and the prize office, and to abandon other favoured bills, including one to provide for a union between England and Scotland. It had been, William groaned, 'the most dismal session I have ever had'[4] and in its wake he dismissed Lord Chancellor Somers, who had absented himself rather than assist in managing the Irish forfeitures bill. It effectively put the Junto ministry to an end. In December 1700, having failed to persuade the ailing Charles Talbot, duke of Shrewsbury, to return to gov-

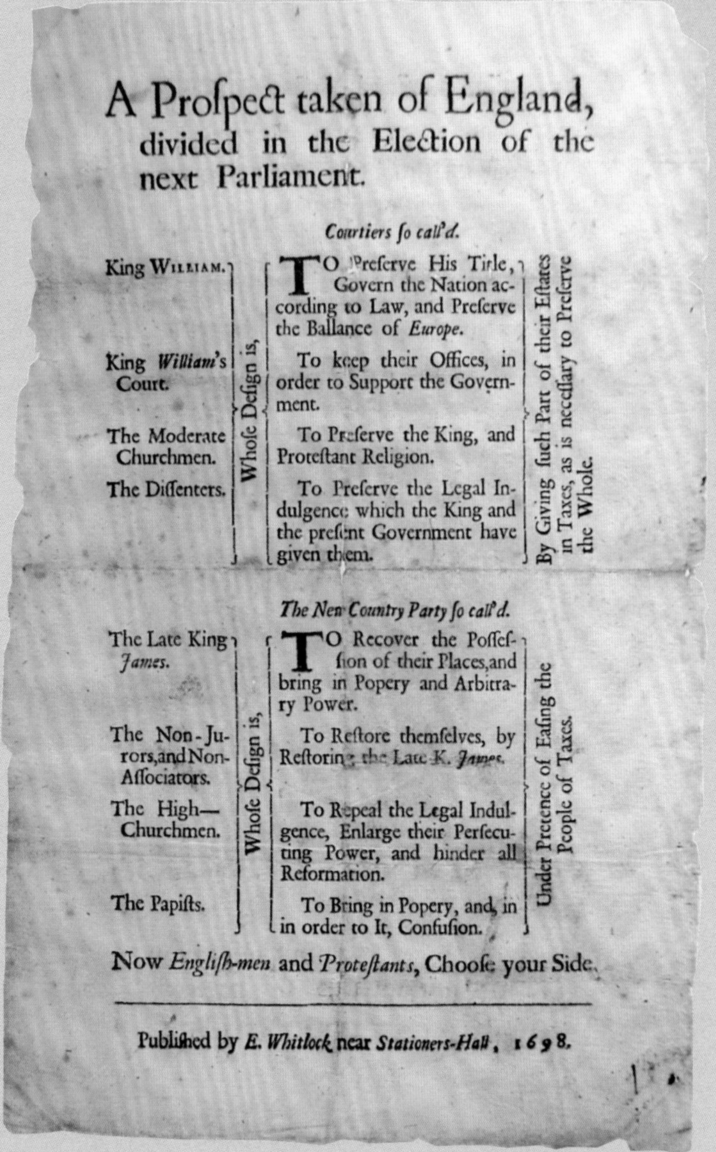

FIG. 132 *Money was a central issue in the 1698 election, when the prospect of peace suggested that government expenditure could be reduced. This rare election handbill suggests that the 'new country party' which was resisting taxation was really composed of Jacobites: taxes need to be kept up in order to support the King, the Protestant religion and the Revolution.*

The handbill reads:

A Prospect taken of England,
divided in the Election of the
next Parliament.

Courtiers so call'd.

King WILLIAM.
King *William*'s Court.
The Moderate Churchmen.
The Dissenters.

Whose Design is,

TO Preserve His Title, Govern the Nation according to Law, and Preserve the Ballance of *Europe*.

To keep their Offices, in order to Support the Government.

To Preserve the King, and Protestant Religion.

To Preserve the Legal Indulgence which the King and the present Government have given them.

By Giving such Part of their Estates in Taxes, as is necessary to Preserve the Whole.

The New Country Party so call'd.

The Late King *James*.
The Non-Jurors, and Non-Associators.
The High—Churchmen.
The Papists.

Whose Design is,

TO Recover the Possession of their Places, and bring in Popery and Arbitrary Power.

To Restore themselves, by Restoring the Late K. *James*.

To Repeal the Legal Indulgence, Enlarge their Persecuting Power, and hinder all Reformation.

To Bring in Popery, and, in order to It, Confusion.

Under Pretence of Easing the People of Taxes.

Now *English-men* and *Protestants*, Choose your Side.

Published by *E. Whitlock* near *Stationers-Hall*, 1698.

ernment, William brought the Tory peer Laurence Hyde, earl of Rochester, together with Sidney Godolphin, Baron Godolphin, into the council, and dissolved Parliament.

Prophesying war

Two deaths overshadowed the elections of January and February 1701 and the subsequent parliamentary session. One was that in July 1700 of Princess Anne's young son, the duke of Gloucester. As neither William nor she had another surviving child it cast into doubt the security of the Protestant succession. The other was the long anticipated death of Charles II of Spain in October 1700. Louis XIV and William had been parties to the deals – known as the First and Second Partition Treaties – designed to stop the whole of the Spanish empire from falling into French hands at Charles's death and thus to prevent a renewal of war. Louis, though, now chose to honour Charles's will instead, which, directing the full and undivided inheritance to his own younger grandson, Philip, duke of Anjou (Philip V of Spain), unbalanced the powers of Europe.

Did the Spanish succession pose a threat to Anglo-Dutch security or not? William was convinced that it did. His new ministers, Rochester and Godolphin, disagreed, and thought that the new Parliament would disagree too. When Parliament met in February 1701, the House of Lords voted in favour of entry into an alliance with those 'who are willing to unite, for the preservation of the balance of Europe ... the preservation of the Protestant religion, and the peace of Europe'.[5] The Commons voted a similar resolution and began work on a bill to settle Protestant succession to the crown through the German house of Hanover, which would become the Act of Settlement.

Although many recognised the existence of a major threat to the peace, they could not agree on what to do about it. Country and Tory politicians had no desire to plunge into another war merely to protect foreign – Dutch – interests. As more details emerged about the earlier negotiations between William and Louis, they showed more interest in attacking the king's Dutch adviser, Hans Willem Bentinck, earl of Portland, and the Junto. The Commons voted to impeach Portland and Somers; later they voted to impeach Orford and Halifax as well. But there was little intention of actually starting a set of prosecutions which had almost no chance of success. Instead during May and June both Houses resorted to obstructive political manoeuvring (see below, p. 280). Eventually, one by one, without any evidence being presented on behalf of the prosecution, the Whig lords were solemnly acquitted. Such proceedings would have seemed farcical at the best of times; in the particular circumstances of 1701 they cast considerable doubt on the capacity of Parliament to provide adequate support for a major European war. War, though, moved a step closer when in September 1701 James II died in exile, and Louis XIV provocatively recognised his son James Francis Edward as James III, rightful king of England. In November William called a general election, hoping to catch a moment of popular enthusiasm for war.

The elections did not produce a clear majority for either Whigs or Tories. Remarkably, both parties vied for the favour of the king, voting support for the preparations for war and for supply, although they clashed over a bill for the abjuration of James III which the Whigs were determined to phrase so that it posed more difficulties for scrupulous Tories. Shortly after the bill received the royal assent, William was dead. After breaking his collar bone in a riding accident in late February 1702, he developed a fever which rapidly worsened. He died early on 8 March, leaving England on the brink of a major war and with leading politicians still firmly divided over religion, the role of the monarchy and their own contending ambitions.

Chapter 7

The business of the House

Law making

Much of the legislation that started in the Lords during this period was private in nature, designed for the benefit of a private individual or corporation, rather than to achieve some general, public aim. To a much greater extent than in the Commons, private bills were the bread and butter of daily business in the Lords. Of a sample of almost 500 bills dealt with in the House of Lords over the period 1660–1715, 58 per cent originated in the House of Commons. Well over half of the 42 per cent that originated in the Lords were private bills. By contrast, only about 30 per cent of the bills originating in the Commons were private bills. About two thirds of the private bills originating in the Lords received royal assent. Only 30 per cent of the private bills that started in the Commons obtained the royal assent.

Most private bills dealt with the estates, especially landed estates, of individual families. They broke up legally binding entails in order to sell land to pay debts or to settle portions of land on family members; they assigned trustees to manage debt-charged estates more efficiently; they confirmed or annulled controversial land transactions. Often legislation was required because no remedy was available through the courts, sometimes because one or more of the parties was a minor. A private act was passed in 1663, for instance, to give legal backing to the marriage settlement of Anthony Grey, 11th earl of Kent, because as a minor Kent was unable to give his consent to the arrangements made on his behalf by his mother.

Like Kent's, many of the hundreds of private bills which went through the House of Lords were promoted by peers themselves or served their interests. In order to secure the passage of their bills, temporal and spiritual lords called in help from friends, relations and clients in both Houses. In 1660 the committee for the bill to settle the estates of William Cavendish, marquess (later duke) of Newcastle, was chaired by his brother-in-law, John Lucas, Baron Lucas. The Yarmouth fishery bill was introduced in the Commons in 1665 by Sir Robert Paston, later earl of Yarmouth, and given a fair wind by the government in return for Paston's role in proposing an unprecedented supply grant that year. When it came to the bill's committee stage in the Lords, Paston dined with thirteen Members of the House and got his kinsman Montagu Bertie, 2nd earl of Lindsey, to entertain 'a great many others'. As a result when the committee met later the same day, three dukes and some thirty other peers were in attendance – 'a fuller committee than was ever observed'. Lindsey's services were also in evidence during the meeting; when an amendment was suggested, he 'stood up and said he would be bound [Paston] should perform whatever [he] said'.[1] James Annesley, 3rd earl of Anglesey, entertained fifteen peers in 1701 in an attempt to defeat his wife's separation bill. In 1703 when Henry Dillon, Viscount Dillon, an Irish peer, wanted to promote an estate bill, he asked his wife to contact her aunt, the duchess of Marlborough, to secure the backing of the duke. The promoter of a bill would have to secure support in the Commons as well. In January 1667, Lord Roos (John Manners, Lord Roos, heir to the earldom of Rutland) treated the solicitor general (Sir Heneage Finch, later earl of Nottingham) and forty-six members of the House of Commons to a dinner at the Dog Tavern in Palace Yard, before they returned to their committee work in the Commons and recommended the passage of Roos's bill, a controversial measure to illegitimate his adulterous wife's children which had already passed the Lords.

It was not only the lords temporal who were involved in private legislation. The bishops, too, were active promoters of private bills, usually designed to maximize the revenue from church lands. In 1671, Isaac Barrow of St. Asaph and Robert Morgan of Bangor introduced a private bill enabling them to let all lead mines on their diocesan lands for twenty-one years. In 1678 Barrow promoted another to appropriate the profits from two rectories in his diocese to maintain the cathedral and its choir and to unite several sinecures for the augmentation of poor vicarages. Barrow thanked Sancroft for supporting the legislation, 'a work of great charity and indeed necessity' because Welsh vicarages were poorly endowed and the clergy were 'illiterate and contemptible . . . for want of books and all improvements for their ministry'.[2] Some episcopal bills were rather less charitable in purpose: one promoted by William Talbot, bishop of Oxford, was designed to sell a rectory and other lands for the benefit of his own children.

Part of the House's job in considering private bills was to ensure that the parties concerned were agreed. This was largely the responsibility of the committee appointed to examine the bill after its second reading, which called the parties before them or obtained letters and affidavits testifying to their consent. Public notice of impending committee meetings and the bills they were to examine was customarily posted on the doors of the House. In 1670, however, the committee considering the Boston-Trent navigation bill ordered that notice of the bill and the date and time of their next meeting be posted in the market places of the local towns so that 'all persons who conceive themselves in any wise concerned in or by the passing of the said bill may then and there be heard what they have to say for or against the passing of the same'.[3] The bill was plainly a controversial one: some of the Lords' amendments provoked a conference with the Commons and had to be jettisoned before the bill was passed. During a committee's deliberations, objections were investigated and could result in amendments or the abandonment of the bill. In 1670 when Lady Leigh declared that a bill proposed by her husband did not take the interests of their children into adequate consideration 'the committee thought fit to proceed no further'.[4] Similar difficulties arose in 1679 over the attempts of Henry Howard, then styled earl of Arundel (later 7th duke of Norfolk), to settle his family estates. Arundel was on bad terms with his father, the 6th duke of Norfolk, and suspected him of diverting the family's resources for the benefit of his second wife and their children. Arundel rallied all the other adult males in the extended and powerful Howard clan in support of the bill and mendaciously assured the House of his father's agreement to it. Norfolk got wind of the proposal and sent a thundering letter opposing 'this most false and scandalous bill' which was required 'merely because the writer does not die as soon as his son and his governors would have him'.[5] Thomas Bruce, 2nd earl of Ailesbury, attempted to secure the second reading of a private bill for the sale of lands mentioned in his marriage settlement in 1690 by insisting that Henry Somerset, duke of Beaufort, and his duchess (his wife's stepfather and mother) had given their consent. When the House realized that this was untrue the bill was recommitted. The Beauforts insisted that Lady

Loyalty and indemnity:
the Derby estate bills

ost private bills were relatively uncontroversial, and affected only a few individuals. A few raised political issues of major significance. The private estate legislation of Charles Stanley, 8th earl of Derby, was a case in point. His father, the 7th earl, was among the most celebrated of royalist martyrs, executed by the republic in October 1651 following Charles II's catastrophic defeat at Worcester. Large tracts of his land in Lancashire and north Wales had been confiscated by the regime and sold, often to the existing tenants. During the 1650s the new earl of Derby made arrangements with many of the purchasers to buy them back in the future, whenever he was able to reimburse them. But in a number of cases, he further agreed to make legal conveyances of the land in return for badly-needed cash, effectively signing away his title to it altogether.

At the Restoration, although land confiscated by the previous regimes was returned, there was no question that the new government would or could overturn sales which had been voluntarily entered into and properly and legally confirmed. Derby, who claimed he had been tricked into signing his land away, made four attempts to get it back through private legislation. The first of his bills, for the recovery of properties in north Wales, was introduced into the House of Lords in June 1660. The purchasers, all former Commonwealth officials, warned the bill's committee that 'if your lordships shake the security of all purchases the whole nation will be in an earthquake',[1] and this became the crux of the matter. Ironically on the same day when it was reported from committee that there had been 'force and fraud' in the sale of Derby's lands, the bill for the confirmation of judicial proceedings was first introduced in the House. Derby's bill flew in its face and regardless of how sympathetic individuals might have been to his plight, his peers felt they could not make an exception for him. The government of Charles II made it clear that it saw this and the other estate bills which Derby brought into the Convention as a breach of the 'indemnity and oblivion' which it had been trying so hard to foster. Derby's bills were allowed to languish, first in the

Lords and then in the Commons, and none had made progress by the time the Convention was dissolved.

He had better luck in the first session of the Cavalier Parliament which, in this measure at least, lived up to its name and reputation as a body supportive of the interests of the old royalists. The House of Lords passed a more limited version of the bill for the restoration of Derby's Welsh properties in early February 1662, restricted to those estates in which there had clearly been some undue practices used to get Derby's consent.

Even so, twenty-five peers, including ministers and privy councillors Edward Hyde, earl of Clarendon, James Butler, duke of Ormond, Edward Montagu, 2nd earl of Manchester, and Arthur Annesley, earl of Anglesey, signed a protest against the bill's passage, which they saw as 'a breach of the act of judicial proceedings' and 'a trenching of the act of indemnity and oblivion'.[2] This clear indication of government disfavour of the measure was confirmed on the last day of the session, 19 May 1662, when Derby's estate bill was one of only two of the raft of bills submitted to the king which received the royal veto – one of a handful of bills vetoed between the Restoration and the death of Queen Anne. The king attempted to broker a mediation between him and the purchasers, but it failed.

Although Derby had recovered much of the land lost in the Interregnum, the king's veto of his efforts to regain these properties was keenly felt. There were other irritations in his relationship with the government over the 1660s, including his high-handedness in his lord lieutenancies and in the Isle of Man (see below, p. 310). He made no further attempt to promote a bill for the recovery of his lands, but his son and heir, William Stanley, the 9th earl, tried again in 1685 and 1691. The 1685 bill got nowhere in a short-lived session of Parliament; the 1691 bill did not even receive a second reading. One strand of royalist and Tory opinion regarded the 1662 veto as a betrayal of one of the cause's most loyal families: Thomas Bruce, 2nd earl of Ailesbury, blamed Clarendon for it, as his 'maxim in general was, and such he gave as advice, that his Majesty must reward his enemies to sweeten

The Right Honoᵇˡᵉ Charles Earle of Derby Lord Stanley and Strange of Knockin Baron of wee ton Viscount Kinton Lord Mohun Burnell Bassett and Lacy Lord Leiuetenant of the Countyes Pall atyne of Lancaster and Chester and the City and County of Chester Chamberlaine of Chester vice Admirall of the aforesaid Countyes Lord of Man and the Isles &c. A Blooteling fecit

FIG. 133 *Charles Stanley, 8th earl of Derby (1628–72), by Abraham Blooteling.*

them, for that his friends were so by a settled principle, and that their loyalty could not be shaken'.[3] The Stanleys bitterly nursed the memory of the snub. When James Stanley, the 10th earl, rebuilt Knowsley Hall in 1732 he placed above its front door an inscription commemorating the murder of his grandfather, who had died 'for strenuously adhering to Charles II, who refused a bill unanimously passed by both Houses of Parliament for restoring to the family the estates which he had lost by his loyalty to him'.[4]

Ailesbury's consent had been obtained by her husband under duress. They themselves, however, were not innocent, since they had used the marriage settlement in question to strip Lady Ailesbury of much of her own wealth. The earl of Ailesbury proved to be a formidable opponent whose decision to attend the House in person 'gained him a great many friends in both houses'.[6] Descriptions of the passage of this bill suggest that the Commons respected the role of the Lords in dealing with private bills, for Beaufort's agent was advised that objections already considered in the upper House should not be raised after the Lords had passed the bill and sent it to the House of Commons.

After 1689, as parliamentary sittings became more regular and the House faced a burgeoning calendar of legislative business – including a greater number of private bills – there was growing concern about sharp practice. On 16 January 1706 Charles Spencer, 3rd earl of Sunderland, remarked on the 'suspicious contents' of a private bill that had been introduced into the House. His political ally, Lord Keeper Cowper, commented similarly on another. The following month when a bill for the sale of the estates of John Barnes was introduced to the House, Cowper 'laid such an emphasis on the peccant parts of the breviate [a short description of the bill that had to accompany it], that the Lords took notice of the roguery; and threw it out with indignation.' Another ally, the former lord chancellor, John Somers, Baron Somers, then made a speech against the 'perfunctory and careless passing of such bills' and it was agreed that a committee of the whole House should 'consider of the best means to prevent the increase of private bills in parliament, and the surprizing the House in their proceeding thereupon' which resulted in a new and comprehensive series of standing orders.[7]

If it was private legislation which occupied most time, public legislation got the greatest amount of outside attention. The legislation about religion and the succession was central to the politics of the period, but even the great clashes on these issues constituted a fraction of the work of the House on public bills. The distinction between public bills and private ones was in any case often unclear, even after the new standing orders were introduced. Many bills promoted as public measures were in effect intended to benefit private interests, especially because a public bill was not subject to the same fees as a private one. Oliver St John, 2nd earl of Bolingbroke, for example, approached William Russell, 5th earl (later duke) of Bedford in 1679 for his support in developing a navigation scheme extending to the town of Bedford. Bedford assured Bolingbroke of his desire to help, but advised against proceeding too fast, reminding him of his own interest in the Fens, 'upon account whereof it would be thought that I stirred in it, not so much out of public respect as out of a private one'. Only too aware of the passions such developments caused from his own experience with the Bedford Level, he also cautioned Bolingbroke against proceeding with the scheme until he could be sure of the support of the local gentry, who, Bedford warned, 'as yet I find are exceedingly averse'.[8] When Robert Bertie, 3rd earl of Lindsey, supported a huge draining project in Lincolnshire in 1685 one of the most influential local gentlemen wrote that 'all the Berties have lost their esteem in the country very much by voting for the drainers which has done my Lord Lindsey an injury and made him not to be respected amongst the gentry'.[9]

Many public bills were put forward to regulate or promote the interests of specific trades and industries, or agricultural sectors. Although such measures more frequently emerged from the Commons than the Lords, debates on them in the Lords could be just as hard fought as they were in the Commons, for the regulation of trade or fiscal measures might deeply affect the local or sectional interests of individual peers. The Irish cattle bills of 1665 and 1666, in which many peers had personal interests, was a case in point (see below, p. 254). Another was the resistance in the Lords after the Union of 1707 to measures which harmed the Scottish economy. In 1711, during debates on a bill to prevent the export of Scottish flax to Ireland, Charles Spencer, 3rd earl of Sunderland, accused the Scottish peer John Erskine, 23rd earl of Mar, of always preferring 'the interest of Ireland to that of any one county in England'. Mar sharply responded that English peers were working against Scottish interests: 'it was true we had a legal union but it were fit that we had a union of interests and of affection, that this did not seem the way to it for he believed the account of this day's proceedings would appear very strange to the people of Scotland'.

Lobbying was as common for public bills as for private. Some was highly organised, involving the circulation of printed copies of reasons for or objections against individual proposals. Much was more discreet than this, although it could be highly organized and extremely effective. From January 1671 William Willoughby, 6th Baron Willoughby of Parham, and a group of Barbadian merchants in London, known as the 'Gentlemen Planters', began to meet regularly as 'The committee for the public con-

'Irish understandings':
the Irish cattle bill, 1666–67

The early 1660s marked the beginning of a period of low prices and agricultural rents which fuelled the anxieties of the gentry and aristocracy about their incomes and about social stability in an era of heightened unemployment and poverty. Many of them blamed cheap agricultural imports, especially cattle and sheep from Ireland, for their problems. Economic interest was mingled with political suspicion: exporting Irish cattle created, it was believed, enormous profits for Irish landowners. Poverty-stricken Ireland, however, needed as much export income as it could get: the Irish administration, headed by its lord lieutenant, James Butler, the Irish duke of Ormond (himself the biggest landowner in Ireland by far and no doubt a very great beneficiary of the trade), was deeply worried about the impact of the pressure in England to ban the trade.

These issues were ventilated in the last three months of 1666 in the debates on the Irish cattle bill, a measure which sought to prohibit imports of cattle from Ireland. They were exploited by George Villiers, 2nd duke of Buckingham, and the chancellor of the exchequer Anthony Ashley Cooper, Baron Ashley (later the earl of Shaftesbury) as a way to attack Ormond and, indirectly, the lord chancellor, Edward Hyde, earl of Clarendon, twin pillars of an 'old guard' whom they thought to be obstructing their rise.

Their attitudes to the bill also reflected the anti-Irish and anti-Catholic prejudices of the English governing elite. When Edward Conway, Viscount Conway, asked Ashley why he was so determined to ruin Ireland, Ashley acknowledged that the bill seemed like an 'unnatural act', but pointed to wider concerns about the government of Ireland: English settlers were being driven out of the country and replaced with the Irish, who grew fat, like their cattle, on the trade. Ormond's own rents, he suggested, would, if the import trade continued, exceed those of the richest English nobleman.

Ashley's attacks on the Irish in the House at one point provoked Ormond's hot-headed son Thomas Butler, Lord Butler (better known by his Irish title as earl of Ossory), only two months after he had become a Member of the House, to make 'reflections' on the peer's previous career in the revolutionary governments, for which he was reprimanded by the House. The young Irish peer had already been censured for challenging Buckingham to a duel for arguing that 'whoever was against the bill was there led to it by an Irish interest or an Irish understanding which' (as Pepys glossed it) 'is as much as to say he is a fool'.[1]

Richard Boyle, earl of Burlington, Edward Conway, Viscount Conway and Arthur Annesley, earl of Anglesey, other Irish landowners who sat in the House, joined Ossory in speaking vehemently against the bill. For a time, their strategy to oppose the bill was to concentrate on its description of the import of Irish cattle as a 'nuisance', designed to prevent the king from using his prerogative to allow any individual a special dispensation from its provisions. Many peers could be persuaded to oppose so direct an assault on the royal prerogative and throughout December 1666 the court's strategy was to use the argument to sink the bill altogether: Clarendon ridiculed Ashley's compromise suggestion that a different word be used by suggesting that 'adultery' might be appropriate. By the beginning of January 1667 an impasse had been reached.

In the end necessity prevailed: the king, engaged in a costly war with the Dutch, desperately needed supply from the Commons which was being held up by the row. At a meeting at Clarendon's London house on 13 January 1667, ministers decided (despite Clarendon's opposition) to drop their resistance. The Lords withdrew their objections to 'nuisance' the next day, although eight peers entered their protests against the bill (including the three Irish peers who were in the House).

The Irish Cattle Act failed to improve the English economy and only forced the Irish to strengthen theirs by diversifying their trade. The disruption the argument had caused in the attempt to secure funding to continue the war with the Dutch contributed to the failure to set out a fleet in the early summer of 1667 and the consequent success of the Dutch assault on the Medway in June. The debates on the bill were also a precursor of the more comprehensive assault on Clarendon, led by the same figures

in the House, that ended in his impeachment and banishment in late 1667 and the removal of Ormond from the Irish lieutenancy two years later.

FIG. 134 *James Butler, duke of Ormond (1610–88), after Sir Peter Lely, c.1665.*

FIG. 135 *A letter written in January 1702 by Robert Harley (later earl of Oxford but at this time Speaker of the House of Commons) to Thomas Tenison, archbishop of Canterbury, reveals something of the collaborative mechanisms of managing parliamentary business. Harley advocates a new law to control the print trade and prevent the publication of 'scandalous lying pamphlets' and sends a draft bill to the archbishop, suggesting it would be best introduced in the Lords rather than the Commons.*

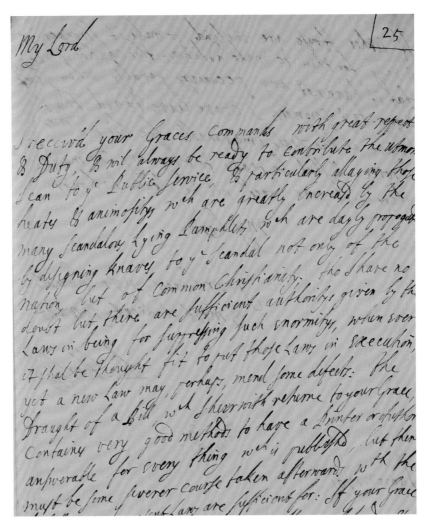

cerns of Barbados'. The catalyst was a bill that would increase the duty on West Indian sugar, then before the Commons. Having failed to make much headway there, the committee arranged to meet Willoughby at Westminster to make arrangements to petition the Lords. In the Lords, the bill went to a committee in which Willoughby was a constant and active member. The House accepted amendments that favoured the West Indian planters and chose Willoughby as one of the managers of the ensuing conference with the Commons. The bill was lost but, in their report to the Assembly of Barbados, the Gentlemen Planters attributed their success in the Lords to Willoughby:

who was one of the committee and infinitely concerned for you, [and] with great efficacy convinced the Lords of the mistake the merchants were running them upon . . . We think it our duty also to let you know that my Lord Willoughby hath shewed himself wonderful affectionate and zealous in your concerns, and very instrumental with the Lords in the ease you have.[10]

Although free from the direct pressure of constituents which their colleagues in the Commons had to endure, the Lords were not immune from more public protest against legislation. In August 1689 the House was besieged by a crowd of silkweavers protesting against a bill to support the wool trade by requiring the wearing of woollens. Several lords addressed them and were forced to promise that nothing would be done until counsel had been heard against the bill. The House ordered a guard of troops to prevent a similar incursion in the future – and it rejected the bill.

Bishops were active in public legislation too, and their concerns were closely reflected in many of the bills introduced into the Lords. In August 1681, Archbishop Sancroft was working on drafts of a bill for the union of small livings in Exeter. The division and unification of parishes to meet the needs of the population was a routine concern for bishops and other clergy: an act was required on each occasion. Sancroft's successor, Archbishop Tenison, pursued his own legislative agenda through the Lords: it included the bishops' perennial concern about the reform of the laws on marriage, on which he helped to draft two bills, one of which received the royal assent in 1696. Another bill, the church statutes bill, was drafted by Somers as a result of the bitter dispute between Bishop Nicolson of Carlisle and the Tory cleric Francis Atterbury (later bishop of Rochester) over Atterbury's rights as dean of Carlisle. Tenison instructed all the bishops to support it and it passed the Lords by a huge majority despite the doubts of the queen and the opposition of Archbishop Sharp of York. When Tenison allowed his directive to the bishops to be re-used in lobbying the Commons, Atterbury published an unsuccessful counter-attack; Tenison told Nicolson that he 'would not have seen [the act] miscarried for £500'.[11]

Divorce

Towards the end of William III's reign the House began to develop a novel jurisdiction in divorce cases, a hybrid legislative and judicial procedure.

FIG. 136 *In this printed statement supporting his case for divorce in the House of Lords in 1670, Lord Roos established that his wife had been found guilty of adultery in the ecclesiastical court of arches and advanced as a precedent an act of Parliament in 1552 retrospectively validating the second marriage of the powerful courtier William Parr, marquess of Northampton. He omitted to mention that the act in question had been repealed a year later.*

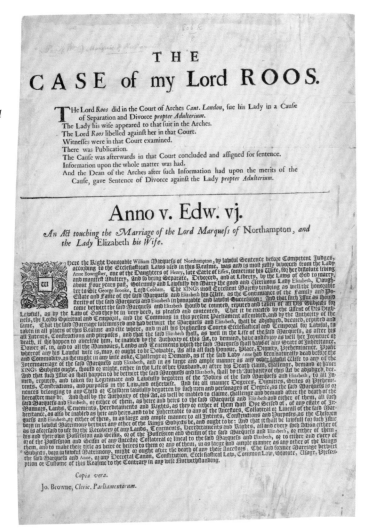

Although a form of divorce had always been available through the church courts, it was by no means clear that this permitted the divorced parties to remarry. Parliamentary divorce started with a bill of Lord Roos's, three years after his 1667 bill to illegitimate his wife's children. Now wanting to remarry, Roos, who had already divorced his wife in the Church courts, sought and obtained an act of Parliament. The act specifically stated that it was not to be regarded as a precedent; nevertheless, when in the 1690s Henry Howard, 7th duke of Norfolk (see below, p. 260) and Charles Gerard, 2nd earl of Macclesfield (see above, p. 88), wanted to divest themselves of their spouses, both of them turned to the Lords.

AN
ABSTRACT
OF
Bishop Cozen's Argument;
PROVING,

That *Adultery* works a Diffolution of the Marriage, and that it is Lawful for the Man in fuch Cafe to Marry again, during the Life of her that is Divorced.

Which he Argues from

THE 19th of St. *Matthew*, from our Saviour's Words therein exprefs'd, That if the Wife be put away for *Fornication*, the Man is left Free to Marry again, which Freedom is not allow'd to the Adulterefs, nor any Man elfe that fhall Marry her.

And he Anfwers the Objection, That this was not fpoke by our Saviour to *Chriftians*, but to the *Jews*, by Saying, That it was fpoke to Chrift's Difciples.

And that it was a full Anfwer to the *Pharifees* Queftion, *That it was not Lawful for a Man to put away his Wife, and Marry again, for any Caufe but only in the Caufe of* Adultery.

And that Exception confirms the Rule, as in many other Cafes, viz. *Except ye Repent, ye fhall all likewife Perifh.* Which certainly infers, *That if ye do repent, ye fhall not Perifh.* And in 1 *Kings* the 3d and 18th, *None were in the Houfe, except we Twain:* From whence no Body can infer but Two were in the Houfe.

And that our Saviour did clearly determine, That if a Man, after the Difmiffion of a Firft Wife, Marryed a Second upon any other Caufe except for *Fornication*, it was no lefs than *Adultery*; thereby Inferring, That upon a juft Difmiffion for *Fornication* a fecond Marriage cannot be branded with *Adultery*.

And that the *Pharifees* very Queftion [*Is it Lawful for a Man to put away his Wife for every Caufe?*] was not without a plain Implication of Liberty to Marry another; and therefore our Saviour well-knowing what he meant, gave a full Anfwer to it.

He anfwers the Objection, That the *Rhemifts* and College of *Doway* urge for the *Popifh Doctrine*: *Romans* 7. 2. *The Woman which hath an Hufband is bound by the Law to her Hufband as long as he liveth.*

Firft, That that Place was to be expounded by Chrift's Words.

Secondly, That it was to be underftood of a Marriage whole and found, as it ftands by God's Ordinance, and not where a Divorce was.

Thirdly, From 1 *Corinthians* 7. 10. *Let not the Woman depart, as if it were in her Choice whether fhe would depart or not*; whereas, by Fornication, *fhe has departed from him, or rather ought to be put away, whether fhe would or no.*

Fourthly, It was of a Woman that was under her Hufband, and not of one that was divorced from him.

That a Conjugal Promife is the Bond of Marriage, *That each of them fhall live together, according to God's Holy Ordinance, during their Lives.* Separation from Bed and Board doth plainly break that Part of the Bond whereby they are ty'd to Live together.

And the Diftinction betwixt *Bed*, and *Board*, and the *Bond* is new, and was never mentioned in Scripture, and unknown to the Antient Church, devifed only by the *Canonifts* and *School-men* in the *Latin Church*, (for the *Greek Church* knew it not) to ferve the *Pope's* turn the better, till he got it eftablifhed in the Council of *Trent*, at which Time, and never before, he laid his Anathema upon all them that were of another Mind, forbidding all Men to Marry, and not to make any ufe of Chrift's Conceffion.

The Co-habitation is the Effence and Subftance of Matrimony; and that the Diftinction between Bed, and Board, and the Bond of Matrimony, was purely Chimerical and Fancy, as attefted by *Erafmus* and Bifhop *Hall*.

And that nothing in the Conjugal Promife extends to Tolerating *Adultery*.

That a Divorce is to break or cut off the Marriage; and that the Antient Canons, Councils, and Fathers of the Church did agree therewith.

And Quotes

Council. *Neocafar.* and *Alib.* Forbidding the Retaining an Adulterous Wife.

Council. *Eliber. Aurelian.* and *Arelatens* give Liberty in fuch Cafe to Marry again.

Clements Conftitution, *Tertullian*, St. *Bafil* in his Canons, approved by a General Council, are for Marrying again.

Council. *Venet.* Council *Wormat.* and Council *Lateran.*

Lactantius, St. *Jerome*, *Epiphanius*, *Chryfoftom*, *Theophilact*. The Eaftern Bifhops in the Council of *Florence*, *Juftin, Martyr*, St. *Ambrofe*.

All the *Greek Church* to this Day allow it.

Erafmus, *Cajetan*, and other *Papifts*, the Civil-Law, and the Laws of the Emperor are clear for it.

And the Conftitution of the *Church of England*, in the Time of *Henry* VIII. *Edward* VI. and Queen *Elizabeth*.

Gratian fays, In the Caufe of Adultery, *Lawful Marriage ought not to be denied.*

Bellarmine owns, That the Bond of Marriage of Infidels is Diffolvable.

Juftinian, a *Jefuit*, confeffes, That it is fimply Lawful for the Innocent Party to Marry again.

That the Canon againft Marrying again is contrary to Two Acts of Parliament, made 25 *Henry* VIII. and 3 and 4 *Edward* VI. wherein no Canons be allowed that be any way repugnant to the Laws of God, or the Scriptures, the King's Prerogative, and the Statutes of this Land.

He Quotes the Opinion of

Lancelot, Juft. Jur. Can.

Selden, Dr. *Hamond*, *Anafius*, Dr. *Taylour*, Bifhop *Hall*, Dr. *Ffulke* are for Second Marriages.

FIG. 137 *Roman catholic theology held that marriage was a sacrament and that it created a humanly indivisible union of souls and bodies. After the Reformation many Protestant theologians denied that marriage was a sacrament and justified divorce for adultery on the basis of Christ's words, as reported in Matthew 19.9. In the debates over the Roos divorce in 1670 John Cosin, bishop of Durham, and John Wilkins, bishop of Chester, were the only English bishops to agree with this view. Cosin probably absented himself from the final vote but his arguments, summarised in this pamphlet, were repeatedly reprinted over the next two centuries whenever the legalisation of divorce was discussed.*

Parliamentary divorce: Henry Howard, 7th duke of Norfolk (1655–1701)

During the crisis caused by the invasion of William of Orange in the autumn of 1688, Henry Howard, 7th duke of Norfolk, sat decisively on the fence until the outcome was clear. The new regime purchased his allegiance with appointments to important local and national offices. He may also have exacted a less obvious reward – a promise to assist him to obtain a parliamentary divorce. Norfolk's marriage had broken down several years earlier and he was desperate to remarry.

Parliamentary divorce was controversial, particularly in a case like Norfolk's, in which both parties had committed adultery and were therefore barred from an action in the Church courts. Like the Roos divorce twenty years earlier, the Norfolk case entwined personal and financial issues with procedural and constitutional ones as well as with questions of national politics. Norfolk had once been a Catholic but was now a Protestant and a prominent supporter of the government of William and Mary. His wife, Mary, daughter and heiress of Henry Mordaunt, 2nd earl of Peterborough, had been a Protestant but was now a Catholic; she was reputed to be a Jacobite, although her lover, Sir John Germain, had fought for William III and was even rumoured to have been his illegitimate half brother. If Norfolk could not remarry, the premier dukedom of England would pass at his death to his nephew, brought up as a Catholic at the court of James II in exile. Finally, although Norfolk wanted to be rid of his wife, he wanted to hang on to her fortune.

Norfolk discovered his wife's affair with Germain in 1685. His first reaction was to take her abroad and try to have her put in a nunnery. She was back by 1687, but at the Revolution the duchess fled over to France with her father and the king. Although she returned again in 1691, her association with the Jacobites was irrefutable and plainly useful to Norfolk. In January 1692 he launched his first attempt at divorcing her. The bill barely scraped through its initial reading and a protest was signed by nineteen Tories. Three of them were bishops: the failure of the other bishops to sign encouraged suspicions

His GRACE the
Duke of Norfolk's
CHARGE
Againſt the
DUTCHESS,
BEFORE THE
Houſe of Lords,
AND THE
Dutcheſſes Anſwer.

With the Depoſitions at large, of the Witneſſes that were Examined on both Sides.

LONDON,
Printed in the Year, 1692.

FIG. 138

that they were following political instructions, rather than their consciences. The debates on the bill turned on a number of abstruse legal and procedural questions, though the allegations about the duchess's sexual misconduct, published in London and in translation in the Netherlands, were of rather more general interest: one foreign newsletter described the evidence as so filthy as scarcely to be repeatable (fig. 138). The king attended the debates incognito, though he was said to have found the evidence of the adultery – tame by modern standards – 'so obscene that he stayed but little'.[1] The bill failed at its second reading.

Norfolk tried to bolster his case by suing Germain for criminal conversation (an action in which a husband claimed damages from his wife's lover for their adultery). He won, although he was awarded only £66, rather than the £50,000 he had demanded. In December 1692 Norfolk's second bill was rejected on its first reading. Norfolk was furious, threatening the printer of an account of the proceedings with an action of *scandalum magnatum* and planning to take out a writ to seize the duchess and 'keep her from all company'.[2] By 1694 he seems to have decided to come to terms with his wife, and they agreed to separate. Then in 1698 his hopes of a divorce were rekindled by the success of the Whig Charles Gerard, 2nd earl of Macclesfield. Realising

FIG. 139 *Thomas Howard, 7th duke of Norfolk, by John Smith, after Sir Godfrey Kneller.*

The Duke of Norfolk

G Kneller pinx: I Smith ex:

that Macclesfield's divorce not only provided an appropriate precedent but might also signal a shift in opinion, Norfolk embarked on his third attempt at divorce in 1700. It was accompanied by a propaganda war. Norfolk emphasised that he stood in danger of being succeeded by spurious issue. Since the duchess was by now forty-two and had been sexually active for more than twenty years without producing a child, this was hardly convincing, and Norfolk's real concern was to retain his wife's substantial dowry. Although his loyalty to the government was by now questionable, the divorce remained as much of a party political question as ever. Its opponents were over-whelmingly Tory; its supporters, Whig. An amendment which required Norfolk to return the £10,000 marriage portion finally rendered the bill acceptable to the House, and it received the royal assent in April 1700. Under the terms of the act, Norfolk was required to raise the money within a year for the divorce to be finalised. Norfolk, though, was in no position to repay his wife. In the following Parliament he tried to amend the act to give him more time. A week after the deadline passed, he died suddenly in his sleep. Six months later his discarded duchess married Sir John Germain.[3] His estate, and the title, were inherited by his Catholic nephew.

FIG. 140 *Order to Edmund King to attend as a witness in the countess of Anglesey's separation bill, 11 March 1701. King (1630–1709) was a prominent surgeon and scientist, who had been admitted to the Royal Society on the proposal of John Wilkins (see above, p. 66). He retired from practice around 1702. A note on the back says that King found the affair very difficult as he had been physician to both parties for many years.*

Their example was followed by others. Some of the actions were probably collusive. In 1701 Elizabeth Box did not contest her husband's demand for a divorce because he had agreed to repay £3,000 from her £4,000 marriage portion within eighteen months; the agreement only came to light when the House accepted an amendment providing her with alimony of £100 a year instead. That this was a case in which both parties sought divorce did not make it any less controversial, especially to high churchmen. What were probably notes for a speech delivered on 3 April 1701 by William North, 6th Baron North and Grey, reveal a deep-seated belief that parliamentary divorce was an exceptional remedy that should be restricted to the very highest members of society. It was one thing to allow it for 'the chief nobility' but quite another to grant a divorce to Mr Box, a mere 'Grocer and citizen of London' and thus open 'a way for infinite suits of the same nature'.[12]

If it was difficult for Mr and Mrs Box, divorce by act of Parliament was practically impossible for a woman trying to rid herself of her spouse. In 1701 the details of the physical and mental cruelties the countess of Anglesey had suffered at the hands of James Annesley, 3rd earl of Anglesey, were considered so appalling that the House ordered that nothing was to be entered in its journals on the subject. The countess had gone into hiding; a petition presented on her behalf detailed how she had arranged for her own kidnapping in order to escape from her mentally unstable, vicious but possessive husband. Anglesey had invoked privilege of peerage to prevent an action in the Church courts and wanted to force her to cohabit. The countess did not even attempt to secure a divorce, but sought an unprecedented act of Parliament that would legalise their separation and prevent her husband from forcing her to return to the marital home.

To have got even that far was exceptional, and the countess of Anglesey, the child of James II and Catherine Sedley, countess of Dorchester, was unquestionably exceptional herself: she had brought to her marriage a dowry worth at least £16,000 which she not unnaturally wanted returned. It was not until after 1750 that divorce became relatively common and the House discovered a need to establish a series of standard procedures (such as a firm requirement for a previous action in the Church courts) in order to process the cases coming before it.

Enquiry

It was the House of Commons which was meant to be the 'grand jury of the nation', investigating grievances and seeking redress for them; but the House of Lords was an investigative forum too. Moreover, its ability to question witnesses on oath – an option not available to the Commons – made it in some respects a more powerful one. Major investigations in the Lords were, however, not common before 1689 – the inquiry into the 'decay of trade' in 1669 (see above, p. 82) was unusual – and the Lords usually left it to the lower House to conduct investigations either of a general or a specific kind, such as the enquiries into the causes of the Fire of London in 1666 and the division of the fleet during the first Anglo-Dutch war in 1668. The Popish Plot seems to have spurred the upper House into more strenuous activity. In October 1678 the Lords requested all of the papers collected for the government's investigations and over the next couple of months they conducted their own investigation, parallel to the one going on in the Commons, dragging individuals in to give evidence before their committee, ordering arrests and seizures of documents, and sending messages to the king concerning the conditions under which prisoners were kept. The Lords committee met twice a day, and soon spawned a sub-committee to gather evidence on the murder of Sir Edmund Berry Godfrey. Some aspects of the enquiry, such as into the failure of the deputy governor at Chepstow castle to take Anglican communion, were plainly aimed at particular individuals (in this case, Henry Somerset, 3rd marquess of Worcester, later duke of Beaufort: see below, p. 298). A few years later, the enemies of Anthony Ashley Cooper, earl of Shaftesbury and his political allies would accuse the committee of bullying their witnesses in an attempt to secure more evidence of Catholic conspiracy. The prorogation and dissolution of the Cavalier Parliament put an end to the Popish Plot enquiry, although in November 1680 some peers made another attempt at a party-driven enquiry, into the recent purges of the local justices of the peace. Such enquiries helped to create a sense of crisis, as they were uncomfortably reminiscent of the days leading up to the Civil War.

In the months after the Revolution the Lords resumed their interests in the detail of administration and political management. In the summer of 1689 a committee of the whole House looked into failures in the war in Ireland. More significant, in some ways, was the peers' close inspection of the circumstances surrounding the trials and executions ('murders', the Journal stated) of William, Lord Russell, Algernon Sydney and the rest of the Whig martyrs of 1682–83, encouraged by the king and a passionate plea from Russell's widow, Lady Rachel Russell. Having got their teeth into one highly political enquiry, the following year the House was pushed into another, on changes made to the command of the militia within London – again, a Whig move against officials implicated in the political trials of the 1680s.

Over the next few years, the Lords would from time to time become the forum for highly political investigations into wartime irregularities and disasters: the state of the fleet and defensive fortifications in 1699; allegations that the admiralty had failed to protect merchant shipping in 1707; and in 1711 an enquiry, held mainly in a committee of the whole House, into the military disaster at Almanza in Spain, which concentrated on whether sufficient troops had been available to the allied forces there.

Many of these investigations were used as sticks with which to beat a ministry: as the Lords said on the Almanza affair, 'whatever defects there have been, they are most of them justly to be imputed to those who had the management of your Majesty's affairs here; whose duty it was, to give the necessary orders, and require the due execution of them, for a service which the nation had so much at heart, as the recovering Spain out of the hands of the French'.[13]

Judicature and impeachment

The role in which the House was most clearly distinguished from the Commons was as a court of law. After 1660 the House consolidated its claim to be regarded as England's highest court of law. It received a setback in 1668 over its attempt to exercise its jurisdiction in cases of first instance, rather than simply on appeal, in Skinner's suit against the East India Company (see above, p. 24). The king's determination to suppress the consequential dispute between the two Houses allowed the Lords to save face; and although they never explicitly gave up their claim to be able to hear cases of first instance ('original jurisdiction'), they never attempted to do so again. The House already had a statutory right to hear appeals from the court of king's bench and as a result of the dispute over *Sherley v. Fagg* in 1675 it managed to extend its appellate jurisdiction to the court of chancery.

The mechanism that brought appeals before the House was a writ of error, which commanded the judges to send the record of their judgment to the Lords for examination in order to correct some alleged mistake. All of the Members of the House – not just those who had legal training – were entitled to debate and vote on the issues. The Speaker, if he were lord chancellor or lord keeper, presided over the court of chancery, as well as over the House of Lords. Speakers were not always Members of the House and therefore able to participate in debate, but if a Speaker both presided in the chancery and was a Member he could intervene to explain the rationale that lay behind the decisions in the court of chancery, from which the majority of the appeals came. The judges, who attended as assistants to the House, were sometimes asked for their opinions and sometimes not. Sometimes they were listened to, and sometimes not.

It was scarcely to be wondered at that litigation in the Lords was

The accidental martyr: William Howard, Viscount Stafford (1612–80)

rought up a Protestant, William Howard, a younger son of Thomas Howard, earl of Arundel, had become a Catholic by the time of his marriage in 1637 to his father's ward, the daughter of Henry Stafford, 5th Baron Stafford. His wife, a wealthy heiress, brought him a title as well as her wealth: following their marriage Charles I had controversially removed the Stafford barony from the man who had inherited it, because of his 'very mean and obscure condition', and gave it to Howard instead. Howard was created Viscount Stafford two months later (see above, p. 146).

An exceptionally assiduous member of the House of Lords, Stafford was regarded with distaste by many of his contemporaries. It may have had something to do with his arrest and imprisonment in Germany in the 1650s for a 'vice that need not be named', according to the diarist John Evelyn;[1] it may have had something to do with the quarrels and lawsuits he conducted with his nephews over his parents' estates; it may have been to do with his religion, which ultimately brought him to death and beatification.

In 1678, among his bogus allegations about a Popish Plot, Titus Oates named Stafford as the paymaster of an invading papal army; other witnesses, Stephen Dugdale and Edward Turberville, accused him of planning the assassination of Charles II. Placed in the Tower of London, he remained there for more than two years before he was put on trial in the court of the high steward. The trial opened on 30 November 1680. By then the recent acquittal of Sir George Wakeman had shown the weakness of the Popish Plot allegations. Stafford, nevertheless, virtually assured his own conviction by putting up an astonishingly poor defence. He failed to prepare properly; he concentrated on minor issues (he argued that the prosecution had failed to advance any proof that he was a Catholic, something that was notorious) and claimed, erroneously, that the prosecution was out of time.

The most telling evidence was given by Dugdale who claimed that Stafford had attended a Jesuit 'consult' to plan the assassination of the king and that

FIG. 141 *William Howard, Viscount Stafford, by an unknown artist, c. 1670.*

subsequently, on 21 September 1678, he had offered Dugdale money to kill the king. Stafford could prove that he was not at the consult but he could not deny meeting Dugdale on 21 September. His attempts to attack Dugdale's character backfired and he made a fool of himself in challenging the evidence of Edward Turberville. Stafford's best effort was his cross examination of Oates: it had little impact, however, as the assembled Protestant peers did not share his outrage at the way Oates had misused the Catholic sacraments.

Stafford was probably correct in arguing that the prosecution had failed to meet the legal requirement for two witnesses to an overt act of treason, as the witnesses had testified to different acts. Stafford was nevertheless found guilty. Both he and another Catholic, James, duke of York, drew parallels between his fate and the conviction of Strafford in 1641 and the subsequent descent into the Civil War. The king, though, seems to have been genuinely convinced of Stafford's guilt. Predictions that Stafford would barter for his life by revealing full details of the Plot proved ill founded. His 'confession' simply confirmed

The Tryall of William Howard Ld Viscount Stafford in Westminster hall.

His Execution on Tower hill.

A The High Steward. CC The Commons. F The Prisoner. [...]
B The Peers in y Robes. D The Judges. E The K's Box. [...]

FIG. 142 *Heneage Finch, earl of Nottingham, sitting just below the throne, presides over the trial of William Howard, Viscount Stafford, in Westminster Hall in this engraving published as a frontispiece to the record of the trial proceedings in 1682. Stafford himself stands with his back to the viewer at the bottom of the main picture. The judges sit on their woolsacks and the peers sit in the body of the hall wearing their hats and robes. Boxes on either side of the throne house the king and other dignitaries whilst Members of the Commons sit, hatless, on the tiered seats to both sides of the hall. The execution on Tower Hill is depicted below the main picture.*

what everyone already knew: that he had campaigned with York for the reintroduction of Catholicism. When he added that he had also conspired with Anthony Ashley Cooper, earl of Shaftesbury, to bring about the dissolution of the Cavalier Parliament, Shaftesbury declared 'that it was evident my Lord Stafford trifled with their Lordships' and successfully moved that he be heard no more.[2]

In death Stafford was transformed into a martyr. James II declared that it was 'the will of God … to crown him with the blessing of dying for his religion'.[3] Dressed in white satin, he was beheaded on 29 December 1680 before a crowd of some 20,000 people. Many of the Catholics who gathered to witness his death dabbed their handkerchiefs into his martyred blood. His estate was later conveyed to the use of the Catholic church for the celebration of masses in his honour and in hopes of canonization. Stafford was declared Venerable in 1886; he was beatified in 1929.

open to lobbying and that friendships and family or political alliances could easily be more important determinants of the eventual decision than evidence or law. Planning for an appeal that was to be heard in the House in 1660, Carey Gardiner relied on Sir Ralph Verney 'to make my lord chamberlain our friend, who is a very considerable person and he will draw many after him.'[14] When a dispute over the estate of Sir Francis Windham went to the House of Lords in 1689, friends of his widow had no hesitation in using their contacts 'to make interest' with Thomas Crew, 2nd Baron Crew, and other peers.[15] Early in 1693, Lady Anne Fitch approached Simon Patrick, bishop of Ely, Henry Compton, bishop of London, Charles Sackville, 6th earl of Dorset, George Compton, 4th earl of Northampton and Algernon Capell, 2nd earl of Essex, in connection with her appeal against a chancery decree. In January 1699 John Lowther, Viscount Lonsdale, explained his case in detail to William Savile, 2nd marquess of Halifax, hoping to enlist his support. He could also rely on the assistance of his political ally, Lord Chancellor Somers. Lonsdale won his case.

After the Revolution of 1688 the Lords began to stake a claim to extend their jurisdiction beyond England and Wales. It started with Ireland. A right of appeal from the Irish court of king's bench to the English king's bench was already well established. It naturally resulted in a possible further appeal to the English House of Lords. A series of appeals from the Irish court of chancery was decided in the English House of Lords in the 1690s at a time when the Irish parliament was not sitting. The House of Lords' decision in 1698 in a dispute involving the bishop of Derry was, however, highly provocative: it declared some decisions of the Irish House of Lords when sitting as a court to be null and threatened a crisis in Anglo-Irish relations, exacerbated still further by a similar ruling a year later. In 1702 Lord Chancellor Somers went to considerable lengths to calm the row, deliberately ensuring that the underlying conflict was forgotten, rather than settled. The unresolved issue was revived after the accession of George I.

The Union with Scotland brought another opportunity to extend the Lords' jurisdiction. The system of law in Ireland was at least based on the same common law principles as English law; that of Scotland shared its origins with the Roman law systems of continental Europe. The articles of Union guaranteed the continuation of Scots law and Scots courts as they then existed, but they did not make specific provision either for an appellate jurisdiction to replace that of the Scots Parliament or for the removal of appellate jurisdiction altogether. In the interval between the last sitting of the Scots Parliament and the opening of the first session of the new British Parliament, two litigants in the Scots court of session entered appeals (protestations). That of the Scottish peer, Alexander Bruce, 4th earl of Kincardine, in March 1707, was directed 'to the queen and Parliament, and after the Union to their next competent judicatory for determining such appeals' but the Scots judges (the lords of session) 'would not determine whether appeals now to the Parliament of Great Britain are legal or not'.[16] The first Scottish appeal actually brought into the Lords was that of *Rosebery v. Inglis* in February 1708, although the dissolution ensured that it was never decided. Other cases followed and were decided; but they were overshadowed by the controversy that was caused by the Greenshields case (below, p. 330), sometimes said, incorrectly, to be the case that established the Lords' jurisdiction over Scotland. Although it was at first thought that Scottish appeals to the Lords would be rare because of the cost and distance, the Lords' decision in April 1709 that any appeal froze the proceedings in the court below rendered appeals to Westminster an attractive option for litigants, especially vexatious ones.

Impeachment was a very different form of judicature. Although it was also a form of criminal jurisdiction, it was distinct from the trials of peers in the court of the high steward, even when that body, after the Revolution, became effectively the same as the House of Lords itself (see above, pp. 185-6). Impeachment could be applied to anyone – peers, bishops and commoners. It was inherently a political process. The offences alleged were either too nebulous to be indicted in the ordinary courts or, if they could be indicted, relied on evidence that would be unlikely to survive the scrutiny of normal trial procedures. During this period (as in the earlier part of the century) the characteristic use of impeachment was as part of a political attack on ministers, servants and allies of the crown who were difficult to remove. Sometimes the purpose was as much to focus attention on the ministry's abuse of power as to secure a conviction. Even the 1667 attempt to impeach John Mordaunt, Viscount Mordaunt, a courtier of trifling importance, for false imprisonment and sexual assault was widely interpreted as a way of testing the procedures for an attack on the lord chancellor, Edward Hyde, earl of Clarendon. The impeachments of Catholic peers during the outcry over the Popish Plot were as much motivated by concern about James, duke of York, as by the activities of the five individuals concerned. The impeachments of Thomas Osborne, then earl of Danby, in 1678 and the Junto Whig leaders in 1701 (see pp. 116, 246, 280-1) were moves in a more general attack on the ministries of the day. The impeachment of Dr Sacheverell in 1710 was the only occasion in this period when impeachment was used as a government rather than opposition tactic; it proved to be a disastrous miscalculation that contributed to the ministry's fall from power as a result of the elections later that year (see below, pp. 333-5).

In cases of impeachment the accusations were formulated by the House of Commons. The Commons also took on the role of managing the prosecution when the case was heard in the House of Lords, a process that inevitably encouraged intra-parliamentary rivalry. Impeachment proceedings were sufficiently rare after 1660 for each instance to spark genuine arguments over procedure which were often exploited to hamper the prosecution.

Managing the House

Success in the House of Lords – whether in the passage of a bill, an appeal, or the promotion of some enquiry or impeachment proceedings – was at least as much a matter of careful and effective management as it was of rhetoric and force of argument. Private individuals pursuing business in the House of Lords spent time and money lobbying and entertaining in order to persuade peers to turn up and to back them. For governments and their opponents, faced with political battles of increasing length and difficulty in both Houses, the process of securing and maintaining majorities in the House of Lords was a growing preoccupation.

The first struggle was to ensure the appearance of Members, many of whom might be too ill, too old, or too uninterested to make the journey to Westminster (see above, pp. 153-7). Any absence from the House was supposed to be covered by permission from the crown for special leave. It was usually the House itself, however, that tried to enforce attendance. Those who lacked royal permission to be absent offered their excuses to the House. It was the House which accepted or rejected them. On a number of occasions it asked to see evidence of the Member's incapacity. Henry Pierrepont, marquess of Dorchester, was absent throughout the first exclusion Parliament. On 18 March 1679 and then again on 21 April his servants William Colgrave and Charles Pelham swore at the bar that

FIG. 143 *Robert Harley, earl of Oxford (1661–1724), by Sir Godfrey Kneller, 1714. Regarded as an adept but slippery politician (he was nicknamed 'Robin the Trickster' when in the Commons in the 1690s) Harley struggled to wrest power out of the hands of the Junto Whigs, and then from the 'duumvirs', Marlborough and Godolphin. His uneasy relationship with the Tories helped to bring about his downfall in 1714.*

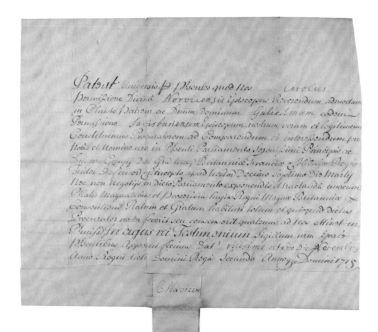

FIG. 144 *Proxy dated 18 November 1715, by which Charles Trimnell, bishop of Norwich, authorised Gilbert Burnet, bishop of Salisbury, to vote on his behalf. This is an unusually elaborate form of proxy.*

he was too ill to attend the House without endangering his life. The House accepted the excuse. It was more sceptical of that offered by Bishop Anthony Sparrow of Norwich to explain his absence from the second Exclusion Parliament. Sparrow's aggressive attack on dissenters had made him powerful political enemies and his failure to attend aroused suspicions that he was a closet Catholic determined to avoid the Test Act (see below, p. 316). Hauling him back to Westminster would have forced him to take the oaths. In 1689 Philip Stanhope, 2nd earl of Chesterfield, took exception to a demand that he send witnesses to excuse his attendance on oath, declaring that 'I think an oath is so solemn a thing that I am very unwilling to engage any man to take one upon such an account, and therefore I shall rather submit to such a fine as the House shall think fit to lay upon me'.[17]

Peers who sought leave of absence from the crown were supposed to appoint a proxy to vote on their behalf. The rule was confirmed by the committee for privileges soon after the Restoration: it implies that the right to make a proxy was originally designed to bolster support for the monarch, rather than regarded as a privilege. Chesterfield revealed the basic assumption that proxies were still expected to be used in favour of the crown and the collective interests of the peers when in 1689 he responded to criticism for giving his proxy to John Sheffield, 3rd earl of Mulgrave (later duke of Buckingham and Normanby), a man closely identified with the policies of James II. Chesterfield explained that Mulgrave was 'accounted a good courtier, and by consequence, one who having much to be forgiven him, will be sure to be for those who are in power; and lastly, his lordship not loving to part with any thing that he can keep, made me think that the privilege of the lords would be very safe in his custody, at a time when they were like to be invaded by a powerful House of Commons'.[18] But if it had once been the assumption that proxies would be exercised on behalf of the king, it was one that was becoming obsolete. In January 1690 the House decided that lords who did not have the king's permission to be absent nevertheless had the right to appoint proxies.

Since the early seventeenth century the rules of the House had prevented individual members from holding more than two proxies each. Only bishops could hold the proxies of bishops; only peers could hold the proxies of peers. Proxies had to be registered and were automatically cancelled when the member assigning the proxy attended the House or when the holder of a proxy made a proxy of his own. Theoretically (though not always in practice) they were also cancelled at the end of the session. Proxies could be given to friends and allies, something that helped to bind peers and groups of peers together. In February 1673 Theophilus Hastings, 7th earl of Huntingdon, was expected to be flattered when the duke of York accepted his proxy in preference to that of Charles Dormer, 2nd earl of Carnarvon, and in 1697 Thomas Thynne, Viscount Weymouth, explained that he was obliged to give his proxy to Robert Shirley, 8th Baron (later Earl) Ferrers rather than William Savile, 2nd marquess of Halifax, because he had himself held Ferrers' proxy for three years so that 'I cannot without disobligation commit it to another.'[19]

Arranging for proxies to be placed in reliable hands had always been part of the process of parliamentary management. Before the Revolution the crown was by far the most assiduous manager of proxies: even so it was a fairly casual business. In 1675, for example, Secretary Williamson sent blank proxy forms to two peers whose interest in the races at Newmarket exceeded their interest in taking their places in Parliament. Successive archbishops of Canterbury put much greater effort into marshalling the proxies of the episcopate in defence of crown and Church. In advance of the session of autumn 1685, Archbishop Sancroft was hard pressed to persuade a doubtful episcopate to attend, when it was already alienated by James II's plans to revive the Catholic Church in England. John Dolben agreed only grudgingly to come up; William Lloyd also acceded 'to that which I cannot avoid', and John Lake (mistakenly in the event) assured Sancroft that he could delay his arrival because 'usually little [was] done in the first two or three days of the session'.[20]

Opponents of the court were just as capable of exploiting the proxy system. Proxies were used on both sides in important political divisions such as those on the Irish cattle bill and the Roos divorce. In 1670 Lord Roos's controversial divorce bill would have failed at its first reading by one vote had it not been for proxies: the bill eventually passed with a majority of eight. Shaftesbury used proxies in the 1670s, although they secured the defeat in November 1675 of the motion he and others had proposed that Parliament had been dissolved by the long prorogation. His ally George Villiers, 2nd duke of Buckingham, commented, as others must often have thought, that the system of proxy voting allowed divisions to be won by 'those lords who never heard the arguments'.[21] The point could help those peers reluctant to become involved in politically controversial decisions. In 1679 the terminally ill Benjamin Mildmay, 17th Baron Fitzwalter politely refused to commit his proxy vote in favour of Thomas Osborne, earl of Danby, explaining through his wife that 'he believes he should not use that great privilege so justly as he ought to do it without hearing the business he gives his vote for'.[22] On 10 and 11 June 1689 the House decided that proxies were not to be used in giving judgment on appeals.

After 1689, politicians on all sides began to exploit more systematically the potential of proxies and also started to tighten the rules. 'There are expresses on all hands to the country for proxies' noted the Scottish representative peer John Elphinstone, 4th Lord Balmerinoch, as he prepared for the battle over the malt bill in the summer of 1713.[23] Managing proxies had become by then a matter for party leaderships. The rules for their use became more elaborate. In 1697 the House decided that proxies could not be used in votes on quasi-judicial legislation such as divorce or attainder, or in committee. Checking the register for proxies before an

FIG. 145 *Predicting and calculating the voting intentions of Members was essential for effective management of the House. In this list, compiled early in 1703, the Tory leader Daniel Finch, 2nd earl of Nottingham, tried to assess support for and opposition to his cherished bill to prevent occasional conformity.*

'Whig the first letter of his name': Thomas Wharton, 5th baron and 1st marquess of Wharton (1648–1715)

Whig the first letter of his name
Hypocrisy the second of the same
Anarchy, his darling and his aim
Rebellion, discord, mutiny and faction
Tom captain of the mob in soul and action
O'er grown in sin, corrupted, old, in debt,
Nob's soul and Ireton's liver within him yet.[1]

When Samuel Johnson composed his Dictionary, his entry for 'leader' ran, 'One at the head of any party or faction: as the detestable Wharton was the leader of the Whigs'. Whig politics ran in Wharton's blood. His father, Philip Wharton, 4th Baron Wharton, variously known as 'the good lord Wharton' and 'Saw Pit Wharton' depending on political bias, had been at the forefront of the impeachment of Strafford in 1641, a friend of Oliver Cromwell and a leading opponent of the court in the 1670s, before finally retiring from front-line politics after the Revolution of 1689.

What the younger Wharton did not inherit from his father was his puritan principles. In 1682 he took part in an infamous frolic in the church at Great Barrington, during which he indulged in a variety of crude acts of desecration; three years later he and another band of young bucks broke into the house of Charles Dormer, 2nd earl of Carnarvon, where they whipped the unfortunate peer and indulged in 'some other peccadilloes in his castle besides'.[2] Concern about the proclivities of the young man and his brother, Goodwin Wharton, had been highlighted by their tutor at the Protestant academy they had attended in Caen in Normandy, who warned 'lest they should suck in any atheistical or unchristian principles which, though they continue civil in their conversations… for the present, may at last end in open wickedness.'[3]

His political opponents reckoned that Whiggism and atheistical principles were synonymous anyway. Almost from his first entry into the House of Commons in 1673, Wharton aligned himself with Anthony Ashley Cooper, earl of Shaftesbury, and the opposition to the court, and then with the emerging Whig party. He avoided becoming entangled in Monmouth's rebellion of 1685, but he was among the first of the English notables to join the army of the Prince of Orange in 1688 following its landing in the west country. Two years previously Wharton had composed the satirical ballad, Lilliburlero, which became well known after it was set to music by Purcell: its popularity at the time of the Revolution enabled Wharton to claim to have been responsible for whistling King James out of three kingdoms.

Wharton was made comptroller of the royal household. The post was traditionally associated with the role of party manager in the Commons, and Wharton's management of the Whigs in the lower House, backed by his remarkable electoral influence in Buckinghamshire, Westmorland and Wiltshire (see below, pp. 329-31) was crucial to the party during the 1690s. Despite his prominence in the Commons, though, the king's distaste and distrust prevented him from attaining high office. Frequently proposed as the obvious candidate to replace the sickly Charles Talbot, duke of Shrewsbury (see above, p. 212) as secretary of state, he was overlooked time and again.

In February 1696, on the death of his father, he succeeded to the peerage. Later that year his remorseless efforts on behalf of the duke of Shrewsbury to secure the conviction of Sir John Fenwick revealed to the peers Wharton's ruthlessness in support of the cause of the Revolution, and his loyalty to those close to him. Observers such as Gilbert Burnet, bishop of Salisbury, and William Nicolson, bishop of Carlisle, thought that Wharton brought to the Lords a more informal and aggressive style of debating.

If sometimes, as with his contributions to the debate over the regency bill of 1705, he 'charmed the whole House',[4] at other moments, as in his interventions the following year during the debates on 'the Church in danger', his combative style caused offence. Thomas Osborne, duke of Leeds, retaliated with a reference to his earlier indiscretions at Great Barrington: 'if there were any [in the ministry] that had pissed against a communion table, or done his other occasions in a pulpit, he should not think the Church in safe hands' (upon which, it was said, Wharton was 'very silent for the rest of that day and desired no further explanations').[5]

FIG. 146 Thomas
Wharton, marquess
of Wharton, *by
John Smith after
Sir Godfrey Kneller.*

The most Hono.^ble *Thomas Lord Marquiss of
Wharton Lord Privy Seal.*

Kneller S.R.I. et Magna Brit. Baro.^t Aur. Pinx: Simon fecit.   Sold by I. Tonson in the Strand.

Wharton continued to be denied the high office that he sought and that his colleagues in the Whig Junto thought his due. Although Queen Anne reluctantly advanced him in the peerage as earl of Wharton in 1706 it was only the Whig triumph in the polls in 1708 that finally secured for him significant office as lord lieutenant of Ireland. Separated from his colleagues, Wharton soon found himself isolated, and the Tory electoral success in 1710 brought to a close his inglorious tenure of the lieutenancy. Finally, after the accession of George I, Wharton was restored to office as lord privy seal and he was also promoted a further step in the peerage with his creation as marquess of Wharton and Malmesbury. But by then Wharton was a sick man and he enjoyed his new honours for little more than six months before his death on 12 April 1715 at his house in Dover Street.

important debate and division soon became commonplace. On 16 January 1703 when the political issue of the moment was the bill to prevent occasional conformity, the Whig peer John Thompson, Baron Haversham, discovered that a proxy had been entered only after prayers that morning on behalf of Meinhard Schomberg, 3rd duke of Schomberg. Haversham successfully objected to its use. However, a messenger was despatched to secure Schomberg's presence and he arrived just in time to vote in person. The Scots peers inspected the register before the debate over the malt tax in 1713 and as a result did not call for the use of proxies in the subsequent division, knowing them to be equal.

The increasingly minute concern with attendance and proxies is one illustration of how the domination of politics by parties was creating a more sophisticated culture of parliamentary management. It was already present, though, at the beginning of our period. The papers of Philip Wharton, 4th Baron Wharton, from the early 1660s show him trying to estimate the outcome of divisions, as well as drafting provisos and amendments and bills to defend nonconformists against the legislative assault coming from the Cavalier House of Commons. Danby, a decade or so later, was doing the same on behalf of the court in both Houses. Likeminded peers would naturally flock together: during the long series of prorogations before the second exclusion Parliament, Charles North, 5th Baron North and Grey, dined regularly with Anthony Ashley Cooper, earl of Shaftesbury, and the other opposition peers at the Swan Tavern in order to discuss strategy (see above, p. 232). By the reign of Queen Anne, parties had evolved routines to provide peers with a lead on a regular basis. In the spring of 1713 William Legge, earl of Dartmouth, summoned William, 6th Baron North, to a pre-sessional meeting of Tory peers at his house. A week before the April session was to start Henry St John, Viscount Bolingbroke, asked North to come to an evening meeting 'with several other lords' at the office of Robert Harley, earl of Oxford.[24] On 29 June 1713, during the parliamentary session, Oxford himself addressed a brief note to North, 'tomorrow an attack being designed directly against the queen's message for the payment of her debts, I hope it will not be uneasy to your Lordship to be in town tomorrow'.[25] North obediently turned up the following day.

The assumption that peers would support the crown had always been a qualified one; maintaining their loyalty and support through the grant of office and favour had been a constant and crucial aspect of royal political management. But from the 1670s onwards, the link between parliamentary support and financial or other favours became more explicit and, especially after 1690, the evidence of peers exchanging their votes for material advantage more abundant. The greater duration, difficulty and importance of Parliaments raised, in crude terms, the value of individual votes to government and to its opponents. For impoverished peers, a court post, pension or annuity could be vital: on prompt payment of it their solvency, their attendance at the House and their willingness to back the government could rest. Aubrey de Vere, 20th earl of Oxford, possessed a prestigious ancient peerage but very little money, and looked to Danby in the 1670s to 'befriend us in an especial manner' and ensure the prompt payment of his pension.[26] Throughout 1678 and 1679 Danby consistently reckoned Oxford as a supporter in his numerous lists. Robert Carey, 6th Baron Hunsdon, relied on a government pension of £500 a year, granted 'for his support and in consideration of the loyalty of his family', and stayed throughout the 1680s a supporter of the court.[27] It was not only the government that was in the market for votes: in 1677–81 the French ambassador, Barillon, distributed cash payments to Members of both Houses, including Lord 'Barker' (almost certainly either Charles Howard, 2nd earl of Berkshire or his son Thomas, 3rd earl). In May 1695, Danby, by now duke of Leeds, was said to have 'kept open house at Hell [one of the taverns at Westminster] with roast beef and pot ale to debauch Lord Morley, Hunsdon, Culpepper, and the rest of the mumpers.'[28] ('Mumper' was contemporary slang for a genteel beggar.)

After the Revolution, as the support of the House of Lords became rather less reliable than it had been for the pre-Revolution regimes, bidding for the votes of such poverty-stricken peers had become even more competitive. By the end of the reign of Anne, the political stakes, especially over the Hanoverian succession, were high enough to create a bidding war for peers' votes. Both Oxford and the Whigs kept lists of those poor lords who might be susceptible to a financial inducement to maintain or change their loyalties. The 3rd earl of Sunderland proposed to the elector of Hanover the distribution of £9,000 a year in pensions which, he suggested, would be sufficient for Hanover to retain the allegiances of ten Whig peers and to turn three of those lords who usually voted with the ministry. The elector refused to risk that much money and probably for good reason, as it is not at all clear that these bribes and pensions were effective.

There may have been around twenty-eight such 'necessitous' peers.

A pretended trial?
The impeachment of
Lord Somers, 1701

An outstanding lawyer and politician, famed for his oratorical skills, John Somers was a prominent member of the group of Whig leaders known as the Junto. Elected to the Commons after the Revolution, he rapidly rose to high office. In 1693 he became Speaker of the House of Lords by virtue of his appointment as lord keeper. He was made lord chancellor four years later.

So critical to political management during the war years, once peace was concluded the Junto's power began to falter under pressure from a resurgent Tory party and from Whigs impatient for a peace dividend. One by one, the Junto members were eased out of high office. By the end of 1699, Somers was the only one left. Tories in the Commons singled him out for attack in November and December 1699. They voted to investigate suspicions that (like many chancellors before him) Somers had used his office to exercise indirect electoral influence, controlling the appointments of local justices of the peace; they called for the commission which Somers had issued to the privateer-turned-pirate Captain Kidd, suspecting that Somers's private interests had been involved in the mayhem Kidd had caused (Somers had been an investor in Kidd's original venture against pirates in the Indian Ocean).

Somers was eventually dismissed as lord chancellor on 27 April 1700. His removal was the signal for a major reconstruction of the ministry. The election which followed in January 1701 brought into the Commons more Tories hungry to claim Whig scalps, Somers's chief among them, and eager to unearth any evidence that would make it possible. What they found related to his involvement in the signing of the First and Second Partition Treaties. Agreed in 1698 and 1699 without Parliament's knowledge and without formal consultation with the privy council, the two treaties with Louis XIV had settled the succession to the Spanish throne. When Louis reneged on the agreements by allowing his grandson to become king of Spain in 1700, information about the second treaty leaked out.

The king's Dutch aide, Hans Willem Bentinck, earl of Portland, who had been responsible for nego-tiating the treaties, was the first target, and the Commons voted to impeach him. When Portland defended his conduct over the second treaty in the House of Lords, he also revealed the existence of the first, hitherto secret, treaty as well as the irregularities in the way it had been concluded. Those irregularities were the consequence of the haste with which it had been done in August 1698, when the death of Charles II of Spain was thought to be imminent. William III – in the Netherlands at the time – deemed it essential that the treaty be concluded before Charles died. Somers was forced to send over to William a sealed commission authorizing the formal conclusion of the treaty with blanks for the names of the commissioners and without going through the normal procedures.

The Tories homed in on all of those involved, although Somers was the most deeply implicated. Somers addressed the Commons eloquently, arguing that he had acted lawfully, in the public interest and on instructions from the king, but it was not enough to avoid the passage of a motion for impeachment, albeit by a very small majority. Votes to impeach Portland and Somers's Junto colleagues, Charles Montagu, Baron Halifax and Edward Russell, earl of Orford, followed.

The following day the Commons petitioned the crown to remove the four Whig peers from his council and presence for ever. By asking the king to take action, they may have been implicitly recognizing that the impeachment was unlikely to be successful. The Lords, certainly, quickly identified it as a device to bypass them and cried out about a breach of their privilege. Anxious to cool down the dispute as quickly as possible, William sent an evasive answer to the Commons and, to their chagrin, none to the Lords at all. The Commons made no attempt to draw up articles of impeachment until prodded by the Lords four weeks later. Their procrastination prompted the Whig propagandist Daniel Defoe to describe the delay as an 'illegal and oppressive' attempt 'to blast the reputation of the persons, without proving the fact'.[1] Detailed articles of impeachment against Somers and Orford were finally produced in May. Somers was to be tried first. Yet, despite the customary wrangling

FIG. 147 *John Somers, Lord Somers as lord keeper, engraved by Robert White after Sir Godfrey Kneller, 1693.*

The Right Honble Sr John Sommers Kn.^t LORD KEEPER of the GREAT SEAL of ENGLAND. And one of their Maties most Honble Privy Council. 1693.

over precedents, there was little indication that the Commons genuinely intended to proceed to trial. Indeed, as the situation in Europe deteriorated, there was increasing popular sympathy for those who had tried to avert a war that now seemed inevitable.

By June, with the end of the session in sight, the Lords had lost patience. Following a series of indecisive and bad tempered squabbles with the Commons, they set a date for Somers' trial. The Commons refused to present any prosecution evidence, and the peers went through the motions. Some Tory peers voted for Somers' conviction despite the absence of a case for the prosecution. They were outnumbered, and Somers was acquitted on 17 June. The Commons affected outrage, declaring it only a 'pretended trial ... repugnant to the rules of justice; and therefore null and void'.[2] The young Tory hothead, Henry St John, later Viscount Bolingbroke (see above, p. 52), fumed about the absurdity of a trial in which the impeached seemed to be managing all the business of the impeachment: 'never man behaved himself with that insolence this little fellow has done upon this occasion. He was the chief manager of the debate concerning himself ... 'twas he that framed the question of his own acquittal... and all this done without hearing any evidence to those facts he denies in his answer or judging whether those he has confessed be crimes or not. I believe no age can parallel such proceedings as these are.'[3] Acquittals followed for the other impeached peers. A dissolution was announced duing the recess and there was no attempt to revive the prosecutions in the new Parliament.

They were a diverse lot, who had come to their parlous financial situations by different routes. John Colepeper, 3rd Baron Colepeper, was left out of the will of a vindictive elder brother. Thomas Willoughby, a minor Lancashire landowner, suddenly found himself in 1679 the 11th Baron Willoughby of Parham when his distant cousin, the last heir of the elder Lincolnshire branch of the family, died without male issue. Stories later circulated that the 11th baron's grandson, Charles Willoughby, the 14th baron, had been either a carpenter or a weaver when he inherited the title in 1713 and was worth only about £150 a year. William Ferdinand Carey succeeded his first cousin once removed to become the 8th Baron Hunsdon in 1702. As he was of a branch of the family that had been settled in the Netherlands for generations he knew little of England when he arrived in the country with a title but no land or income.

The poor lords were an important, but unpredictable contingent. Some of them used their vote without embarrassment to get even more money out of the ministry: Lord Hunsdon purposely withheld his deciding vote during a close-run division on the peace in December 1711 in order to force Oxford to double his pension. The 18th Baron Fitzwalter, in receipt of a court pension worth £600 a year, nevertheless voted against the ministry in the same crucial 'no peace without Spain' motion. When the 3rd earl of Sunderland offered him £1,200 on behalf of the Hanoverians to turn his coat and oppose the ministry, he accepted with alacrity. Charles Finch, 4th earl of Winchilsea, 'being very poor … complied too much with the party he hated', in the words of his 'particular friend', Jonathan Swift.[29] A Tory by inclination and by family connections, his 'unhappy circumstances' drove him uncharacteristically to support the Whigs in the Sacheverell trial of 1710.[30] In 1712, the Hanoverian agent Bothmer told Charles VI of Austria that Winchilsea's opposition to the Anglo-French peace could be bought for a pension of £1,000.

As a result of the pensions and offices they were given, some of the least wealthy peers, such as Baron Hunsdon, were among the most assiduous attenders and the most heavily involved in the proceedings of the House. Their financial necessity belied one of the ideological underpinnings of the House, that the peers should act independently as the king's counsellors without pressure from external influences. Their presence in the House starkly revealed that not all peers were equal in estate, dignity or independence and that some could be bought when the government or a faction chose to dangle an estate-saving pension before them.

The Church in danger?
1702–09

ishop Gilbert Burnet of Salisbury was the first to give Queen Anne the news of William's death. 'Upon his knees by her Majesty's bedside', he 'kissed her hand and assured her he would be her Majesty's loyal & faithful subject, excusing his zeal to the service of his late Majesty'.[1] Robert Spencer, 2nd earl of Sunderland, hastened to tell her that 'she has not a more dutiful nor a more affectionate subject than I am' and that 'Those who were his friends and those who were his enemies, will be hers',[2] not omitting to pay court to the queen's influential favourites, the Marlboroughs.

The new queen made it clear enough that her political and religious sympathies lay with the Tories and the Church rather than Whigs. Three of the Junto peers were dropped from the privy council, and the political career of Thomas Osborne, duke of Leeds, briefly flickered back into life when he was re-appointed to it. John Churchill, earl of Marlborough, was appointed general of all the queen's forces. Laurence Hyde, earl of Rochester, the queen's uncle, was made lord lieutenant of Ireland. Although initially unwilling to take the new abjuration oath, Daniel Finch, 2nd earl of Nottingham, allowed Archbishop Sharp of York to assuage his conscience and in May 1702 he became secretary of state once more. Sidney Godolphin, Baron Godolphin, became lord treasurer and started the most famous phase of his long political collaboration with Marlborough. Having forged an alliance with the Speaker of the Commons, Robert Harley, the former 'country' leader now identified with the Tories, it seemed that the new ministry would be able to combine the confidence of the monarch with support in the House of Commons in a way that none of William's had ever managed. In reality, the ministry was far weaker than it seemed. A substantial group of Tories in the Commons disliked and distrusted Harley, the Junto Whigs still commanded a loyal following, especially in the House of Lords, and there were divisions within the ministry itself, especially over the conduct of the war against France, declared on 4 May 1702. Tories prepared to make the most of their opportunity to protect the Church from Whigs and dissenters; but for

Godolphin and Marlborough, the civil servant and the general, these were of little moment compared to the great European conflict just beginning.

The Tory onslaught began soon after their success at the elections of 1702: 'I hope now we are pretty sure of a Church of England Parliament which will settle the affairs of England a little better than they have been of late' wrote Basil Feilding, 4th earl of Denbigh, to Nottingham, reporting the results of the elections in Leicestershire and Warwickshire.[3] Tories planned to call to account the previous administration. The Commons voted by an overwhelming majority 'that right had not been done' them in the previous year's impeachments of the Junto peers.[4] A new Commons commission of accounts enthusiastically pursued the ex-minister Charles Montagu, now ennobled as Baron Halifax.

The Tories' principal aim was a bill that would force occasional conformists from office. Occasional conformity – by which moderate dissenters took the Anglican sacraments as directed by the Test Acts in order to qualify for public office, but continued to worship at conventicles – was perceived by the defenders of the Church as a hypocritical and cynical manipulation of the law that undermined state and Church. The bill imposed substantial fines on those guilty of the practice. It was doggedly fought in the Lords. A series of amendments designed to restrict the impact of the bill and reduce the fines produced, no doubt intentionally, a quarrel with the Commons over interference with their financial privileges. The queen made public her support for the Commons bill, despite the fact that her Lutheran husband, Prince George of Denmark (who sat in the Lords as duke of Cumberland), was himself an occasional conformist. He was said, probably apocryphally, to have voted for the bill whilst remarking to Thomas Wharton, 5th Baron Wharton, teller for the opposing side, that 'My heart is vid you'.[5] The Commons responded to the Lords' amendments with a threat to tack occasional conformity to a money bill. The Lords countered with a resolution, on 9 December 1702, against tacking (see above, pp. 242-3, 244). Debates on the subject descended into abuse: the House had to prevent a duel after Leeds accused Halifax (with whom Leeds and his son were in dispute over a private matter) of coming from a family that had been 'rais'd by rebellion'.[6]

At the opening of the next session of Parliament, and seemingly chastened by the chaos the bill had caused, the queen exhorted both Houses to remain 'in perfect peace and union' and to 'carefully avoid any heats and divisions, that may disappoint me ... and give encouragement to the common enemies of our Church and state.'[7] The pragmatic 'duumvirs' (as Marlborough and Godolphin came to be known) consolidated their dominant position in the ministry, and the queen's uncle, Laurence Hyde, earl of Rochester, one of the most uncompromising Tories, was dismissed. This time, when a new occasional conformity bill was rejected outright by the Lords – itself an indication of the ambiguity of the court's position on the subject – the reaction in the Commons was muted. In December 1703 Whigs targeted Nottingham, accusing him of having failed properly to investigate the Scotch Plot, a convoluted tale of Jacobites, double agents and factional rivalries in Scotland centred on plans for a highland rising in favour of James III. The Lords set up a committee to investigate. Although elected by secret ballot, it was composed entirely of leading Whigs. Nottingham hit back with claims that the Lords had invaded the royal prerogative, but after the end of the session, dismayed by the lack of support he had received and by the dismissal of some of his Tory colleagues, he resigned from the ministry.

The row over the Scotch Plot paled into insignificance beside the one that erupted in January 1704 when the House of Lords, acting in its judicial capacity, reversed a judgment of the court of queen's bench concerning a Whig elector, Matthew Ashby, whose vote had been refused by the Tory borough constables at the 1701 Aylesbury election. A Tory House of Commons chose to see the Lords' decision in *Ashby v. White* as an infringement of their privilege. Any lawyers who assisted further suits on the same grounds, they declared, would be guilty of a high breach of privilege. Although it would become a key case in demarcating the boundaries of the jurisdiction of the House of Lords, the origin of the case was a matter of low politics rather than of high constitutional principle. Aylesbury had long been the subject of a struggle for control between the high Church Tory Sir John Pakington and the Junto Whig, Lord Wharton. Ashby was a supporter of Wharton; it was Wharton who financed his legal actions and the Whigs who benefitted from them. Disputed election results were handled by the Commons themselves; Ashby's case, very different in substance, had gone through the ordinary common law courts. By claiming to adjudicate in it, the peers, Tories argued, were deliberately undermining the freedom of the House of Commons: 'this will be a way to destroy all checks', Sir Humphrey Mackworth told the lower House, 'and to make the House of Commons dependent on the Lords; and then I cannot see upon what foundation you can be said to sit here to do any service for your country'.[8] The Lords, for their part, were united in defence of their judicature and resolved

> That the deterring electors from prosecuting actions in the ordinary course of law, where they are deprived of their right of voting, and terrifying attornies, solicitors, counsellors, and serjeants at law, from soliciting, prosecuting, and pleading, in such cases, by voting their so doing to be a breach of privilege of the House of Commons, is a manifest assuming a power to control the law, to hinder the course of justice, and subject the property of Englishmen to the arbitrary votes of the House of Commons.[9]

The session was brought to an early end in April 1704 in order to stop the quarrel.

Over the summer Marlborough and Godolphin worked to strengthen their ministry with moderate Tories who could command a following in the Commons. Robert Harley replaced Nottingham as secretary of state and his associate, the young Henry St John (later Viscount Bolingbroke), was appointed secretary of war. Parliament reconvened in October 1704 amid the euphoria created by Marlborough's

FIG. 148 *Sir Godfrey Kneller painted this allegorical and triumphant portrait of John Churchill, duke of Marlborough (1650–1722), in or about 1706. Relatively fresh from his great victories at the battles of Blenheim (1704) and Ramillies (1706), Marlborough wears his armour with the blue sash of the order of the garter; his horse tramples Discord beneath its hooves, Justice sits above him in the clouds and Victory extends a crown of laurels. To the left are Hercules and a woman offering a castle.*

victory at Blenheim in August. A group of Tories with Nottingham at their head gathered their forces for another fight over occasional conformity, but efforts to tack it to the land tax bill were soundly defeated by the careful management of Harley. The new occasional conformity bill again failed in the Lords.

What was not so easily disposed of was *Ashby v. White*. When, late in November 1704, the Commons learned that five more Aylesbury voters had commenced actions against White, they committed them to prison for breach of privilege (Wharton saw to it that they were maintained in luxury while they were there). When the court of queen's bench refused their application for *habeas corpus* the voters turned to the Lords instead. The Commons addressed the queen declaring that if the Lords set them free it would 'tend to the overthrowing the undoubted rights and privileges of the Commons of England'.[10] As both Houses erupted in further outrage, the queen and her ministers stalled until the end of the session released the 'Aylesbury men' anyway. Parliament was shortly afterwards dissolved.

At the 1705 elections, despite Tory efforts to mobilise their supporters with their slogan 'the Church in danger', there were gains for the Whigs. The duumvirs, Marlborough and Godolphin, found themselves (to Harley's dismay) increasingly reliant on the Junto Whigs for a voting majority in the Commons: in their most important concession to the Junto, William Cowper was appointed lord keeper. When Parliament met for the first time after the elections, on 27 October 1705, with Cowper presiding in the Lords, the queen's speech hit back at those who were 'so ... malicious' as to suggest that the Church was in danger and 'to distract us with unreasonable and groundless distrusts and jealousies'.[11] In a debate in December, the Tories responded: the earl of Rochester accused Whig ministers of putting words into the queen's mouth that misrepresented her real views. The Whigs hit back with a series of attacks on mischief-making Tories, with the contributions of Whig bishops coordinated by Archbishop Tenison. The Whigs carried the vote that the Church was not in danger, and twenty-six Tories registered their protest. Despite its failure at the polls in 1705, the rallying cry of the 'Church in danger' would remain central to the Tories' increasingly successful political propaganda.

Nottingham and Rochester tried other ways to wreck the duumvirs' relationship with the queen, using John Thompson, Baron Haversham to propose that the Electress Sophia of Hanover – heir apparent to the English throne under the terms of the Act of Succession – should be invited to reside in England, to help to prevent disturbances and disorder whenever the queen should die. Anne, exceptionally sensitive on the point, was furious. The duumvirs elegantly substituted their own proposal, agreed with the queen and the Junto Whigs, the Regency bill, to secure the succession on her death. In April 1706 the three old Junto whigs, John Somers, Baron Somers, Halifax and Wharton were appointed to a commission charged with negotiating a Union with Scotland. The following December, after months of pressure from the duumvirs, the queen, still extremely wary of 'throwing myself into the hands of a party'[12] agreed, at last, to appoint Marlborough's son in law, the Whig Charles Spencer, 3rd earl of Sunderland, as secretary of state. Sunderland, the son of the Junto's *bête noire*, had become closely associated with it even before his father's death in 1702.

Whigs helped the ministry to see the Union with Scotland through both Houses, despite a determined, but unsuccessful, rearguard action against it by a small band of Tory peers on the grounds that Scottish Presbyterianism might endanger the integrity of the English Church. One of them was William, 6th Baron North, who presented an unsuccessful last-ditch proviso stating that nothing in the act was to imply an 'approbation or acknowledgment of the truth of the Presbyterian way of worship' or agreement with the Presbyterian Church's designation of itself as 'the true Protestant religion'.

All this strained the patience of Harleyite Tories, as well as the queen herself, to breaking point. Marlborough's privileged position as a close friend of the royal couple was also crumbling as the relationship between his wife and the queen deteriorated.

FIG. 149 *The Articles of Union (1706), the precursor to the Act of Union which united the kingdoms of England and Scotland into the single sovereign state of Great Britain. It is signed and sealed by the commissioners for both kingdoms, including Cowper, Godolphin, Sunderland, and Wharton.*

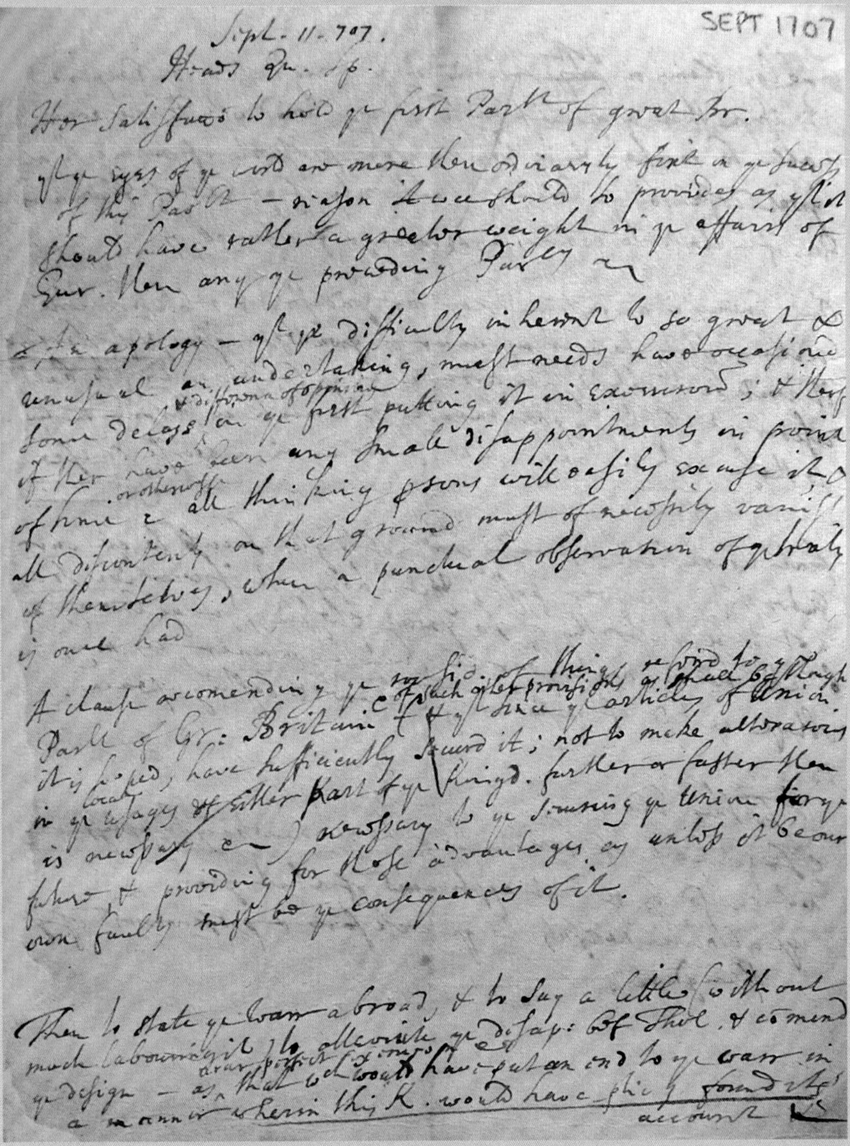
Sept. 11. 707.

SEPT 1707

Heads Qu. Sp.

Her Satisfaction to hold ye first Parl^t of great Br.

FIG. 150 *By 1707 the monarch's speech to Parliament was a matter for his or her ministers, who spent much time drafting and re-drafting it. These documents from the papers of Lord Chancellor Cowper show different stages in the preparation of Queen Anne's speech to the first Parliament of Great Britain. The earlier version, dated 11 September 1707, consists only of brief notes or 'heads'. The later version is much closer to the text of the speech as it was delivered, which was not until 6 November 1707.*

Harley bitterly resisted the Junto's advance, while quietly taking advantage of the queen's growing friendship with his cousin, Abigail Hill, to build up his own interest at court.

A dispute over bishops grew into the crisis which would wreck the duumvirs' fragile coalition. After their success in the 1705 elections, the Whigs began to demand appointments to high ecclesiastical as well as secular office. Early in 1706 Godolphin and Marlborough – in defiance of the wishes of Harley and of Anne's spiritual adviser, Archbishop Sharp – came to an agreement with them over the sharing out of bishoprics. It was put to the test the following November when the death of Bishop Peter Mews left the valuable see of Winchester vacant. The Whigs wanted it for one of their own; Godolphin, though, was already under an obligation to promote his west country ally, Jonathan Trelawny, bishop of Exeter. When Nicholas Stratford, bishop of Chester, died in March 1707 and created a second vacancy, Godolphin believed he had the solution. The queen, however, insisted on appointing Tories to both vacancies, Offspring Blackall and William Dawes. The Whigs threatened to withdraw support for the min-

My Ld & Gentlemen

all humble

entire

Tis wth ye greatest thankfulness to Almighty God & ye utmost satisfaction to my self, yt I meet you here in this first Parliamt of Great Britain: not doubting but you come wth hearts prepar'd as mine is, to make this Union so prosperous as may answer ye Hopes of all my good Subjects, & ye favourable apprehensions of our Enemys.

materiell

To that end nothing is so im-mediatly necessary as the letting both our friends & enemys whose eys must be more then ordinarily fixed on ye proceedings of this Parlt &c. convinced as soon as possible, yt this uniting our Interests hath ... far from abating but rather ... improved our ... ability to prosecute this just & necessary warr; & to put no end to it.

to convince as soon as possible both our friends & our enemys that the uniting of our Interests hath not only ... improved our abilitys but ...

istry altogether. The death of a third bishop, Simon Patrick of Ely, in May 1707 did not help either, as the Whigs now demanded all three bishoprics. Godolphin was in no doubt that the crisis over the bishoprics 'will give the Whigs a handle to be uneasy and to tear everything in pieces if they can't have their own terms' and was convinced that the crisis was being orchestrated by Harley out of enmity to the Junto.[13]

When Parliament sat again in October 1707, the ministry came under more pressure after a military disaster at the battle of Almanza in south eastern Spain. The Junto Whigs made it very clear that they held the balance of power in Parliament and could make or break the ministry. The Queen refused to be browbeaten: in January 1708 she appointed Blackall and Dawes to two of the vacant bishoprics, although the Whigs were handed the third, a regius professorship at Oxford and a vacant deanery. Robert Harley was already planning (with the queen's connivance) a ministerial coup, one that would detach the more moderate Whigs from their Junto leaders. Before he was ready, however, Godolphin and Marlborough got to hear about it. Marlborough told the queen that after Harley's 'false and treacherous proceedings…

no consideration can make me serve any longer with that man.'[14] Dropped by the queen, Harley had to resign.

Harley's exit stumped his plans for a coup; but it left the ministry highly vulnerable in both Houses. It lacked reliable support from the Tories, yet the queen (still closely in touch with the ousted Harley) adamantly refused to be pushed any further in the direction of the Whigs. When, in April 1708, she was pressed to take Somers into the ministry, she dug in her heels, 'looking upon it to be utter destruction to me'.[15] Her stance became even less practical after the general election of May, the first in which both England and Scotland went to the polls to elect representatives to the Westminster Parliament, and the first test of the system for elections of Scottish representative peers. The result was a stronger Whig presence in the Commons. Only after her husband's death in October did the queen give way. In November Somers became lord president of the council and Wharton was appointed lord lieutenant of Ireland. In return, the Junto rallied behind the court. By the end of 1708, although the alliance was still not an enthusiastic one – Godolphin remained wary of the Junto and keen to build up a personal connection among the Whigs – it was more effective than a demoralised and disunited Tory party, split between Harley on the one hand, and Nottingham and Rochester on the other.

As the war meandered into a bloody and expensive stalemate, the Tories saw an opportunity. Marlborough's pyrrhic victory at Malplaquet in August 1709 – the allied army lost 21,000 men, twice as many as the French – was a turning point. Marlborough and the Whigs were determined to fight on, refusing to conclude a peace without achieving the allies' original aim of removing Philip V from the throne of Spain. To many others, however, it seemed that they wanted to keep on a war which served only their own interests. For the last four years of Anne's reign, politics in Britain were driven by peace and the succession, and an irritating clergyman whose antics would suddenly and dramatically deepen the deep divide that had existed since the Revolution.

FIG. 151 *Offspring Blackall (1655–1716), son of a London alderman, owed his curious name to his puritan maternal grandfather, Charles Offspring. Taught at Cambridge by the famous Presbyterian Edmund Calamy, he nevertheless became a Tory polemicist, who after his elevation to the see of Exeter engaged in a particularly vicious pamphlet debate in 1709 with the notorious Whig clergyman Benjamin Hoadly.*

Chapter 8

Interest: the Lords and the nation

The landed interest

Most peers were important at Westminster because they were important at home, able to dominate local society and the affairs of the county and nearby towns, including their parliamentary elections. The influence of the peerage depended on land, kinship and clientage. The enormous estates of families such as the Monck dukes of Albemarle, the Somerset dukes of Beaufort, or the Holles dukes of Newcastle provided them with wealth and an extensive field over which they could deploy their 'interest'. Intermarriage with other leading peerage and gentry families provided them with partners and collaborators. The family of George Monck, duke of Albemarle, had been resident in Devon for many generations and claimed kinship with almost every gentry family in the county; Francis Newport, 2nd Baron Newport (later Viscount Newport and earl of Bradford) was related through blood or marriage to all the prominent gentry families in Shropshire. Peers' social standing, connections at court and influence within government enabled them to help friends, families and supporters into jobs and other benefits.

Not all of the country was dominated by great noblemen. Some counties had few, or no, great estates: there, influence was shared or contested among less exalted gentry families. But even where great noblemen did dominate, as they did in many counties, they still had to be constantly active and vigilant to protect their social and political dominance against rival peers or independent-minded local gentry. They had to engage with the court to maintain the regard and attention of the monarch and principal ministers whose favour added lustre to the grandest local grandee; they had to ingratiate themselves with local communities by the judicious distribution of favours and benefits; and they had to negotiate marriage

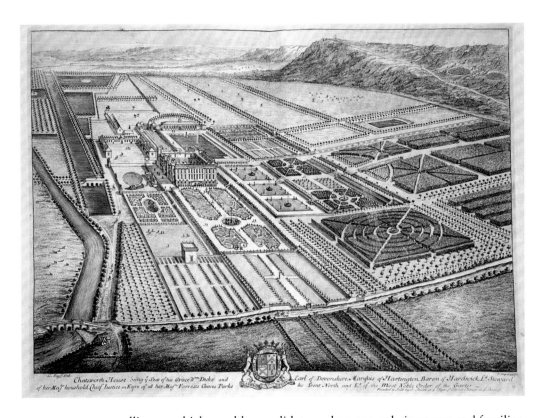

FIG. 152
Chatsworth House, seat of William Cavendish, duke of Devonshire, engraved by Johannes Kip after Leonard Knyff. Forced out of public life during the reign of James II, the Whig William Cavendish, then 4th earl (later duke) of Devonshire, concentrated instead from 1686 on rebuilding and modernising his stately home at Chatsworth, in Derbyshire.

alliances which would consolidate and preserve their estates and families. Governments relied on the leading peers to secure order in the localities; the towns and cities looked to them to promote and mediate their dealings with government (though they might also come into conflict over their rights and privileges); individuals sought help from them in obtaining jobs or other benefits. Power, position and wealth mattered in the deferential society of late seventeenth and early eighteenth century England and Wales but influence, that intangible quality usually referred to as 'interest', needed more than these qualities: it had to be won and consolidated through openhandedness and hard work.

Nursing interest

It meant, among many other things, a routine round of fundraising and donating to local causes. Fulke Greville, 5th Baron Brooke, contributed £40 towards the relief of those who had lost property in the fire at Warwick in 1694 and played a continuing role in rebuilding the town. In

January 1685 William Feilding, 3rd earl of Denbigh, headed the list of the local nobility and gentry who petitioned secretary of state Robert Spencer, 2nd earl of Sunderland, for £200 to add to the £1,200 they had already raised towards building a new hall and gaol in Warwick. Regular small donations, such as a gift of five guineas for the poor of Hastings, by John Ashburnham, Baron Ashburnham, were essential; Edward Russell, earl of Orford, began to take a close interest in the Suffolk borough of Orford in 1698, but it was noted when he visited that year that 'he paid his reckoning but gave not one penny to the poor'.[1]

Generosity was not always enough. Patronage of a scheme for almshouses at Woodstock by John Lovelace, 3rd Baron Lovelace, was insufficient to shore up an interest damaged by his Whig politics and competition from a rival married to one of Charles II's illegitimate daughters. Local communities were adept at sensing when a peer was unable to help them and unimpressed by empty threats, as Thomas Bruce, 2nd earl of Ailesbury discovered in 1696 when he objected to plans by his wealthier rival, Lord Ashburnham, to build a private gallery in the church at Ampthill. Ailesbury's agent made it clear to the parish that if the project – a very visible statement of the relative current fortunes of the two families – went ahead, Ailesbury would 'never come to that church any more nor none of his family, his lordship will take off all the charity given to the poor there, and never employ one tradesman nor workman for the future'.[2] Despite the threat, Ashburnham got his gallery.

Ostentatious hospitality was just as important as charitable giving. John Poulett, 2nd Baron Poulett, fostered his position in post-Restoration Somerset with (as a local militia officer remarked) 'generosity in plentiful housekeeping'.[3] In July 1681 Robert Bertie, 3rd earl of Lindsey, hosted a magnificent entertainment at Grantham to help secure signatures to the county's loyal address. Among the guests was Sir John Reresby, who reported approvingly that, 'if good meat and drink will make men loyal (which used to be a good argument with Englishmen) my lord spares no cost to effect it in his lieutenancy'.[4] For bishops, hospitality was a religious obligation but it nevertheless served a similar purpose. William Beaw of Llandaff insisted that he lived 'not according to my revenue, but answerable to my dignity'. His gates 'stood open to all comers' and bread and beer were distributed on a daily basis.[5]

Gifts to the local gentry helped to consolidate friendships and ensure their loyalty. Venison was highly prized and often given as a

'A thousand lies': electing the Scots representative peers in 1708

iven the difficulties ministries found in securing a majority in the House of Lords in the reign of Queen Anne, and the assumption that Scottish peers were indigent and easily suborned, the sixteen Scottish representative peers added to the House of Lords under the Treaty of Union offered a promising source of cheap and reliable lobby fodder. Ensuring that the right peers were picked who would obediently fulfil expectations nevertheless required some management, for the Scottish peers were as deeply divided by personal and factional rivalries as their English counterparts.

The elections were held under the articles of the Union and subsequent Scottish legislation. The first election, a provisional choice of representatives to the existing Westminster Parliament which still had a year and a half to run, took place in the Scots Parliament itself on 13 February 1707, just a month after it had ratified the Treaty of Union. On behalf of the 'Court' party, which had promoted the Union, the queen's commissioner, James Douglas, 2nd duke of Queensberry in the Scottish peerage, presented a list of sixteen court candidates. Fourteen of them were elected, but the opposition group known as the New Party, or the 'Squadrone Volante', managed to secure the remaining two places for candidates of their own.

Eighteen months later, on 17 June 1708, the first election under the full statutory system took place following the dissolution of Parliament. Party political manoeuvres on both sides of the border and the new, untried and vague electoral procedures helped to make it the most controversial election of first half of the eighteenth century. In England, the duumvirs, Sidney, earl of Godolphin, and John Churchill, duke of Marlborough, were bound in an uncomfortable parliamentary alliance with the Whig Junto to which the queen was implacably opposed. In Scotland three political parties vied for power: the Tories, Queensberry's Court party and the Squadrone. A failed French and Jacobite invasion attempt in March 1708 had led to the arrest of several Scots peers, including the nominal leader of the Tories, James Hamilton, 4th duke of Hamilton, suspected of Jacobite sympathies. The duumvirs signalled their support for the Court party by granting Queensberry a title in the British peerage as duke of Dover and publicised the decision of Marlborough (who also held a Scottish peerage) to register his proxy with a Court party supporter. Hamilton brokered a deal with the Junto that led to a revivial of the Scottish Country party based on an alliance between his Tories, the Squadrone and the Junto Whigs.

It was a battle to convince the small electorate of what they might gain personally from exercising their vote. Hamilton went chasing after the votes of the imprisoned Scots peers, although he found that they 'have been all most grossly imposed upon and have had a thousand lies told them, so that I assure you we have much more difficulty here than I expected'. He entreated his Whig allies to confer 'distinguishing marks' on their supporters and to secure the release of those arrested in order to prove their access to patronage and influence. Queensberry's supporters, he claimed, 'stick at nothing and commit all the irregularities in the elections that's possible'.[1] The Squadrone leader James Graham, duke of Montrose in the Scots peerage, complained in turn that the 'threats and promises' of David Leslie, 5th earl of Leven, 'have gained more upon people here than can be imagined'.[2]

The Scottish Court party and the duumvirs were particularly alarmed by the intervention of secretary of state, and leader of the Junto Whigs, Charles Spencer, 3rd earl of Sunderland, on the side of Hamilton and the Squadrone. His letters of support were taken to indicate royal backing, as Anne realised only too well, but rather too late:

> Lord Sunderland has assured me he has neither directly or indirectly made use of my name, but at the same time owned he had writ his own thoughts about the elections to some lords of the Squadrone, as they call them, and I find by all his discourse on that subject he intends to continue in opposition to what I think for my service. Now though he did not

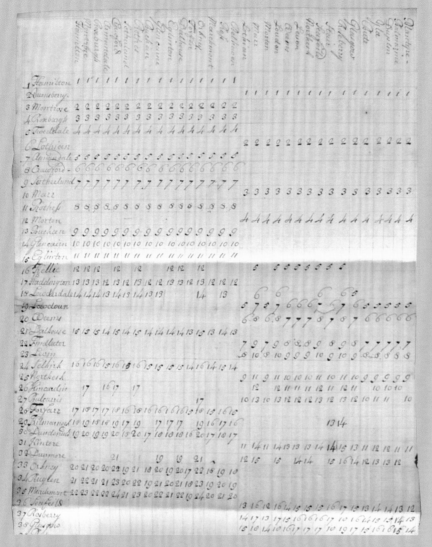

FIG. 153 *An elaborate checklist, laid out as a grid, records who voted for whom in the 1708 election of the Scots representative peers.*

mention my name, I think in effect what he has done is the same thing, for whatever comes from one in such a post, on such a subject, must be looked upon as done by my approbation, so that I cannot but still resent this usage very much.[3]

It was only with difficulty that she was prevailed upon to keep him in office.

The election itself took place at Holyrood House and lasted until 4 a.m. When the votes were counted, ten Court party supporters and six of the Country party's list were returned. The Country party determined to challenge the result in the House of Lords itself, where Hamilton believed a sympathetic hearing would hand it another three or four members. Many of the complaints were technical; one of them was closely connected to a much more substantial issue. Hamilton claimed that Queensberry was disqualified from voting by virtue of his creation as duke of Dover in the British peerage the previous summer. The House decided, by a narrow majority, that a Scots peer who sat in the House by virtue of a British peerage was unable to vote in the elections for Scottish representative peers. As a result of the objections raised, one representative peer was replaced by another: but in the end, despite the intense fuss of the election, even most of those elected for the Country party proved to be fairly amenable to the government's influence.

compliment. The removal in 1702 of the Junto Whig Thomas Wharton, 5th Baron Wharton (see above, p. 276) from the office of chief justice in eyre south of the Trent was attributed in some quarters to his having been 'a little too free' with the queen's venison, 'bestowing it up and down to promote the elections of his friends', although the real reason was more straightforwardly political.[6] Robert Creighton, bishop of Bath and Wells, was delighted to receive a gift of a buck from Sir Ralph Verney; Verney in his turn was pleased to receive venison from William Henry Lee, earl of Lichfield. The fashion for gardening, and especially for exotic fruits grown under glass, set a premium on gifts of unusual plants and seeds. The renegade Whig Charles Mordaunt, 2nd Viscount Mordaunt (later 3rd earl of Peterborough) supplied the Tory Lord Ashburnham with vines and fig trees. Thomas Osborne, earl of Danby (later duke of Leeds) and George Jeffreys, Baron Jeffreys, both received presents of orange trees from political allies. In 1667, a correspondent gently remonstrated with Richard Boyle, earl of Burlington, over his failure to distribute gifts of venison to local notables, 'an usual respect which they receive from common gentlemen that have parks, which discourse I thought fit to discover to your honour that your lordship may understand what they expect'.[7]

Such small courtesies were essential, but in order to build up a real interest in a locality or region, peers and bishops had to be prepared to use their influence with their fellow peers, with ministers and other notables to secure multiple advantages for their individual and corporate clients. They were approached to obtain rich livings or promotions for clergymen; lucrative or prestigious appointments for gentlemen; nominations for admission to charity schools and hospitals for the needy. Key boroughs needed to be filled with supporters, borough corporations flattered and the benefits of the family's patronage made manifest. Noblemen and bishops were expected to use their social and political networks to facilitate the submission of petitions or the passage of private or local legislation to secure advantages for friends, relatives and supporters or to protect local workers and industries. The earl of Burlington and Marmaduke Langdale, 2nd Baron Langdale, lent their support to a petition from the inhabitants of Bridlington for a new tax to finance the rebuilding of their pier in 1672; Robert Paston, Viscount (later earl of) Yarmouth, high steward of the corporation of Great Yarmouth, oversaw the passage of a bill to repair its pier in 1677. Early in Anne's reign, Thomas Johnson, who represented Liverpool in the Commons, tried to get the assistance of local grandee James Stanley, 10th earl of Derby, in a campaign to secure the lease of Liverpool Castle and its grounds for the corporation. Initially he complained that the earl 'often talks of things, but is a long time before he does it'; within a short time, though, he was writing of the town's obligations to the earl for his help.[8]

Power and perquisites: local office

Those who aspired to local dominance needed to grasp one or more of the major local and regional offices that conferred power, prestige and the chance to distribute patronage. The grandest of them all was the duke of Beaufort's presidency of the council of the marches which gave him an almost vice-regal status in Wales and its marches until its abolition after the Revolution (see below, p. 298). Before the Civil Wars a sister body, the council of the north, had provided a similar position for Thomas Wentworth, earl of Strafford, but it was abolished at almost the same time as Strafford was executed in 1641. After the Restoration several noblemen urged that it be re-established, hoping to use it as the foundation of their own regional pre-eminence. Strafford's son William Wentworth, restored to the earldom, was one of them; George Villiers, 2nd duke of Buckingham, another. Opposition from those whose own claims to local power would be undermined by a restored council of the north was fierce. Algernon Percy, 4th earl of Northumberland, headed a delegation of ten lords and six commoners to Lord Chancellor Clarendon to express their hostility to the measure. In the House of Lords in early 1662 Buckingham and Northumberland nearly came to blows over the issue. Although the council's reinstatement was frequently rumoured, it never happened.

Apart from these councils, the pre-eminent position in the politics and society of each county was the lord lieutenancy, conferring on its holder honour, prestige and the deference of the county community. Lords lieutenant headed the county militia and so stood at the head of the local structures for the maintenance of order and defence. They were able to offer prized commissions as deputy lieutenants or militia officers to members of the lesser nobility and local gentry. After the Revolution it became almost standard practice for the lord lieutenancy to run concurrently with the post of *custos rotulorum* which controlled the appointment of magistrates – the justices of the peace who undertook a significant role in local government as well as enforcing the law as unpaid lay judges.

The power of Beaufort: Henry Somerset, duke of Beaufort (1629–1700)

In his classic *History of England* in the late seventeenth century, the peer and politician Thomas Babington Macaulay described the splendour and influence of Henry Somerset, duke of Beaufort, at the beginning of the reign of James II:

> The power of Beaufort bore some faint resemblance to that of the great barons of the fifteenth century. He was president of Wales and lord lieutenant of four English counties. His official tours through the extensive region in which he represented the majesty of the throne were scarcely inferior in pomp to royal progresses. His household at Badminton was regulated after the fashion of an earlier generation. The land to a great extent round his pleasure grounds was in his own hands; and the labourers who cultivated it formed part of his family. Nine tables were every day spread under his roof for two hundred persons. A crowd of gentlemen and pages were under the orders of his steward. A whole troop of cavalry obeyed the master of the horse. The fame of the kitchen, the cellar, the kennel and the stables was spread over all England. The gentry, many miles round, were proud of the magnificence of their great neighbour, and were at the same time charmed by his affability and good nature.[1]

Beaufort undoubtedly lived in magnificent style, ostentatiously displaying his wealth at every possible opportunity. It had not been acquired without a struggle. In the early seventeenth century the Somerset family had possessed extensive lands and influence in Monmouthshire, Gloucestershire and beyond, but the Civil Wars, combined with the family's royalism and Catholicism, had been financially disastrous for the estate. Long before he inherited his original title as 3rd marquess of Worcester and a place in the House

FIG. 154 *Henry Somerset, duke of Beaufort, by Robert White, after Sir Godfrey Kneller (1679), depicted wearing his garter robes and regalia.*

of Lords in 1667, the young Henry Somerset had single-mindedly set about rebuilding the family fortunes. He fought his relatives through the law courts, married a wealthy widow and diverted assets from his step-children, converted to Protestantism, and obtained (through hard bargaining with Oliver Cromwell) the right to buy back family lands sequestrated during the Civil Wars because of the family's Catholicism. After the Restoration, he started to rebuild the family's political influence as well. Having found his house at Badminton inadequate to entertain Charles II in 1663, he invested in a building programme that turned his properties into the social and political powerhouses of the region. Already lord lieutenant of Monmouthshire, Gloucestershire and Herefordshire, in 1672 he was made lord president of the council in the marches of Wales (the institution established under the Tudors to bring order to the lawless Welsh border country) and a member of the privy council. In 1682 he became duke of

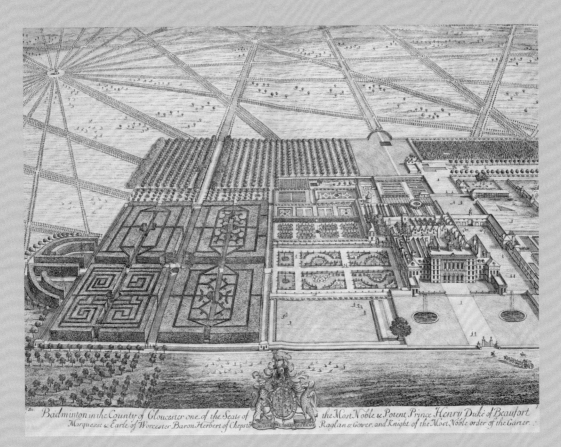

Badminton in the County of Gloucester one of the Seats of [...] the Most Noble & Potent Prince Henry Duke of Beaufort Marquesse & Earle of Worcester Baron Herbert of Chepsto [...] Raglan & Gower, and Knight of the Most Noble order of the Garter.

Beaufort, and in the summer of 1684 he embarked on the magnificent progress Macaulay described through the marcher counties and through North and South Wales.

Beaufort's apparent hegemony in Wales and the marches was, though, far from as secure and effortless as Macaulay implied. When he was elevated to the Lords he failed to secure the election of his son and heir to the Monmouthshire seat in the Commons he had vacated. He upset the local gentry by packing the deputy lieutenancy and the magistracy with his supporters. He caused resentment in Wales by attempting to administer the principality from Badminton or his house in Monmouth rather than from the traditional centre of government at Ludlow. During the political crisis surrounding the Popish Plot, his family's Catholic past and his own doubtful commitment to Protestantism opened him to a series of attacks, inspired by his local enemies. His estate steward was named as one of the ringleaders of the Plot. Anthony Ashley Cooper, earl of Shaftesbury, claimed that Worcester had turned the garrison of Chepstow castle into a nest of Catholics. His son, styled Lord Herbert of Raglan, was elected to the first exclusion

FIG. 155 Badminton House in the county of Gloucester, *engraved by Johannes Kip after Leonard Knyff.*

Parliament but after his election to the second he was unseated in favour of one of his father's bitterest local enemies (who later claimed to be in fear of his life from Worcester's henchmen). There were further attacks in the Commons in late 1680, including a proposal that the council of the marches be abolished. In 1681 his candidates were beaten in Monmouthshire and Breconshire and there were murmurs of revolt from the deputy lieutenants in Denbighshire. Even the 1684 progress produced trouble in Herefordshire, where the behaviour of some of the local gentry so infuriated Beaufort's followers that they threatened to torch the area.

The accession of James II, an old friend and ally of the now duke of Beaufort, probably represented the height of Beaufort's power. Even so, when he tried to exercise his influence in Bristol in the election of 1685, his candidate 'was so treated… the first day of voting, that for the peace of the city and avoiding of bloodshed, he and three hundred of his friends fore-

Justices of the Peace not Dep: Leiv:ts

Sr William Keyte		Liues in Worcestersh:
Sr Robert Southwell		as formerly not by King Known's
Sr Fleetwood Dormer		Refuse's ye 2: first, Consents to ye 3:
Sr Samuell Astrey		Consents to all.
Thomas Rawlins serj at law.		
Henry Hall	Esqr	A Catholick now Sherriffe
John Hill	Esqr	A Catholick now Mayor of Gloucest: consents to all.
Robert Brent	Esqr	A Catholick
Nicholas Veale	Esqr	Refuse's ye 2: first, consents to ye 3:
John Ashton of Ashton.	Esqr	A Catholick, consents to all.
Philip Draycott.	Esqr	A Catholick, Sherriff of Staffordsh:
Henry Powle	Esqr	A Cisnt
John Vaughan	Esqr	A Catholick, consents to all.
Philip Sheppard	Esqr	Refuses ye 2: first, Consents to ye 3:
Charles Trinder	Esqr	A Catholick
William Rogers	Esqr	A Catholick.
Thomas Harris	Esqr	Liues in Wiltshire.
Robert Price	Esqr	As formerly to ye King.
Giles Parsons	Esqr	Absent
Anthony Sambach } John Parsons Jun	Esqr	Not Sworen.
Benedict Wakeman	Esqr	A Catholick, consents to all
Thomas Bartlett	Esqr	A Catholick
Francis Creswick	Esqr	Consents to all
George Raymond	Esqr	Refuse's ye 2 first consents to ye 3:
Christopher Cole	Esqr	Lame in his Shouder & notable worm:
Henry Benedict Hall	Esq	A Catholick
John Wagstaffe	Esqr	Consents to all
David Warren.	Esqr	Refuse's ye 2: first, Consents to ye 3:
Rich: Parsons Lo: ce Baralow		Refuse's ye 2 first Consents to ye 3:

FIG. 156 A page from Beaufort's report on the response in his own jurisdiction to the survey required by James II of the views of all deputy lieutenants and justices of the peace on the repeal of the Test Acts. Many of the justices in his area were already Catholic.

bore to appear, for of about two hundred that had voted for him, many were so beaten and trod under foot that he rather chose to send in a protest against their tumultuous behaviour'.[2] Beaufort, closely associated with an increasingly unpopular regime – despite his unease with it, and despite James's decision to remove him from the command of Chepstow castle – toured his bailiwick in 1687 to establish the level of support for the king's project of repealing the Test Acts. At the Revolution he was one of the few to remain – for a time at least – loyal to James. Unwilling to accept that James II had abdicated, and despite being snubbed by Willliam of Orange, he nevertheless took the oaths to William and Mary. It did him little good. The council of the marches was abolished and he lost virtually all of his offices. Late in 1689 he withdrew from Parliament and spent the rest of his life in retirement on his estates, holding himself aloof from politics until his death eleven years later.

The position of lord lieutenant and *custos rotulorum* was almost always held by a peer or a peer's son. Sometimes one or other or both of these posts became virtually hereditary. Until the Revolution the Stanley earls of Derby routinely took the lieutenancies of Cheshire and Lancashire. The lord lieutenancy of Buckinghamshire was held by successive earls of Bridgwater after the Restoration; after the death of the 3rd earl in 1701 his son was still under age, so it was put into other hands during his minority. Many peers held more than one lieutenancy. In 1682 Henry Howard, then styled earl of Arundel (later 7th duke of Norfolk) became lord lieutenant of Berkshire and Surrey; the next year he got Norfolk too. The decidedly Protestant chronicler Roger Morrice remarked with concern that between them, Arundel and his uncle, the duke of Beaufort (both with strong Catholic connections), controlled some twenty counties in England and Wales.

In counties where there was no obviously dominant family or where the government wished to re-shape local allegiances, competition for the lord lieutenancy and other posts could become intense. At the Restoration, the routine jockeying for local hegemony was sharpened by the legacy of Civil War hostilities. In Oxfordshire in 1660 it was rumoured that the lord lieutenancy would go either to the parliamentarian Viscount Saye and Sele or the inactive royalist Montagu Bertie, 2nd earl of Lindsey. The young royalist conspirator Henry Carey, 4th Viscount Falkland in the Scottish peerage, bitterly complained that Lindsey 'never did anything for the king's service... He thought my lord Saye so much more unworthy... that in case he were the man, he would oppose whatsoever he would do by all the interest he had there'.[9] An appeal by Oliver St John, 2nd earl of Bolingbroke, to secretary of state Nicholas – 'Sir, my desire is in which I beg your favour to be lord lieutenant of Bedfordshire where all my land lies. My name is Bolingbroke' – was ignored in favour of a former royalist, Thomas Wentworth, earl of Cleveland.[10] The Revolution saw many other examples of the replacement of lords lieutenant on political grounds. The appointment of Charles Gerard, 2nd earl of Macclesfield, to the lord lieutenancies of Gloucestershire, Herefordshire and North Wales in 1689 was part of a concerted attempt to undermine the Beaufort (and Tory) interest in the region and to build an alternative Whig power structure in its place.

Peers who were appointed as lords lieutenant were not necessarily the wealthiest in the county. Aubrey de Vere, 20th earl of Oxford, who held the lord lieutenancy of Essex from 1660 to 1675 and then jointly with the 2nd duke of Albemarle until dismissed by James II in 1687, was one of the poorest of peers. There were several reasons for his appointment. Despite his relative poverty, Oxford enjoyed a prestigious peerage of great antiquity; he was also a soldier and a royalist and, given the strategic maritime position of Essex, it was crucial that the county defences be placed in safe hands.

Peers were always on the lookout for opportunities to extend their political and social grasp, or to head off threats to it. In 1662 Charles Stuart, 3rd duke of Richmond, already lord lieutenant for Dorset, cast covetous eyes on the lieutenancy of Kent. When he heard of the departure of the incumbent, Heneage Finch, 3rd earl of Winchilsea, on embassy to the Levant in 1662, he offered to share the lieutenancy. Winchilsea thought Richmond planned to 'crowd me out' and managed to get his brother-in-law Thomas Wriothesley, 4th earl of Southampton, to act as caretaker until his return.[11] After Southampton's death in May 1667, however, Winchilsea, still in Turkey, was forced to accept Richmond as joint lord lieutenant.

A handful of other posts provided power and influence on a similar scale to the lieutenancy. One was the lord warden of the Cinque Ports and constable of Dover Castle. The office was prestigious and largely honorific. Its holders were often royal, including James, duke of York, and Queen Anne's husband, Prince George of Denmark: its duties were exercised through a deputy, usually also a peer. The chancellorship of the duchy of Lancaster traditionally went to a courtier, with little connection to the county, rather than to a prominent local landowner. The convention was broken in 1706, with the appointment of James Stanley, 10th earl of Derby. Some of these offices in the gift of the crown offered valuable perquisites. The exploitation of the ancient forest law as a source of royal revenue had created friction between crown and subjects before the Civil War. At the Restoration it seemed that it was to be revived, for the two posts responsible for implementing it, the chief justices in eyre north and south of the Trent, were both filled and the new appointees, William Cavendish, earl (later duke) of Newcastle (north), and Aubrey de Vere, 20th earl of Oxford (south), proceeded to hold their courts, known as forest eyres. Oxford, dependent on court handouts, was enthusiastic about his role in reviving a lucrative source of revenue for the crown, as well as for himself. The two Restoration forest eyres were, however, the last to be held, and the judicial powers of the two chief justices came to an end.

The office nevertheless conferred considerable powers of patronage in the appointment of forest officials and equally considerable profits from the right to license breaches of forest law, ranging from running ale houses to felling trees, enclosing plots of land and erecting buildings. The posts were not grand in themselves – although Charles Spencer, 3rd earl of Sunderland, was probably understating matters when in 1705 he pressed for the reappointment of the 5th Baron Wharton as chief justice in eyre south of the Trent, advising that 'little things done with a good air, do often please more than greater'.[12] Little as they might be in the estimation of some, they were highly prized. In 1711 John Holles, duke of Newcastle, made the grant of the office of chief justice in eyre north of the Trent a condition of his continued support for the administration of Robert Harley, earl of Oxford.

There were many lesser offices in the Crown's gift, often associated with royal palaces, castles, estates and forests. They included some important military posts as governors of garrisons and arsenals, but many were undemanding, their main function and benefit that they provided local patronage. After Thomas Thynne, Viscount Weymouth, was appointed warden of the Forest of Dean in 1712, at least one of his poor Tory relations approached him, eager to secure a place 'proper for a sportsman, and some profit too'.[13] The office of keeper and warden of the New Forest was held by a string of high ranking noblemen, including the 4th earl of Southampton and Charles Powlett, 6th marquess of Winchester (later duke of Bolton). Charles Stanley, 8th earl of Derby, lord lieutenant of Lancashire and Cheshire from 1660, was also forester of Macclesfield Forest in Cheshire, steward of Furness Liberty in Lancashire and (jointly with his son and heir) chamberlain of the exchequer of the county palatine of Chester.

Peers played a role in town governments too, as recorders and high stewards of corporate boroughs. Appointments to both offices were governed by borough charters. Recorderships, like lieutenancies and *custodes rotulorum*, could become virtually hereditary. At his succession to the peerage William Seymour, 3rd duke of Somerset, was only eight years old. He never took his seat in the House of Lords but he did become the recorder of Lichfield, a place traditionally held by the Devereux family and passed to the young duke through his Devereux grandmother. Many peers collected multiple offices of this kind. During the 1680s the 5th Baron Brooke, who played an active role in securing new charters for

The malt tax and the Union, 1713

The Scots representative peer John Elphinstone, 4th Lord Balmerinoch, recognised in 1711 that a plan to arrange weekly dinners with all of the Scottish members of the House of Lords was doomed to failure, as he was 'convinc'd we will all of us agree to dine very well (at half a guinea the head beside our wine) and never mind or agree in anything else'[1] for the Scottish peers, just like the English ones, were divided by ideology and personal interests. Nevertheless by the parliamentary session which opened in 1713, shortly after the queen had ratified the Treaty of Utrecht, a fragile national unity had been fostered by resentment at a series of political decisions that were perceived as an attack on Scottish national interests. As a result the Scots were prepared to mount an attack on the Union in the House of Lords. Their initiative presented Robert Harley, earl of Oxford, who had only dragged himself out of his previous parliamentary crisis in the winter of 1711–12 by means of his notorious dozen creations, with another predicament of similar proportions.

The crisis began with the proposal to impose a tax on malt, which came from a group of 'country' politicians in the Commons on 12 May 1713. Because the tax would fall harder on the poorer quality malt produced in Scotland, it was interpreted as breaking the Union treaty principle that the two countries would be treated equitably in tax affairs; it also, technically at least, violated the guarantee in the Union that Scotland would be exempt from a malt tax for the duration of the war. That evening Balmerinoch called a meeting of the Scots Members of both Houses. They were not yet prepared, as he had hoped, to seek the dissolution of the Union, but they did plan to demand a reduction in the tax on Scottish malt. When they failed to achieve it, they resolved to subordinate their many party and factional rivalries to a common assault on the Union. One of the representative peers, John Campbell, 2nd duke of Argyll, led a deputation to tell the queen of their decision on 26 May.

The Scots' best chance of putting real pressure on the ministry lay in forming an alliance with the Whigs in the Lords. The Whigs were keen to desta-bilise the ministry, but somehow it had to be done without jeopardising the Union and the linked issue of the Hanoverian succession – both regarded as major Whig achievements. Negotiations between the Scots and the Whigs resulted in a deal in which the Whig leaders paid lip service to Scots grievances without any real intention of assisting them. James Ogilvy, the Scottish earl of Seafield, introduced the motion to dissolve the Union on 1 June. The subsequent debate lasted between two and three hours, giving the Scots, supported by the Junto Whigs, an opportunity to catalogue the grievances heaped upon their nation. The Whigs sidestepped actually doing anything about them. Although on a procedural motion to bring the matter to a vote the ministry won by a mere four votes, a vote on the main motion for a dissolution was avoided: many of the Whigs had already left the chamber rather than risk being forced to declare themselves for or against a dissolution of the Union.

Few expected the Scots to succeed in dissolving the Union; but the malt tax bill still had to pass the Lords, where it was apparent that the opposition groups would join with the sixteen Scots peers to fight it. The Junto Whig Charles Spencer, 3rd earl of Sunderland, approached Balmerinoch to concert tactics, insisting that the Scots should oppose the tax not only for Scotland but also for England and that they must endeavour to throw the bill out in its entirety rather than amend it. The government fought hard to secure the tax for, having been forced by the Commons to declare what was in effect a peace dividend by accepting a substantial cut in the land tax, government finances were dependent on securing extra revenue. The bill scraped through its second reading by a mere two votes. One of those voting for the tax, the independent Whig George Booth, 2nd earl of Warrington, effectively sold his vote (see above, p. 100). At the third reading on 8 June government support rallied a little, providing it with a majority of eight. Victory over the malt tax meant that Oxford broke the brief alliance in the upper House between the Scots representative peers and the Junto Whigs.

Nevertheless, the crisis had shown how fragile was Oxford's majority in the Lords, and how depend-

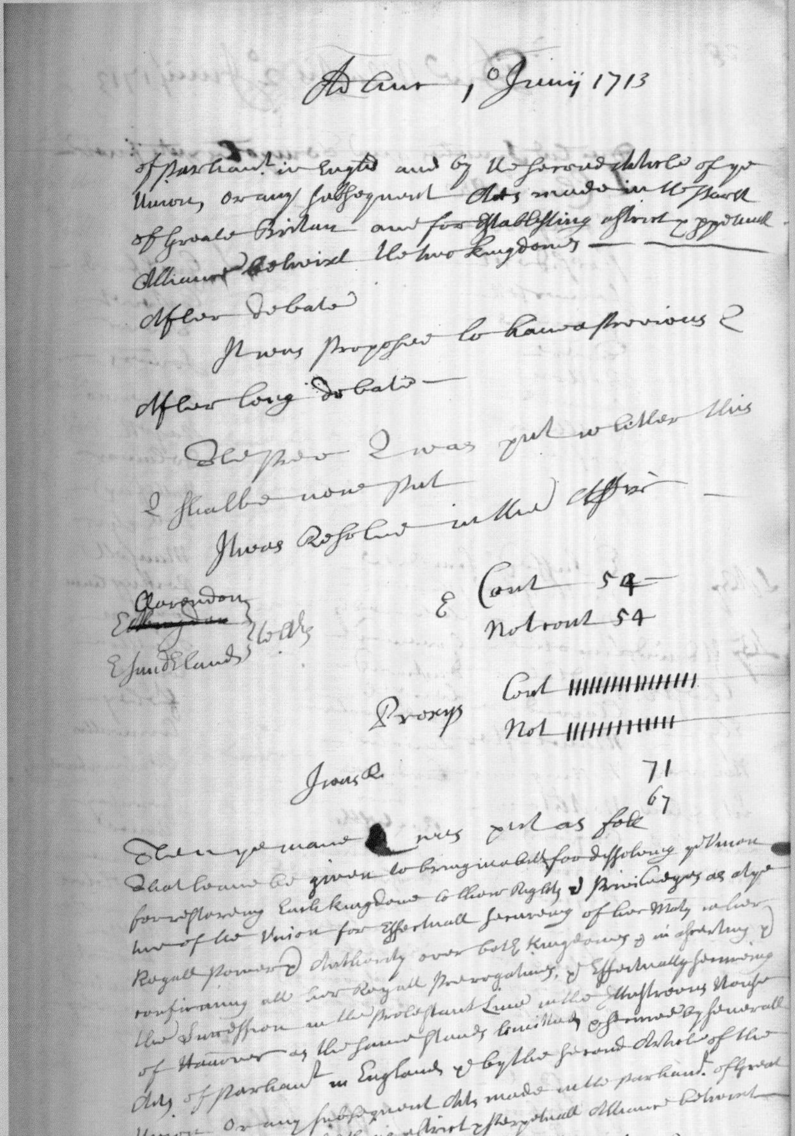

FIG. 157 *The manuscript minutes of the House of Lords showing the vote on 1 June 1713 on whether to put the question on the motion to dissolve the union. The contents and not contents were tied at 54 votes; proxies altered the result to 71 to 67.*

ent it was on the representative peers. Within two days the loss of another bill was a reminder of how weak it was in the Commons as well. Although Parliament had no role to play in the ratification of the peace treaty, an associated commercial treaty required the repeal of anti-French trade statutes. It was not popular. William Berkeley, 4th Baron

Berkeley of Stratton, wrote that the commercial treaty was 'understood by so few that it gives a large field to those who have a mind to find fault, and it hath been so long a received opinion that a trade with France is prejudicial to this kingdom, that it is no easy task to beat them out of it'.[2] On 10 June, the bill was rejected on its second reading.

A SPEECH spoken in the Council-Chamber of the City of OXFORD, the 16th of September, 87. by William Wright, Esq; Deputy Recorder of the said City, being the Day on which the Right Honourable James Earl of Abingdon took the Oath, and accepted the Office of Lord High Steward of the City aforesaid.

Mr. MAYOR,

 IT was the Custom of the ancient *Romans*, the greatest and wisest People that ever liv'd, to dedicate their Cities and Free-towns to the care and protection of some God, to whom they fled in all their Calamities, if they were invironed by their enemies, or threatned with any impendent danger, there they sought and there they expected to find relief.

IN conformity to this great example, we of this place, tho' we do not pretend to such a choice, have sought and gain'd; too the protection of one of the greatest men; a person, who for his temperate zeal, for the establish'd religion, his firm adherence to the Laws of *England*, his steady and unshaken loyalty to the Crown, is deservedly the glory of the present, and will be the wonder as well as the example of all succeeding Generations.

WE have seen his unwearied pains in serving the Crown, we have tasted his pious care of us, our Liberties and Franchizes, and have in all respects found him a zealous asserter of the public Good; and that which makes him more dear to us now, a Champion for the Rights and Priviledges of this Corporation. Therefore he that shall search the Records and look into the former Triumphs and Glory of this City, will at no time find a greater occasion of Joy than is now afforded us; for what can he that consults the honour and reputation of this City desire greater than to see this noble Lord become our Patron and Protector, to see him that has always made it his choice now make it his Duty to assist and defend us?

MY LORD,

OUR unanimous Choice, the joyful Acclamations and general Satisfaction which attended your Lordship's Election, do sufficiently evince how much you are the Darling of this City, and your Lordship's constant Inclination to assist us, even when you were under no Obligation, doth give us all possible Assurance that we shall never fail of your Lordship's Care, Shelter and Protection.

In humble Confidence of this, we do repose in your Lordship's Care, a City in some measure worthy of so noble a Patron, a City compos'd of wise, discreet, and understanding Members, that have been in all Times famous for their Loyalty and Integrity to the Crown, and have therefore, in every King's Reign, since *Henry* II. been adorned with fresh Grants of Royal Franchizes, as Monuments, and noble Rewards of their couragious, and brave Adherence to their Sovereign. And lastly, a City that has been always honoured with the Protection of the Prime and Flower of the *English* Nobility, such as amongst many other were Ch. *Brandon*, Duke of *Suffolk*, *Tho.* Lord *Cromwell*, *Francis* Earl of *Bedford*, *Robert*, Earl of *Essex*, *John* Lord *Williams*, the Lord *Hunsdon*, Sir *Tho. Knollys*, the Lord *Eleemore*, Lord High Chancellor of *England*, the Lord *Knollys*, the Earl of *Berks*, and the late Duke of *Buckingham*, and we have now obtained the Protection of your Lordship also, as the Crown and Glory of them all.

MY LORD,

To perform well the Office of *Lord High Steward* of this City, requires no other measures, than what you have always practised, It hath been your Lordship's continual Study to do us good, and thereby you have performed that Office, without the least View to your Lordship's Person.

Your Lordship is now become as a Guardian Angel to this Place, and have given us a Title to bring our Complaints, and to pray your Assistance in all our Difficulties; and by the Security of so Noble a Patronage, your Lordship has given us an everlasting Establishment, and made us the Envy of all other Corporations, and thereby, as an humble Acknowledgement of the great Honour your Lordship has done us, I do, in behalf of myself, of this House, and of the whole Body of this City, return your Lordship our humble and hearty Thanks, making this our most earnest Request to Heaven, that your Lordship may flourish in all Honour and Greatness, and that there may never be wanting one of your Lordship's Name and Blood to protect us so long as this Corporation last, which I hope will be to the World's End.

Price Two-pence.

the boroughs of Warwick and Coventry, became recorder of both. Such offices provided influence within a town, though not control. George Fitzroy, duke of Northumberland, high steward of Windsor, was unsuccessful in his efforts to have a client elected a freeman of Windsor in May 1704, but the corporation was at pains to retain his goodwill by explain-

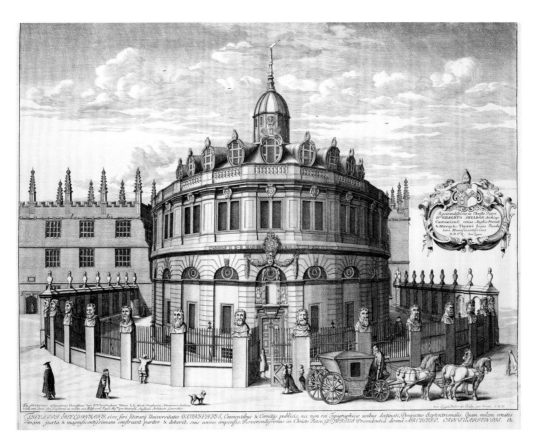

ing the grounds for their refusal and hoped that the duke would 'not take it amiss'.[14] In November 1707 they made some amends by electing Northumberland's butler as a freeman, waiving the usual fees.

FIG. 159 *The Sheldonian Theatre, Oxford, engraved by David Loggan, from* Oxonia Illustrata (1675). *Sheldon provided the money for Oxford's new theatre during his temporary tenure of the vice-chancellorship of the University in 1667.*

A handful of other offices enhanced their holders' stock of influence and patronage, not so much because they conferred additional power but because they amounted to public recognition and endorsement of an individual's existing stature. The most prestigious were the chancellorships of the two universities, Oxford and Cambridge. The 2nd duke of Albemarle became chancellor of Cambridge in 1682. His subsequent installation, which took place at the former Clarendon House, was a lavish social occasion, involving hundreds of students and alumni and an elaborate (and extremely expensive) entertainment. In 1669 Gilbert Sheldon, archbishop of Canterbury, proposed that James Butler, the wealthy and powerful duke of Ormond, was more suitable than himself for the position of chancellor of Oxford, for, 'besides the eminency of

Elections and family feuds:
the earls of Coventry

The Coventrys, locked up in their private feuds, were reluctant politicians. Thomas Coventry had unexpectedly inherited a peerage – as 5th Baron Coventry – from his nephew in 1687. Although he also gained an extensive estate and influence in Worcestershire and although he worked hard to turn the barony into an earldom, which he achieved in 1697, he was an erratic attender of the House of Lords. He attracted attention mainly by his injudicious second marriage to the daughter of his housekeeper, Elizabeth Grimes, forty years his junior, and by his poor relations with his spendthrift and resentful younger son, Gilbert, whom he starved of cash. He died in 1699, leaving a large amount of money and the duty of constructing a suitable memorial for him to his wife: she discharged the latter obligation with a monument which twinned his coat of arms with a wholly spurious set of her own, and to the irritation of the rest of the family, she continued to flaunt her supposititious ancestry.

The first earl's son, Thomas, 2nd earl of Coventry, inherited his father's attitude to Westminster politics, his feud with his brother Gilbert, and his influence in Gloucestershire, Warwickshire and Worcestershire. Elections consequently found him besieged with requests to employ his interest on behalf of a plethora of candidates, an annoyance that was exacerbated by the activities of Gilbert, to whose provocations he found it hard to respond 'without falling into Billingsgate'.[1] In 1702 the family division found its focus in the election for Worcestershire, where the earl appeared in support of William Walsh while his brother plied the electors with gifts of meat in support of Sir John Pakington. Gilbert's intention of attending the poll in person was only prevented by the intervention of their kinswoman, Lady Throckmorton, but it was with an ill grace that he agreed to stay away, complaining that 'I will not pretend to advise one way or other not knowing how far the nobility ought to concern themselves in elections, but it is very hard that my brother should pretend to forbid me any place, because he is there present. I hope I may be allowed the liberty... to serve my friends and country as others do without disobliging anybody.'[2]

The earl himself became thoroughly disenchanted with the whole business of elections. By 1708 he was complaining – ironically, given his own prominence – that a small number of people in the county were trying fix the election: 'as England has been remarkable for a heptarchy, or government by seven kings, so Warwickshire is like to be no less famed for an attempt made to govern that branch of the kingdom by seven electors'.[3]

The battle within the Coventry family was eased after 1705 as the two brothers found common cause in a dispute with another local magnate, Sir Richard Newdigate, over the leasing of coal mines on Coventry's land. The 2nd earl died young in 1710, and was followed soon after by his heir, a young boy at Eton. Gilbert therefore inherited the earldom in 1712, and set about trying to perpetuate the dynasty: he married a second time, to his 'Indian Queen', the daughter of the director of the New East India Company (despite their combined riches, they spent a mere £6 5s 4d on a wedding breakfast in a hotel on Hampstead Heath). A Tory, unlike his brother, the new earl further extended the family interest into Cornwall, and showed some enthusiasm for politics: his 'zeal' on behalf of the ministry in Worcestershire gained him the praise of Charles Talbot, duke of Shrewsbury. Like his father and his brother, however, it did not extend to exerting himself to attend much at Westminster, nor to rallying to the side of the Tory Robert Harley, earl of Oxford, when he was impeached by the Whigs in 1715, after Anne's death. He dismissed any reproach: 'my Lord Oxford's enemies carried it by so great a majority that had I been there it would have been no service to him.'[4]

FIG. 160 *Funeral monument for Thomas Coventry, earl of Coventry, at Elmley Castle, by William Stanton. The second wife of Thomas Coventry, earl of Coventry, incorporated a false coat of arms into the design of the monument she erected to commemorate her husband in order to misrepresent her genealogy and social status. The 2nd earl, also named Thomas Coventry, refused to allow his stepmother to erect the elaborately designed tomb in the parish church at Croome D'Abitot, close to the family seat. The dowager Lady Coventry married Thomas Savage of Elmley Castle in 1700 and arranged instead for the monument to be erected there.*

birth and dignities, he hath made himself more illustrious by his virtue and merits; by constant integrity ... in all fortunes, to king and Church; and ... by his love of letters and learned men'.[15]

Agents of the crown

Peers who became lords lieutenant and *custodes rotulorum* needed not only the authority of their status and office, but also enough political dexterity to command and retain the confidence of both the monarch and their local communities. Some individuals were better able to juggle these demands than others. The over-zealous determination of the 8th earl of Derby to suppress nonconformity in Cheshire and Lancashire during the early 1660s embarrassed the court, and ultimately infuriated it when Derby exploited his position as hereditary lord of the Isle of Man to seek revenge against William Christian, who had helped deliver Man to Commonwealth forces a decade earlier. Christian, confident that he was protected by the Act of Indemnity, returned to the island in 1662, whereupon Derby had him charged him with treason, convicted and condemned to death by a packed local court. By the time the privy council had heard of the sentence and ordered a reprieve, Christian had already been shot. Summoned to London to explain his actions, Derby claimed that the Act of Indemnity did not extend to Man, as the island had never been 'taken anciently as a part of England (though in homage and subjection to it)'. Christian's judges were punished and his widow and children compensated; Derby was chastised, but he remained in office until his death in 1672. The 2nd Baron Lovelace's lax attitude to the suppression of nonconformists in Berkshire brought a number of protests, including one from Dr Peter Mews, later Bishop of Winchester, who complained that one ejected minister, Christopher Fowler, refused to desist from holding meetings at his house, protesting that he had 'satisfied the lord lieutenant'.[16] Lovelace nevertheless also stayed in office until his death.

The divisive politics of the 1670s and the aftermath of the exclusion crisis and the Rye House Plot in 1682 saw more rigorous efforts on the part of the crown and its ministers to control the political life of the localities, especially urban communities. In this, as in every other aspect of government, they relied on the peers to help them to persuade towns to surrender their charters in return for new ones, offering valuable advantages in return for increased royal control. Hereford's new charter, granted in 1682, was drawn up in close association with Henry Somerset, then 3rd marquess of Worcester (the future duke of Beaufort). Worcester increased his electoral hold, the town acquired an additional fair and the king got the right to approve the high steward, the town clerk and all the aldermen. Similarly Thomas Windsor, earl of Plymouth, was closely involved with the drawing up of new charters for Evesham, Worcester and Hull. Theophilus Hastings, 7th earl of Huntingdon, pulled the strings that secured the surrender of Leicester's charter.

James II tested to destruction central government's reliance on the aristocracy to control the localities when he required his lords lieutenant to cooperate with his deeply unpopular plans to secure the repeal of the Test Acts. Lords lieutenant were charged with enforcing a new round of charter surrenders and were instructed to gather information about the attitudes of local gentry towards repeal. The process was transparently concerned with preparing for a rigged set of elections. Lords lieutenant who either refused to cooperate or who were deemed to be insufficiently enthusiastic were replaced by men on whom the king could rely, many of whom had little standing in the county concerned. They included the Catholics Richard Graham, Viscount Preston and Walter Aston, 4th Lord Aston (both Scottish titles), Christopher Roper, 5th Baron Teynham, and Thomas Petre, 6th Baron Petre. To make matters worse Aston had been accused of involvement in the popish plot and had spent the final years of Charles II's reign imprisoned in the Tower. Petre's older brother William, 4th Baron Petre, had suffered a similar fate and their relative, the Jesuit Father Petre, was one of James II's most hated advisers. Petre's commission as lord lieutenant of Essex explicitly dispensed with the requirement to take the oaths of supremacy and allegiance. In Essex, as in other counties where Protestant lords lieutenant were displaced by Catholics, the gentry refused to take commissions because of doubts about the legality of Petre's appointment. As a result, the militia was 'very much out of order, the officers dead, or unwilling to act.'[17]

The new lords lieutenant struggled to impose the king's will. By October 1688 James began to realise that he had squandered his political capital, rendering unworkable a system of local government that depended on the goodwill of the lieutenants and the acceptance of their authority by the local gentry. As he absorbed the news of the Prince of Orange's impending invasion, he began to reverse some of the measures of the last few months. He removed Teynham as lieutenant of Kent,

'How much depends upon new elections': Thomas Thynne, Viscount Weymouth (1640–1714)

y the time of the Restoration there were two distinct branches of the Thynne family, one based at Longleat in Wiltshire and the other in Gloucestershire and Shropshire. The head of the former, Thomas Thynne ('Tom of ten thousand'), famously enjoyed an annual income in excess of £10,000. When he was murdered in 1682 (see above pp. 109-11), the majority of the family's estates were reunited in the hands of his cousin, Sir Thomas Thynne of Drayton Bassett. With another vast inheritance in Herefordshire, Staffordshire and Ireland through the will of his wife's grandmother, the duchess of Somerset, Thynne was one of the wealthiest gentlemen in England. His elevation to the peerage in 1682 as Viscount Weymouth acknowledged the vastness of his estate, his closeness to a group of powerful families, including the Finches (he had married the daughter of Heneage Finch, 3rd earl of Winchilsea) and to George Savile, marquess of Halifax, and his support for Tory principles and court politics.

With interests in so many parts of the country, Weymouth represented an important gain for the court, looking to consolidate its hold in the country after the turbulence of the crisis over exclusion. His significance in Wiltshire was registered with appointment as the county's *custos rotulorum*, but he had to tread warily with the other dominant peer, the notoriously unstable Philip Herbert, 7th earl of Pembroke. In August 1683 Weymouth visited him at Wilton House in an attempt to arrive at some sort of understanding, though he wrote that Pembroke 'was very ceremonious, but when the wine is in, his jealousy breaks out.'[1]

Weymouth was instrumental in overseeing Wiltshire's loyal address in response to the Rye House Plot, excusing himself for failing to present it to the king in person, because he was busy at the assizes, 'securing the peace and watching the motions of that restless faction'.[2] In Staffordshire the Legge family were his rivals, especially in Lichfield. Annoyed not to have been included the city's new charter as its Recorder, Weymouth grumbled to his successful rival, William Legge, Baron Dartmouth, 'that they have made an infinitely better and discreter choice of your lordship I do most readily acknowledge, though their carriage towards me is not very obliging'.[3]

The Revolution severed Weymouth's links with the court. His frosty reception by William of Orange in December 1688 deepened his profound unease at the turn of events. In the Convention he consistently opposed moves to see William and Mary acclaimed as king and queen. He took the oaths of allegiance to the new regime, although he would later offer sanctuary to a number of non-juring clergy, including Thomas Ken (see above, p. 150). It annoyed the local bishop, Gilbert Burnet, who complained to Daniel Finch, 2nd earl of Nottingham, of Weymouth's flagrant refusal to offer prayers to the king and queen and his employment of a non-juror as chaplain, 'the most insolent affront that is put on the government in the west of England':

> The whole neighbourhood cry out of this. They indeed do all tell me that the earl of Nottingham is his great friend who will still maintain him *custos rotulorum* and master of the justices of this county though it be the jest of every one in it.[4]

After the Convention's dissolution, Weymouth anticipated bitter struggles ahead, telling James Bertie, earl of Abingdon 'how much depends upon new elections, and how absolutely the welfare of the Church, nay possibly of the monarchy, are concerned at this time'.[5] His brother, hampered by accusations of Jacobitism, was defeated in Gloucestershire, and at Tamworth he threw away his dominance by his dilatoriness and inconsistent instructions to his agents. By the autumn of 1692, Weymouth was thoroughly disenchanted with politics, writing to his kinsman, Halifax, that 'the slender consideration is had of the House of Lords, or that they have indeed for themselves, makes home and quiet very desirable'.[6]

Weymouth found it increasingly hard to promote the election of his favoured candidates. His removal as *custos rotulorum* of Wiltshire in 1696 may have influenced his resolution to abandon Longleat

and return to his original home in Staffordshire. Although the accession of Queen Anne and subsequent Tory ascendancy saw his reinstatement as *custos rotulorum* and a revival in the political and electoral fortunes of Weymouth and his family, the sudden death of his son, Henry Thynne, in 1708, and his own declining health threatened the survival of a significant Thynne family interest. When he died in 1714, Weymouth's fortune and titles passed to his five-year-old great-nephew, leaving the Thynne interest to be managed by trustees.

FIG. 161 *Thomas Thynne, Viscount Weymouth, by Richard Gibson after Sir Peter Lely, c. 1675.*

replacing him not with his predecessor, Heneage Finch, earl of Winchilsea, but an experienced and loyal military commander, Louis de Duras, 2nd earl of Feversham. When James fled from London and was captured and imprisoned in Kent, it was Winchilsea who rescued him, and James promised to reinstate him in his old offices. From 15 December Winchilsea again styled himself lord lieutenant of Kent and warden of the Cinque Ports, 'all which his lordship published to all the company with his usual vanity', although no formal commission had been issued.[18] The 7th duke of Norfolk managed to hang on to his lord lieutenancies (Berkshire, Surrey and Norfolk) throughout the crisis. In November 1688 he was trying to rally support for the king in Norfolk; by the end of the month he had joined the local gentry in calling for a free parliament, stating that 'no man will venture his life more freely for the defence of the laws, liberties and protestant religion than I will do'.[19] Barely a week later he declared his support for a settlement based on the declaration of the Prince of Orange. Only when the outcome was certain did he come off the fence and throw in his lot with William. Norfolk retained his lieutenancies after the Revolution. William Stanley, 9th earl of Derby, who had been reinstated in his by James II in October 1688, was less fortunate. In Lancashire after the Revolution he was replaced by Viscount Brandon (later 2nd earl of Macclesfield). Brandon, who had been forced into collaborating with James II after being sentenced to death for treason in 1685, showed his loyalty to the new regime by a strenuous prosecution of the county's Catholics and energetically promoting the Whig cause. Snubbed in Lancashire, Derby refused to act as lord lieutenant in Cheshire either, and retreated to become the (sometimes reluctant) figurehead of the north-west's now embattled Tories.

Factionalism had always been rampant in the localities. From the 1680s, and especially after the Revolution, local rivalries began to wear party political labels, a process stimulated by the frequency of elections. By the reign of Anne lieutenancies and other local offices were changing hands with the mood of the electorate. A few months after the election of 1702, the reliable Tory Basil Feilding, 4th earl of Denbigh, replaced the Whig John Manners (about to be promoted from earl to duke of Rutland) as lord lieutenant of Leicestershire. He was displaced himself when Rutland was reinstated, months after the 'Church in danger' election of 1705. Along with these changes went party political purges of deputy lieutenants and magistrates, although they were rarely totally systematic, and were often tempered by the favour of lords lieutenant and other peers. The struggle over local leadership was part of a struggle for national dominance. Success in counties and boroughs could deliver election gains that would in turn determine the direction of national policy and politics. Elections had become the key battlegrounds over which campaigns for power at county and national level were fought, a barometer of the interest of the individual peer and the strength of the party. After the 1694 Triennial Act, as elections came round with relentless frequency, they became, to some peers at least, a consuming concern.

Elections

In 1701, the Commons resolved that 'for any peer to concern themselves in the election of Members to serve for the Commons in Parliament is a high infringement of the liberties and privileges of the Commons of England'.[20] The resolution was an empty one. Peers had always attempted to influence elections: Members of the House of Lords routinely deployed their interest to secure the return of their and their friends' relations and clients. Most of the time it was accepted as the natural order of things, although it could, occasionally, be resented and challenged. In 1701 one of the candidates in Westmorland, incensed by the involvement of Charles Howard, 3rd earl of Carlisle, in the county election, told the freeholders 'that it is a new thing for any man who has no lands in a county to concern himself in elections there', something which the first two earls of Carlisle, also lieutenants of the county, had never dared to do.[21] Peers were, in theory, unable to vote themselves in elections to the Commons. Nevertheless, Charles Montagu, 4th earl (later duke) of Manchester, voted in the 1698 election at Maldon, in his capacity as an honorary freeman; and in 1701 three dukes – Charles Beauclerk (St Albans), Charles Lennox (Richmond) and Charles Powlett (2nd duke of Bolton) – claimed the right to vote for Bolton's brother, Lord William Powlett, at Winchester, where Bolton was high steward. When the case was debated in the House of Commons, the defeated candidate argued that their votes should be rejected; one Member, Sir Richard Cocks, thought 'there was never a fairer cause'. Nevertheless, the result stood.[22]

Cases of peers actually voting in elections were rare. But many peers worked strenuously to influence their outcome. Theatrical demonstrations of their magnificence were commonplace. In the Essex election

A bishop at the polls: Anthony Sparrow (1612–85) at Exeter and Norwich

uring the Civil War the ardent royalist and high-flying Churchman Anthony Sparrow had been ejected from his Cambridge fellowship for failing to take the Presbyterian Covenant, and ejected from his first living for using the proscribed Book of Common Prayer in his Church services. After the Restoration he cut his political teeth as the archdeacon of Sudbury, battling against Suffolk nonconformity. Approved of by Archbishop Sheldon, he was made bishop of Exeter in 1667, a provocative appointment in a region dominated by powerful Presbyterian sympathizers, especially George Monck, duke of Albemarle. Sparrow basked in liturgical ceremony, wore elaborate vestments and incorporated organ music and Gregorian chant into the worship of the cathedral. He told nonconformists that 'if they were not satisfied with the legal assemblies, they should keep their faith to themselves'.[1] At the polls he supported candidates who shared his religious politics, brought to bear his own influence on elections (for example, as lord of the manor in Penryn) and provided Sheldon with a stream of political intelligence. At a by-election in 1671 he reported gleefully that the 'loyal party' had forced 'a cunning busy Fifth Monarchy man' (a member of one of the radical religious sects regarded as particularly dangerous by the Restoration establishment) to withdraw his candidature before the poll.[2] Dismayed by the 1672 Declaration of Indulgence, which, he claimed, saw his 'poor sheep' being 'snatched out of the fold by cunning wolves', he rallied the gentry and justices in a punitive campaign against religious dissent.[3]

Sparrow was translated to Norwich in 1676, where he was in the forefront of the Church's political renaissance under the patronage of Thomas Osborne, earl of Danby. Lord lieutenant Robert Paston, Viscount Yarmouth, was delighted. Sparrow, Yarmouth told his wife, 'carries himself like a bishop'.[4] The two men established a close political alliance. They purged the commission of the peace of 'goats' and campaigned against 'a most seditious infuser of ill principles',[5] a chaplain to their political opponent. Sparrow received a death threat in June 1678: 'I will kill you … the day is fixed … it is not traditions and ceremonies … will save you … you are grown a viper not fit to live, you limb of Satan'.[6] It made no difference to him. In the contentious county election in spring 1679 he boasted that he and Yarmouth had 'overcome all the crafty attempts of the parties' and secured the election of two 'loyal and pious' parliamentary candidates. But the result was disputed and the eventual election of Yarmouth's opponent encouraged 'the disaffected populacy'.[7] In the similarly heated city election, Sparrow complained, there were 'all arts … used to cross us to prevail for a good choice',[8] but he and Yarmouth prevailed.

Exclusionists won the February 1681 county election only, according to Sparrow, 'by the favour of an ill undersheriff and some arts of splitting votes and a cunning way of swearing'.[9] After the end of the Oxford Parliament there was a strong reaction towards the Tories in Norfolk. Sparrow should have been pleased, but chronically ill with kidney and bladder complaints (some of his enemies who suspected he was really a Catholic attributed his failure to turn up to the House of Lords in 1680 to his unwillingness to take the Test Act), Sparrow was unable to keep up with a new breed of Tory extremists, including his own son-in-law, 'a drunken physician'.[10] Claiming that they were taking the fight against nonconformity beyond legal means, he was sued for libel by the Tory sheriff. Sparrow died the day James II's first Parliament assembled, on 19 May 1685. It was perhaps a mercy: he would, no doubt, have found the subsequent trials of the Church very hard to bear.

The Bishop of EXONS

CAUTION

TO HIS

DIOCESE

Against False Doctrines,

Delivered in a SERMON

AT

TRURO in *CORNWALL*

at his Primary Visitation.

Anthony Sparrow

by Ralph Brownrigg

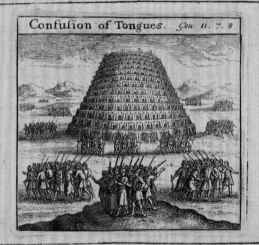

Confusion of Tongues. *Gen: 11. 7. 8*

London, Printed for *Timothy Garthwait*, 1669.

(4), 15 p.

FIG. 162 *In this 1669 sermon, delivered at one of the routine visitations of his diocese, Sparrow likened the 'false doctrines' of the non-conformists to the 'confusion of tongues' in the biblical account of the building of Babylon – the city which was regarded as the fountainhead of false religion. The title page underlines the point by showing the Tower of Babel.*

317

of 1685 the 2nd duke of Albemarle and the Catholic 6th Baron Petre led a cavalcade of court supporters to the hustings. A similar cavalcade in Rutland in 1710 consisting of 'about 1,000 horse ... 500 of whom were entertained with a sumptuous cold treat, and wine and ale' by Daniel Finch, 2nd earl of Nottingham, secured the election of Nottingham's son. There was however a difference between impressing the electorate and trying to overawe them which peers did not always grasp. When, from the spring of 1677, Robert Bertie, 3rd earl of Lindsey, started canvassing for the seat at Grantham, his robust use of the militia to support his agents produced vigorous complaints from his opponents and caused his kinsman, the earl of Yarmouth, to fear an impeachment. A cavalcade at the poll at Lewes in 1705 by the duke of Richmond and Charles Seymour, 6th duke of Somerset, provided a rare example of local independence. Initially it seemed that 'such a sight having been seldom seen at Lewes, it was thought by all the inhabitants it must of necessity carry the election' but the two dukes were ordered out by the sheriff, who cited the Commons order of 1701 and insisted that peers had no right to participate in the election. They spent the remainder of the day kicking their heels at a puppet show, and Richmond later complained about his failure to secure the election of both of his candidates: 'I did what I could', he lamented, 'to throw out a damned Jacobite and get in an honest Whig'.[23] During the 1698 election at Warwick, the 5th Baron Brooke was said to have 'arbitrarily and corruptly discontinued' the offices of a number of assistant burgesses who had voted for the wrong candidate.[24] Even when they were not trying to browbeat voters, some peers, like many others involved in elections, were buying them. Open bribery was a risky business, as it was relatively easy to prove and could invalidate an election. Nevertheless, the 5th Baron Brooke ran a campaign in 1705 to secure the election of his sons at Warwick which included the payment of 'a crown for two votes and half a crown for one vote'.[25]

Some borough constituencies were easily dominated by peers. In some of them, a local magnate was so important to the social and economic life of the area as to be able to impose his will. As lord of the manor of Christchurch, Henry Hyde, Lord Cornbury (later 2nd earl of Clarendon), expected to nominate both Members of Parliament for the borough. The earls of Carlisle similarly enjoyed a virtual monopoly on candidate selection in the Northumberland borough of Morpeth. Interest in many boroughs, however, was a much more complicated business. It

Robert Lord Brooke Baron Brooke of Beauchamps Court in the County of Warwick Lord Liev.t of y.e County of Stafford. Obijt Feb 15.1678.

FIG. 163 *Robert Greville, 4th baron Brooke (1639–77), by Gerard Valck, 1678. An influential political figure in Warwickshire and Staffordshire, regularly concerned with the outcomes of parliamentary elections, Brooke was nevertheless an infrequent attender at the House of Lords.*

might, for example, be divided between two or more families, who could either cooperate (as most boroughs had two Members, it was easy to come to an amicable arrangement) or compete to win over the electorate. The competition between the earls of Carlisle and the Musgrave family at Carlisle was given added piquancy by the fact that the earl, when a loyal agent of the Protectorate, had harassed the royalist Sir Philip Musgrave. At the Restoration, although Carlisle received his earldom and the lord

Peeresses and politics:
Baroness Rockingham,
Baroness Lovelace and the
countess of Rochester

ristocratic women may not have been able to vote, but they could exercise a formidable influence on elections nevertheless, which they used to promote their family fortunes and the ambitions of their sons. In many cases, this was by using the networks they had built up through marriage and family connection. In advance of the elections of early 1679, for example, Lady Rockingham, wife of Thomas, 2nd Baron Rockingham, was frustrated with her husband's reluctance to use his interest on behalf of their son, Lewis Watson, in Northamptonshire. She wrote instead to her kinsman, John Wentworth, requesting that he might reserve one of the places at his disposal in Yorkshire. Watson, she pleaded, was anxious 'to become a Parliament man' and was well qualified for it, 'being a right Englishman, well-affected to Church and state'.[1] Watson failed to find a seat and he had to wait until 1681 to enter Parliament: then he was returned at Canterbury, thanks to the interest in the town of his wife, daughter of Louis de Duras, 2nd Earl Feversham.

Some women went further, and engaged very actively in the complex negotiation and deal-making of electoral politics. The involvement in elections of Sarah, duchess of Marlborough, is well known; less so is that of her neighbours in Oxfordshire, Martha, Lady Lovelace and Anne, countess of Rochester. Lady Lovelace, married to the 'hot Whig' John, 3rd Baron Lovelace, was a fearsome figure in county society. During the bad-tempered city elections in Oxford in 1681 she was noted as being 'very busy at all businesses in the town to influence them her way... By her and some other that come hither our Oxonians are made so courageous that they talk nothing now but of waging war with the king'.[2] She was credited as 'the sole contriver' of the plan to offer the freedom of the city to Arthur Annesley, earl of Anglesey, in the hope that he would agree to act as a bulwark against the power of Lord Norreys (later earl of Abingdon), though Anglesey proved more interested in conciliation and refused.[3]

In the other camp in Oxfordshire politics was Anne, dowager countess of Rochester, from the St

John family in Wiltshire, the widow of one of the principal royalist generals in the Civil War and mother of the poet, rake and favourite of Charles II, John Wilmot, earl of Rochester. From the Resoration, Lady Rochester was able to wield significant electoral interest, initially on behalf of her granddaughters in Wiltshire. In March 1660 she complained to Sir Ralph Verney about how she was being solicited to use her interest there: 'it has been very troublesome to me but I put them all off with telling them that I am already promised as far as my interest goes'.[4] It was promised at Great Bedwyn for Sir Ralph, who conveyed his thanks to her for her 'great care' in securing his election.[5] At Malmesbury her son by her first marriage was elected in 1660 and 1661. In Oxfordshire in the 1680s she was an important ally of her Tory Bertie relations, although by that stage she regarded her interest as in decline: 'in the county alas I have no power there now for as I am already a dead woman in my own opinion so I am I believe esteemed in the country, but if my name can do my lord any service pray make use of it to any friends you know'.[6] Although Lady Rochester outlived the family's principal rival, Lord Lovelace, by the time of her own death in 1696 her interest in Woodstock in particular was under direct assault from that of the Marlboroughs.

PROGENIES STRAFFORDIANA.

A. Vandyke pinx 1639.   G. Vertue sculp 1739.

The R.t Honourable {
William Lord Wentworth, afterwards Earl of Strafforde.
Lady Anne Wentworth, married to Edward Lord Rockingham.
Lady Arabella Wentworth, married to the Honourable Justin Maccartie Son of the Earl of Clincartie.
}

FIG. 164 *Anne, Lady Rockingham (1629–1695) was daughter of Thomas Wentworth, earl of Strafford, who was attainted and executed in 1641. She is shown here as a child in the 1630s with her brother, the 2nd earl, and her sister.*

lieutenancy, Musgrave was given the governorship of the castle. In 1661 and for the next three parliaments the two families lived in reasonable harmony, with Carlisle's younger brother Sir Philip Howard returned along with Christopher Musgrave, son of the governor. The arrangement broke down in the 1690s, after Carlisle's son, the third earl, was appointed governor and joined with the Lowther family against the Musgraves.

The extraordinary 1677 by-election in Stamford showed the competition that could develop between local aristocratic families. Baptist Noel, 3rd Viscount Campden and Robert Bertie, 3rd earl of Lindsey, together with John Manners, then styled Lord Roos (later duke of Rutland), formed a formidable triumvirate in Rutland, Leicestershire and Lincolnshire. When they promoted the election of Campden's son Henry Noel in Stamford, a number of other peers, all laying claim to influence within the borough, piled in. Among them were John Cecil, 4th earl of Exeter (owner of Burghley House, next door to the town), Thomas Grey, 2nd earl of Stamford, and John Egerton, 2nd earl of Bridgwater. Campden 'furiously treated' the town and Lindsey spent £1,000 campaigning on Noel's behalf; their opponent was forced to give up. Later that year Campden was elected recorder in place of Exeter. Exeter protested to the king, but was rebuffed; his son John Cecil, styled Lord Burghley (later 5th earl of Exeter) was furious at the affront to the family's honour and challenged Campden's son to a duel (though no-one was hurt).

Whatever the strength of their interest, peers could rarely take the whole business for granted. At a by-election in 1706 James Stanley, 10th earl of Derby, only recently appointed chancellor of the duchy of Lancaster, discovered that the duchy officials were already committed to a rival candidate. He fretted about the damage that electoral failure would do to his prestige, for 'I am sure, we shall be scoffed at, which must be prevented, if possible'. In more normal circumstances, in 1708, he was able to nominate a successful candidate. Lord Brooke was delighted to secure the election at Warwick of both of his sons, Algernon and Francis, in 1701, and wrote to the corporation to express his pleasure that he was 'not forgot by those for whom I have ever had a cordial and sincere respect and whose interest (however I may have been misrepresented) I have and shall constantly advance and promote'.[26] Nevertheless, there was resistance within Warwick to Brooke and to the corporation that was so much in his pocket. A strong feeling against his domination of both seats was registered at the following election and Brooke had to resort to buying votes in the one after that, in 1705. The dukes of Norfolk adopted a more tactful approach in their borough at Castle Rising where, wary of over-playing their hand, they usually nominated to only one of the two seats.

The cost of elections, especially when they were hotly contested, could make it impossible for impoverished peers to compete. The only known foray into electioneering by Robert Lucas, 3rd Baron Lucas, came at the by-election for Colchester in 1694 when his support for Sir Thomas Cooke was actually financed by a London merchant, Thomas Haynes. Lucas agreed to 'write to the town and go down afterwards and lay out what moneys were necessary'. During the course of the election – which was not even contested – Lucas spent nearly £1,000 towards 'taking up of several houses for entertainment of the electors', £400 of which he borrowed from another London financier, Sir Stephen Evance, on Haynes's behalf. After the election, Lucas was forced to sue Haynes for the £400 still owed to Evance.[27]

County elections were more difficult to control than most boroughs. The right to vote was held by those holding freehold land worth 40 shillings (£2) a year, and electorates could amount to well over a thousand. In some counties where they held great estates, however, peers could wield great and often decisive influence. Elections in Shropshire were dominated by the Newport interest; those of Carmarthenshire by the Barons Vaughan (better known by their Irish peerage title as earls of Carbery). More often the county interest was divided – in Cumberland, for example, between the Howards of Naworth (who became earls of Carlisle) and the Lowthers of Whitehaven. There was considerable pressure to avoid the expense and divisiveness of an election contest, and it was common for county elections to be settled at pre-election meetings of the county elite. The lord lieutenant could play a crucial role in securing the necessary compromises. Robert Greville, 4th Baron Brooke, lord lieutenant of Staffordshire, boasted of his success in averting a contest for the county seat after the sitting Member's death in 1662: 'I heard of great contests like to be between the gentry … about the choice of another which … I did endeavour to settle and appease, which happened to have so good success that all the parties agreed'.[28] Failure to secure local agreement could perpetuate long lasting rifts in local society. In Warwickshire Fulke Greville, the 5th Baron Brooke, was determined to control the county together with William Feilding, 3rd earl of Denbigh. In November 1679 he had Sir Richard Newdigate and Thomas Mariot put out of the commission of the peace in retaliation for their standing against the court candidates the previous August; at the 1680 summer assizes Denbigh prosecuted Newdigate for 'a pretended riot'. In July 1681 Lady Newdigate approached Lady Denbigh in an attempt to end the feud between their warring husbands. Lady Denbigh turned her down:

> Time I hope may efface what is past if no new subject be given for unkindness, but my lord was credibly informed that at the last elections Sir Richard to lessen my lord's interest in the country, publicly bid them remember my lord voted not guilty in my lord Stafford's business, which exasperated my lord very much, for what he did according as his conscience and honour directed him, ought not to be mentioned with reproach.[29]

Peers with extensive landed interests and offices were able to deploy their influence over a wide area, in county and borough elections. The Howard family, dukes of Norfolk, were influential in a number of boroughs in the south-east and East Anglia. In 1685 the 7th duke used his interest to support court candidates in Berkshire, Norfolk and Surrey as well as in the boroughs of Arundel, Castle Rising, Horsham, King's Lynn and Thetford. Lords lieutenant were expected to support government candidates in their counties: as secretary of state Robert Spencer, 2nd earl of Sunderland, put it in a letter to them in 1685, they were requested to secure the return of 'people of approved loyalty and affection to government'.[30] The 9th earl of Derby worked at the county elections for Lancashire that year to prevent the election of two sons of peers who had been among Monmouth's leading supporters in the north-west: Richard Savage, Lord Colchester (later 4th Earl Rivers) and Viscount Brandon. Bishops could also deploy their own interest in elections, often on behalf of the government. In Norfolk, Anthony Sparrow, appointed to the diocese of Norwich in 1676, formed a formidable partnership with Robert Paston, Viscount Yarmouth (see below, p. 316). In the west country in 1685 Jonathan Trelawny of Bristol promised to employ his interest with 'such full measures as may be of use in those corporations where I have an helping influence, as well as in such where my authority is absolute'.[31]

Most noblemen saw parliamentary elections as an opportunity to add to the local and national lustre of themselves and their families. The earl of Plymouth used his influence in Droitwich to secure the return of his 16 year-old son in 1685. James Bertie, earl of Abingdon, failed to get his son, aged just 12, returned for Woodstock that same year, although

FIG. 165 *James
Bertie, second son
of James Bertie, earl
of Abingdon, after
Sir Peter Lely. The
younger Bertie was
born in 1674.
Unlike his brother,
destined to succeed
as earl, he had to
wait until coming of
age, in 1695, to find
a seat in parliament,
at New Woodstock.*

his grandmother, Lady Rochester (see above, p. 320), vehemently (but inaccurately) claimed that there were younger Members in the House at the time. Two years later, still underage, he was elected for the much more prestigious Berkshire seat and the following year for Oxfordshire, which he continued to represent until he succeeded as 2nd earl of Abingdon in 1699. When a peer was unable or unwilling to look after his family's electoral interests, it was common for his widow, wife, or mother to do so instead. The duchess of Marlborough famously kept a close eye on politics in Oxfordshire, Woodstock and St Albans while her husband was on campaign in Flanders. Richard Lowther, 2nd Viscount Lonsdale, inherited his father's title and estate in 1700 when he was only eight years old, and his mother Katherine, Viscountess Lonsdale, kept her late husband's political influence alive during her son's minority. The first viscount appears to have provided his wife with specific instructions on his deathbed to promote the candidacy of his uncle Richard Lowther in a by-election held shortly after his death ('in my opinion a very improper legacy to his country, for I never heard that knights of the shire were disposed of by will' grumbled the father of Lowther's opponent).[32] Lady Lonsdale claimed that she was 'resolute to do as my lord would have done had he been alive' and consistently promoted Whig rivals to her husband's old antagonists the Musgraves.[33] Some strong-willed noblewomen were closely involved even while their husbands were alive and in the country. The estate of Edward Montagu, the weak-willed 3rd earl of Sandwich, was the subject of a tug-of-war between his Tory wife Lady Sandwich (daughter of John Wilmot, the notorious 2nd earl of Rochester, and granddaughter of the active electoral patroness, the countess of Rochester) and his Whig uncle Sidney Wortley Montagu, the trustee and principal manager of the estate. In January 1701 the countess of Sandwich decided to pit her own interest against Wortley Montagu in the Huntingdon seat. 'Vive la guerre', her admirer the poet Matthew Prior wrote when he heard that she was promoting the candidacy of Charles Boyle (later 4th earl of Orrery in the Irish peerage and raised to the British peerage in 1711 as Baron Boyle). In a petition against the outcome of the subsequent election, Lord Sandwich was accused of having weighed in on Boyle's behalf:

> with the assistance of others, with swords and clubs, [he] did menace, assault and strike the recorder of the borough and others of the petitioner's voters. Some being wounded, others were carried under a strong guard to give their votes for Mr Boyle, but were not permitted to give their second votes, which they would have done, for the petitioner, nor his friends, could speak with them.

In his maiden speech in the Commons Boyle defended Sandwich from allegations of interference in the election, asserting that he had only been exercising a legitimate influence as lord of the manor and took umbrage at the Commons' insistence that peers remove themselves from all involvement in elections. Boyle and his fellow member for Huntingdon, Francis Wortley Montagu, fought a near-fatal duel over some of the claims.[34]

Family interest and party interest

Although previous elections had seen court candidates pitted against country candidates and 'presbyterians' against 'cavaliers', in the two elections of 1679, the first 'general' elections since 1661, national political concerns were imposed on local rivalries more explicitly than ever before. The Popish Plot crisis and the prospect of a Catholic successor to the throne stimulated a much more partisan politics, and were used both to challenge and to defend powerful local interests. In the second 1679 election in Essex the young 2nd duke of Albemarle, as joint lord lieutenant, attempted to preserve the united front of the county by promoting a local gentleman together with a courtier, a strategy supported by much of the local gentry and clergy. However, an opposition group led by the 3rd Baron Grey of Warke (see above, p. 238), put up 'country' candidates against them. In the rowdy and bitter election that ensued, Albemarle's candidates were trounced. Grey appeared at the election in 'a most sumptuous habit' and horse in 'rich trappings' and then together with his candidate, Henry Mildmay, led a formidable cavalcade:

> about 2000 horse attending him; then the Lord Grey with the colonel began to march into the town, where they were met with near 2000 horse more, and so passing through the town into the field in very good order, with their mouths loudly hollowing for A Mildmay only and crying out, God bless my Lord Grey.[35]

Grey organised the second 1679 Middlesex election as well. In support of Sir Robert Peyton's bid he led a group of voters to the hustings at Brentford (trying to provoke a fight with a company of royal soldiers along the way), where they were joined by another convoy of 1,000 voters led by the duke of Buckingham and the other 'country' candidate for Middlesex, Sir William Roberts.

The political divisions of the late 1670s and 1680s were perpetuated through the labels of Whig and Tory, and came to channel local and electoral as well as parliamentary politics. During the 1690s, although political alignments became complex and unstable, elections were suffused with partisan hostilities. Held every three years under the Triennial Act of 1694, they changed from occasional events into a constant and consuming preoccupation for peers and gentry alike. Not all elections were run along party lines: old contests about a family's standing within the community survived despite the new realities of party politics. The traditional rivalry between the Berkeley and Somerset families in Gloucestershire, for example, persisted even though both men were regarded as Tories. The appointment of Charles Berkeley, 2nd earl of Berkeley, as lord lieutenant of the county in 1708, seen by some as offering the Tories in Gloucester relief 'from the hardships they groan under by the bare-faced bribery of men in power in that place',[36] was greeted with horror by another Tory, the duke of Beaufort, who complained to Robert Harley (later earl of Oxford) that:

> we lie under the greatest hardship that ever men did, to have it given out by all the other side, that this earl of Berkeley has kissed the queen's hand for lord lieutenant and that the interest of her majesty and her officers is to influence all that is possible against us.[37]

Nevertheless, by the first decade of the eighteenth century, many peers were routinely deploying their interest strategically on behalf of a political party and party political leaders jockeyed to secure the support of young peers like William Henry Granville, 3rd earl of Bath, still a minor but in command of prodigious electoral influence in the west country.

A number of peers became key electoral managers. In the elections of the summer of 1702, the earl of Winchilsea, as deputy warden of the Cinque Ports, managed the Cinque Port constituencies for the Tories, sending secretary of state the earl of Nottingham an analysis of electoral prospects in each Kent constituency. Probably the most assiduous electoral manager of all was the 5th Baron Wharton, a central figure in the Whig Junto (see above, p. 276). Wharton inherited his peerage and an estate reputed to be worth £16,000 a year in 1696 and proceeded to build up a powerful influence on behalf of the Whigs. At his most successful, he commanded support in Buckinghamshire (the centre of his estates), Wiltshire (by property in Malmesbury acquired by marriage), and Westmorland and Yorkshire (the foundation of the Wharton patrimony). Wharton also tried, largely unsuccessfully, to inveigle his way into Oxfordshire, dominated by the interest of his Tory brother-in-law, James Bertie, earl of Abingdon. In 1696 he wrecked John Hampden the younger's chances of election in Buckinghamshire after Hampden had suggested that the Rye House plot of 1683 – the alleged assassination attempt on Charles II, which had resulted in the executions of a number of prominent Whigs, and whose falsity was a central point of Whig faith – might have been a

FIG. 166 *Jane Hyde, countess of Clarendon and Rochester (c. 1672–1725), by Michael Dahl, c.1691–2. Jane Hyde married Henry Hyde, the son of the prominent Tory, the earl of Rochester, who became the 2nd earl in 1711, and became 4th earl of Clarendon too on the death of his cousin in 1724. A famous beauty, Jane Hyde was particularly admired by Tory literary figures including Jonathan Swift and Alexander Pope.*

real conspiracy. Hampden, who had himself been caught up in the plot, committed suicide not long afterwards. Ruthless though he might be, even Wharton could be successfully opposed in his heartlands. The antiquarian Browne Willis turned to Wharton's rival Scroop Egerton, 4th earl (later duke) of Bridgwater, when he stood for the small borough of Buckingham with its electorate of only 13, in 1705; he managed to win, though only on a deciding vote cast by a member of the corporation who was brought out of prison for the purpose. At Malmesbury, Wharton tried to extend his influence by buying up burgages (properties that carried the right to vote). He also invested heavily in burgages in Appleby (Westmorland) in

James Greenshields: episcopacy, the Union, and appeal to the House of Lords

eligion had been one of the most difficult issues in the discussions on the Union of England and Scotland, and continued to play a major role in tensions between Scottish and English politicians after the Union. Following the Revolution of 1688 the religious paths to England and Scotland had diverged. Scotland rejected its bishops, and readopted the Presbyterian system for its national church. There remained Episcopalians in Scotland, but they had the status of a dissenting, and sometimes persecuted sect, often regarded as Jacobite sympathisers. Much to the annoyance of the Scots, the Union enabled their Anglican brethren in Westminster to meddle in Scottish affairs by coming to the assistance of the Episcopalians.

James Greenshields was a Scottish Episcopalian minister who was ordained in 1694 by James Ramsay, the deprived bishop of Ross. He served briefly as a curate in Ireland before returning to Scotland in 1709 where he was invited to hold Episcopalian services in Edinburgh. His opponents alleged that he did so as an *agent provocateur* for the Jacobite cause. He was certainly provocative. He moved his meetings from the then suburban Canongate to a house opposite St Giles on the Royal Mile. During the late summer the Edinburgh magistrates moved to close Greenshields' meeting house; when he defied them, Greenshields was imprisoned in the Tolbooth.

In a letter from the Tolbooth to John Sharp, the high Tory archbishop of York, who had expressed grave doubts at the time of the union about its effects on the Episcopal cause in Scotland and who had long believed that Scottish Episcopalian clergymen were subject to persecution by the Presbyterian Kirk, Greenshields expressed his own view that the struggle against Jacobitism was hampered by the persecution:

> It is the great misfortune of the Episcopal interest here that all our surviving bishops, and most of the clergy, the men of very good lives, and even zealous for the church, yet being not well affected to the present government, can't therefore promote her true interest, and therefore have rather

hitherto obstructed than advanced a legal toleration in this place, which was really the reason of this my undertaking ... I thought to do considerable service to the church ...by setting up a meeting house for the use of the English from South Britain, and for these in this place that were well affected both to the queen, and to the Church of England and did not in the least doubt but that the civil government here (who always declared it was not Episcopacy but Jacobitism that they were persecuting, and which gained belief everywhere) would at least connive at this my undertaking.[1]

His Anglican supporters agreed: despite the argument that his ordination had been invalid and allegations that he had sworn to serve James II at his ordination his Edinburgh services included prayers for the queen and Princess Sophia. As a result it was alleged that he 'may probably draw great numbers of the Pretender's friends to join in common prayers for Her Majesty'.[2]

When Greenshields' appeal to the court of session in Scotland was dismissed on the grounds of his invalid orders he took his case to the House of Lords. It was not the first Scottish case to be heard by the House but it was the most controversial. Entertaining it was easily characterized as a deliberate abrogation by the English of the articles of union which had guaranteed Scots religion as well as Scots law and which made no mention of a new appellate jurisdiction at Westminster. A propaganda war turned Greenshields into a celebrity, feted on one side of the border as the heroic defender of the English liturgy and on the other as the perfidious instrument of English oppression. On 1 March 1711 the Lords overturned the magistrates' decision, thus creating *de facto* a toleration for Scots Episcopalians as long as they were prepared to take oaths of allegiance and abjuration. The following year Parliament affirmed its commitment to Episcopalianism in Scotland by passing a Toleration Act. It was the first in a series of Scottish grievances against the way in which the Union had worked in practice.

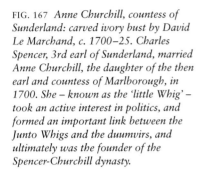

FIG. 167 *Anne Churchill, countess of Sunderland: carved ivory bust by David Le Marchand, c. 1700–25. Charles Spencer, 3rd earl of Sunderland, married Anne Churchill, the daughter of the then earl and countess of Marlborough, in 1700. She – known as the 'little Whig' – took an active interest in politics, and formed an important link between the Junto Whigs and the duumvirs, and ultimately was the founder of the Spencer-Churchill dynasty.*

an attempt to wrest control from his Tory rival, Thomas Tufton, 6th earl of Thanet, pooling his interest there with the bishop of Carlisle, William Nicolson. Wharton's influence in Yorkshire centred on Richmond, where three other families also had electoral interests and where he again invested in burgages. In November 1705 one of his rivals for control of the borough, James Darcy, claimed that Wharton and his supporters had succeeded only 'by splitting of votes and of houses and lands to multiply votes, and by Lord Wharton's meddling with the election, and by bribery and other corrupt practices'.[38] The election of 1708 proved to be the summit of Wharton's achievement, and gave the Junto the extra leverage they needed to demand governmental rewards. The new House of Commons boasted a Whig majority of 60, with Wharton responsible for perhaps 20 of the seats.

Wharton spent £12,000 on his campaigns around the country during the 1705 election campaign. Purchasing burgages was one way to spend ruinous sums. Some burgage holders and voters realized that they had in their hands a much-desired commodity. John Holles, duke of Newcastle, who built up a major electoral interest after he inherited the Cavendish/Newcastle estate from his father-in-law and in 1705 was said to control as many as ten Members of the Commons, complained early in 1710 about Boroughbridge in Yorkshire that 'the buying little single burgages at such extravagant rates has given the townsmen a handle to enhance their prices beyond measure'.[39] When financial difficulties forced Henry Howard, 7th duke of Norfolk, to relinquish control of Castle Rising, a buying war pushed the price of burgages there from between £20 and £30 each to near £300.

Elections were already expensive enough before the Revolution. Now, more frequent and harder fought than before, the growing cost of election campaigns meant that serious involvement was becoming a hobby for only the wealthiest of aristocrats and oligarchs. In 1710 Robert Darcy, 3rd earl of Holdernesse, was said to have abandoned plans to promote the election of his brother for Yorkshire 'only on the account of the vast expense (which he sustained last time) … he declines it when he's pretty sure of success and 'tis only for want of money that we shrink.'[40] 'Interest', made out of local landownership and local prestige, close connections to the local community and services, large and small, to local people, would remain the essential element of local electoral and political success for peers and gentry for many years afterwards. But in a world imbued with party politics, in which frequent election campaigns were run by party managers on a nationwide basis, the way in which elites competed for local and regional ascendancy was changing. Family interest might be tempered or shaded by party interest; the interest created by prestige and service alone might be overcome by the interest of money. The political world – and the position of the nobility and the House of Lords within it – that welcomed the arrival of George of Hanover as king in September 1714 was already a very different one from that which had welcomed Charles II in May 1660.

Sacheverell and the peace, 1710–14

In retrospect, it was a catastrophic mistake for the ministry to rise to the inflammatory sermon preached by the high Churchman Henry Sacheverell before the lord mayor of London in St Paul's Cathedral on 5 November 1709. But such a provocative challenge could scarcely be ignored. The sermon, on 'The perils of false brethren in church and state', disparaged the Revolution, vilified the ministry in general and Sidney Godolphin, earl of Godolphin, in particular as enemies of the Church, and suggested that the 1689 Toleration Act had resulted in schism and heresy.

When John Churchill, duke of Marlborough, asked what should be done with Sacheverell, Thomas Wharton, 5th Baron Wharton, was said to have replied, 'Quash him and damn him'.[1] They chose to proceed by impeachment on the grounds of seditious libel, calculating that such a high profile trial would frighten their high church enemies into silence. It was an exceptionally risky strategy, as many of them recognised. Lionel Sackville, the young 7th earl of Dorset, called it a 'nasty trial' and hoped it would be over as soon as possible.[2] Instead, the trial became a phenomenal public event. The prosecution crystallised growing popular discontent over the Whigs and their war, and turned Sacheverell into a popular hero. As a temporary structure was built in Westminster Hall, admission tickets were like gold dust; the hard-drinking bully Sacheverell became a favourite among Tory women, who bought the many versions on sale of his engraved portrait. Sacheverell's name was even said to be 'a ticket which admits you into the best favours of all the Phyllises [prostitutes] in Drury Lane'. More to the point, rather than frightening them into silence, the prosecution rallied Tories to the cause. While Sacheverell was held in comfortable custody he received a stream of visitors and gifts (including a crate of claret and a purse of fifty guineas from Henry Somerset, 2nd duke of Beaufort) and worked with the ablest Tory lawyers on an unapologetic eighteen page answer to the charges. Thomas Leigh, 2nd Baron Leigh, rarely attended the House but he struggled in from Warwickshire despite his gout so 'that he might have an opportunity of showing his zeal for the Church'.[3] Richard Verney, 11th Baron Willoughby de Broke, who had attended Parliament only twice since 1702, turned up assiduously to support Sacheverell. Riots in his support broke out in London and elsewhere. Wharton's speech pressing for a conviction brought out the fundamental divide between the two parties:

> If the Revolution is not lawful, many in that House, and vast numbers without, were guilty of blood, murder, rapine and injustice; and the queen herself is no lawful queen, since the best title she had to the crown, was her Parliamentary title, founded on the Revolution.[4]

Sacheverell was convicted by the House of Lords on 20 March 1710 by 69 votes to 52. The vote was narrower than expected and many of the peers who voted him guilty did so with little enthusiasm. An exemplary punishment was out of the question, and the one imposed – a three-year ban on preaching – was derisory. 'So all this bustle and fatigue ends in no more but a suspension of three years ... and burning his sermon at the Old Exchange', Godolphin bitterly complained. Sacheverell was exuberantly celebrated with nationwide bonfires, bellringing and drunken carousing, and 'huzza'd by the mob like a prizefighter'. Marlborough was shocked by how many peers who usually supported the court had defected to Sacheverell's cause – he asked uncomprehendingly 'how were these lords influenced to be for Sacheverell?'[5] He and Godolphin, the duumvirs, were convinced that the answer lay in the intrigues of their former ministerial colleague, Robert Harley.

After the humiliation of Sacheverell's trial the power of the duumvirs began to disintegrate. Over the next few months (while Sacheverell made a victory tour through the most Tory parts of the country) Harley began to build an alternative ministry through an alliance with independent Whig peers, in particular Charles Talbot, duke of Shrewsbury, who had voted for Sacheverell on 20 March, and he coaxed the queen to support it. Shrewsbury was appointed lord

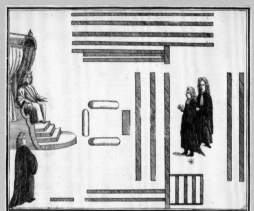

FIG. 168 *A broadside verse in support of Sacheverell, and showing schematically the layout of Westminster Hall for the trial.*

FIG. 169 *One of many pamphlets and satirical prints inspired by the Sacheverell trial, this is a direct response to a print that had accused Sacheverell of being in alliance with the devil, popery and the Jacobites. The accused cleric is shown sitting companionably with a bishop. He 'flurts' (i.e. jerks) his pen at the devil who is forced to fly away; a papal tiara and cope lie rejected on the ground.*

chamberlain in April. Godolphin, kept in the dark, protested furiously to the queen when he found out:

> to bring him into your service and into your business at this time, just after his being in a public open conjunction in every vote with the whole body of the Tories, and in a private constant correspondence, and caballing with Mr Harley in everything, what consequence can this possibly have, but to make every man that is now in your cabinet council, … run from it, as they would from the plague.[6]

Godolphin was dismissed in August. Harley returned to the council and became chancellor of the exchequer. He tried to prevent some court-supporting Whigs from leaving with Godolphin, hoping to maintain a moderate mixed ministry in which his own enemies amongst the Tories would have no place. He told the lord chancellor, William Cowper, Baron Cowper, that it was 'a Whig game intended at bottom'. Cowper refused to believe it and, convinced 'that things were plainly put into Tories' hands', left office.[7]

The elections of October 1710, called early in order to reverse the Whig majority in the Commons, succeeded rather better than Harley had intended. Still in the grip of Sacheverellite fever, the electorate delivered a Tory landslide, leaving Harley precisely in the position he had hoped to avoid, dependent on the

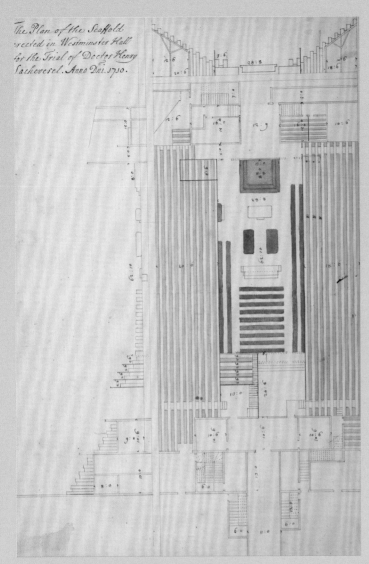

The Plan of the Scaffold erected in Westminster Hall for the Trial of Doctor Henry Sacheverell. Anno Dni. 1710.

FIG. 170 *A plan of Westminster Hall for the trial of Sacheverell, showing the construction of an arrangement close to that of the House of Lords' usual chamber.*

votes of determined Tories in the House of Commons, many of them eager young zealots sitting for the first time. Looking with intense suspicion on Harley's preference for moderates, they organised themselves into the October Club and openly declared that they planned 'to have every Whig turn'd out, and not to suffer that the new ministry shou'd shake hands as they do with old'.[8] Tories prepared, as Nottingham told Harley at a meeting around February 1711, to 'make it impracticable for [the Whigs] ever to rise again'.

Early in 1711 the Tories launched their well-planned assault against the previous ministry and its works. In January they raised the case of the Scottish episcopalian minister James Greenshields (see above, p. 330). A debate in the House of Lords on the con-

duct of the war in Spain in 1706–7 resulted in the censure of the three generals in charge of the campaign (allies of the duumvirs) for advising an offensive strategy. Matters began to move beyond Harley's control, although a desperate attempt by a French spy under interrogation to assassinate him with his penknife in March 1711, and the emotional reaction to it, did help to subdue the October Club and get key financial legislation through Parliament. Fully recovered by May, Harley was appointed lord treasurer and ennobled as earl of Oxford. But he was still trapped between the two parties. After Rochester's death in 1711 it was said that 'the Tories are a party without a head. And the treasurer is a head without a party.'[9]

An Alphabetical LIST of the Right Honourable the LORDS, and also of those Members of the Honourable House of COMMONS, in England and Wales, that were for Dr. HENRY SACHEVERELL.

Een Alphabetise LYST van de seer achtbare HEEREN, als mede van de Leden van het seer agtbaar Huys van de GEMEENTENS, in Engeland en Walles, die geweest zyn voor Doctor HENRY SACHEVERELL.

Henricus Sacheverell S.T.P.

DUKES of
Beaufort,
Buckingham,
Hamilton,
Leeds,
Northumberland,
Ormond,
Shrewsbury.

EARLS of
Abingdon,
Anglesey,
Berkshire,
Denbeigh,
Jersey,
Mar,
Northampton,
Northesk,
Nottingham,
Pembroke,
Poulet,
Plymouth,
Rochester,
Scarsdale,
Scarborough,
Sussex,
Thanet,
Wymes,
Yarmouth.

VISCOUNTS of
Say and Sele,
Weymouth.

BISHOPS of
Bath and Wells,
Chester,
Durham,
London,
Rochester,
York, Archbishop.

BARONS
Berkley of Stratton,
Butler,
Chandos,
Conway,
Craven,
Dartmouth,
Ferrers,
Gernsey,
Guilford,
Haversham,
Howard of Escrick,
Leigh,
Lexington,
Leimpster,
North and Grey,
Osburn,
Stawell,
Willoughby of Brook.

Of the House of COMMONS.
Annesly, Francis
Annesley, Hon. Arthur
Arundel, Francis, Junior
Ackland, Richard
Alcock, Lawrence
Archer, Andrew
Aislabie, John
Blagrave, Anthony
Bromley, John
Bunbury, Sir. Hen. Bar.
Buller, James
Bankes, Sir Jacob, Kt.
Borlace, John
Bankes, John
Bathust, Allen
Bromley, William
Beaumont, Sir Geo. Bar.
Baldwyn, Acton
Barker, Sir William Bar.
Bruce, Lord, Right Hon. Cha.
Bruce, Hon. Rob.
Bruce, Hon James
Benson, Rob.
Beverley, Rob.
Bland, Sir John Bar.
Boteler, John
Bulkeley, Right Honourable Richard Lord Viscount
Bertie, Honourable Henry

Bertie, Charles
Bertie, the Honourable Henry
Cotton, John Hynde
Conyers, John
Curzon, John
Courtenay, Sir William, Bar.
Courtenay, George
Conyers, Thomas
Child, Sir Richard, Bar.
Cox, Charles
Cecil, the Honourable Charles
Colston, Edward, Jun.
Campion Henry
Cotes, John
Currance, Clement
Conway Sir. John Bar.
Cary, William
Chaffin, Thomas
Cartwright, Thomas
Dering, Sir Cholmley, Bar.
Drake, Sir William, Kt. and Bar.
Dolben, Sir Gilbert, Bart.
Davers, Sir Robert, Bar.
Duncombe, Edward
Duncombe, Sir Charles, Kt.
Down, Right Honourable Hen. Lord Viscount
Duncombe, Francis
Docminique, Paul
Etheridge, Sir James, Kt.
Eliot, Edward
Eden, Sir Robert, Bar.
Ettricke William
Eversfeild, Charles
Fownes, Richard
Foley, Thomas
Freeman, Ralph, Jun.

Fleetwood, Henry
Ferrier, Richard
Forster, Thomas, Jun.
Farringdon, Sir Richard, Bart.
Fox, Charles
Foley, Edward
Griffith, William
Grahme, James
Garrard, Sir Samuel, Bart.
Gape, John
Gwyn, Francis
Girdler, Joseph, Serjeant at Law.
Greville, the Honourable Francis
Greville, Honourable Dodington
Grandville, George
Gorges, Henry
Halsey, Thomas
Hyde, Right Honourable Henry Lord
Herne, Thomas
Hooper, Nicolas, one of her Majesties Serjeants at Law.
Herne, Nathaniel
Herne, Frederick
Harley, Edward
Heysham, Robert
Heysham, William
Harvey Edward
Halsford, Richard
Holmes, Henry
Hamer, Sir Thomas, Bar.
Hide, Robert
Harvey, William
Hungerford, John
Harcourt, Sir Simon, Kt.
Harley, Thomas
Harley, the Right Honourable Robert

How, Sir Richard, Bar.
Isham, Sir Justinian, Bar.
Jenkinson, Sir Robert, Bar.
Johnson, James
Johnson, Sir Henry, Kt.
Johnson, William
Jeffreys ——————
Lewen, William
Lister, Thomas
Levinz, William
Lambert, Edmund
Long, Sir James, Bar.
Langharne, John
Lawson, Gilfrid
Manley, John
Morice, Sir Nicolas, Bar.
Manaton, Henry
Mervin, Richard
Meres, Sir Thomas, Kt.
Moor, Arthur
Medlicot, Thomas
Milburn, Clayton
Mordaunt, Sir John, Bart.
Middleton, Sir Richard, Bar.
Mansell, Sir Thomas of Margam, Bar.
Nicholas, Edward
North, the Hon. Charles
Newland, Sir George Kt.
Oglethorp, Theophilus
Pitt, Robert
Pendarves, Alexander
Praed, John
Pole, Sir William, Bart.
Pitt, George
Prise, John, of Westeston
Probey, John
Parker, Christopher
Palmer, Jeffery
Powys, Sir Tho. her Majesty's serjeant at Law
Portman, Henry
Prowse, John, deceas'd
Phelips, Edward
Paget, the Right Honourable Henry
Parsons, Sir John, Knight
Popham, Francis
Packington, Sir John Bart.
Price, Lewis
Renda, Thomas
Rolle, Robert
Rowney, Thomas
Randyl, Morgan
Stonehouse, Sir John, Bart.
Scobell, Francis
Seymour, Sir Edward, Bart.
Strangeways, Thomas
Strangeways, Thomas, Jun.
Scudamore, Right Honourable James, Lord Viscount
Shuttleworth, Richard
Stewart, Simeon
Stephens, William
Swift, Samuel
Sharpe, John
Stapylton, Sir Bryan, Bart.
Seymour, Sir Henry, Bart.
Shepheard, Samuel, Jun.
Shakerley. Peter
Trevanion, John
Trelawny, Harry
Trotman, Samuel
Trevelyan, Sir John, Bart.
Vaughan, Richard
Vaughan, Edward
Windsor, the Hon. Dixey
Wood, Nicolas
Webb, Thomas
Walpole, Horatio
Ward, John, of Capesthorn
Winstanley, James
Wynne, Richard
Withers, Sir William, Kt.
Ward, John
Windsor Right Hon. Thomas Lord Viscount
Wentworth, the Hon. Thomas
Whitlock, Sir William, Kt.
Walter, Sir John, Bart.
Ware, Sir Francis, Bart.
Wortseley, John
Weld, Joseph, Serjeant at Law.
Winnington, Edward
Wharton, Sir Michael, Bart.
Williams, Sir Edward, Bart.
Williams, Sir William, Bart.
Willoughby of Eresby, Rt. Hon. Peregrine, Lord.

FIG. 171 A list, published in English and Dutch, of the peers and Members of the House of Commons who voted for Sacheverell in the various divisions on the impeachment.

The peace and the succession

The arguments over the war and the Church reached a climax in the session of 1711–12. After Oxford came to power in the summer of 1710, the ministry had opened its own negotiations with France (without involving Britain's allies). To the delight of most Tories, peace preliminaries had been agreed in September 1711. For most Whigs, the headlong rush towards peace was sheer folly. In Marlborough's view the negotiations 'did sully the triumphs and glories' (many of them his own) of the queen's reign.[10] A few Tories agreed with him. Daniel Finch, 2nd earl of Nottingham, the veteran Tory leader and opponent of Oxford, was deeply hostile to a settlement that would leave Philip V on the throne of Spain. In return for his, and his supporters', backing on the peace, the Whigs agreed not to oppose Nottingham's cherished ban on occasional conformity in the Lords, an achievement which Nottingham hoped, vainly, might 'reconcile me to my old-friends... [and] bring 'em to think better of my opinion about the peace'.[11]

The House of Lords would be a key battle-ground as Oxford prepared to force the peace through Parliament. Shrewsbury nervously pointed out the weakness of the ministry's support there, 'so many of our friends in the Lords House being dead and many more soured or at least become lukewarm by disappointments in their expectations'.[12] Oxford hastily prepared for the confrontation with six new peerages or promotions for supporters in early September (including, highly controversially, an English dukedom, of Brandon, for James Hamilton, the Scottish 4th duke of Hamilton) and by lobbying Tory peers to come to the House to 'disappoint the designs of all that are enemies to peace'.[13] The Tory Basil Feilding, 4th earl of Denbigh, responded that he had not intended to come to Westminster so early, 'knowing that our house used to have little to do at the first setting till the Commons had cut us up some work, but I find now the case is altered. It's we that are doing that and indeed fine work'.[14] Nottingham joined battle on 7th December when he carried the House by a single vote on a motion to condemn any

FIG. 172 *Francis Atterbury (1663–1732), champion of the Tory clergy against what was perceived to be an erastian episcopate, became bishop of Rochester in 1713. At the death of Queen Anne he accepted the Hanoverian succession but he was widely believed to have Jacobite sympathies and was implicated in a plot against the crown for which he was arrested in 1722. In the absence of adequate legal evidence he was deprived of his spiritual dignities and exiled by means of a bill of pains and penalties.*

peace that left Spain in the possession of Louis XIV's family. Shortly afterwards the occasional conformity bill sailed rapidly through both Houses, as Oxford, dependent on Tories for the peace, barely put up any resistance to it. Upsetting 'Dismal' Nottingham's calculations, the achievement of occasional conformity won few Tories to his attitude on the peace. (He grumbled bitterly about their ingratitude and their failure to recognise his success over the bill, 'their darling bill which they could never have had but by me and ... they know the Great-Man [Oxford] would never have given it them nor suffered it if he could have helped it'.[15]) But a further series of ministerial defeats on 20-22 December, including one over Hamilton's English dukedom, underlined that Oxford would almost certainly fail in his bid to secure the Treaty.

At some point over the next few days he decided

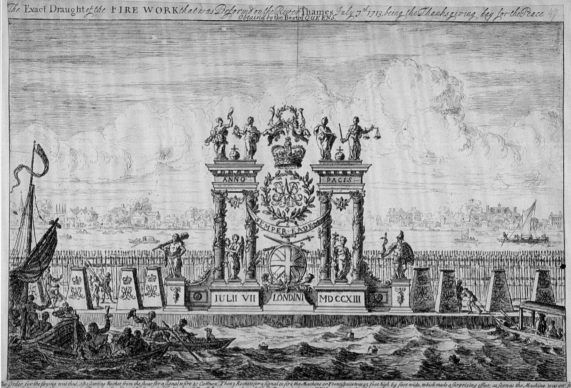

FIG. 173 *Fireworks to celebrate the conclusion of the Treaty of Utrecht in July 1713.*

on an unprecedented mass creation of peers. On 31 December 1711 and 1 January 1712 letters patent were issued creating ten new peers; a further two were summoned by writ of acceleration. All were, in the words of the Huguenot and Whig journalist Abel Boyer, 'blindly devoted to the court'.[16] It was an outrageous piece of political chicanery. It was the queen's undoubted right to create peers; and most of the new crop had unexceptionable credentials to seats in the Lords. James Compton, styled Lord Compton, was the heir to the earldom of Northampton and was called up by writ of acceleration in his father's barony, as was Charles Bruce, styled Lord Bruce, who was the heir to the earldom of Ailesbury; Thomas Windsor, Viscount Windsor, was already an Irish peer and an uncle of Other Windsor, 2nd earl of Plymouth; Henry Paget was the heir to a barony; George Hay, Viscount Dupplin, was a Scots peer and Oxford's son-in-law. Nevertheless, the mass creation was greeted with howls of derision from the Whigs, one of whom (Wharton) enquired whether the new members 'voted by their foreman, like a jury'.[17] Even with his 'dozen', Oxford had to cajole and coerce members in order to get his way on the peace. In spite of further Whig efforts to disrupt it during the summer, by raising in

the House the 'restraining orders' that had prevented the commander-in-chief James Butler, 2nd duke of Ormond, from engaging the enemy during the period of negotiation, the peace was ratified and on 30 March 1713 the Treaty of Utrecht was signed. By September, it was clear that Oxford had survived the storm.

Oxford was at the height of his power in 1712. 'These people', the Junto Whig Charles Spencer, 3rd earl of Sunderland, wrote disgustedly to Nottingham, 'have by corruption, and one way or other, got such a majority in both Houses, that … it seems to be running our heads against a wall'.[18] Despite his despondency, over the remaining two years of Anne's life, Oxford's power drained away. A new rival emerged, his protégé, the ambitious Henry St John. Raised to the peerage in July 1712 as Viscount Bolingbroke, St John had been irritated not to receive the earldom that he craved (see above, p. 52); sent to negotiate the peace at Utrecht, he had fallen out with Oxford over its terms and his contacts with the Jacobite pretender. The intrigues which surrounded the Treaty of Utrecht

FIG. 174 *Queen Anne and the knights of the Garter, by Peter Angelis: a garter ceremony, believed to be that of 4 August 1713, when the knights installed in the order included Charles Talbot, duke of Shrewsbury, Henry Somerset, 2nd duke of Beaufort, Henry Grey, duke of Kent, Robert Harley, earl of Oxford, John Poulett, earl Poulett, and Charles Mordaunt, 3rd earl of Peterborough.*

had served to reawaken concerns about a possible Jacobite restoration; the queen's illness over the winter of 1712–13 was a reminder of the fragility of peace and stability at home. The succession once again became a major preoccupation for British politicians, as most Whigs and some Tories began to suspect that Oxford was covertly supporting the Jacobites. The achievement of the peace had itself removed the principal glue that kept Oxford and the Tories together. Tories expected that their support over the past two years would now receive its reward, with a purge of Whigs from the administration and a wholehearted pursuit of Tory measures.

In advance of the Parliamentary session which opened in April 1713, a coalition of Whigs and pro-Hanoverian Tories mobilised to protect the Protestant succession. They secured the rejection in the Commons of the commercial treaty with France negotiated by Bolingbroke, who assumed that the opposition had been, if not orchestrated, at least secretly encouraged by Oxford. The Scots hammered at Oxford's door, too, complaining about the way in which Scottish national interests had been ignored or belittled. Scots in the Lords moved to dissolve the Union: the ministry saved it on a majority of only four votes. The malt tax bill, whose application to Scotland had been regarded as a breach of the articles of union, passed its second reading in the Lords by a majority of only two (see above, p. 304).

An election in the summer of 1713 consolidated Tory dominance and set the scene for the final crisis

The Right Honble Charles Earl of Sunderland. &c.

FIG. 175 *Charles Spencer, 3rd earl of Sunderland, mezzotint by John Simon after Sir Godfrey Kneller. Sunderland, the second son of the 2nd earl (see above, p. 134), was closely associated with the Junto Whigs from his entry into the House of Commons in 1695. His marriage in 1700 to Lady Anne Churchill, daughter of John Churchill, duke of Marlborough made him an important conduit between the Junto and the duumvirs (see fig. 167). After his succession to the earldom in 1702, he became secretary of state in 1706, until sacked in the aftermath of the Sacheverell trial in 1710. He eventually returned to office after the accession of George I, jointly heading a ministry from 1717 which collapsed amid the scandal of the South Sea Bubble in 1720.*

of Anne's reign. The queen's worsening illness and expected death hung over the session. Oxford's relationship with her, so important to his political power, broke down. In September 1713 he asked her to confer the dukedom of Newcastle on his son, recently married to the old duke's daughter. She refused. She was disgusted when, after the death of his own daughter Elizabeth, marchioness of Carmarthen, he turned to drink to drown his sorrows and the intense pressure he was now under. As the queen's illness worsened and she became more querulous she believed that Oxford was neglecting her; Bolingbroke willingly supplied his place as he chipped away at Oxford's tenuous hold on the parliamentary Tories.

Throughout the gruelling session of 1714 Oxford and Bolingbroke battled for leadership of the Tories, and Hanoverian Tories and Whigs struggled to bring down a ministry which they had little confidence would secure the succession. In April 1714 the Lords debated whether the ministry was putting the Protestant succession in danger. It survived a vote by just twelve votes – so low a majority 'that it may be said they have got a mortal wound'.[19] Bolingbroke seized on the schism bill, a measure to suppress dissenting schools, as an opportunity to wrench the Tories from Oxford. If Oxford opposed it, he would lose the last vestiges of his credibility with Tories; if he supported it he would alienate the Whigs. In a vintage performance of customary ambiguity, he managed to appear to be doing both, or neither.

The struggle between the two ministers continued throughout the spring and summer of 1714, rumour sometimes predicting the triumph of Oxford, sometimes that of Bolingbroke. As late as 17 July it was 'the chat of the Town' that Oxford 'will hold where he is' unless he wished to resign and become a duke.[20] Ten days later he was dismissed. Five days after that, on the morning of Sunday, 1 August 1714, Queen Anne was dead.

Epilogue

The Hanoverian succession and the 1719 peerage bill

Despite the tensions of early 1714, on the death of Queen Anne the arrangements made for the transition of power to the new Hanoverian king under the 1706 Regency Act rolled smoothly into action. King George I's nominations to the regency council were disclosed at a privy council meeting the day the queen died. Apart from three leading Hanoverian Tories (Daniel Finch, 2nd earl of Nottingham; Montagu Bertie, 2nd earl of Abingdon and Arthur Annesley, 5th earl of Anglesey) they were all Whigs, although two Tories had turned down an invitation to participate. The king was proclaimed that afternoon and even though it was a Sunday, Parliament met in the evening so that the assembled peers could take the oaths. The new king arrived on 18 September, amid scenes of celebration throughout London. He soon made his preference for the Whigs and his dislike for Robert Harley, earl of Oxford, very clear. He did not even attempt to construct a balanced ministry. 'From the changes that are made' wrote Oxford's brother Edward Harley,

> it is easy to conclude what is further to be expected. It's surely in vain to withstand such a torrent, therefore humbly hope you will only pursue those measures that will most conduce to your own ease and safety, which in my poor opinion would be to get out of town as soon as possible.[1]

The Whig bias was visible too in the promotions to the peerage of October. Parliament was dissolved on 15 January 1715 and in the elections that followed the Tories were routed. If the Tory split of 1714 had started the decline in the party's fortunes, the king's partiality for the Whigs was decisive. In the new Parliament the Whigs sought to punish their enemies. Tories of all hues found themselves tainted with allegations of Jacobitism and pushed into the political wilderness. Two of them,

Henry St John, Viscount Bolingbroke and James Butler, 2nd duke of Ormond, fled to France. In July 1715, Oxford was impeached by the House of Commons; the long series of charges against him included the creations of 1712, an attempt 'at one fatal blow, as far as in him lay, to destroy the freedom and independency of the House of Lords, the great ornament and nearest support of the imperial crown of these realms'.[2]

After the failure of the Jacobite rebellion of 1715, the Whigs consolidated their hold on power. The 1716 Septennial Act, replacing elections every three years with elections every seven, meant that the existing Whig Parliament would remain in being until 1722. It helped to calm party rivalries, at the cost of violating principles that had once been at the core of the ideology of the Whigs (for the Triennial Act of 1694 had been regarded as one of the most significant Whig achievements).

Peers were painfully aware of threats to the dignity and exclusivity of their order. Indeed, alarmists could point to a rapid increase in the pace of creations and promotions in the peerage after the accession of George I – twenty-two promotions and fifteen new peers in the four years up to the end of 1718, compared to fifteen promotions and twenty-five creations by Queen Anne in her whole twelve years. In 1719 a concerted effort was made to halt a further slide. The peerage bill of that year played on the growing concerns that the peerage could easily be emasculated by an unscrupulous ministry. It originated in the factional politics of the Whig party, and was designed by one faction, that of James Stanhope, earl of Stanhope, and Charles Spencer, 3rd earl of Sunderland, to prevent another, that of Sir Robert Walpole and Charles, 2nd Viscount Townshend, from establishing their control over the House of Lords. The bill imposed severe restrictions on the royal prerogative of creating new peers. It also replaced the elective Scottish representative peers with a similar number of Scots peers who would have a hereditary right to sit in the House of Lords. It would have virtually frozen the size of the House, preventing the addition of any more than six new peers and replacements for those whose hereditary line failed. Its supporters claimed that it would create a more independent House of Lords, less susceptible to ministerial pressure. Its detractors worried that the peerage was already independent enough. According to one newspaper, the '*Moderator*', whose author identified himself as a 'whimsical' (i.e. a pro-Hanoverian Tory), the bill would add thirty-one new peers to the House. Not only were the privileges of the peers, he argued, 'very extraordinary above the rest of their fellow-sub-

jects, that a commoner cannot wish to see the species increased' but the
bill would diminish the prerogative of the crown, threatened to promote
unrest in Scotland and might be used to justify the establishment of a
standing army.[3] According to Robert Walpole, its most effective opponent,
the bill was likely to destroy the balance between the two Houses

FIG. 176 *The arrival of George I at St James's Palace, London, in September 1714.*

> and consequently subvert the whole constitution, by causing one of
> the three powers, which are now dependent on each other, to
> preponderate in the scale. The crown is dependent upon the Commons
> by the power of granting money; the Commons are dependent on the
> crown by the power of dissolution: the Lords will now be made
> independent of both.[4]

The failure of the first systematic effort to rebalance the constitutional
relationship between the Lords and the Commons since the Civil War, and
the last for many years more, showed not only that reform of the House

of Lords was a matter of exceptional difficulty but also that governments were reluctant to encourage the development of an upper House less susceptible to government pressure. The House grew in size during the eighteenth century, even more so after 1784 when William Pitt the younger used peerage creations to bolster his new ministry in a much more systematic fashion than Oxford had ever done, but attendance levels fell.

The Lords would continue to produce occasional upsets for the administration. They were responsible in 1716 for the defeat of the select vestries bill; they caused major problems for the ministry over the excise bill in 1733; and the scale of opposition in the Lords to the cider bill in 1763 forced the resignation of the king's favourite, John Stuart, 3rd earl of Bute (in the Scottish peerage). Opposition in the Lords again caused difficulties for the administration during the regency crisis of 1788–9. Even more, Members of the House continued to be an active governing class. They dominated the political and social life of the nation, monopolising office in national and local government and senior posts in the military, the diplomatic corps and at the king's court. They remained intensely aware of their status as a privileged elite, convinced that they were born to exercise power over the great mass of the people. Complacent about their position in political and social life, the lords temporal and spiritual expected the House of Lords to serve their interests and regarded it as a fundamental constitutional truth that in serving the needs and expectations of the upper ranks of society the House served those of the nation as a whole.

Notes

REFERENCES

The following abbreviations or abbreviated titles are used throughout the notes:

Abbott	*The writings and speeches of Oliver Cromwell,* ed. W.C. Abbott (reprint, 4 vols., 1988)
Add.	BL, Additional mss.
Ailesbury Mems.	*Memoirs of Thomas, earl of Ailesbury written by himself* (2 vols., 1890)
Bath	Bath mss. at Longleat House Wiltshire
BIHR	*Bulletin of the Institute of Historical Research*
BL	British Library (manuscript collections)
Bodl.	Bodleian Library (manuscript collections)
Bolingbroke Corresp.	Henry St John, Viscount Bolingbroke, *Letters and correspondence, public and private, of Viscount Bolingbroke: during the time he was secretary of state to Queen Anne; with state papers ... And a translation of the foreign letters* (1798)
Boyer, *Anne Annals*	Abel Boyer, *A History of the reign of Queen Anne: digested into annals* (10 vols., 1703–10)
Burnet, *History*	*Burnet's History of my own time* ed. Osmund Airy, (2 vols, 1897–1900)
Burnet, *History* (1833)	*Bishop Burnet's History of his own time* (6 vols., 1833)
Burton's Diary	*The Parliamentary Diary of Thomas Burton, MP for Westmorland from 1653–59* ed. John Towill Rutt (1828)
CCSP	*Calendar of the Clarendon State Papers preserved in the Bodleian Library* eds O. Ogle, W.H. Bliss et. al. (5 vols., 1869–1970)
Chatsworth	Chatsworth muniments at Chatsworth House, Derbyshire
CJ	*Journal of the House of Commons*
Clarendon, *Life*	Edward Hyde, earl of Clarendon, *The Life of Edward earl of Clarendon* (Oxford, 1857)

Clarendon, *Corr.*	*The Correspondence of Henry Hyde, earl of Clarendon* ed. S.W. Singer, (1828)
Clarke, *Life of James II*	J.S. Clarke, *Life of James II, edited from the King's own Memoirs* (1816)
Cobbett, *Parl. Hist.*	William Cobbett, *The Parliamentary History of England from the earliest time to the year 1803* (36 vols., 1820)
CSP Dom.	*Calendar of State Papers, Domestic*
CTB	*Calendar of Treasury Books*
Eg.	Egerton MSS, British Library
Evelyn, *Diary*	*The Diary of John Evelyn* ed. Esmond S. De Beer (6 vols., 1955)
EHR	*English Historical Review*
Gregg, *Queen Anne*	Edward Gregg, *Queen Anne* (1980)
Haley, *First Earl of Shaftesbury*	K.H.D. Haley, *The first earl of Shaftesbury* (Oxford, 1968)
HHM	Hatfield House manuscripts
HMC	*Historical Manuscripts Commission*
Holmes, *British Politics*	G.S. Holmes, *British politics in the Age of Anne* (revised edn., 1987)
Hist. Parl. Commons, 1690–1715	*History of Parliament: The Commons, 1690–1715* ed. D.W. Hayton, Eveline Cruickshanks and S.N. Handley (5 vols, 2002)
Hist. Parl. Commons, 1715–1754	*History of Parliament: The Commons, 1715–1754* ed. Romney Sedgwick (2 vols, 1970)
'Letter from a Person of Quality'	*A Letter from a person of quality* in John Locke, *An Essay Concerning Toleration* eds J.R. and Philip Milton (2006)
Letters and Memorials of State	Letters and memorials of State...written and collected by Sir Philip Sydney,... ed. Arthur Collins (1746)
LJ	*Journal of the House of Lords*
Luttrell, *Brief Relation*	Narcissus Luttrell, *Brief historical relation of state affairs 1678–1714* (1857)
Marlborough-Godolphin Corresp.	*The Marlborough-Godolphin correspondence* ed. Henry L. Snyder (3 vols, 1975)
Poems and Letters of Andrew Marvell	*The poems and letters of Andrew Marvell,* ed. H.M. Margoliouth (revised edn. 1971),
Mellerstain Letters	Mellerstain House, Berwickshire, Mellerstain Letters
Morrice Entring Bk.	*The entring book of Roger Morrice (1677–1691)* ed. Mark Goldie et al. (6 vols, 2007)
NAS	National Archives of Scotland
Nicolson, *London Diaries*	William Nicolson, *The London Diaries of William Nicolson, bishop of Carlisle, 1702–18* ed. Clyve Jones and Geoffrey Holmes (Oxford, 1985)

Pepys, *Diary*
Diary of Samuel Pepys ed. R. Latham and W. Matthews (Berkely, 1970–83)

Prideaux Letters
Humphrey Prideaux, *Letters of Humphrey Prideaux, sometime dean of Norwich, to John Ellis, sometime under-secretary of state, 1674–1722* (Camden n.s., xv, 1875)

Reresby Mems.
John Reresby, *Memoirs and travels of Sir John Reresby, Bt.* ed. A. Browning (2nd edn., 1991)

Robbins, *Wharton*
Christopher A. Robbins, *The earl of Wharton and Whig party politics, 1679–1715* (1992)

Somerville, *King of Hearts*
Dorothy Hunter Somerville, *The king of hearts: Charles Talbot, duke of Shrewsbury* (1962)

Sidney, *Diary*
Diary of the times of Charles the Second, by the Honourable Henry Sidney ed. R.W. Blencowe (2 vols, 1843)

Sidney, *Discourses*
Algernon Sidney, *Discourses concerning government* (1698)

Swift, *Journal to Stella*
Jonathan Swift, *Journal to Stella* ed. Harold Williams (2 vols, 1948)

Timberland, *Hist. and Procs.*
History and proceedings of the House of Lords (1742)

TNA
The National Archives, Kew

UNL
University of Nottingham Manuscripts and Special Collections

Vernon-Shrewsbury corr.
Letters illustrative of the reign of William III… addressed to the duke of Shrewsbury by James Vernon ed. G.P.R. James (1841)

Wentworth Pprs.
The Wentworth Papers ed. J.J. Cartwright (1883)

The House of Lords restored, 1660–61 (pp. 2–4)

1. *CJ*, vi, 132.
2. *CJ*, vii, 879-80.
3. *Letters and Memorials of State*, ed. Collins, ii. 685.
4. *LJ*, xi, 48.
5. *Letters and Memorials of State*, ed. Collins, ii. 722.

CHAPTER 1: 'The ancient land mark': the House of Lords in the constitutional landscape (pp. 5–35)

1. *His majesties answer to the xix propositions* (Cambridge edn., 1642), 14.
2. Henry Parker, *Jus populi* (1644), 61.
3. Richard Overton, *The commoners complaint* (1647), 2.
4. *CJ*, vi, 111.
5. *The political works of James Harrington*, ed. J.G.A. Pocock (1977), 172.
6. Abbott, iv, 412-13.
7. Abbott, iv, 417.
8. *Burton's Diary*, ii, 391.
9. *Burton's Diary*, ii, 390.
10. Abbott, iv, 729-30.
11. Burton's *Diary*, iii, 405.
12. [Silius Titus] *A Seasonable Speech* (1659), 3.
13. Timberland, *Hist. and Procs.* i. 177.
14. BL, Harleian 1223, fo. 205.
15. William Salt Library, Bagot Letters, D/1721/3/291.
16. Sidney, *Discourses*, 419-20.
17. *The Earl of Shaftesbury's Speech in the House of Lords* (1675).
18. 'Letter from a Person of Quality', 374.
19. Sidney, *Discourses*, 385.
20. *The prose works of Andrew Marvell* ed. Annabel M.Patterson et al. (2 vols, 2003), ii, 299.
21. *A speech made by the Duke of Buckingham* (1677), 5.
22. Burnet, *History* (1833), vi, 220.

Saviour of the nation: George Monck, duke of Albemarle (1608–70) (pp. 8–10)

1. Clarendon, *Life*, ii, 277
2. HMC *5th Report*, 184.
3. TNA, PRO 31/3/107 p. 30-1.
4. *CSP Dom.* 1666-7, p. 99.
5. Bodl., Tanner 45, f.53.

'There is no pleasure in the memory of the past': William Fiennes, Viscount Saye and Sele (1582–1662) (pp. 14–15)

1. Edward Hyde, earl of Clarendon, *The History of the Rebellion and Civil Wars in England*, ed. W.D. Macray, 6 vols, (1888) ii, 547, 548.
2. *HMC Hatfield* xxiv, 277.
3. *Broughton Castle, Banbury* (1960).
4. C. Firth, 'A letter from Lord Say and Sele to Lord Wharton', *EHR*, x (1895).
5. Bodl., Carte 80, f. 749.
6. *HMC 8th Report*, 65.
7. Anthony Wood, *Athenae Oxonienses*, ed. P. Bliss (4 vols., 1813-20), iii, 548-50.

Skinner v. the East India Company (pp. 24–5)

1. Grey, *Debates of the House of Commons, 1667–1694* (10 vols., 1769), i, 189-95.

'Apt to go forward and backward in public affairs': Charles Howard, earl of Carlisle (1628–85) (pp. 32–3)

1. Burnet, *History*, ii. 277.
2. Cobbett, Parl. Hist., iv. 83.
3. James Macpherson, *Original Papers*, (2 vols, 1775), i. 70.
4. *HMC Ormonde*, n.s. vii. 61.

Religion and faction, 1661–73 (pp. 36–42)

1. *HMC Hastings* iv, 130.
2. *LJ*, xi. 482-92.
3. Wiltshire and Swindon Archives, Ailesbury 1300/653.
4. Bodl., Carte 77, f. 392.
5. Bodl., Rawlinson A 130, f. 56; C. Robbins, 'The Oxford session of the Long Parliament of Charles II', *BIHR*, 21 (1948), 221-4.
6. Bodl., Carte 44, f. 513.
7. *English Historical Documents 1660–1714* ed. A. Browning (1966), 387-8.
8. *LJ*, xii. 525.
9. TNA, SP 104/177, f. 144v.

CHAPTER 2: The peerage: recruitment, extinction and the inflation of honours (pp. 43–75)

1. Chatsworth, 27.4.
2. Burnet, *History*, ii, 19-20.
3. *HMC 10th report*, vi, 190.
4. *CCSP*, v. 21.

5. TNA, SP 29/49/97
6. *CSP Dom.* 1694–95, p. 138.
7. Add. 70251, Paget to Oxford, 19 Feb. 1714.
8. *Wentworth Pprs*, 203.
9. *The reasons which induced her majesty to create Samuel Massam Esq; a peer of Great-Britain* (1712), 3.
10. *Wentworth Pprs*, 133.
11. *Reresby Mems.*, 90-1.
12. *HMC Portland*, vii, 160.
13. *Wentworth Pprs*, 347-8.
14. Add. 70140, Oxford to his son Edward Harley, 13 Aug. 1713.1.
15. UNL, PwA 1217/1.
16. Add. 61459, ff.155-7.
17. Pepys, *Diary*, iv, 38.
18. Pepys, *Diary*, v, 21.
19. *HMC Ormond*, n.s. v, 67.
20. *LJ*, xiii, 154, 163, 174.
21. *CSP Dom.* 1670, pp. 179, 196, 264, 293, 311, 329.
22. *HMC Ormond*, n.s. vi, 223.
23. Add. 27357.
24. *Morrice Entring Book*, v, 84.

Henry St John, Viscount Bolingbroke (1678–1751) (pp. 52–3)

1. *Works of Mr Jonathan Swift* (1745), xv, 48; *HMC Portland*, vii, 164.
2. Swift, *Journal to Stella*, 545.
3. *Bolingbroke correspondence*, ii, 484-5.

Married to the king's daughter: Edward Henry Lee, earl of Lichfield (1663–1716) (pp. 58–9)

1. TNA, C104/109, countess of Rochester to [John] Cary, 5 May 1691.
2. Bodl, Tanner 26, f.50.
3. *Reliquiae Hearniae* ed. P. Bliss (3 vols., 1869), ii, 55.

The great experiment: John Wilkins (1614–72), natural philosophy and toleration (pp. 66–8)

1. Pepys, *Diary*, ix, 485.
2. Burnet, *History*, i, 473-4.
3. Bodl., Lister 34, f.37.
4. Bodl., Tanner 44, f.196.

'Faithful services'? Christopher, Baron Hatton (1605–70) (p. 74)

1. Add. 15856, f. 84.
2. Add. 29551, f. 71.

3. *CCSP*, v, 446.
4. *CCSP*, v, 498.

'Livy and sickness has a little inclined me to policy': country and court, 1673–78 (pp. 76–8)

1. 'Letter from a Person of Quality', 376.
2. *LJ*, xiii, 33.
3. 'Letter from a Person of Quality', 337-8.
4. Quoted in C Goldsworthy, *The Satyr* (2001), 197.
5. *LJ*, xiii, 37-9.

CHAPTER 3: Getting and spending (pp. 79–115)

1. *CSP Dom.* 1663-4, 239.
2. Chatsworth, Halifax Collection B.7,
3. Chatsworth, Halifax Collection B.59.
4. *CSP Dom.* 1663-4, pp. 5-6.
5. *My Lord Lucas his speech in the House of Peers, Feb. the 22. 1670/1 … in the presence of His Majesty* (1670 [i.e., 1671]).
6. Add. 75361, Strafford to Halifax, 16 Feb. 1687.
7. Bodl., Clarendon 74, fo 71.
8. BL, Verney, M636/30, John Verney to Edmund Verney, 19 Feb. 1677.
9. Pepys, *Diary*, viii, 460.
10. Bodl., Carte 34 ff.459-60.
11. *HMC Montagu of Beaulieu*, 177.
12. Add. 34223, f.4.
13. Add. 75375, f. 47.
14. *Vernon-Shrewsbury corr.* ii, 287.
15. Berkeley Castle mss, Select Books, 35 (J), p. 55.
16. *HMC Buccleuch (Montagu House)*, I, 356.
17. Add. 61450, f. 199.
18. *CCSP*, v, 291.
19. Add. 61546, f.112.
20. *CSP Dom.* 1695, p.274.
21. *Samuel Pepys' Naval Minutes* (Navy Records Soc. lx), 257.
22. Pepys, *Diary*, v, 336.
23. *Clarendon's Four Portraits*, ed. R. Ollard (1989), 121.
24. *CSP Dom.* 1664–5, p. 22.
25. *CSP Dom.* 1697, p. 486.
26. C. Jones, ' "The Scheme Lords, the Necessitous Lords, and the Scots Lords'", *Party and Management in Parliament* (1984), ed. C. Jones, 164.
27. Eg. 3330, f.101; Add. 46376B, f.10.
28. Eg. 3330, f.101.
29. Add. 63465, f.87.
30. BL, Verney, M636/32, Edmund Verney to Sir Ralph Verney, 26 Dec. 1678.

31. *HMC Portland*, ii, 149.
32. BL, Verney, M636/36, Cary Gardiner to Sir Ralph Verney, 14 Oct. 1681.
33. *CTB* xiii, 406, xiv, 326, xv, 360, xvi, 66, xvii, 75, xviii, 215, xxviii, 404, 449.
34. *Ailesbury Mems*, ii, 562.
35. T.L. Kington Oliphant, *The Jacobite lairds of Gask* (1870), 17.
36. Burnet, *History* (1833), vi, 69.

'All trade is a kind of warfare': the 1669 committee on the decay of trade (pp. 82–4)

1. *LJ*, xii, 254.
2. Parliamentary Archives, HL/PO/JO/10/1/334/215.

'Cecil the Wise': James Cecil, 4th earl of Salisbury (1664–94) (pp. 96–7)

1. TNA, C 5/71/86.
2. HHM, Estate Papers, General 131/21.
3. *HMC House of Lords 1690–91*, 141.
4. HHM, Estate Papers, General 131/22, 23.
5. HHM, Genealogies, 65.

A poor lord? George Booth, 2nd earl of Warrington (1675–1758) votes on the malt tax (pp. 100–1)

1. John Rylands Library, Manchester, Dunham Massey Papers.
2. Add. 70212, Warrington to Oxford 10 June 1714.

'Jove the fulminant': Edward Hyde, earl of Clarendon (1609–74) and corruption (pp. 104–5)

1. Clarendon, *Life*, i, 317.
2. *The Poems and Letters of Andrew Marvell* ii, 156.

'I pray God restrain the minds of unquiet and tumultuous men': exclusion and reaction, 1678–88 (pp. 116–24)

1. Bodl, Ms.Eng. lett. c.210, fol. 239.
2. Timberland, *Hist and Procs.*, i, 221.
3. Add. 19253, f.197v.
4. Burnet, *History* (1833), vi, 36n.
5. Add. 29582, f.3.
6. *The E. of Shaftesbury's expedient for settling the nation* (1681).
7. *CSP Dom.* 1680–1, pp.545-6.
8. Reproduced in *The works of John Dryden*, xvii (1971), ed. S. Holt Monk, 516.
9. Quoted in Richard L. *Greaves, Secrets of the Kingdom* (1992), 195.
10. Bodl., Carte 78, ff.403-4, 407.

11. *The Letters of Philip, 2nd earl of Chesterfield* (1835), 301.
12. *HMC Buccleuch*, II, i, 32.
13. National Register of Archives, Library of Congress MSS 1675–99, Norfolk to Howard of Effingham, 10 Sept. 1687.
14. K.H.D. Haley, 'A list of the English Peers, c. May, 1687', *EHR*, lxix, no. 271 (1954).

CHAPTER 4: The Lords in Parliament (pp. 125–57)

1. *CSP Dom.*, 1664–5, pt 2, 498.
2. Add. 70230, Memorandum by Harcourt to Oxford, 4 Apr. 1714.
3. Bodl., North c.4, ff. 126-7.
4. Parliamentary Archives, HL/PO/JO/10/1/378, 595.
5. TNA, PRO 30/24/7, 573.
6. Bath mss, Wiltshire, Prior pprs, ix, f.31.
7. Add. 61589, ff.167-8.
8. *LJ*, xii, 121.
9. *LJ*, xii, 126.
10. *LJ*, xii, 174.
11. Parliamentary Archives, HL/PO/CO1, 14 June 1660.
12. *LJ*, xii, 673.
13. *Wentworth Pprs*, Peter Wentworth to Strafford, 21 Dec. 1711.
14. *LJ*, xix, 346-7.
15. Add. 70319, Memorandum from earl of Cromartie, 16 Jan 1712.
16. Pepys, *Diary*, viii, 364-65.
17. *LJ*, xiii, 253.
18. Add. 32095, f. 401.
19. Nicolson, *London Diaries*, 498.
20. Staffordshire RO, Paget papers, D603/K/2/2, f.60.
21. *Letters and Memorials of State*, ii, 700.
22. *HMC Buccleuch*, i, 329-30.
23. *The Correspondence of Robert Boyle*, ed. M. Hunter, A. Clericuzio and L.M. Principe (8 vols., 2001), iv, 319-20.

'The soul of an old stubborn Roman': Denzil Holles, Baron Holles (1598–1680) (pp. 130–1)

1. *Morrice Entring Book*, ii, 95.
2. TNA, PRO 31/3/143, ff.34, 112.
3. *Morrice Entring bk.*, ii, 224.
4. Burnet, *History*, i, 175.

'The subtillest, workingest villain that is on the face of the earth': Robert Spencer, 2nd earl of Sunderland (1641–1702) (pp. 134–5)

1. *Sidney Diary*, ii, 125.

2. *Ibid.*, ii, 129.
3. *Ibid.*, ii, 159.
4. BL, M636/37, Sir Ralph Verney to John Verney, 3 Aug. 1682.
5. Burnet, *History* (1833), iii, 263
6. Anne to Princess Mary, 20 Mar. 1688, quoted by J.P. Kenyon, *Robert Spencer, earl of Sunderland* (1958), 329.

The bishops restored (pp. 142–4)

1. *The correspondence of Bishop Brian Duppa and Sir Justinian Isham, 1650–60* ed. Gyles and Justinian Isham (Northants. Rec. Soc., XVII, 1955), 52, 180.
2. Pepys, *Diary*, i, 210.
3. *CSP Dom. 1660–1661*, 324; *The correspondence of Bishop Brian Duppa and Sir Justinian Isham*, 184.
4. BL, Lansdowne 986, f.50.
5. Add. 4224, f. 76.
6. *LJ*, xi, 80.
7. Bodl., Tanner 49, f.23.
8. Bodl., Smith 22, f.21.
9. Quoted in John Rouse Bloxam, *A register of the presidents, fellows, demies, instructors ...* (8 vols, 1853–5), iv, 254.
10. Bodl., Tanner 141, f.102.
11. *The articles and charge proved in Parliament against Doctor Walton* (1641), 1.
12. *The autobiography of Richard Baxter*, ed. N. H. Keeble (1974), 77.
13. Anthony Wood, *Athenae Oxonienses*, ed. P. Bliss (4 vols., 1813–20), iv, (*Fasti Oxonienses*, part ii, 83).

A non-juring bishop: Thomas Ken (1637–1711) (pp. 150–1)

1. Quoted in M.H.StJ. Maddocks, 'Bishop Ken', *Church Quarterly Review*, 164 (1963), 174.
2. Bodl., Tanner 28, f. 261.

Philip Bisse: a political bishop (1666–1721) (pp. 154–5)

1. Philip Bisse, *A sermon preached before the Honourable House of Commons on Wednesday March 15, 1709/10* (1710), 10.
2. Philip Bisse, *A sermon preached before the Right Honourable House of Peers, on Tuesday the 29th of May, 1711* (1711), 9-11.
3. Quoted in G.H. Jenkins, *Literature, religion and society in Wales, 1660–1730* (1978), 276.
4. *Hist. Parl. Commons 1715–54*, I, 570.
5. Quoted in P. Monod, *Jacobitism and the English people, 1688–1788* (1989), 148, 172.

6. Quoted in G.S. Holmes, *The trial of Dr Sacheverell* (1973), 329 n.36.

Revolution, 1688–89 (pp. 158–66)

1. *Letters of Philip, 2nd earl of Chesterfield* (1832), 338.
2. *Letters of Lady Rachel Russell* (7th edn., 1809), introduction, cxxviii.
3. R. Beddard, *A Kingdom without a King* (1988), 37.
4. *Morrice Entring Bk*, iv, 509.
5. *Clarendon Corr.*, ii, 261.
6. *Clarendon Corr.*, ii, 261-2.

CHAPTER 5: Honour, power and privilege (pp. 167–191)

1. *Remembrances for order and decency to be kept in the Upper House of Parliament* (1735), order 7, 37, 10.
2. BL, Althorp mss, Savile pprs. C5, Weymouth to Halifax, 25 July 1685.
3. *LJ*, xii. 197.
4. *LJ*, xii, 477.
5. *LJ*, xii, 182
6. *HMC 12th Rep* v, 41.
7. *Letters and Memorials of State*s, ii, 722.
8. *LJ*, xiv, 78-9.
9. *LJ*, xii, 355-6.
10. *LJ*, xiii, 659.
11. *LJ*, xv, 241.
12. *LJ* xi, 637.
13. *LJ*, xi, 655.
14. *LJ*, iii, 417.
15. *LJ*, xi, 340, 341.
16. *The speeches, discourses, and prayers, of Col. John Barkstead, Col. John Okey, and Mr. Miles Corbet, upon the 19th of April being the day of their suffering at Tyburn*, (1662), p. 8.
17. *LJ*, xi, 474.
18. *HMC Finch*, i, 511.
19. *LJ*, xiv, 247,
20. *LJ*, xiv, 309.
21. *LJ*, xiv, 441
22. A.S. Turberville, 'The "protection" of the servants of Mmembers of Parliament', *EHR*, xlii, no. 168, 596-7.
23. Quoted in D. R. Hainsworth, *Stewards, lords and people: the estate steward and his world in later Stuart England* (1992), 41.
24. *LJ*, xvi, 71.
25. *Marlborough-Godolphin Correspondence*, 1056.
26. BL, Stowe 396, ff.178-190.
27. 6 Anne c. 78.

28. *Reresby Mems*, 59-61.
29. Bodl. Tanner, 45, f.254.
30. Add. 36913, ff.302-309.
31. Add 28046 ff.53-6.

Edward Stillingfleet (1635–99) and comprehension (pp. 170–1)

1. *Morrice Entring bk.*, iii, 254.
2. Add. 27448, f. 340.
3. B. Southgate, ' "The fighting of two cocks on a dung-hill": Stillingfleet versus Sergeant', *Judaeo-Christian intellectual culture in the seventeenth century* (1999), 225-36.
4. A.T Hart, *Life and Times of John Sharp, Archbishop of York* (1949), 238.

Getting away with murder? Charles Mohun, 4th Baron Mohun (1677–1712) (pp. 182–4)

1. Bodl, Carte 79, f.477.
2. Bodl., Carte 79, f.479.
3. Bodl., Tanner 25, f.7.
4. Bath mss, Thynne papers xliv, f.40.
5. Woburn Abbey mss HMC 8 volume VII. f. 11.
6. Add 36772, ff. 18-19.

Scandalum magnatum: libel and politics (pp. 188–9)

1. Bodl., Tanner 47, ff. 66-7.
2. Northants. RO, Montagu Letters, xvii, p. 48.
3. *Ibid.*, p. 45.
4. *Ibid.*, p. 46.
5. *Ibid.*, p. 47.
6. *Ibid.*, p. 69.
7. BL, Verney ms mic. M636/34, Edmund Verney to John Verney, 20 July 1680.
8. *The Life and Times of Anthony Wood*, ed. A. Clark (3 vols, Oxford Historical Society, 1891–4), iii, 31.
9. Bodl., Carte 222, ff. 322-3.

Allegiance, conspiracy and confusion: the legacy of revolution, 1689–97 (pp. 192–200)

1. *Clarendon corr.*, ii. 275.
2. Bodl., Ballard 45 fo. 58.
3. Burnet, *History* (1833), iv.5n.
4. *HMC Finch*, v, 243.
5. UNL, Portland mss, PwA 1233/1, Sunderland to Portland, 18 May 1694.
6. *HMC Portland*, ii, 173.

7. *LJ*, xv, 683.
8. *LJ*, xv, 684.
9. Add. 19253, fols. 190v-189v.

CHAPTER 6: The House of Lords at work (pp. 201–43)

1. *HMC, Ormond MSS*, n.s., v. 109-10.
2. Mellerstain Letters, iii, Baillie to his wife, 14 Mar. 1709[/10].
3. Pepys, *Diary*, viii, 34.
4. Evelyn, *Diary*, iv, 619.
5. *LJ*, xiii, 233.
6. *LJ*, xv, 461.
7. *LJ*, xii, 591.
8. *The earl of Shaftesbury's speech in the House of Lords, the 20th of October 1675* (BL, LR 41 d12).
9. Bodl. MS Eng. hist. c. 46 f. 40.
10. *Post Boy*, 25 Nov. 1708.
11. *Morrice Entring Bk*, iv, 89-90.
12. BL, Verney ms. mic. M636/39, John Verney to Edmund Verney, 9 Apr. 1685.
13. *LJ*, iii, 676.
14. *LJ*, xii, 413.
15. Clarendon, *Life*, ii, 338-9.
16. Bodl., Carte 217, ff.354-5; *LJ*, xii. 31.
17. Bodl., Carte 79, ff. 37-8.
18. Hertfordshire ALS, DE/P/F26.
19. *LJ*, xii, 318.
20. Bodl., MS Eng lett c. 210, f. 141.
21. Add 36916, f.212.
22. *Poems and Letters of Andrew Marvell*, ii, 322-3.
23. TNA, PRO 31/3/124 pp. 157-8.
24. J.C. Sainty and D. Dewar, *Divisions in the House of Lords: an analytical list 1685–1857* (1976).
25. Pepys, *Diary*, v, 110-111.
26. *LJ*, xi, 79.
27. Harold Love, *Scribal publication in seventeenth century England* (1993), 21.
28. *LJ*, xiv, 123.
29. *LJ*, iv, 296.
30. Add 23215, ff. 40-1.
31. *CJ*, viii, 311.
32. Clarendon, *Life*, ii. 223.
33. TNA, PRO 30/24/7/531.
34. *LJ*, xv, 91.

35. *LJ*, xvi, 575.
36. *LJ*, xvii, 185.

'So much pain and so little pleasure': Charles Talbot, duke of Shrewsbury (1660–1718) (pp. 212–3)

1. Quoted in Somerville, *king of hearts*, 143.
2. Holmes, *British Politics*, 306.
3. Somerville, *king of hearts*, 262.
4. Gregg, *Queen Anne*, 310.

The Fenwick attainder, 1696 (pp. 216–8)

1. *Private and original correspondence of Charles Talbot, duke of Shrewsbury*, ed. Coxe (1821), 430-1.
2. Wiltshire & Swindon Archives, 2667/25/7.
3. *Ibid.*
4. *Lexington papers*, ed. H. Manners Sutton (1851), 236-8.

A committee chairman: Edward Hyde, 3rd earl of Clarendon (1661–1723) (p. 228)

1. Thomas Babington Macaulay, *The History of England from the accession of James II* (1856), ii, 389.
2. *Clarendon corr.*, ii. 301.
3. Add. 70293, Clarendon to Oxford, 13 Feb. 1713.
4. Add. 22211, f. 55.

'High feeding and smart drinking': clubs, dinners and party politics (pp. 232–4)

1. Aphra Behn, *The city-heiress, or, Sir Timothy Treat-all* (1682), 31.
2. *CSP Dom.* 1679-80, 296.
3. Quoted in Newton Key, ' "High feeding and smart Drinking" ' in *Fear, Exclusion and Revolution: Roger Morrice and Britain in the 1680s* (2006), ed. Jason McElligott, 168.
4. Quoted in Holmes, *British Politics*, 21.
5. TNA, C 104/116, pt 1, entries for 17 Dec. 1703 and 13 Feb. 1704.

The radical Whig: Ford Grey, 3rd Baron Grey of Warke and earl of Tankerville (1655–1701) (pp. 238–40)

1. 'Reception of the duke of Monmouth at Chichester in 1679', *Sussex Archaeological Collections*, vii (1854), 169.

War and peace, 1697–1702 (pp. 244–6)

1. *CSP Dom.* 1699–1700, p. 27.
2. Northants RO, Montagu Letters, xlvii, no.180.

3. Bodl., Ballard 10, f.107.
4. Quoted in H. Horwitz, *Parliament, policy and politics in the reign of William III* (1977), 269.
5. *LJ*, xvi, 601.

CHAPTER 7: The business of the House (pp. 247–82)

1. Add. 27447, f. 338.
2. Bodl., Tanner 146, f.39.
3. Parliamentary Archives, HL/PO/CO/1, vol. 2, p.364.
4. *Ibid.*, 369.
5. *HMC, 11th rep.* pt. 2, 141.
6. Wilts & Swindon Archives, 1300/787, Geoffrey Harcourt to Lady Beaufort, n.d. [1690].
7. Nicolson, *London Diaries*, 376.
8. Woburn Abbey ms (*HMC 2nd Rep.* viii), iii. f. 124.
9. Bodl., Tanner 31, f. 119.
10. TNA, CO 31/2, pp. 44-5, 48-9, 98-101.
11. Nicolson, *London Diaries*, 463.
12. Bodl., North MSS, a.3, fols. 9-10.
13. *LJ*, xix, 218.
14. BL, Verney, M636/17, Cary Gardiner to Sir Ralph Verney, 31 Oct. [1660].
15. *HMC 11th Rep*, vii:109.
16. John Lauder Fountainhall, *The decisions of the Lords of Council and Session from June 6th, 1678, to July 30th, 1712* (2 vols, 1759–61), ii, 368, 381.
17. Add. 19253, f.163v-4.
18. Add. 19253, f. 160v.
19. Add. 75368, [Weymouth] to Halifax, 11 Dec. 1697.
20. Bodl., Tanner 31, f. 228.
21. Bodl., MS Eng. misc c. 300, ff.127-132.
22. Add. 28053.
23. National Archives of Scotland, GD45/14/352/22, Balmerino to Harry Maule, 6 June 1713.
24. Bodl., MSS North b.2, f. 8.
25. Bodl., MSS North b.2, f. 17.
26. BL, Eg. 3331, f. 109
27. CTB, vii, 1166.
28. *HMC Portland* ii, 173.
29. Swift, *Journal to Stella*, ii, 555.
30. *HMC Portland* iv, 551.

Loyalty and indemnity: the Derby estate bills (pp. 250–1)

1. Parliamentary Archives, HL/PO/CO/7/3, 27 June, 3, 7 and 12 July 1660.
2. *LJ*, xi. 378-9.
3. *Ailesbury Mems*, i, 6-7.
4. Peter Edmund Stanley, *The House of Stanley* (1998), 201.

'Irish understandings': the Irish cattle bill, 1666–67 (pp. 254–5)

1. Pepys, *Diary*, vii. 342-3.

Parliamentary divorce: Henry Howard, 7th duke of Norfolk (1655–1701) (pp. 260–1)

1. *HMC Portland*, iii, 488.
2. Luttrell, *Brief Relation*, iii, 16.
3. Luttrell, *Brief Relation*, v. 99.

The accidental martyr: William Howard, Viscount Stafford (1612–80) (pp. 266–7)

1. Evelyn, *Diary*, iv, 234.
2. *HMC Ormonde*, n.s. v, 529.
3. Clarke, *Life of James II*, I, 637.

'Whig the first letter of his name': Thomas Wharton, 5th baron and 1st marquess of Wharton (1648–1715) (pp. 276–7)

1. Gateshead public library, CN/1, Burgh 29.
2. *Memoirs of the Verney family during the seventeenth century*, ed. F and M. Verney (2 vols, 1907), ii, 402.
3. John Stoye, *English travellers abroad 1604–1667* (rev. ed., 1989), 305-6.
4. Burnet, *History* (1833), v, 234.
5. *Ibid.*, 242n.

A pretended trial? The impeachment of Lord Somers, 1701 (pp. 280–1)

1. Daniel Defoe, *Mr. S——r, The enclosed memorial you are charg'd with, in the behalf of many thousands of the good people of England* (1701), 4.
2. *CJ*, xiii, 639.
3. *HMC Downshire*, I, ii, 803.

The Church in danger? 1702–09 (pp. 283–90)

1. Add. 70073-4, Newsletter, 10 Mar. 1702
2. Add. 61126, ff.12, 14-15.
3. Add. 29588, f.117.
4. *CJ*, xiv, 12.
5. Quoted in Gregg, *Queen Anne*, 163.

6. Badminton House, Gloucestershire, FMT/B1/1/1/20.
7. *LJ*, xvii, 332.
8. *State Trials*, xiv, col. 764.
9. *LJ*, xvii, 535.
10. CJ, xiv, 549-50.
11. *LJ*, xviii, 7-8.
12. Add. 61118, ff.6-7.
13. *Marlborough-Godolphin corresp.* 830-1.
14. Add. 61101, ff.109-10.
15. Add. 61101, f.111.

CHAPTER 8: Interest: the Lords and the nation (pp. 291–332)

1. West Sussex RO, Winterton Mss. (Ac.454 series), nos. 974.
2. East Sussex RO, ASH 840, 187.
3. *HMC 15th Rep.* vii, 163.
4. *Reresby Mems.* 228n.
5. Add. 4292, f.66.
6. Add. 70073-4, newsletter, 21 July 1702.
7. Add. 75356, R Graham to Burlington, 30 July 1667.
8. *Norris papers* ed. T. Haywood (Chetham Soc. 1st ser. ix (1846)), 104.
9. Quoted in Victor Stater, *Noble government* (1994) 76-7.
10. *Ibid.*, 75.
11. *HMC Finch* i, 206-7, 225-6.
12. *Private Correspondence of Sarah, Duchess of Marlborough* (2 vols, 1838), i, 39.
13. Worcestershire RO, Hampton mss, 705:349/4739/2 (vii) /1.
14. *Hall book of the borough of New Windsor* (2 vols., 1972), i. 111.
15. Bodl., Carte 69, f. 160.
16. *CSP Dom.* 1663-4, 18.
17. *Autobiography of Sir John Bramston* (Camden Society, 1845), 325-6.
18. Add. 33923, fol. 453v.
19. *HMC Lothian*, 135.
20. *Hist. Parl. Commons, 1690–1715*, i, 199
21. Bodl., Ms Eng. misc. b. 44, f. 160; *HMC 10th Rep.* pt 4, 334-5.
22. *The Parliamentary diary of Sir Richard Cocks*, ed. D.W. Hayton (1996), 153-4.
23. West Sussex RO, Goodwood MS 19.
24. Philip Styles, 'The corporation of Warwick 1660–1835', *Transactions of the Birmingham Archaeological Society*, lix, (1938), 42-3.
25. Add. 61496, f.87.
26. Warwickshire CRO, CR 1618/W21/3.
27. TNA, C 9/144/9.
28. *CCSP*, v, 279.
29. Warwickshire CRO, CR 136/B/86.

30. *CSP Dom.* 1685, p. 21.
31. *CSP Dom.* 1685, p. 36.
32. *HMC 10th Report*, iv, 335.
33. Cumbria Archive Centre, Carlisle, Lowther Archive, D/Lons/W2/2/4, James Lowther to Sir John Lowther of Whitehaven, 5 April 1701
34. *Hist. Parl. Commons, 1690–1715*, ii, 303.
35. *Essex's Excellency* (1679), 3.
36. Bath mss, Thynne pprs. 47, ff. 63-4.
37. *HMC Portland*, iv. 611.
38. Christopher Clarkson, *The History of Richmond in the County of York* (1821), 117-8.
39. UNL, Portland (Bentinck) mss Pw2 37/1, 206-9.
40. Add. 61475, ff. 10-11v.

'A thousand lies': electing the Scots representative peers in 1708 (pp. 294–5)

1. Add. 61628, f.90.
2. Add. 61628, ff.135-7.
3. Add. 61101, ff.121-2.

The power of Beaufort: Henry Somerset, duke of Beaufort (1629–1700) (pp. 298–300)

1. Thomas Babington Macaulay, *The History of England from the Accession of James the Second* (5th edn., 1849), i, 589.
2. Quoted in Nicholas Rogers, *Whigs and Cities: Popular politics in the Age of Walpole and Pitt* (1989), 264.

The malt tax and the Union, 1713 (pp. 304–5)

1. Quoted by Holmes, *British politics*, 338.
2. Wentworth Pprs, 330-32.

Elections and family feuds: the earls of Coventry (pp. 308–9)

1. Cornwall RO, Antony mss, CVC/Z/20.
2. Cornwall RO, Antony mss, CVC/Y/2/13.
3. Badminton House, Gloucestershire, mss, FMT/B1/1/1/34.
4. BL (India Office), Mss Eur. E210, f. 97.

'How much depends upon new elections': Thomas Thynne, Viscount Weymouth (1640–1714) (pp. 312–13)

1. BL, Althorp mss, Savile pprs, C5, Weymouth to Halifax, 4 Aug. 1683.
2. *CSP Dom.* 1683 July-Sept., p. 110.
3. *HMC Dartmouth*, i. 122.
4. *HMC Finch*, iv, 442.
5. Bodl., Ms. Eng. Lett. d. 310, f.219.

6. BL, Athorp mss Savile pprs. C5, Weymouth to Halifax, 10 Oct. 1692.

A bishop at the polls: Anthony Sparrow (1612–85) at Exeter and Norwich (pp. 316–7)

1. Bodl., Add. C 305, ff. 251-3.
2. Bodl., Add. C 305, ff. 225, 229.
3. Bodl., Add. C 305, f.267.
4. Quoted in John Miller, *After the Civil Wars* (2000), 231.
5. *HMC 6th Report.*, 385.
6. Bodl., Tanner 39, f.39.
7. Bodl., Tanner 38, f.22.
8. Bodl., Tanner 39, f.179.
9. Bodl., Tanner 36, ff.6, 230.
10. *CSP Dom.* 1682, 54-5.

Peeresses and politics: Baroness Rockingham, Baroness Lovelace and the countess of Rochester (pp. 320–1)

1. *HMC Var. Coll.* ii. 393.
2. *Prideaux Letters*, 90-1.
3. *Prideaux Letters*, 98-9.
4. BL, Verney ms mic. M636/17, Anne countess of Rochester to Sir Ralph Verney, 9 Mar. 1660.
5. *Ibid.*, Sir Ralph Verney to John Carey, 30 Mar. 1660.
6. TNA, C104/110, Lady Rochester to John Carey, 27 Sept. [1685].

James Greenshields: episcopacy, the Union, and appeal to the House of Lords (pp. 330)

1. Gloucestershire RO, Sharp papers, Box 78, 55
2. Christ Church, Oxford, Wake Mss, 17, f.264.

Sacheverell and the peace, 1710–14 (pp. 333–340)

1. Quoted in G.S. Holmes, *The Trial of Dr Sacheverell* (1973), 97.
2. *HMC Stopford-Sackville*, i, 35.
3. Boyer, *Anne Annals*, ix, 428.
4. Cobbett, *Parl. Hist.*, vi, 831.
5. Quoted in Holmes, *British Politics*, 389.
6. Add. 61118, ff. 30-5.
7. *Private Diary of William, first earl Cowper* (Roxburghe Club 49 (1833), 43.
8. *Wentworth pprs.*, 180.
9. Wodrow, *Analecta* (Maitland Club, lx) vol. i, 336.
10. Timberland, *Hist and Procs.* ii, 375.
11. Quoted in D. Szechi, *Jacobitism and Tory Politics* (1984), 106.

12. *HMC Bath*, i, 207.
13. Add. 70214, William Bromley to Oxford, 3 Dec. 1711.
14. Quoted in Holmes, *British Politics*, 383.
15. Quoted in H. Horwitz, *Revolution Politicks: the career of Daniel Finch second earl of Nottingham* (1968), 235
16. Abel Boyer *The History of Queen Anne* (1735) 533.
17. Abel Boyer, *The political state of Great Britain*, ii, 14,
18. Leicestershire RO, Finch MSS, DG7, box 4950, bundle 24, Sunderland to Nottingham 26 Sept. 1712.
19. Quoted in Eveline Cruickshanks, 'The Tories and the Succession to the Crown in the 1714 Parliament', *BIHR* 46 (1973), 180-1.
20. Bodl, North c.9, ff. 80-1.

EPILOGUE: The Hanoverian succession and the 1719 peerage bill (pp. 341–4)

1. Add. 70236, Edward Harley to Oxford, 28 Sept. 1714.
2. *LJ*, xx, 97-112 (9 July 1715).
3. *The Moderator* (1719).
4. William Coxe, *Memoirs of the life and administration of Sir Robert Walpole* (London, 1798), 123.

Further reading

Although there are few books specifically on the House of Lords and the peerage in the late seventeenth and early eighteenth century, the subject encompasses much scholarship on politics, society and government. The works listed here constitute only a very small selection of the published material available.

Primary sources

Bishop Burnet's history of his own time, ed. M.J. Routh (Oxford, 6 vols, 1833)
The diary of John Evelyn, ed. E.S. De Beer (Oxford, 6 vols, 1955)
The entring book of Roger Morrice (1677–1691), eds Mark Goldie,
    John Spurr, Tim Harris, Stephen Taylor, Mark Knights, Jason McElligott
    (Woodbridge, 6 vols, 2007)
The London diaries of William Nicolson, Bishop of Carlisle 1702–1718
    eds C. Jones and G.S. Holmes (Oxford, 1985)
The diary of Samuel Pepys, eds R. Latham and W. Matthews (London, 11 vols,
    1971–3)

The House of Lords

Clyve Jones (ed.) *Party and management in Parliament 1660–1784*
    (London, 1984)
Clyve Jones (ed.), *A pillar of the constitution: the House of Lords in British
    politics, 1640–1784* (London, 1989)
Clyve Jones and David Jones (eds), *Peers, politics and power: the House of
    Lords, 1603–1911* (London, 1986)
Clyve Jones, Philip Salmon and R.W. Davis *Partisan politics, principle and
    reform in Parliament and the constituencies* (Edinburgh, 2005; supplement
    to Parliamentary History vol. 24)
Andrew Swatland, *The House of Lords in the reign of Charles II* (Cambridge,
    1996)
A.S. Turberville, *The House of Lords in the reign of William III* (Oxford, 1913)
A.S. Turberville, *The House of Lords in the eighteenth century* (Oxford, 1927)

The aristocracy in society and government

John Cannon, *Aristocratic century: the peerage of eighteenth-century England* (Cambridge, 1984)

John Habbakuk, *Marriage, debt and the estates system* (Oxford, 1994)

D.R. Hainsworth, *Stewards, lords and people: the estate steward and his world in later Stuart England* (Cambridge, 1992)

Anna Keay, *The magnificent monarch: Charles II and the ceremonies of power* (London, 2008)

Molly McClain, *Beaufort: the duke and his duchess, 1657–1715* (New Haven, CT, 2001)

Victor Stater, *Noble government: the Stuart lord lieutenancy and the transformation of English politics* (Athens, GA, 1994)

Susan E. Whyman, *Sociability and power in late Stuart England: the cultural worlds of the Verneys, 1660–1720* (Oxford, 1999)

National politics and the peers

Edward Gregg, *Queen Anne* (rev. edn, New Haven, CT, 2001)

D.W. Hayton, *The History of Parliament: the House of Commons, 1690–1715* (5 vols, Cambridge, 2002), I, Introductory Survey

G.S. Holmes, *British politics in the age of Anne* (revised edn, London, 1987)

G.S. Holmes, *The trial of Doctor Sacheverell* (London, 1973)

Henry Horwitz, *Parliament, policy and politics in the reign of William III* (Manchester, 1977)

Mark Knights, *Politics and opinion in crisis, 1678–1681* (Cambridge, 1994)

Mark Knights, *Representation and misrepresentation in later Stuart Britain* (Oxford, 2005)

Douglas Lacey, *Dissent and parliamentary politics in England, 1661–89* (New Brunswick, NJ, 1969)

John Kenyon, *Robert Spencer, earl of Sunderland, 1641–1702* (London, 1958)

Paul Langford, *Public life and the propertied Englishman* (Oxford, 1991)

John Miller, *Charles II* (London, 1991)

John Miller, *James II* (rev. edn, New Haven, CT, 2000)

Steven Pincus, *1688: the first modern revolution* (New Haven, CT, 2009)

Craig Rose, *England in the 1690s: revolution, religion and war* (Oxford, 1999)

Lois Schwoerer, *The Declaration of Rights 1689* (Baltimore, MD, 1981)

Paul Seaward, *The Cavalier Parliament and the reconstruction of the old regime, 1661–1667* (Cambridge, 1989)

W.A. Speck, *Reluctant revolutionaries: Englishmen and the Revolution of 1688* (Oxford, 1988)

W.A. Speck, *Tory and Whig: the struggle in the constituencies, 1701–15* (London, 1970)

Grant Tapsell, *The personal rule of Charles II, 1681–85* (Woodbridge, 2007)

Picture credits

Cover: The Royal Collection © 2010 Her Majesty Queen Elizabeth II
Frontispiece: Palace of Westminster Collection

Fig. 25	© National Portrait Gallery, London
Fig. 26	Conway Library, The Courtauld Institute of Art, London
Fig. 27	© British Library Board shelfmark 816.m.23(132)
Fig. 28	© National Portrait Gallery, London
Fig. 29	© Trustees of the British Museum
Fig. 30	Private Collection © Philip Mould Ltd, London/The Bridgeman Art Library
Fig. 31	© Crown copyright: UK Government Art Collection
Fig. 32	© Victoria and Albert Museum, London
Fig. 33	© Victoria and Albert Museum, London
Fig. 34	© British Library Board shelfmark: S22.h.30
Fig. 35	Hyde ec65 w6563 668e. Houghton Library, Harvard University.
Fig. 36	The Royal Society
Fig. 37	Reproduced by permission of The Huntington Library, San Marino, California
Fig. 38	© National Portrait Gallery, London
Fig. 39	© Victoria and Albert Museum, London
Fig. 40	© National Portrait Gallery, London
Fig. 41	© National Portrait Gallery, London
Fig. 42	© National Portrait Gallery, London
Fig. 43	© National Portrait Gallery, London
Fig. 44	© British Library Board shelfmark1891.d.(76)
Fig. 45	Skyscan Photolibrary/Alamy
Fig. 46	Conway Library, The Courtauld Institute of Art, London.
Fig. 47	David Lea
Fig. 48	Private Collection/The Stapleton Collection/The Bridgeman Art Library
Fig. 49	© Trustees of the British Museum
Fig. 50	© National Portrait Gallery, London
Fig. 51	© National Portrait Gallery, London
Fig. 52	© Trustees of the British Museum
Fig. 53	© British Library Board shelfmark 815.m.1. (115)
Fig. 54	© British Library Board shelfmark 1852.d.1.(5)
Fig. 55	Hyde ec65 b6465 682t. Houghton Library, Harvard University
Fig. 56	© National Portrait Gallery, London
Fig. 57	© Trustees of the British Museum
Fig. 58	©Victoria and Albert Museum, London
Fig. 59	RB 133234, Reproduced by permission of The Huntington Library, San Marino, California
Fig. 60	By Permission of the The Folger Shakespeare Library
Fig. 61	© Museum of London, UK/The Bridgeman Art Library
Fig. 62	© National Portrait Gallery, London
Fig. 63	Reproduced by courtesy of the Essex Record office
Fig. 64	Northamptonshire Record Office, Montague Boughton vol 77 f.7

Fig. 65   With permission of The Rare Book & Manuscript Library of the
           University of Illinois at Urbana-Champaign
Fig. 66   Harriet Mills
Fig. 67   RB 141461. Reproduced by permission of The Huntington Library,
           San Marino, California
Fig. 68   The collection at Althorp
Fig. 69   Private Collection/© Philip Mould Ltd, London/The Bridgeman Art
           Library
Fig. 70   © Trustees of the British Museum
Fig. 71   RB 143022. Reproduced by permission of The Huntington Library,
           San Marino, California
Fig. 72   Reproduced by permission of the Master and Fellows of Trinity
           College, Cambridge
Fig. 73   © Lambeth Palace Library, London, UK/The Bridgeman Art Library
Fig. 74   The Bodleian Library, University of Oxford. Firth b.21(27*)
Fig. 75   © Victoria and Albert Museum, London
Fig. 76   National Library of Scotland. L.C.Fol.77(106)
Fig. 77   Reproduced by kind permission of the Syndics of Cambridge
           University Library. E.10.10(5)
Fig. 78   © National Portrait Gallery, London
Fig. 79   © Timothy Millett Collection/The Bridgeman Art Library
Fig. 80   The Royal Collection © 2010 Her Majesty Queen Elizabeth II
Fig. 81   The National Archives, PRO 30/11/268 f. 95-9
Fig. 82   National Library of Scotland. L.C.Fol.77(78)
Fig. 83   Northamptonshire Record Office, Montague Boughton vol 77 f.6
Fig. 84   Northamptonshire Record Office, Montague Boughton vol 77 f.8
Fig. 85   Parliamentary Archives, P1215
Fig. 86   Parliamentary Archives, HL/PO/JO/10/1/403D
Fig. 87   Parliamentary Archives, P1216
Fig. 88   RB 142905. Reproduced by permission of The Huntington Library,
           San Marino, California
Fig. 89   Palace of Westminster Collection
Fig. 90   © National Portrait Gallery, London
Fig. 91   Parliamentary Archives, HL/PO/JO/10/1/33/144
Fig. 92   Centre for Kentish Studies U269/O34
Fig. 93   Hertfordshire Archives & Local Studies. DE/P/F/101
Fig. 94   Warwick Castle, Warwickshire/The Bridgeman Art Library
Fig. 95   © National Portrait Gallery, London
Fig. 96   London Metropolitan Archives, City of London
Fig. 97   EC65 J2310 684a. Houghton Library, Harvard University
Fig. 98   RB 358046. Reproduced by permission of The Huntington Library,
           San Marino, California
Fig. 99   RB 482019. Reproduced by permission of The Huntington Library,
           San Marino, California

Fig. 100   Art Archive/Museum of London
Fig. 101   By Permission of the The Folger Shakespeare Library
Fig. 102   © Trustees of the British Museum
Fig. 103   © Trustees of the British Museum
Fig. 104   © Trustees of the British Museum
Fig. 105   The Royal Collection © 2010 Her Majesty Queen Elizabeth II
Fig. 106   Parliamentary Archives, HL/PO/JO/10/7/980A
Fig. 107   © Trustees of the British Museum
Fig. 108   London Metropolitan Archives, City of London
Fig. 109   The Art Archive/Museum of London
Fig. 110   © Trustees of the British Museum
Fig. 111   London Metropolitan Archives, City of London
Fig. 112   © British Library Board shelfmark 604.I.19
Fig. 113   © National Portrait Gallery, London
Fig. 114   © National Portrait Gallery, London
Fig. 115   © British Library Board
Fig. 116   Staffordshire Record Office D260/M/F/1/6
Fig. 117   Northamptonshire Record Office, F.H. 2852
Fig. 118   © National Portrait Gallery, London
Fig. 119   © National Portrait Gallery, London
Fig. 120   Palace of Westminster Collection
Fig. 121   Palace of Westminster Collection
Fig. 122   Hertfordshire Archives & Local Studies. DEP F69
Fig. 123   Centre for Kentish Studies U269/040
Fig. 124   Lebrecht Music and Arts Photo Library/Alamy
Fig. 125   RB 133276. Reproduced by permission of The Huntington Library, San Marino, California
Fig. 126   RB 133277. Reproduced by permission of The Huntington Library, San Marino, California
Fig. 127   Guildhall Library, City of London
Fig. 128   The Bodleian Library, University of Oxford. 8°S 185 Art
Fig. 129   The Bodleian Library, University of Oxford. Firth c.15(35)
Fig. 130   © Trustees of the British Museum
Fig. 131   London Metropolitan Archives, City of London
Fig. 132   Hertfordshire Archives & Local Studies. DE/P/F/127
Fig. 133   © National Portrait Gallery, London
Fig. 134   © National Portrait Gallery, London
Fig. 135   The Trustees of Lambeth Palace Library
Fig. 136   © British Library Board shelfmark 806.k.15(8)
Fig. 137   © British Library Board shelfmark 516.m.18
Fig. 138   hyde_ec65_n7675_692h Houghton Library, Harvard University
Fig. 139   © National Portrait Gallery, London
Fig. 140   Northamptonshire Record Office, F.H. 2912
Fig. 141   © National Portrait Gallery, London

Index